A "Topping People"

A "Topping People"

The Rise and Decline of Virginia's Old Political Elite, 1680–1790

Emory G. Evans

University of Virginia Press · *Charlottesville and London*

University of Virginia Press
© 2009 by the Rector and Visitors of the University of Virginia
All rights reserved
Printed in the United States of America on acid-free paper

First published 2009

9 8 7 6 5 4 3 2 1

LIBRARY OF CONGRESS CATALOGING-IN-PUBLICATION DATA
Evans, Emory G.
   A "topping people" : the rise and decline of Virginia's old political elite,
1680–1790 / Emory G. Evans.
      p.   cm.
   Includes bibliographical references and index.
   ISBN 978-0-8139-2790-9 (cloth : alk. paper)
      1. Virginia—History—Colonial period, ca. 1600–1775. 2. Virginia—Politics
and government—To 1775. 3. Elite (Social sciences)—Virginia—History—
17th century. 4. Elite (Social sciences)—Virginia—History—18th century.
5. Politicians—Virginia—Biography. 6. Landowners—Virginia—Biography.
7. Gentry—Virginia—Biography. 8. Upper class—Virginia—Biography.
9. Virginia—Social conditions—18th century. 10. Virginia—Economic
conditions—18th century. I. Title.
   F229.E9 2009
   305.5'209755109033—dc22

                                                            2008043124

For Winifred

Contents

Acknowledgments

I BEGAN TO THINK ABOUT the Virginia elite in a serious way in the 1960s, but administrative responsibilities kept me from working systematically on the project until the late 1980s. The need for such a study grew out of my work on planter indebtedness and the Revolution in Virginia. Many of the wealthy carried a heavy debt into the Revolution and did not recover from it once the war was over. Their political role was also diminished. Because the elite had dominated Virginia society for so long, I wanted to find out more about them and how they attained this position and lost it.

In the process of this work, I have acquired substantial debts myself. Without the help of many people I would not have been able to complete this study. Thad Tate and Don Higginbotham read all of the manuscript with friendly and careful eyes as it emerged. Unfortunately Don died before he was able to see the final result. John Hemphill and John Selby read substantial portions before their deaths and provided the insight that can only come from serious scholars of eighteenth-century Virginia. Owen Ireland, Warren Billings, Ira Berlin, Ronald Hoffman, Kevin Hardwick, Camille Wells, Calhoun Winton, and Jack P. Greene, as well as Jean Russo, Lois Carr, and George Callcott, read one or more chapters to my great benefit. Others who helped in various supportive ways are Jeffrey Evans, the late Henrietta Goodwin and the late Jane Carson, John C. Dann, W. W. Abbot, Rebecca Wrenn, Angie Hogan, Richard Holway, and Mark Mones. Portions of the study were presented to the Washington Area Early American Seminar at the University of Maryland, from which I received helpful comments. And, finally, none of this would have been possible without the support of the one to whom this book is dedicated.

Three sabbatical leaves and a General Research Board award from the University of Maryland–College Park, as well as a Mellon summer research grant from the Virginia Historical Society, provided me with the time to complete the research. Most of the research was done at the then Research Library of the Colonial Williamsburg Foundation, the College of William and Mary, the Library of Virginia, the Virginia Historical Society, the University of Virginia, and the Manuscript Division of the Library of Congress. The staffs of those institutions were generous with their time and help. I should especially mention the late Edward M. Riley, who headed the then Research Library of Colonial Williamsburg and the late William M. E. Rachal of the Virginia Historical Society.

The dates in this book are the New Style that the English adopted in 1752. All British manuscript material, unless otherwise noted, is available on the Virginia Colonial Records Project microfilm, which can be obtained from the University of Virginia Library, the Library of Virginia, the Virginia Historical Society, and the John D. Rockefeller Library of the Colonial Williamsburg Foundation.

A "Topping People"

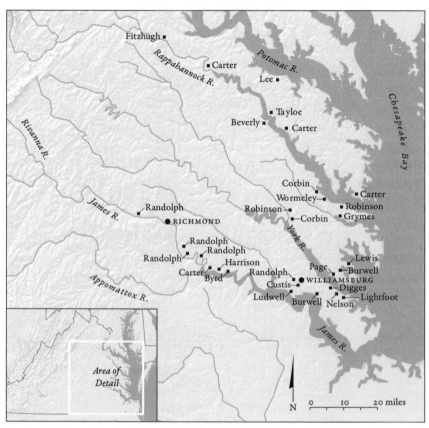

Locations of Virginia's twenty-one leading families. (Map by Rebecca Wrenn)

# Introduction

Few of "the topping people" have a house ... of their own in
Williamsburg, but they all "live on their Estates handsomely
and plentifully."

—LORD ADAM GORDON, 1765

THE ORIGINS, GROWTH, AND INFLUENCE of Virginia's upper class have long
fascinated scholars and the wider public. Louis B. Wright writing in 1940 set
forth what is the generally accepted view: "The tight little aristocracy that developed in Virginia in the later years of the seventeenth century quickly gained
a power and influence far in excess of the numerical importance of its members,
who were vastly outnumbered by the yeoman class. Planter-aristocrats ruled
Virginia as by prescriptive right and from the ranks of their descendants came
statesmen who helped weld thirteen colonies into a nation."[1] Others before and
after Wright have devoted much attention to this group.[2] And there is no denying their importance in Virginia and the nation, a point cogently argued by
Charles Sydnor in his *Gentlemen Freeholders: Political Practices in Washington's
Virginia.*[3]

Here I examine this Virginia elite between 1680 and 1790 in their political,
social, and economic context. I do so through the history of twenty-one families, all but one of whom had two or more members on the Council of State
in the seventeenth and eighteenth centuries (table 1). The Council of State,
composed usually of twelve men appointed by the reigning monarch, was the
advisory body to the governor, the upper house of the General Assembly, and
the court of last resort in Virginia, and it wielded powerful authority. Men of
wealth who desired to combine political, social, and economic power and thus

Table 1   Twenty-one elite Virginia families

Family	Approximate date of arrival	Place of origin	Virginia residence
Beverley	1663	Yorkshire	Middlesex
Burwell	1640	Bedfordshire	Gloucester
Byrd	Before 1670	London	Henrico
Carter	1635	London	Upper Norfolk or Nansemond to Lancaster
Corbin	1654	Warwickshire / London	Maryland to Middlesex
Custis	1650	Gloucestershire / Rotterdam	Northampton
Digges	1650	Kent	York
Fitzhugh	1670	Bedfordshire	Stafford
Grymes	1644	?	Gloucester to Lancaster / Middlesex
Harrison	1632	Northamptonshire	James City / Surry
Jenings	1680	Yorkshire	York
Lee	1639	Worcestershire / London	Charles River (York) to Northumberland
Lewis	1653	Monmouthshire	Gloucester
Lightfoot	1670/71	Northamptonshire	Gloucester
Ludwell	1648	Somerset	James City
Nelson	1705	Cumberland	York
Page	1650	Middlesex	York
Randolph	1670	Warwickshire	Henrico
Robinson	1660	Yorkshire	Middlesex
Tayloe	Before 1681	Gloucestershire?	Richmond
Wormeley	1636	Yorkshire	Lancaster / Middlesex

Sources: Cynthia Miller Leonard, *The General Assembly of Virginia, July 30, 1619–January 16, 1978: A Bicentennial Edition* (Richmond, 1978); Earl Gregg Swem, *Virginia Historical Index* (Roanoke, VA, 1934–36); *Cavaliers and Pioneers.* I have used the *VMHB* and the *WMQ* to supplement Swem's index, which ended in 1936.

become the most influential people in the colony sought membership in this select body. Wealth is difficult to assess precisely in Virginia because, unlike Maryland, few probate records are extant. But in Jackson Turner Main's study of the one hundred wealthiest Virginians, gleaned from the land tax and personal property records of 1787 and 1788, sixteen of the twenty-one families emerge, and what had happened to the remaining six is known. I also draw information from another group of twenty families.[4]

Members of these families also held other appointive positions and were elected to the House of Burgesses. But using long-term membership on the Council of State simplifies the selection of a representative elite group. The Fitzhugh family had only one member on the colonial Council of State, but William Fitzhugh and his descendants were very wealthy, and his letters, along with those of William Byrd I, are among the few surviving records left by the seventeenth-century Virginia elite. The Blair and Parke families, both of whom had two members on the council, are in the second group. James Blair served almost continuously from 1694 to 1743, and his nephew John from 1745 to 1770. James had no children and left a considerable fortune to John. Daniel Parke served from 1670 to 1678; his son Daniel served from 1695 to 1697, but he left Virginia in the latter year and never returned. The Blairs could easily be substituted for the Jenings or Lightfoot families, whom I have included in the first group of leaders. Peter Jenings served on the council in 1670–71, and his relative Edmund from 1691 to 1726. John Lightfoot was on the council from 1697 to 1706, and his nephew Philip from 1733 to 1747. The experiences of all these and other families are included here.

I begin the story at about 1680 even though eighteen of these families were in Virginia before that date and not a few of them were well established and an important force in the colony. But after 1680 the relationship between the crown and the colony began to change as the government tried to exercise greater control over Virginia. The response to British efforts was strong, and the result was a redefined relationship between the mother country and Virginia as well as between the colony's political leadership and the people. There emerged over the next two decades a clearly identifiable group of political leaders who, in their resistance to British efforts, forged a closer relationship with the wider public and began to think of themselves as Virginians. By the early eighteenth century, this group dominated not only the colony's political life but its economic and social life as well.[5] Finally, I chose the ending date of 1790 because by then the decline in their political and economic influence, which began in midcentury, was virtually complete, and a new elite was taking their place.

Beginnings

They have few Scholars so that everyone studies to be halfe
Physitian halfe Lawyer & with naturall accuteness would amuse
thee for want of books they read men the more.

—THE REVEREND JOHN CLAYTON, 1684

THE MIGRATION OF LARGE NUMBERS of people from one part of the world
to another is an endlessly fascinating process, and none more so than the movement of English-speaking peoples to North America and the Caribbean in the
seventeenth century. The twenty-one families that are treated in this study represent only a minute part of the total group, but they played an inordinately
important role in the creation of society in Virginia. By studying them more can
be learned about Chesapeake culture, its roots and influence.

Where did the immigrants come from? It has been argued that most of
the people who migrated to Virginia in the seventeenth century came from the
south and west of England. But of the nineteen out of the group of twenty-one
whose place of origin can be definitely established, five came from the north
(Cumberland and Yorkshire), three from the west (Monmouthshire, Gloucestershire, and Somerset), four from London and the Home Counties (London,
Middlesex, Kent), and seven from the West and South Midlands (Warwickshire,
Worcestershire, Northamptonshire, Bedfordshire). So it is difficult to identify
them with any particular regional English culture. Even adding another twenty
elite families, whose names are as familiar as the twenty-one but only a few of
whom had a member on the council, does not change the pattern much. There
were three from the north, including one from Scotland. Another six were from

the West and South Midlands (Worcestershire, Staffordshire, Gloucestershire, Buckinghamshire, Oxfordshire). Five were from London, and four from the east (Essex, Kent, Norfolk). Finally, two were from Hampshire. Those characteristics attributed to the south and west of England, from where it is argued the bulk of the 40,000 to 50,000 immigrants to Virginia came between 1645 and 1670—a highly developed sense of honor, a hierarchical conception of liberty, predatory sexual habits, a long custom of slavery, etc.—do not apply, unless they were also characteristic of England's other regions.[1]

Several other factors, common to most of the group, are of great importance. Six of the group can positively be identified as younger sons of county families who had little or no inheritance, and another nine, including two of the younger sons, had relatives and/or sponsors in Virginia when they arrived. Fifteen were merchants or came from mercantile backgrounds; five were either born in or had spent substantial time in London, and there is reason to believe that many of the remainder had London connections. Martin H. Quitt, looking at a much larger elite group, has asserted that the two primary factors in loosening the ties of these men with the mother country were that they were younger sons and that they had London mercantile experience. London merchants, Quitt explained, were a "competitive, achievement-oriented lot" as opposed to county families, who in general had a disdain for trade. Experience in London provided "an alternative role model" for young men who spent time there. These factors apply equally well to most of the twenty-one council families in this study. Adding the fact that many of them had relatives in Virginia makes the impulses that led them to leave home clearer.[2]

The early careers of several of the immigrants show how the process of migration worked. Richard Lee I (1618–1664) was the younger son of a cloth merchant from Worcester. His older brother John had been apprenticed in 1633 to a merchant kinsman in London, and Richard probably joined him there. Circumstances also suggest that it was in London that he met Sir Francis Wyatt, who brought Lee to Virginia with him when he came as governor in 1639–40 and who, on their arrival, made him clerk of the quarter court. The next year Lee married Anne Constable, a member of Wyatt's household. This was a good beginning in a new land. William Byrd I (1652–1704) provides another example. The son of a London goldsmith, he was sent to Virginia to live with his merchant-planter uncle Thomas Stegge before 1670. Stegge, who was a member of the council and auditor general, had no children and on his death in 1671 left most of his estate to his nephew. In 1673 Byrd married Mary Horsmanden

Filmer, a cousin of the wife of Governor Sir William Berkeley, Frances Culpeper Stephens Berkeley. This too was a good beginning. William Fitzhugh I (1651–1701) presents an additional interesting example. The seventh and last son of a Bedford woolen draper, Fitzhugh seems to have migrated to Virginia in 1671 with the help of Bedford natives Nicholas Spencer and Nicholas Hayward. Spencer had been a London merchant before he came to Virginia in 1659, and he later became a member of the council and secretary of state. Hayward was a London merchant who maintained close relations with Fitzhugh throughout his life. And then there is Henry Corbin I (1629–1675), who was the third son of Thomas Corbin of Hall's End, Warwick. His younger brother was a London merchant, and after inheriting £400 from his father, Henry came to Maryland in 1654 perhaps as a representative of his brother's firm. Soon thereafter he was in Virginia where he married Alice Eltonhead Burnham, daughter of Richard Eltonhead and widow of Rowland Burnham, both of whom were members of well-established Virginia families.[3]

All of the twenty-one came from gentry or mercantile families. Not only were fifteen from mercantile backgrounds and merchants in Virginia; for at least ten of them, their entry to Virginia was made easier by having relatives or good connections in Virginia and/or being well connected in England. Christopher Robinson, for example, arrived in Virginia from Yorkshire in 1660. He joined two of his cousins in Lancaster (later Middlesex) County. His younger brother John became bishop of London, suggesting that the family in England was one of position and influence. Edmund Jenings arrived in 1680, as attorney general, from Yorkshire. His father had been sheriff of York and a member of Parliament, while his mother was the daughter of the lord mayor of London. His relative Peter Jenings had preceded him to Virginia and had been a member of the council and attorney general under Governor Berkeley. At least nine of these men were Royalist or came from Royalist backgrounds, which did not hurt their chances in Virginia after the Restoration. Both Philip Ludwell I and Henry Corbin were firm Royalists. Ludwell joined his brother Thomas in the colony shortly after 1660 and was on the Council of State by 1675. Corbin, in Virginia by 1654, was appointed to the council in 1663. It is also reasonably clear that these people came with substantial financial backing, that theirs was not a "rags to riches" story. William Fitzhugh, who arrived in 1670, had made a fortune by 1690 when he wrote that it took £300 to £400 to get started properly: £150 to £200 for land and a similar amount for slaves. This estimate may be high, especially for earlier years, but it is clear that this group had enough money to ease their entrance to Virginia. Finally, the twenty-one had to live long enough in this disease-ridden land to leave sons. They were survivors, and they, or their children, got through hard times. They hung on and prospered.[4]

Twenty of these families arrived in Virginia between 1630 and 1680. In this period when the population was largely immigrant and male, the ratio of men to women was roughly 3 to 1. The population grew from about 8,000 in 1640 to 40,000 in 1680, mostly the result of white servant immigration rather than natural increase because life expectancy was short. Most people did not live much past forty. This dominantly male society was predictably a "rough and ready" one, and the men had to be tough and lucky to survive. The average age at death of the fifteen for whom that age is known was fifty-seven, so in longevity, as in many other things, these men were exceptional.[5] They had to be out of the ordinary in a time that began with the governor, Sir John Harvey, knocking out a councillor's teeth with a cudgel and ended with tobacco riots during which angry and frustrated planters tried to solve the problem of excess tobacco production by destroying tobacco seedlings and plants. In between were a major Indian uprising, economic depression, Bacon's Rebellion, and more.[6] Even by the 1680s Virginia was, by European standards, still a place with rough edges. The Reverend John Clayton writing in 1684 explained that "I would now give you a further account of the Country but that now my thoughts might be as wild as the place where plenty makes poverty, Ignorance ingenuity, and covetousness causes hospitality that is thus every one covets so mch. & There is such vast extent of land that they spread so far they cannot manage well a hundred pt of wt they have every one can live at ease & therefore they scorne & hate to work to advantage themselves so are poor wth abundance." Clayton went on to say that inns were very expensive so Virginians, "with comon impudence . . . goe to a mans house for diet & lodgeings tho they have no acquaintance at all rather than be at the expense to lie at an Inn & being grown into rank custom it makes them seem Liberall."[7]

Three years later a French Huguenot nobleman, Durand of Dauphiné, wrote that Virginia was a refuge for those

> who, unable to earn a livilhood in England, take ship, & are brought over and sold for the price of their passage. They are also the English galleys, for whom a person is convicted of a crime not punishable by hanging, he is banished to America to serve a sentence. They are likewise the refuge of bankrupts & the retreat of women who are thieves or lax in matters of chastity & modesty. Therefore it is not surprising that little honesty is to

be found among the populace; but this does not apply to the people of quality. They are attracted by the richness of the country, for in England among the nobility, the estate is given almost entirely to the eldest child, & the younger get only a small legacy, so some of them settle in this new world, & where they live in high state on little wealth, & abide in virtue and honor.[8]

Durand may have exaggerated. Although William Fitzhugh called the Frenchman's "book . . . a most impolite piece," even he admitted that in Virginia "society that is good & ingenious is very scarce, & seldom to come at except in books"; good education for children was "almost impossible"; and the colony was "barren" of "spiritual help & comforts."[9] Clearly the outsiders Durand and Clayton, as well as Fitzhugh the longtime resident, captured something of the 1680s Virginia where the few were already set apart from the many in both visible and tangible ways.

Seventeenth-century English society was a hierarchical one in which a small minority maintained political, economic, and social power: this was the accepted norm. There were few men from the upper orders of English society in Virginia, and those who came were almost automatically singled out for positions of leadership. Sir William Berkeley, who governed through most of the period from 1640 to 1680, suggested in 1662 that younger brothers of good families for a small "summe of money" could "erect a flourishing family" in Virginia. And when such men migrated, he rewarded them. His cousin by marriage Nathaniel Bacon provides an exceptional example. From a good family, Bacon had been packed off to Virginia in 1674 because of some fraudulent activities. There he joined Colonel Nathaniel Bacon, a cousin and member of the council. Within six months Berkeley had appointed the younger Bacon to the council.[10] The first generation of the twenty-one elite families examined here did not achieve such instant recognition, although by 1683 nine of them had been advanced to the council.[11] Four of the nine also eventually held the important and remunerative appointive offices of either auditor, secretary, or deputy surveyor general of the colony. And twelve held other positions that were not only important, and in most cases profitable, but also gave them access to information and important people. These posts included attorney general, clerk of the county court or House of Burgesses or council, sheriff, naval officer and collector of customs, and surveyor.[12]

The post of surveyor suggests how these positions helped ambitious men rise in wealth and status. Four of the elite men were surveyors, with ready access to the best land: between them they patented 88,415 acres. Robert Beverley I, the surveyor for Gloucester and Middlesex counties, patented 27,788 acres. He was also clerk of the House of Burgesses and deputy to the auditor. These activities, plus his law practice, brought him an estimated annual income of £425, plus additional income from tobacco planting and mercantile activity. Surveying was not the only way to find choice land. The council, with the governor, approved land grants, and the nine councilors in the elite group did quite well. John Carter I and Henry Corbin (who died in 1669 and 1675, respectively) patented 10,721 and 18,250 acres. As a group the first generation patented 246,114 acres. It is not known how much total land they held because of the scarcity of probate records. But William Fitzhugh, William Byrd I, and John Custis II, for whom the only accurate records remain, patented 33,168, 17,260, and 15,658 acres, respectively, and had at their death 56,631, 26,000, and 4,000 acres.[13]

Appointive public office was then extremely important, especially positions such as secretary, auditor, naval officer, collector, escheator, and sheriff. These offices were profitable, and being appointed to most of them required the support of the governor and connections with the proper authorities in England. Nicholas Spencer explained how the process worked in 1672. A customs collector for the lower Potomac River, he had just been appointed to the council. Writing his brother, Spencer explained that he was in favor with Governor Berkeley, "but he is antient, and by the course of nature can not be expected long to continue, and it may be expected that" the next governor "will putt all commissions of places of profits upon sale, and hee that bidds most carys it, but that I may stand on firmer Ground, I request you, to procuer the place [customs collector] to be to mee confirmed by his Maiests Letter, which by any friend at Court will be an eassie matter for you to procuer." Spencer's colleague William Byrd I spent the year 1687–88 in England gaining a commission for the profitable post of deputy auditor, which paid a salary of 7½ percent on all public money collected, such as quitrents and export duties on tobacco. Because Robert Ayleway had been appointed auditor for life in 1676, the deputy's post was not secure, and a division of fees was involved. For the next four years Byrd worked assiduously to purchase the permanent position from Ayleway. The governor, Francis Howard, fifth Baron Howard of Effingham, now in England, the London mercantile firm of Perry & Lane, and William Blathwayt, auditor general of plantations and clerk of the Privy Council, assisted him. John Povey, Blathwayt's deputy on the Privy Council, received a £20-a-year retainer to make sure no impediments were placed in his way. Byrd initially offered Ayleway 100 guineas, but by 1690 he was prepared to go as high as £300 and then £350. How much he ultimately paid is not clear, but in March 1693 he was made auditor. The auditor's position brought in an estimated £350 to £400 a year, so even if he paid £350 to get the position, it was well worth the price.[14]

Byrd's quest for place and profit is the only one for the late seventeenth century that is fully documented, but his case seems not to be exceptional: the process went on continuously for all income-producing posts. The pursuit of these places was avid, the thanks when one was attained were effusive, and the posts were held onto tenaciously. William Fitzhugh even sought to be appointed to offices that did not exist in Virginia (but presumably could): high sheriff for life and head of the probate office where he would serve the bishop of London. And although he was unsuccessful in securing these positions, as well as most existing appointive ones, he did not hesitate to give advice as to how to gain them. To his brother-in-law George Luke, who desired a sheriff's or customs collector's post, he wrote that he was talking to council members William Cole and Isaac Allerton and that Luke, who was in England, should seek the help of London merchant Nicholas Hayward. He should also apply to "his Lordship," Governor Effingham, as well as his uncle, Sir Humphrey Winch, who was a commissioner for foreign plantations. Luke was to be "diligent" in obtaining the post of collector for the upper district of the Potomac River "either for your self or me, for if I have it, it shall be as convenient to you & easie for trade as if you had it your self."[15]

The key to obtaining places of profit, as Fitzhugh explained, was the recommendation of the governor. He controlled most profitable positions (collectors, naval officers, escheators) except for those of auditor and secretary of state, and even for them the governor's support was important. Chances of gaining profitable office were obviously enhanced if a candidate was a member of the council. Here too the governor's recommendation, if not absolutely decisive, carried great weight. Support from England was also necessary. Daniel Parke enlisted his cousin John Evelyn, the gentleman antiquary, to write William Blathwayt requesting that he support Parke's appointment to the council. Council membership, if not in itself profitable, was important to holding "places of honor" that gave access to positions that were. There is no evidence between 1680 and 1700 that governors sold positions they controlled as Spencer had suggested earlier, but the authority to make and/or influence appointments gave them great power in Virginia's seventeenth-century political world. As Henry Hartwell stated, "places of profit" were "the Governors gift, and during his pleasure, which I have always observed has restrained them [members of the council] from due freedome of Councill and debate." In fact, the governor's power and influence were soon to begin a slow decline. In the competition for "places of honor" and "places of profit," the twenty-one families did quite well. In 1696 they held five of the twelve council seats, and on a list of twelve to supply vacancies, the names of nine appear. In the decade of the 1690s, they held the most profitable offices of auditor and secretary, and they dominated others such as collectors, naval officers, receivers of Virginia duties, escheator, clerk of the council and of the House of Burgesses, and attorney general. They were also in position to take advantage of other profitable places. Collection of quitrents is a good example. Earlier governors farmed this task out to councillors. By 1690 quitrent collection in a county or counties was sold for a varying percentage of the amount collected, and councillors seem to have again dominated. In 1690 three members, including William Byrd I and Ralph Wormeley II, were collecting quitrents in fifteen of the twenty-one counties. And although it was not always the case, the governor when announcing the sale of quitrents in 1700 ordered that if any members of the council were "desirous to purchase the same . . . they shall have the Preference before any other." They were also frequently appointed by the House of Burgesses as treasurer to administer new taxes. Or there were cases such as when the governor of New York in 1696 requested militia to aid in the defense of that colony: William Byrd I, a merchant, was selected to supply and transport them. The expedition did not materialize, but Byrd's influence is clear. Finally, thirteen of the twenty-three militia colonels, a "place of honor," came from these families.[16]

Public office, then, was a part of the key to the success of these men, but only part. All of them were, of course, tobacco planters. At least twelve were also merchants, but probably most of them were involved in some form of mercantile activity. Eight can be identified as attorneys. And speaking more generally, seven of the twenty-one can be classified as planter-attorney-merchant. What is clear is that they did anything they could to improve their economic status. They planted tobacco, wheat, and corn, functioned as merchants, operated sawmills and gristmills, and leased land to tenants. Robert Beverley I combined public offices with a law practice and mercantile activity. Member of the council, auditor, and colonel of the Henrico County militia, William Byrd I was a merchant as well, operating several stores, ran an extensive fur-trading business, was involved in the slave trade, had sawmills and gristmills, owned at least part of two vessels, and was a substantial planter. These men presided over extensive and complicated business operations.[17]

By the 1680s most of the twenty-one families were firmly established. Their success continued despite the fact that for the next twenty years, the price of tobacco rarely exceeded and was frequently below 1 pence a pound. William Byrd I and William Fitzhugh provide the best evidence. By 1685 they had been in the colony at least fifteen years, and both were merchants and planters. Byrd in 1684 shipped the London mercantile firms of Perry & Lane and Arthur North 459 hogsheads of tobacco and 10 hogsheads of furs. In 1691, after he had become deputy auditor, Byrd asserted that he could ship as many as 900 hogsheads of tobacco. He grew part of this tobacco on his plantations and received the remainder in fees for his work as deputy auditor and from the sale of goods at his stores. At 1 pence a pound, this amount of tobacco would have been worth £1,725 sterling. Byrd was also growing corn and wheat in not inconsiderable amounts that kept his gristmills busy. He also had a sawmill, the only known product of which was pipe staves. Most of the corn, wheat, and pipe staves were shipped to the West Indies, primarily Barbados. In return came rum, sugar (refined and raw), molasses, lime juice, oranges, chocolate, and sweetmeats. Indian trade to the southwest brought in skins and furs that were shipped to England. Byrd's trade involved not just England and the West Indies but included Ireland, New England, Madeira, and Africa, and it was carried out in vessels that he often owned in part. The slave trade provided additional income. By 1698 he owned a slave-trading vessel, but he had been involved in this commerce as early as 1684 (and probably before), both with the West Indies and Africa. A final source of income was rent from an unknown number of tenants. Further, he was constantly exploring other income possibilities. For example, he ordered a book on minerals and tools to explore for and extract stone, crystal, iron, lead, and coal samples that he promptly shipped to England for testing. His total earnings are impossible to estimate, but Byrd was a very wealthy man by the 1680s.[18]

William Fitzhugh had been similarly successful. Anticipating that he might move back to England, he reported in 1687 that he possessed a thirteen-room house sitting on 1,000 acres that were divided into three quarters manned by twenty-nine slaves. At the house quarter were a dairy, dovecote, stable, barn, henhouse, and kitchen as well as a 100-foot-square garden. There were also cattle, sheep, hogs, and horses. Half a mile away was a "good water Grist mill." Fitzhugh also owned an additional 23,496 acres. He had on hand a "Stock of Tobo., with Crops and good debts," amounting to "about 250,000" pounds, part of which must have come from his mercantile activities, which he claimed were producing 60,000 pounds annually. At his stores he sold largely coarse goods such as "Kersey Cottons, & Bedminster Cottons," coarse canvas, ironware, shoes, "nails . . . & hoes & axes" in addition to silk thread and "Gloucershire Cheese." He also operated as a commission merchant selling other people's goods for a percentage of the proceeds. He estimated the production of "yearly crops of corn & Tobo. together with a surplusage of meat" would "amount annually" to 60,000 pounds of tobacco. This, he asserted, at his somewhat inflated estimate of 1.2 pence per pound, would total £300 a year. The sale of treenails, pipe staves, and walnut plank, not to mention his substantial law practice, added even more income. From time to time he invested in merchant ships, and he seems to have had additional earnings from rents and the buying and selling of land. A letter in July 1690 to London merchant Nicholas Hayward points to the variety of Fitzhugh's activities. He wrote of having shipped iron ore to be assayed after having consulted José de Acosta's *Naturall and Morall Historie of the East and West Indies* and Robert Boyle's *Sceptical Chymist,* of plans to settle tenants on 21,996 acres, of a proposition to buy additional land, of handling the affairs (shipping tobacco, selling goods, collecting debts) of Madam Susanna Letten in England, and of shipping his own tobacco. By 1687, after only seventeen years in the colony, Fitzhugh was wealthy and could, as he did on one occasion, entertain twenty overnight guests with "three fiddlers, a jester, a tight rope dancer, an acrobat who tumbled around," and "good wine & all kind of beverages."[19]

By the first decade of the eighteenth century, nineteen of the twenty-one families were financially secure. Landholding can be determined for seventeen (table 2). The average for the group, which includes those of the first generation who were still living and descendants of others who continued to be politically prominent, was 11,572 acres. For others, such as Robert Carter and Richard Lee II, landholdings can only be approximated. Robert Carter inherited 1,000 acres from his father in 1669 and most of his brother John's estate in 1690. The latter was divided into six quarters that in 1690 produced 122,586 pounds of tobacco and was worked by 115 slaves and 3 indentured servants. In 1700 Carter had 84 tithables in Lancaster County, which at a 1–3 ratio produces 251 individuals, most of whom must have been slaves. Richard Lee II was another man of substance. In his 1715 will he bequeathed 7,150 acres plus additional unspecified acreage in both Virginia and Maryland and over 50 slaves. John Custis IV, at the time of his marriage to Frances Parke in 1706, valued his estate at £8,839. The estate included, in addition to about 4,650 acres, a three-story brick house measuring 60 by 80 feet, at least 25 slaves, 500 cattle, 100 sheep, 200 hogs, 40 horses, substantial amounts of wheat, oats, and tobacco, a sloop, boats, harrows, and carts. Lewis Burwell II, holding 17,100 acres in four counties, at his death left money bequests of nearly £6,000 plus substantial amounts of plate. Benjamin Harrison III, whose 20,000 acres do not appear on the 1704–5 rent rolls instituted by Governor Francis Nicholson, had more than 80 slaves at his

Table 2 PROMINENT LANDHOLDERS

Name	*Acres*
Robert Beverley	10,663
Lewis Burwell	17,100
William Byrd	29,631
Gawin Corbin	6,260
John Custis IV	4,650 approx.
Dudley Digges	6,126
William Fitzhugh	56,631
John Grymes	2,300
Benjamin Harrison III	20,000
Edmund Jenings	6,700
John Lewis	15,000
Philip Lightfoot	1,650
Philip Ludwell	7,726
Matthew Page	7,900
William Randolph	12,395
John Robinson	1,350
Ralph Wormeley	8,200

Sources: Thomas J. Wertenbaker, *The Planters of Colonial Virginia* (Princeton, NJ, 1922), Rent Roll of Virginia, 1704–5, appendix; will of Henry Corbin, July 25, 1675, Beverley Fleet, *Virginia Colonial Abstracts* (34 vols., rept. Baltimore, 1961), 4:54–55; will of William Randolph, March 6, 1709, Ambler Family Papers, 1638–1809, LC. Gerald S. Cowden, "The Randolphs of Turkey Island: A Prosopography of the First Three Generations, 1650–1806" (Ph.D. diss., College of William and Mary, 1977), 51, says that Randolph acquired at least 16,000 acres in his lifetime, but how much he retained is not clear, so I use the rent roll figure of 12,395. Robert Beverley Title Book, MSS 5:9 B4676, VHS; John Custis IV, estate evaluation, c. 1705–6, Custis Family Papers, 1683–1858, MSS 2 p2205 a1, VHS; will of Lewis Burwell II, Oct. 11, 1710, Berkeley Family Papers, box 1, UVA. For Benjamin Harrison III's land and slave holdings, see Hening, *Statutes* 3:538–40; will of Benjamin Harrison II, April 16, 1711, *WMQ* (1), 10 (1901–2): 109–12; Christ Church Parish, Lancaster County, Wormeley Estate Papers, 1701–10, 1716, photostats, LOV; [Robert Carter] to [Francis?] Lee, July 15, 1702, ibid.; *Cavaliers and Pioneers*, vols. 2 and 3.

death in 1701. William Fitzhugh had more than doubled his landholdings in the 1690s, and when he died in 1700, his estate included 51 slaves, 7 indentured servants, 122 pieces of plate, an enormous amount of cloth in his stores, and a calash and two coaches. Ralph Wormeley left 8,200 acres at his death in 1701; in 1686 his workforce had included 26 slaves and 20 indentured servants. And though his estate was heavily encumbered, he had lived a life of "Grandure"; it was reported that his son Ralph would have "a fine Estate" and his son John "a Tolerable good one."[20]

By the early 1700s many of these estates, as in the case of the Wormeleys, had been divided among numerous sons and daughters. For example, Henry Corbin I, who died in 1675, left his eldest daughter, Letitia, who married Richard Lee II, £400 and 2,000 acres; each of his four younger daughters were to get 1,000 acres and £450; and his two sons, in addition to most of the remainder of the real estate, were allotted £500 each. Yet on the rent rolls for 1704–5 the younger son, Gawin, from whom the subsequent Corbins descended, possessed at least 6,200 acres. Similarly, Edward Digges, who died the same year as Corbin and appears to have had thirteen children, left money bequests of £3,200. While his landholdings are not known, his son Dudley held 6,126 acres in 1705, and his daughter Mary, who married Francis Page, left at her death in 1692 an estate valued at £1,102, including 108 slaves. The Harrison family provides an interesting albeit somewhat different case. They do not appear to have acquired great quantities of land by the turn of the century, yet Virginia-born Benjamin Harrison II (1645–1713) was appointed to the council in 1698 and after his death was replaced in that post by his son Nathaniel. They were a powerful family, but on the 1704–5 rent rolls, Benjamin and Nathaniel paid taxes on only 2,900 and 2,177 acres, respectively. Appearances may be deceiving, though, for the family's rising star, Benjamin Harrison III, who paid taxes on only 100 acres in 1704–5, had patented 7,000 acres by then and at his death in 1711 owned 20,000 acres and over 80 slaves. The possibility that he was not paying taxes on most of his land is clear, and it may be that his father and brother were also less than forthright concerning their holdings. It is also possible that the bulk of the Harrison wealth came from mercantile activity. In any case, the relatively equal division of estates among sons and daughters, so uncommon in England, does not appear to have substantially affected the growth in wealth and power of these Virginia families.[21]

That wealth and power were being consolidated by 1700 or so is demonstrated by the sons and daughters of nineteen of these families marrying into at least one of the others. Intermarriage with two other families was most common, but the Wormeleys and the Corbins led the list. By this time five Corbins had married a Lee, a Tayloe, a Wormeley, a Lightfoot, and a Jenings while soon thereafter three Wormeleys had married a Tayloe, a Page, and a Corbin. Governor Nicholson explained this development well in 1701 when he wrote that newcomers had difficulty finding "Widows or Maids of any Fortune" for wives because "the Natives for the most part get them for they begin to have a sort of Aversion to others calling them strangers." Here was the beginning of a process that by the third quarter of the eighteenth had created such a complicated web of relationships that almost everyone was a cousin; in fact, cousins, even first cousins, not infrequently married. So by the early eighteenth century, most of these families had gained and consolidated wealth and attained political preferment.[22]

These grandees were also by then a self-conscious group, very aware of their place and role in society and sensitive to any slight or criticism. When John Custis II, a member of the council and collector of customs for the Eastern Shore, arrived for the election of burgesses in Accomack County in the spring of 1688, he found a list of grievances posted complaining of "his great Exactions, & extorting . . . unjust and unreasonable fees." He flew into a rage. Ripping the grievances down and "shaking his Cane with much fury," he asserted that the "Inhabitants" were "presuming on the dignity of his place & great authority" and "expressed many threatening and menacing words." The assembled group was "terrified & affrighted" and "drew up no other aggrievances." Other councillors were haughty and removed, such as William Churchill, who, it was asserted, refused to be involved in a suit to settle an estate for which there was no will because he was "so great as to be Employed." All were concerned with their antecedents. Philip Ludwell I bluntly dismissed the allegation that Daniel Parke was upset about his daughter Frances's marriage to John Custis IV because she had "fallen so much below the honor of his noble family." "I take Custis to be of as good extraction as Byrd [who married the other daughter] or Park himself," Ludwell declared.[23]

But it appears that these families had not always reached their position in Virginia society by functioning within the letter of the law. For example, John Custis's practices as collector probably were extortionate. William Fitzhugh appears to have overcharged Stafford County for services performed and to have imported slaves illegally. William Byrd I may have also illegally imported slaves. Benjamin Harrison III, who accused many "Collectors" and "Naval Officers," including Ralph Wormeley, of defrauding the public, was himself charged with illegally trading in tobacco with Scotland.[24]

Finally, this consolidation of wealth and status had been carried out in the twenty-five years after Bacon's Rebellion, a time of great stress. A series of royal governors tried, as directed by English authorities, to exercise greater control over Virginia affairs; tobacco prices were consistently low; and the colony experienced a dramatic shift in its labor force from white indentured servants to black slaves.[25]

The impact of this period of adjustment can best be seen in the realm of politics. When Thomas Culpeper, second Baron Culpeper of Thoresway, arrived as Virginia's new governor on May 3, 1680, five members of the leading families—John Custis II, Richard Lee II, John Page I, Philip Ludwell I, and Ralph Wormeley II—were on the Council of State, soon to be joined by William Byrd I and Christopher Wormeley. In the House of Burgesses, or soon to be, were seven others from the families: John Carter, John Custis III, William Fitzhugh, Benjamin Harrison II, Francis Page, William Randolph, and Christopher Robinson, as well as Robert Beverley, clerk of that body. These men, who represented the cream of Virginia's political leadership, were faced with seemingly insurmountable problems. The colony, still suffering from the destructive effects of Bacon's Rebellion, was occupied by 1,000 soldiers and faced two governors in a row who were instructed to bring the colony under stricter control. Further, low tobacco prices led to a sluggish economy that produced continued unrest among a wide spectrum of the public.

The leaders' response to these circumstances was in some degree governed by their relationship, or lack of it, with the personal rule of Sir William Berkeley. Those who had benefited from Berkeley's largesse and who served under him during the rebellion generally resisted the efforts of Culpeper and his successor, Lord Howard of Effingham, to strengthen the central government. Philip Ludwell and Robert Beverley best illustrate this position. Another group who had been supporters of Berkeley and the Stuarts but did not play an active role in the rebellion despite the fact that some of them suffered at the hands of the rebels were John Custis II, Richard Lee II, John Page I, and Ralph Wormeley II. Unlike Ludwell and Beverley, they appear to have not outwardly resisted the efforts of Culpeper and Effingham. Both of these groups dated their beginnings in Virginia from 1663 or before. Finally, there are William Byrd I and William Fitzhugh, both of whom arrived around 1670. Byrd had been a marginal supporter of Nathaniel Bacon, but toward the end of the rebellion, when he saw the way the wind had shifted, he switched sides and aided in the arrest of former comrades. None of these actions seemed to hurt him politically, and from 1680 on he was able to get along with various governors without evincing any political position. Fitzhugh's role in the rebellion is not known. He entered the pro-Berkeley House of Burgesses in February 1677 and until the mid-1680s was an important member of that far from malleable body. He also served as Robert Beverley's lawyer during the latter's manifold difficulties. But Fitzhugh was a loyal and outspoken Stuart supporter and seems, because of his lack of discretion, and unlike Byrd, to have lost the opportunity for place and profit. But the role of Fitzhugh in the House of Burgesses, and that of William Randolph who joined him in 1684, is significant and has to be seen in relation to the behavior of Ludwell and Beverley. The latter two represented that small group who for fifteen years under Berkeley had had things pretty much their own way. English authorities did not interfere with Virginia's internal affairs, and despite economic difficulties this group prospered, in part, because of their relationship to the governor. The Berkeley faction was not prepared for the radical change that occurred after 1677, and they did not remain quiescent. The increased assertion of English authority must have appeared to them to be a terrible threat to their position in society.[26]

Both Ludwell and Beverley were removed from their offices in 1677, Ludwell from the council for his criticism of the new governor and Beverley as clerk of the House of Burgesses for failure to turn over its journals and papers to royal commissioners. As it turned out, the House of Burgesses ignored Beverley's removal and continued him in office, an action that Culpeper and the council did not challenge until Beverley was again removed from office because of his role in the tobacco-cutting riots of 1682. He was arrested and in and out of jail for the next two years, escaping on several occasions. Beverley eventually was brought to trial in May 1684 and convicted of "high Misdemeanours," but he was pardoned when he "supplicated the bench . . . on bended knee," publicly acknowledging his error and giving bond for good behavior. He was again elected clerk in the fall of 1685 and immediately was in trouble for altering a piece of legislation that Effingham then felt forced to disallow. This resulted in what was described as "disputes touching the Negative Voice." The king declared Beverley "incapable of any office or Public Employment" and ordered that he be brought to trial, but Beverley died in March 1687.

Ludwell was returned to the council in 1680 and after Effingham arrived in 1684 entertained his family. The governor knew that Ludwell had been "troublesome to former Governors" and made every effort to get along with him. Ludwell had married Governor Berkeley's widow Frances, and when she went to England in the summer of 1684, Effingham instructed his wife to show this "very well bred woman" who "hath been very Civill to me" every courtesy in "the best manner you can." He even appointed Ludwell collector for the upper James River "in hopes to have gained him by it." But Ludwell was not influenced and from 1685 on seems to have been outwardly in sympathy with the resistance of the House of Burgesses to Effingham's efforts, which increased the governor's own income and extended the range of royal authority. Effingham charged that Ludwell not only attended the council "very little" but supported the resistance of the legislative body "both by his words and actions." The governor reported that the legislative "Caball" opposing his measures met "constantly at Ludwell's house, next door "to the Assembly house." When Effingham ordered Ludwell, as deputy surveyor general, to remove Arthur Allen, the Speaker of the House of Burgesses, from his "surveyors place," Ludwell replaced him with "one all-together as troublesome" and even went so far to as to appoint Robert Beverley's son to the "best surveyors place . . . in the Country." Effingham suspended Ludwell from the council, but the House of Burgesses then designated him to present its grievances to "his Most Sacred Majestie."[27]

Both William Byrd and his other council colleagues must have concluded that a vocal and intransigent posture against the assertion of royal authority was not in their best interests. Byrd, it appears, made every effort to get along with Effingham and was rewarded. A major Indian trader, he supported Effingham's money-raising initiative to limit the number of traders by requiring a license. The governor wrote William Blathwayt, the surveyor and auditor general, that while Byrd was in England, he would present Effingham's case for licensing as well as "an Account that the method" the governor had "used with Col. Ludwell were very necessary." Byrd as a major producer and exporter of tobacco was behind the governor's proposed ban on the exporting of bulk tobacco, a right that benefited the small planter. This must have been only a small portion of Byrd's cooperation, for at this time he was seeking the post of auditor of Virginia. Effingham praised him as "a person very proper both for parts and purse, and one I shall be very well satisfied with," and Byrd got the post. Several years later he smugly reported that "Col. Ludwell I find hath done no great matter by his long stay in England, having rather exasperated matters, than done himself any good."[28]

So Byrd and his colleagues had learned that one did not oppose governors publicly or on major issues. And when Commissary James Blair, also a council member, made "several indecent reflections" on Governor Sir Edmund Andros, they, with the governor, suspended him from the council. Such a posture paid off for most of these men; in the 1690s they dominated places of profit. Writing in 1698 about fraudulent activity on the part of naval officers and collectors,

Benjamin Harrison III, whose father had just been appointed to the council, explained how it all worked. They were appointed to these posts by the governor and were usually members of the Council of State that not only approved "their own" accounts but gave advice on the "Disposal of Money" collected. "The same men also constitute the Supreme Court of judicature in all causes whatsoever so that there is no relief against any judgment they Shall please to give, & therefore the most prudential method for every man, is to Submit—patiently, and make his terms with em as well as He can; for they will always have so great a regard to their own Interest, that they will not fail to stand by each other in opposition to all others." He went on to say that the governor did not discourage such activity; for example, he had taken no action against Ralph Wormeley, whose accounts had been "noted as faulty."[29]

These men also had learned another lesson. For fifteen years under Governor Berkeley, no general elections were called, and the council, with the governor, generally ran things at the colonywide level. But after 1680 the House of Burgesses fought vigorously against the extension of royal authority. Even though it lost some of its prerogatives in the process, it established a precedent for resistance and independence that over time increased its importance in the Virginia political world. Berkeley supporters of the persuasion of Ludwell and Beverley, "irreconcilables" they were called, who never made it to the council, found their way into the House of Burgesses and took a strong stand for Virginia rights. And others from elite families for whom there was no immediate place on the council, such as John Custis III and Benjamin Harrison II, entered the house and played important roles there until a position on the council opened.

Early on Effingham was being told not to submit his instructions to the "Cavile and dispute of the Assembly." Although he began to remove contumacious members from public offices, it seemed to have little effect, for as he said, "Assemblys in this part of the world are not to be managed espetially by a naked and unarmed man." They did not hesitate, he remarked, to "rudely and boldly" dispute "the Kings Authority." His successors Francis Nicholson and Edmund Andros encountered similar problems in dealing with the assembly. The result was that governors, for a while at least, were more careful in their relations with Virginia politicians, and council members became increasingly more aware that all the power did not rest with them. Nicholson reported early in his first administration that he dared not "venture any New Methods" in which the "Great Men" were concerned without a royal instruction. And the "Great Men" of the council, in turn, advised governors to be sensitive to the rights, rules, and procedures of the House of Burgesses, even to the point of suggesting to Nicholson on one occasion that it was "Not for his Majtes Service" to press the house further on a matter on which it had refused to act. And later they urged caution in dealing with that body on matters of defense. It would be better, Nicholson was advised, to urge the house itself to find ways for better "defending the Country" rather than forwarding specific proposals to it. In fact, the council advised in 1701 that it was more proper "for the particular members of the said house of Burgesses" to deal with the problem because it would be more in conformity with "the Customs in Parliament & Assemblys and more likely to take Effect than if it were proposed to them by your Excellency and the Council." That the role and status of the House of Burgesses had risen can be further seen in Robert Carter's reservations about accepting an appointment to the council. The greatest obstacle, he said, was the fact he had had the honor of being a member of the house for a number of years and was now its Speaker. He was convinced otherwise, perhaps easily, but being a member of the House of Burgesses was more important in 1700 than it had been in 1675. The council too had come to recognize that the world had changed and that the well-being and support of its members did not rest solely with governors and patronage in England.[30]

In the twenty-five years since Bacon's Rebellion, Virginia had seen difficult times. Although these difficulties would not all go away, now political, economic, and social affairs were beginning to sort themselves out. The twenty-one families had been immensely successful, but to maintain that success would not be an easy matter.

2 Politics, 1700–1737

A "little factious party" and "a very strange sort of men."
—FRANCIS NICHOLSON, 1705

FRANCIS NICHOLSON WAS SWORN IN as governor of Virginia on December 9, 1698. At this point Virginia's population was about 62,000, more than any of England's other North American colonies. But by any measure it was a small place in which a few families dominated its political, social, and economic worlds. In that year some fifty-nine men made up the Council of State and the House of Burgesses. Of that group seven of the leading twenty-one families were represented on the council and eight in the house. Two of the eight chaired two of the three committees of the House of Burgesses; seven were members, one of them serving as the Speaker, and the eighth was the clerk. Over the next four decades the pattern remained the same. Virginia's political leadership was drawn from this group, and including the next twenty important families makes the view even more striking.[1]

A change occurred in those forty years, one seen in the gradual transfer of political power from the council to the House of Burgesses. Challenges from the Burgesses to the council's authority began early on and continued through almost every administration. The emergence in the 1730s of the Speaker of the House of Burgesses as the most powerful political figure in the colony is a clear indication of the shift. This development began with the speakership of Sir John Randolph and continued after his death in 1737 with his successor,

John Robinson Jr. This shift does not mean that political leadership changed in
the first half of the century; it was still drawn from the same pool of people.

The emergence of this native-born political elite had begun during the last
two decades of the seventeenth century. In this same period England worked to
increase its control, both political and economic, over its colonies. The appointment of strong governors, with strict instructions, was one manifestation of the
mother country's effort. Many of these governors were military men. In Virginia
between 1683 and 1749, six of the seven governors had been army officers.[2]

Nicholson by 1698 already had substantial experience in America. After
military service beginning in 1678 in Flanders and continuing in Tangier and
with the Portsmouth garrison, he was dispatched to America in the winter of
1686–87 as commander of a company assigned to Colonel Sir Edmund Andros,
who was "Captain-General and Governor in Chief of New England." From that
post he moved to New York in 1688 as lieutenant governor, and he then held
similar positions in Virginia in 1690–92 and Maryland in 1692–98. He was
forty-three years old and unmarried when he returned to Virginia as governor.
His career in America, as Stephen Webb has asserted, had been marked by the
effort "to establish both royal authority and its concomitants, social order and
security." Robert Beverley, no friend of the governor, later charged that Nicholson scoffed at the Virginians' belief that they were "entituled to the liberty of
Englishmen," and the governor himself remarked they were an "obstinate people
of Commonwealth principles." Authoritarian by nature and training, he possessed a violent temper and seems to have held the people he was going to have
to deal with in low esteem. Early on he complained of the scarcity of qualified
"natives" to carry out public business and bemoaned the fact that no longer did
English gentlemen of "tolerable parts . . . come hither." He spoke insightfully of
the modest antecedents of "this generation" who "derive their originals, either
as from themselves or at farthest their fathers, but very few Grandfathers," and
who had acquired their "estates and places of honour . . . more by accident than
any extraordinary honesty or ability."[3]

Of "this generation," those with whom Nicholson would come in closest
contact were the members of the Council of State and the leadership in the
House of Burgesses. They were a group of mixed ability, but among them were
a number of formidable characters. Some, like Ralph Wormeley, were on their
last "legs"; Wormeley, who had not attended meetings in several years, died in
1701. But William Byrd I and Benjamin Harrison II were individuals to be reckoned with, as was the commissary of the bishop of London, James Blair, who
had been removed from the council by Andros in 1695 but was soon to be rein-

stated. In the Burgesses, Philip Ludwell II and Robert Carter were emerging as strong figures. Carter, of Lancaster County, had twice been Speaker of the House (1696–97, 1699) and was appointed to the council in 1699. Philip Ludwell II, of James City County, had entered the house in 1696 and would follow Carter to the council in 1702. Especially impressive were the Harrisons. Benjamin Harrison II, of Surry County, after long service as a burgess was elevated to the council on Nicholson's arrival. His son Nathaniel replaced him in the Burgesses, where Nathaniel's brother, Benjamin Harrison III of James City County, whom the governor called one of the two best lawyers in the colony, soon joined him. Most of these men were closely related. Benjamin Harrison III, Philip Ludwell II, and James Blair were, for example, all brothers-in-law. Some were unrefined, even coarse. Councilor Daniel Parke, whose enemy James Blair was protected from a challenge to a duel by his clerical status, had vented his anger against Blair's wife Sarah. Parke's father-in-law, Philip Ludwell, had offered Mrs. Blair a seat in his pew in Bruton Parish Church. Parke rushed in the church in the midst of the service and seized her "by the wrist, and with great fury and violence pulled her out of the Pew," to which he declared she was not entitled. John Lightfoot was not sworn into the council, despite the king's appointment, for over a year because of his "generall ill reputation and known misbehavior."[4] The governor, despite his experience, may not have been fully aware of what faced him that December 1698.

Nicholson's tenure as lieutenant governor in 1690–92 had generally been a popular one. He had endeared himself especially to Commissary James Blair through his support for the clergy and his advocacy of a college. He had hoped to become full governor, but to his chagrin this plum went to his old commander Sir Edmund Andros, and he had to settle for the lieutenant governorship of Maryland. Working through Blair and the clergy as well as the trustees of the newly chartered College of William and Mary, of which he was one, Nicholson orchestrated a campaign to undermine Andros in England. Blair himself was outraged at Andros because he felt the governor was not supportive of the college and the clergy. Things did not improve when Blair was elevated to the council in 1694, an appointment that was partly due to Nicholson's support. Ultimately Blair and Nicholson's efforts were successful. In 1697 Blair went to England, ostensibly to raise money for the college but more importantly to work to have Andros replaced by Nicholson. He met repeatedly with John Locke, a key member of the newly created Lords Commissioners for Trade and Plantations, or the Board of Trade. And in response to a series of questions from that board concerning the colony, he and two other Virginians also in England, Edward

Chilton and Henry Hartwell, gave answers that did not help Andros. Blair, with his brother-in-law Benjamin Harrison III, also presented charges against Andros before the archbishop of Canterbury, the bishop of London, and the clerk of the Privy Council. William Byrd II tried to rebut the charges, but Andros was old and sick and had already been in office five years. He resigned for reasons of health, but he may have seen the handwriting on the wall. Relations between him and Blair had been bad for a long time; he wrote in 1697 that it is "not possible for me to please Mr. Commissary Blair." Nicholson replaced Andros, and it was perceived in Virginia that Blair had played no small role in the change.[5]

The new governor came into office in the wake of a reorganization of the administrative machinery of the empire in an attempt to better control colonial affairs in the interest of the crown and especially to enforce the acts of trade. The Privy Council acquired a new advisory body, the Lords Commissioners of Trade and Plantations, through which most colonial business had to be channeled, and a new Navigation Act was passed. For Francis Nicholson, longtime imperial servant and now full governor of the Old Dominion, such "improvements" were appropriate.

The attitude of the Board of Trade, and probably that of the governor, was certainly influenced by the responses Hartwell, Blair, and Chilton had made to its questions concerning Virginia. None of the three had been born in Virginia, but they all had served the government in various important capacities. They were especially critical of the way the land system was administered and the unchecked power of the governor. They charged that through the abuse of the land system, a few individuals were able to acquire and keep large tracts of undeveloped land, thereby depriving "ordinary planters" of all the good land. Further, quitrents—land taxes that went to the crown—were not being collected. As Hartwell put it, there "is a great concealment of Quitrents. Chiefly by granting vast quantities of land to the richer Sort of inhabitants, Some holding forty fifty or Sixty thousand acres by whom the Sheriffs [tax collectors] are overawd, that they take their accounts as they themselves would have it." The power of the governor was enhanced, in part, because the council members, who should have provided a check on his power, "have all along held places of profit in the Country by the Governors gift and during his pleasure," which "has restrained them from due freedome of Councill and debate." A Virginian, almost certainly Benjamin Harrison III, writing in 1700 disputed Hartwell's assertion. He stated that between October 1697 and May 1700, 157,000 acres had been patented, and not all of it "to the Council and their favourites." And "excluding . . . the Northern Neck, there is not one Man that holds 30,000 acres . . . in the whole

Colony." He also argued that there was plenty of good land available. Harrison's statement, with respect to the twenty-one leading families, appears to be correct. But he did confirm that governors used patronage in ways that made it "almost impossible to lay any restraints upon them."[6]

Nicholson's instructions from the crown mirrored these concerns. He was specifically ordered to bring about reform in the land system and to curtail the use of patronage to control the council. The governor moved quickly on the question of patronage. Members of the council were prohibited from holding "places of profit" such as naval officer and collector, nor could the same person hold two offices. Councillors also lost their exemption from "ordinary forms of process" in civil cases. He moved more slowly on reform of the land system. He did away with headrights granting land to anyone who imported slaves and instituted treasury notes, which could be purchased for five shillings per fifty acres, to be substituted for a headright in the patenting of land. Nicholson also began efforts to limit the size of land grants, a move recommended to representatives of the crown as far back as 1696. To facilitate the better collection of quitrents, he began procedures for developing a rent roll, an accurate list of landholdings, in each county. But he did not follow the board's instructions to change land policy by requiring actual settlement on patented land. Responding to the board's comment that it was "incongruous that the place of receiver and accountant should be . . . in the same person with that of auditor," he recommended that the office of auditor and receiver general be separated, for it was unwise for one person to collect public money and then audit his own accounts. All of these measures affected powerful members of Virginia society, especially councillors who had always held "places of profit."[7]

The response of the council was quick. On June 8, 1699, the day the General Assembly was adjourned, eight councillors wrote Nicholson "as humble suitors" requesting that he represent to the king that "since those few places of profit as the Country doth afford are thought unsuitable for us," they hoped "he will be graciously pleased to settle Such Establishment upon us his Majesty in his Wisdom shall think fitt." These "places" had always been "thought fitt to be in their hands in some measure to compensate their vast expense, cares, Trouble— perils & loss in Attending upon Generall Courts—assembly's and Councills." The governor forwarded their plea but did not recommend any change in his instructions, and none was forthcoming. This reform was a blow to a small number of men, but they seem to have accepted the decision, although Richard Lee II may have resigned from the council in order to keep his position as naval officer. Lee claimed that he was resigning "by reason of his age and many

Infirmities," but he lived for another fifteen years. There was little or no immediate comment concerning the changes in land policy, and in fact, Nicholson was evenhanded in approving patents. He did not restrict the size of grants to 400 or 500 acres, as had been recommended, nor did he discriminate against those who were emerging as bitter enemies. From June 1699 until May 1705, Nicholson signed 775 land patents; 103 were for over 1,000 acres, with the highest being for 6,500 acres. The large majority of the patents were for less than 500 acres. He later said he was, in such matters, only "endeavouring to do my duty." The suggestion of separating the office of auditor and receiver general may have been potentially more dangerous for him because in this case he was challenging the powerful William Byrd I. As early as March 1699, Byrd had expressed concern about Nicholson's questioning of his accounts. In 1700 Byrd requested and was granted permission to go to England for the recovery of his health, but there is every reason to believe that his request also was related to the proposed division of his office. There is no evidence that he went to England, but like many others he was soon complaining, "We live in a storme and continual hurry."[8]

The "storme" had been building from almost the beginning of Nicholson's administration. It related not only to matters that affected the pocketbooks of some of Virginia's wealthiest men but also to the governor's administrative style, his personality and behavior, his thinly veiled contempt for many of those with whom he had close working relations, and an ill-fated love affair.

The governor was experienced and intelligent. On taking office, he probably had a better understanding of the colony than most of his predecessors or, for that matter, those who followed him. He understood that he was going to have to build political support if he was to accomplish much, and in the beginning the chance of a successful administration looked promising. The well-connected James Blair, soon to be, again, a member of the council, was a strong supporter; he had even described Nicholson as "one of the best men and Governors in the world." Nicholson quickly distributed key posts in the legislature to men from prominent families: Benjamin Harrison III was appointed clerk of the council and William Randolph clerk of the House of Burgesses. Others, such as Nathaniel Harrison and Hancock Custis, were appointed naval officers. And even after relations had worsened, in early 1703 he appointed Robert Beverley clerk of the House of Burgesses.[9]

The governor's job had always been difficult, but after 1698 the task became formidable. His instructions changed the relationship between him and the council by removing some of its perquisites and protections. The land system, which had been so congenial to the council's economic interests, was to be altered. The preparation of an accurate rent roll perhaps would indicate that some powerful figures had not revealed all of their holdings. An important official's office was to be carefully examined and perhaps separated. Tensions emerged that were soon heightened by the crown's order that Virginia provide £900 to aid in defending the frontiers of New York against the French and by Nicholson's efforts to improve the colony's militia and strengthen its defenses. This complicated situation was exacerbated when the governor ran afoul of the powerful Harrison family. In 1702 he had opened land for settlement in the Blackwater Swamp area south of the James River. The Harrisons proceeded to take up most of the good land before anyone else had an opportunity, and Nicholson withdrew the area from sale. Further, the new College of William and Mary owned 10,000 acres in the area, and James Blair, president of the college, who had married Sarah Harrison, was looking forward to enhanced revenues from land sales as he attempted to put the infant institution on a firm footing. In the midst of all of this, Nicholson made a fool of himself when he fell in love with young Lucy Burwell and relentlessly sought the hand of this daughter of another powerful family related to the Harrisons and many others of importance.[10]

Nicholson brought to this difficult situation a low opinion of many of those Virginians on whom he had to rely. From the beginning he complained about not being able to get the council together frequently enough to do business. He urged the Board of Trade to appoint a lieutenant governor for Virginia and Maryland so that in the governor's absence the council and its senior member, who stood in as acting governor but whose power was not clear, would not have to be relied on. After all, "self interest may cause them to do things prejudicial to the Kings interest." Further, proper persons, "gentlemen of quality" and others of "good parts," who were capable of carrying on public business were in short supply. A "sober man & a good writer can hardly be gotten in this country," he fumed. To Nicholson, a dyed in the wool Tory, many of the leaders were people of "Commonwealth principles" who if they had the power "might use it as Parliament did to King Charles I." In this small community such attitudes did not sit well with a people who, as a visiting crown official commented, were "a little Jealous of those liberties and priviledges they now enjoy." A Virginian, probably Benjamin Harrison III, expressed the opinion in 1701 that "Arbitrary Governors, and the mischievous contrivances of some Evil Ministers about the Court" which had "injured and oppressed" the plantations were not to be tolerated. If the "Public service requires it" he would "venture to strike one bold stroke" without being frightened "by the Greatness or Power of those Persons, whose Gaudy Tinsel Pomp I despise, as much as I should their mean base Spirits, if I found them in Lower Status." This was heady stuff, a point of view with which Nicholson had little patience.[11]

The governor had great energy and liked to get things done. As William Byrd I said, "We live in a ... continual hurry, as if universal fame depended on us." With no family, Nicholson was able to give full attention to the business of government. Moreover, he was a military man who did not like to be crossed, and he possessed a quick and violent temper. Nicholson himself admitted that he was "very much given to passion," but he insisted "that it" did not last "long" or make "him do an unjust thing not becoming a gentleman." However, if his critics are to be believed, his "passion" went beyond that. They charged that when angry he would call the "best Gentlemen ... scurrilous names, of Dogs, Rogues, Villains, Rascals, Cheats & Cowards, and the best Women with the names of Whores, Bitches, Jades &c." Sometimes he went so far as "actually to beat and buffet Gentlemen in a most, insolent and tyrannical manner."[12]

The first two years of the governor's administration seem to have gone reasonably well. William Byrd I admired his success in collecting quitrents and the fact that he had taken "all imaginable care" to "procure" an accurate "rent roll of all lands." As late as December 1700, relations between the governor and James Blair, a difficult person at best, were good. But early in 1701, with war with France and Spain imminent, King William requested that Virginia and other colonies contribute money and, if necessary, men for the defense of New York's borders. Virginia's assessment of £900 and 240 men was the largest. The General Assembly gathered in Williamsburg in August 1701. The House of Burgesses quickly resisted appropriating money for New York, as well as for internal defense, and went so far as to appoint William Byrd II its agent to present its case to the king. To make matters worse, the council sided with the house and gave the governor unwanted advice. He had approached the problem with his usual vigor, wanting to be involved in every step of the process. Early in the session he asked the council if it would be proper for him to be present when it was "debating bills to return to the House of Burgesses and to hear and debate the matter with them." This, he asserted, had been "the Custom & Practice at his first coming to the Government & Continues so till the present time." The council asked for time to respond to "this nice intricate question," but he appears to have participated, and he suggested increasing taxes to raise the necessary money. This was a sensitive issue, and the council urged caution in dealing with the lower house. It would be better for the initiative to come from the Burgesses, a process "being more agreeable to the Customs of Parliament & Assemblys." And to what must have been his extreme irritation, Nicholson was given a list of things to add to and delete from his address to the House of Burgesses. Byrd, Blair, and Carter even went so far as to advise him that the best approach would be to write the governor of New York telling him that he had laid the king's letter before the House of Burgesses and including as much of its response as he thought appropriate. Nicholson, of course, did not follow the council's advice and urged the house to support both the colony's and the empire's defense needs. His efforts failed, and in early December he wrote the Board of Trade of "his extraordinary great trouble," explaining that the assembly did not "comply about N. York nor the buying of Arms and Ammunition" for the colony's defense. He forwarded the assembly proceedings and dispatched "an old Englander," Dionysius Wright, to fully explain what went on and to counter the efforts of William Byrd II.[13]

The governor had worked hard with no success, and in the process he interjected his personal life into the political scene. In his speech to the House of Burgesses on September 22, he spoke of venturing his "life and fortune" in the service of his "Majesty's most antient and great colony," for which he had "an Exceeding great love and affection" and "for the Natives thereof in particular but principally One of them." The particular native was eighteen-year-old Lucy Burwell, eldest daughter of Major Lewis Burwell of Gloucester County. The forty-six-year-old Nicholson had fallen hopelessly in love with young Lucy. As he wrote her father, she "hath charmed me to a degree beyond expression &c." But by the time he addressed the House of Burgesses, any prospects of winning her hand were gone, for she was already betrothed to Edmund Berkeley II of Middlesex County. Major Burwell had responded to the governor's request for his "leave to make addresses to your Daughter" by telling him that he regretted that "you are in an extacy of trouble" but he had already agreed to the match with Berkeley. Nicholson called this "the greatest misfortune of" his life, but he did not give up, for, as he said, what kept "me from sinking under the great weight of my misfortune" was "that thing [the marriage] is not done." The young couple were married in December 1704, and by that time a variety of things, including his frustrated love, had come together to completely sour the relationship between the governor and an important segment of his council.[14]

The pressure from the home government to support New York continued. In May 1702 Queen Anne, recently crowned, rejected the petition of the council and House of Burgesses and ordered Nicholson to put the matter before the assembly again and to use "his best persuasions to encline them to a voluntary complyance." The governor met with the council and announced that a new assembly would be called for March 13, 1703. In the meantime he began to work actively to get a more cooperative House of Burgesses elected. Earlier the house had voted a gift of 10,000 pounds of tobacco to Speaker Peter Beverley, an action that the council blocked. Toward the end of the August 1702 session, the governor shifted his position and sided with the elective body. It was reported that he met frequently with individual members of the house, and "those days he did not treat" them to dinner himself, he ate "with them at the Ordinary." He seems to have had a measure of success. When several of his opponents, the "little factious party" had left town, the "Country Party" was able to pass a resolution thanking him for his "favours." This was followed by a complimentary address by the grand jury that reported to the council in its capacity as the General Court. The jury's members, Nicholson made sure, included his staunchest supporters, especially the Speaker. And as the meeting of the new assembly approached, he began to electioneer on behalf of candidates on whom he felt he could rely.[15]

It was about this time that relations between the governor and the Harrison family began to deteriorate. When Nicholson first arrived, he wanted to rent a house in Williamsburg from Benjamin Harrison II for which Harrison was asking £40 a year. The governor thought this exorbitant and, irritated, moved into cramped quarters in the college. Harrison, among others, was not as regular in council attendance as Nicholson thought appropriate. On one occasion when Harrison did not attend and sent no excuse, the governor took it as an affront to "the Kings Govr" and sent "an Express for him to come hither forthwith." Then in 1702 the governor opened the Blackwater Swamp lands for settlement, and the Harrisons, in connivance with three surveyors, a son-in-law, and two others whom Nicholson called tools "of theirs," took up most of the good land, causing him to close the area pending an investigation. At the same time the governor was becoming angrier over his failed love affair. Benjamin Harrison III was the son-in-law of Major Lewis Burwell and, of course, sympathized with Burwell, whom Nicholson was now holding responsible for his disappointed courtship.

The web of family relationships contributed further to governor's disenchantment with the Harrisons when he and James Blair, the son-in-law of Benjamin Harrison II, came to a parting of the ways. Blair felt that Nicholson was not appropriately appreciative of the role he had played in securing him the governorship. The governor, on the other hand, resented Blair's counseling him to control his temper and to deal more moderately with the legislature. Blair now believed that Nicholson, like Andros, was not supporting the college. When Blair preached a funeral oration for King William in May 1702 and spoke of the "mildness and gentleness of the King's reign," the governor felt Blair was not only being critical of him but of "King Charles the second, & especially" of King James. Nicholson came to have greater influence with the clergy than the commissary, who seemed to be devoting more time to worldly affairs than clerical duties. Finally, the governor's frequently obscene behavior deeply offended Blair. Nicholson often acted as if he were in an army barracks, using what his critics called "Billingsgate" language, "bloody cursing and swearing" that often came before or "after Prayers, & perhaps the same or next day after receiving the blessed [sacr]ament," convincing "people that he has no sense of Religion.... This is further confirmed by the many gross immoralities & pranks of lewdness, rudeness to Women that he is notoriously known to be guilty of in several parts of the country." Nicholson would respond to most of the charges against him but had nothing to say about his vulgarity.[16]

The governor began to develop a siege mentality. In a quarrel with Blair, it was reported, he asserted "there was a Caball that thought to get him out of the Government but he Swore they should not so long as he had one penny of money or one drop of blood in his body." He began to open opponents' mail and to harass them at every opportunity. Nathaniel Harrison, naval officer for the upper district of the James River, was ordered on short notice to come to Williamsburg to "pay" Nicholson "his Demands arising on Ships and Vessels" and to provide "Lists of Ships . . . and the Invoices of their Loading," which he did. The governor then demanded the militia lists for Surry County, which Harrison had not had time to prepare. This set Nicholson off. He attacked Harrison's father and began to "swear as fast as any slow spoken man could speak," calling Harrison "all the Rogues, Doggs, Villains and Rascalls that he could think of." He accused both Harrisons of not mustering the militia "once a fortnight" out of too much concern for them, and he declared that "by Gods Blood if there should be a War he'd try my father and I both for our lies." He followed Harrison onto the "Porch cursing and swearing & bawling." Harrison stated that on one occasion Nicholson told a colonel of the militia "that it would never be better till he hanged up one half of em." And Nicholson threatened another "gentleman" that "if the Law would not hang him he'd ki[ll] him himself."[17]

With the approach of the new assembly, the governor worked tirelessly on behalf of friendly candidates. He traveled widely and was especially active in James City and Surry counties where he hoped to bring about the defeat of Benjamin Harrison III and Nathaniel Harrison. Supporters helped in other counties. Secretary and Councillor Edmund Jenings was, for example, active in York County, which points to a division in the council. Both Harrisons were elected. The governor does seem to have had some small success elsewhere but not as much as his opponents suggested. Robert Carter spoke despairingly, before the election process was completed, of "the unruliness of the voice of the people," and he was discouraged that Gloucester County had reelected their "Cheif Member," Speaker of the House Peter Beverley, whom Nicholson had cultivated. Benjamin Harrison II explained, "We have had unusual Bussles about our Elections" and saw "no end of Our Calamities." He declared that "nothing but Death, Sickness or Change" would stop him from moving to England. The governor's power of appointment was such, Harrison explained, that "places" were shifted as often as the occasion required "to put out or in, as men will or will not Serve a turn." Remember, he warned, "A Gift will blind the Eyes of the wise." This shifting was not extensive, but the threat was there, as Nicholson reminded all with "browbeating" and "hectoring." And he did remove the possibility of having an additional opponent in the lower house by denying "poor James City . . . the Privilege of Electing a Burgess" because it was no longer the capital. Robert Beverley had represented Jamestown in the House of Burgesses, and it appears that Nicholson tried to buy him off by appointing him clerk of the house, not realizing what a strong opponent he was. In the end, the core of Nicholson's support in the House of Burgesses remained intact.[18]

It was in this context that a coalition of six members of the council—James Blair, Robert Carter, Benjamin Harrison II, John Lightfoot, Philip Ludwell, and Matthew Page—framed a long address "To the Queens most Excellent Majty" pleading relief from "many Grievances and pressures We lye under by reason of the unusuall insolent and Arbitrary methods of Government as well as wicked and Scandalous examples of life" that have gone on "for Divers years past."[19]

The document is a long one which states that for reasons of space the observations are limited to the governor's "behavior towards ourselves, in the several capacities wherein we act," as council, upper house of the legislature, and judges of the General Court, with some examples of "the most publick & Notorious abuses of his Government and bad examples of his Life and conversation." Although the government was vested in the governor, its administration was to be carried out with the advice and consent of the council. Nicholson, they charged, had altered that "good and wholesome method" and in most cases had "taken all of the power himself." He made virtually all appointments—justices of the peace, sheriffs, militia officers, and naval officers—without consultation. He made proclamations, sent orders, spent money, approved accounts of revenue, and appointed agents to represent the colony in England, all without the council's knowledge, thus rendering its members "insignificant Cyphers." He was changing land policy "against both law and custom"; interfering with surveyors "against law"; and altering council minutes. To make matters worse, the governor was squelching "all just freedom of dispute and debate in council." Those who spoke out were rebuked, threatened, and treated "in the most rude insolent and abusive manner." The governor took every opportunity to "debase and villify the Council before the people," implying they had "gott their Estates by cheating the people" and that the members were "no more than dirt under his feet and that he would reduce them to a primitive nothing." Moreover, he "advanced men of inferior Status to command of militia" positions that had formerly been held by "the Council alone." These things were done to "regain the good opinion of the Common People" and to generate in them "Distrust of the council," rendering it "incapable" of withstanding "his arbitrary designs." Further, he interjected himself into the legislative process by presiding when the council met as the upper house of the legislature, thereby encroaching on its "Libertys and Precedences." And he did everything he could to create divisions between the council and the House of Burgesses. The list went on and on, including his hectoring of councillors when they sat as members of the General Court and allowing court meetings to go on to an "unreasonable hour," thereby "endangering the health of Judges Lawyers and People."

The address suggested that he was paranoid, accepting the false stories of "sycophants" and "talebearers" and forcing people to affirm the truth of such allegations under oath without giving the accused person the opportunity of knowing the accuser or the accusation. The treatment of "the best gentlemen" and women went beyond "anger and passion" and was more "like downright madness." Not only was the governor "prophane"; in "ordinary house keeping" he "was Scandously penurious, not suiting the dignity of her Majestie's government having but one Dish of Meat at his Table" unless it was a "public time" when he wished to procure favors. On those occasions "he prepares such treats as he thinks may best" carry out his "sinister purposes."[20]

The writers seem to have thought that if they fired enough shots, some would strike home. The memorial was designed to catch the attention of English officials. Some of it was overdrawn and stretched the truth, and some of it was petty, but the bottom line was that a substantial number of the council members, powerful men on their home ground, not only were being denied their lawful role in government but also were regularly being vilified and threatened, both privately and publicly. In brief, the governor was treating them like "the Common people." And it appeared to them that they were losing the fight among the people's representatives and the people themselves.

The memorialists did not have the public support of the whole council.

William Byrd I, the senior member, was not one of them. Part of his success in political life had resulted from the fact that he played things close to the vest, and he did not now air his views. But his office of auditor and receiver general was threatened, and it is clear that he did not approve of much of what Nicholson was doing. He kept quiet while wishing his colleagues well. Nor did the secretary, Edmund Jenings, join them. Yorkshire born, he had been in Virginia for over twenty years and as early as 1683 was attorney general. Jenings's successful career as a public servant resulted as much from his English background and connections as from his talents. Not only were his parents prominent; no less a person than James, duke of York, had written to Governor Effingham in his support. By 1703 he was a wealthy man, and he was not about to rock the boat. Philip Ludwell II referred to him disparagingly as "Little Coll Jenings" and said he was one of Nicholson's "Minions." Jenings visited England in 1703–4, but he was of no help to the governor. Nicholson thought highly of William Bassett of New Kent County, a "good and honest gentleman" who had "acted like . . . a man of honour" in "this affair." But Bassett, who also was married to one of Major Lewis Burwell's daughters, was fed up with the bickering and the governor's behavior. He was soon to express the desire to resign his post. Finally, the position of John Custis from the Eastern Shore and Henry Duke of James City County is not known. Perhaps they were, as Robert Carter put it, among the "unsteady" ones. They were, in any case, not major players.[21]

There were no vocal defenders of the governor on the council, and when John Smith and John Lewis were added in 1704, they refused to become involved. Nicholson was faced by a formidable and organized group of opponents in Virginia and in England. Blair went to England in the summer of 1703 to deliver the memorial. He was joined by Robert Beverley II who was there to appeal a lawsuit but who supported the memorial. Naval captain James Moody and two clergymen, Stephen Fouace and James Wallace, all of whom had grievances against Nicholson, also aided Blair. Add to these men George Luke, an Englishman who had married William Fitzhugh's sister, and especially Philip Ludwell I, who had been living permanently in England since 1700. Ludwell had long been a thorn in the side of governors.[22]

Holding the fort in Virginia were Councillors Robert Carter, Benjamin Harrison II, Philip Ludwell II, and John Lightfoot. Matthew Page, the remaining signer, died in January 1704. These five individuals were not to be taken lightly, especially Carter, Harrison, and Ludwell. They were wealthy, well-connected, and experienced politicians. Carter, who Nicholson said was sometimes called "King Carter," was treasurer of the House of Burgesses and agent for the proprietors of the Northern Neck. He possessed at least 13,000 acres of land and in Lancaster County alone had around 300 slaves and servants, a phenomenal number for the time. Harrison and Ludwell, if not so wealthy, were not far behind.[23]

The planning for the attack on Nicholson had begun early. A letter-writing campaign started in the summer of 1702 and gained momentum in the spring of 1703, continuing through the year. Most of the letters, which detailed all sorts of alleged misconduct on Nicholson's part, were addressed to Philip Ludwell I, who filed them for future use.[24] In the background were the Glorious Revolution and the emerging ideology connected with it. Council members considered themselves patriots, and early on, when complaining of their exclusion from profitable offices, they explained that they had preserved "order" and "the Revolution." They believed that they now enjoyed new "liberties and priviledges," and past experiences made them sensitive to what might appear to be the arbitrary use of authority on the part of the governor. Nicholson frequently acted without their advice. He "illegally" presided over the upper house and thus encroached on their "liberties." The governor was aware of all of this discontent and later charged that the recalcitrant members were men of "Commonwealth principles," but he was not sensitive to the implications.[25]

Nicholson might have weathered the storm if it had not been for his personal behavior and his abuse of any and all whom he perceived to be critical of him. The councillors were not accustomed to "abuse and affront," as John Lightfoot put it; to being called "Rogues, Villains, Rascalls, Cowards, Dogs"; to being treated as if they were "dirt under his feet." They were proud and important men who valued their reputations and who had not gained place or profit by being shrinking violets. Nicholson might know "how to govern the Moors," but Virginia was not Morocco. Most elite Virginians, as Kevin Hardwick has pointed out, accepted a "model of a good society" in which "civility flowed down from the top of social hierarchy, and rulers embodied virtue . . . setting the pattern to be emulated by their social inferiors, and fashioning the civil character of the entire society." Nicholson did not fit this model for his character was flawed, and this defect "rendered him an unfit governor."[26]

The governor's strategy was to divide and conquer. He pitted the House of Burgesses against the council and elite leaders against each other. Ultimately he gained the support of the majority of the lower house, but he did not make similar progress with the elite leaders. He was never able to get real backing from any of the council members. His efforts were marked with more success among the wider elite. He bestowed important offices on key individuals, such as county clerkships and sheriffdoms, naval officer posts, and clerk of the House of Burgesses. Robert Carter, for example, told London merchant Thomas Corbin that "your brother [Gawin] & most of the rest that hold places of Profit have been Nc's most zealous advocates and continue soe." But in the end none of these appointments helped the governor. His opponents were better organized, and they had James Blair.

Blair thrived on controversy, he was a skilled infighter, he was tenacious, and his sensitivity to slight was matched only by that of Nicholson himself. The two men had supported each other, perhaps more out of need than mutual respect. Once Nicholson became governor and Blair saw the college successfully launched, their shared needs were diminished. They, in fact, had never really trusted each other. Blair also had great influence in England, primarily through the bishop of London but elsewhere as well. Despite his outward support he may have played a role in Nicholson's failure to be appointed full governor in 1692; he was concerned about Nicholson's temper. But when Blair became disenchanted with Andros, he successfully worked to have him replaced by Nicholson. Certainly these achievements bred confidence, and it appears that Blair became an effective leader of the opposition. By early 1703 the dissident councillors had had enough and were prepared for extreme action. Robert Carter put it succinctly when he said that they were exhausted with endless and meaningless meetings while enduring "the avid Heats, the fatigues, the Indignities." He concluded, somewhat disingenuously, that all they could do was "to lay our hands a cross and never let our tongues press our complaints anymore." Soon thereafter, on May 20, the memorial against Nicholson was completed, and in August, Blair was on his way to England, presumably on church business but with the document in hand. The memorial might do no good, Benjamin Harrison II wrote Philip Ludwell I, but he knew of no better way to get to the bottom of things than to have men who went to England bear witness "to the truth of Our Complaints."[27]

The governor was aware of the building opposition as early as the summer of 1702, and a year later he had heard intimations that he would be replaced. In late August he wrote the earl of Nottingham, principal secretary of state, and the Board of Trade concerning reports "spread through this Country of a new Governor," requesting that anyone filing a complaint accusing him of maladministration "give it under their hands, with the liberty for him to answer when & where her Majtie shall please to appoint." But Nicholson did not know the specific charges or, apart from Blair, exactly who was aligned against him. Further, the complainants cleverly waited until March 31, 1704, to present the memorial to the queen, which meant that the governor was not fully informed until early winter. He did receive notice from Edmund Jenings in September that the senior Ludwell had presented the memorial, but Jenings included none of the details. The governor also somehow had gotten his hands on Robert Beverley's supporting complaint that had been included in a letter to Major David Gwyn of Richmond County. But by then the game was virtually over.[28]

The queen referred the memorial to the Board of Trade. The board began its consideration of the matter on April 10 and continued its deliberations through June 13. Ludwell and Blair were questioned closely and submitted affidavits by Beverley, Fouace, Luke, Wallace, and Moody along with supporting letters. Blair himself provided several clarifying affidavits. Ludwell, Blair, Fouace, and Beverley appeared most frequently before the board. John Thrale, solicitor for Virginia affairs and Nicholson's agent, responded to the charges, but by early June he was dead. At this point the board recommended to the queen that all of the documents be forwarded to Nicholson and the councillors who had not signed the memorial. The latter were authorized to examine the charges and receive "affadavits or otherwise as" the governor "shall think fit." Nicholson was also given permission to "come home" if he so desired.[29]

The material was all forwarded to Nicholson on June 21 via Lord Cornbury, governor of New York, on a ship that accompanied "the Newfoundland convoy." The governor did not receive the documents until after December 8. On December 15 he informed the council of the "Petition," as well as the other material, and the request of the Board of Trade that he respond. He made all the documents available to the council. On December 16 and in subsequent meetings in February and April 1705, the charges were hashed over. Nicholson was combative, and he did everything he could to make life uncomfortable for Carter, Harrison, Lightfoot, and Ludwell, but he was at a distinct disadvantage. The charges were so extensive that he indicated in December that he would not be able to respond formally until April. No help came from the nonprotesting councillors, who ignored the Board of Trade's request that they be actively involved in examining the charges. Nicholson did respond to the board in March in four long letters, but the board did not receive them until May 2, and by then the decision had been made. On April 17, 1705, the secretary of state, Sir Charles Hedges, wrote Nicholson that he was being replaced by "Col. Edward Nott," not because of "any information against" him "or any displeasure H[er] M[ajesty] has taken against you" but because "she thinks it to be for her service at this time." Stephen Webb has argued that the complaints by "the Virginia oligarchs" had nothing to do with Nicholson's removal; it occurred "because of his 'high flyer' Tory associations, and to make room for military colleagues of the Duke of Marlborough." This was not the perception in Virginia. Certainly the complaints were substantial enough to give the Board of Trade pause about the governor's continued effectiveness. Nicholson himself brooded about his removal until the end of his life and blamed "the great men." In 1727, one year before his death, he published an extended response to a number of James Blair's charges against him.[30]

The news of Nicholson's removal did not reach Virginia until July 1705. In the meantime the governor had the satisfaction of seeing the House of Burgesses fully support him. He addressed the house on May 1, explaining that apart from the personal charges against him, it had been represented that the "publick peace & Tranquility of the Country was in Danger & its Circumstances Deplorable." The complainants had requested that "the Government . . . be put into other hands" because he, among other things, intended to bring in "Arbitrary Government by a Millitary force particularly by the fifth Men." He delivered all the documents to the house, which indicated that it would consider them on Friday, May 4. That morning Councillors Carter, Lightfoot, and Ludwell appeared "at the Door & Desired to be heard on the Affadavits & Memorials." The request was denied, as was a subsequent one by letter. The house discussed the speech, the memorial, and the affidavits for the remainder of the day. Miles Cary offered a motion that the governor had shown respect for the "Welfare & prosperity of This Country" and had the support of the better part of "her Majestys" subjects, who were not in agreement with the charges of "Male-Administration." The motion was approved on a vote of 27 to 18. The debate and discussion resumed on Saturday with similar results. Once again the house declared that the public peace and tranquillity were not threatened and the greater part "of the inhabitants" were "quiet and well satisfied" and did not desire the governor's removal. The people represented by "This House" had not complained of hardships brought on by maladministration. Nicholson had no "design" to introduce "Arbitrary power" by military force, and he merited the support the house had given him, through addresses, in the past. Whoever had presumed to "Take it upon himself" to represent the views of the country "In general" without "the Consent and Authority of this house . . . is Guilty of an unwarrantable Act tending to the prejudice of the Country." The victory was complete, and early in the day Benjamin Harrison III became ill and went home. The "honble John Lightfoot Robert Carter and Philip Ludwell Esqrs" wrote another letter on Monday, but the house ignored it.[31]

The rebuff by the House of Burgesses must have taken the councillors aback, but they were implacable. Early in June rumor had it that Lord Orkney was to be governor, but they were determined to leave nothing to chance. A meeting was to be held at Ludwell's home, Green Spring, near Williamsburg, where they would "give the finishing Stroke." Remember, Robert Carter said, from the "Apocalyps" that "Beelzebub near the end of his reign will arm himself with double furies For the destruction of his enemies, & that just such I take the violence of our Devils to be." But even Carter sensed that "our troubles of this nature are near at end."[32]

On August 15, 1705, Francis Nicholson "came in to Council and presented a Letter under her Majestys Royal Sign Manual . . . whereby her Majesty is pleased to signify her Royal pleasure that upon the arrival of Edward Nott Esqr whom her Majesty hath appointed to succeed him . . . he should deliver up to her Majtys said Governor the Seal of the Colony . . . and repair to her Royal presence . . . to give an account of the State of the Colony, when he might expect from her Majesty the marks of her Royal favour." Then, after other formalities and the delivering of various "Records and Papers," "Collo Nicholson withdrew."[33]

Major Edward Nott, who had served in the West Indies and most recently had been the deputy governor of Berwick, was reported to be a "man of good character in all respects" and "of Excellent temper." Nott, in contrast to Nicholson, was mild-mannered, but his charge from the crown was no different than Nicholson's, and he was determined not to be pushed around by the council.[34]

That body had changed somewhat, but Blair, Carter, Harrison, Lightfoot, and Ludwell were still members, and they, with their newer colleagues, quickly asserted themselves. The new governor immediately moved to separate the office of auditor and receiver general, something they advised was not necessary so long as that office reported regularly to them. He also appointed a committee composed of Dudley Digges, Lightfoot, Harrison, and Carter to examine the accounts of the office. Nicholson had not made an interim appointment in the wake of the death of William Byrd I and had assumed the responsibilities of the office himself. The councillors took this new opportunity to harass Nicholson, who was still in town. They found nothing illegal but asserted that he had acted irregularly and contrary to custom. The council also moved against Nicholson supporters by working to have them removed from naval officer and collector positions, especially Arthur Allen, Gawin Corbin, and William Wilson, and "put in their owne relations." The governor's right to appoint collectors of Virginia duties was also questioned. But Nott would have none of this, telling the Board of Trade it "is not my turn of temper" to do so.[35]

Nott did agree with the council when the members again complained of being denied naval officer posts. They "think itt a very hard case" to "be at so much trouble and charge and yet be made incapable . . . of those places, if they are vacant." It would be "a great satisfaction," he said, to "have the restriction off." He thought highly of Colonel Miles Cary, who was naval officer for the York River. Cary was "so necessary a man" and of "so good character" that he would appoint him to the council if it were not for that "very odd instruction that incapacitates a Navall officer."[36]

The governor was also ordered to carry out the long-standing instruction limiting the size of land grants and requiring actual settlement on the land. In this case the council may have outwitted him. It argued that small grants would not "encourage any man to go out & Settle in a remote place upon a Small tract . . . which he knew . . . must wear out" in a few years and thus would not promote settlers' "industry" and pursuit of "fortune." The council passed a bill in June 1706 limiting grants to persons who possessed less than five tithables to 500 acres. Those who had five tithables or more could receive an extra 200 acres for every servant or slave, provided no single grant exceeded 4,000 acres. It was clear who would benefit by this act, and it was not what the Board of Trade had in mind. But Nott forwarded the act, with his approval, to London.[37]

The councillors had not changed their position one whit; they were still intent on regaining those rights and privileges they had lost under Nicholson. His removal, of course, had encouraged them. There "are severall in this Governmt," a crown official explained, "who have been for many years endeavouring to have all the power vested in the Councill," and to accomplish that "they have by degrees endeavour'd to lessen the prerogative, and to render the Queens Governor little better than a cypher." He believed that they had "gaind their point," for "they are the sole Judges of law and property," "they have the whole command and regulation of Militia"—one gentleman "hath the command of three countys"—and "the Governor can make no justice or any officer in Government without their advice."[38]

Governor Nott died on August 23, 1706. He had brought some peace and quiet to Virginia's political world, but to the Board of Trade it seemed that not much had been accomplished. His administration did see the office of auditor and receiver general separated. The council had argued that the salary would be too small for two persons, that it would not "be worth any Gentlemans while." But Dudley Digges, who became auditor, and William Byrd II, who became receiver general, gladly accepted appointment. Nicholson had insisted that it was his right to appoint county clerks, and the council wanted the privilege of consultation. The Board of Trade ruled, much to Edmund Jenings's delight, that appointment of county clerks rested solely "in the Secretary, and the Council of Virginia ought not to intermeddle." This was a great victory for Jenings and his successors, for the office of secretary, apart from that of governor, was the most profitable and probably the most powerful one in the colony. Much else that concerned councillors remained unresolved. Land policy was still in limbo, and no decision had been made concerning councillors having the right to be naval officers. Further, the assembly and Nott had jousted over a revisal of the laws which a committee had been working on since 1699, and which had been sent to the Board of Trade for consideration before being passed in Virginia. Jenings had taken the suggested revisions to England in 1703. The board made changes, and Nott brought them back in 1705 and presented them for passage. He reported that the whole process put "the Council and Assembly . . . out of humour that their laws should be sent home without being passed here." Most of the bills were passed by both houses, but three important ones involving clergy, the county courts, and securing "the liberty of the subject" were, the governor said, "very much changed," back to "as they were before revisall, wch is very deplorable." Nott vetoed the court bill, and perhaps the one concerning the liberty of the subject. The former had provided that justices of the peace were to be appointed by the governor with the advice of "at least" five councillors. Nott took the position that this was "intrenching upon HM Perogative" and that the appointment of justices was the governor's sole right. So questions of legislative authority and the authority of the council itself were being raised, and English authorities were well aware of it.[39] Nott may have been mild, but he was no pushover.

The governor's death changed the complexion of things. Edmund Jenings, senior member of the council, now became president—the chief administrative officer in the absence of a governor—and he remained so for four years. Colonel Robert Hunter was appointed governor in 1707, but he was seized by the French on his voyage to America and never took office. So the council, with Jenings at its head, was in charge in Virginia until the arrival of Alexander Spotswood in 1710.

This period has been called the rule of the council, which suggests a more powerful role than was the case. Everything was negotiated, as can be seen in the appointment of a clerk of the court for Prince George County. President Jenings had the right, as secretary, to appoint a clerk, but the county justices would not accept his choice or an alternate one. The justices had their own candidate, and they accepted Jenings's first choice only after he had agreed to share one-half of the salary with their man. The council was also divided. Those who had been instrumental in Nicholson's removal did not trust Jenings. Earlier they had accused him of being one of Nicholson's minions, and his behavior in England in 1704–5 supports this view. Robert Carter considered him a lightweight as early as 1701 when they had worked together as executors of Ralph Wormeley's estate. It appears that Jenings in a memorial, perhaps to the Board of Trade, had accused Nicholson's opponents of "a falsehood," and shortly before Nott's death they had confronted him with this in a council meeting. Carter reported that Jenings "did not know how to make an answer." They then tried, unsuccessfully, to get his profits and perquisites as secretary reduced and began to express doubts about the power of the Presidt." When he asked that the council authorize the payment of his salary as president, the response was that there was no precedent in such a case and that the Board of Trade should be asked for instructions. Jenings ultimately was informed that he was to act with the same authority and receive the same salary as a lieutenant governor, but the council's foot-dragging delayed payment for two years. The councillors' request that they be allowed to serve as naval officers was considered carefully but denied by the Board of Trade. To make matters worse, many of the council suspected that they had a spy in their midst. Robert Quary, surveyor general of Her Majesty's customs, had been appointed to the council in 1703. He was a strong supporter of Nicholson, and it was believed, accurately it turns out, that he continued to forward derogatory information to England. The council was also aware that the Board of Trade was consulting the retired Nicholson regularly on Virginia affairs, giving him the opportunity to "make daily vents against those that were concerned in the complaints agt. him."

Further, Jenings proved to be an inefficient administrator, and attendance at council meetings was poor. Receiver General Byrd said that when councillors "do come, they are in so much hast that the publique business is not performed with due consideration." The General Assembly did not meet during this four-year hiatus. Jenings suggested that an assembly perhaps should be called because "the People might be uneasy that they had no opportunity to represent their grievances," but the council saw no "immediate necessity." Councillors appeared to be pursuing their private agendas to the neglect of the public's business. However, they were not negligent when it came to pursuing public office. Philip Ludwell, hearing that Jenings might have to go to England on family business, sought to be appointed his successor as secretary. William Byrd II, recently advanced to the council, advised his brother-in-law John Custis, who desired a naval officer appointment, that "you and my sister should now & then take a trip to Ripon Hall," Jenings's home. "The President, like all men in post, loves to have respect showd him. . . . Those that woud push their fortunes, must not fall out with great men about a little ceremony. Thats no great price to pay for profitable employment."[40]

Councillors could come together when their interests were threatened, and they were successful in blocking the continued efforts of the Board of Trade to change land policy. A land act that was passed in the summer of 1706 had been disallowed by the board, which called on Nicholson to help redraft it. It appears that the council ignored a letter to Robert Hunter, who never reached Virginia, informing him of this action. The council refused to grant land on the basis of the crown's earlier instructions, and very little land was patented between 1706 and 1710. The board ultimately gave up and insisted only that "every patentee be obliged in the best and most effectual manner to cultivate and improve three acres out of every fifty acres so granted." Even so, when Spotswood informed the council that the 1706 act had not been approved, it brassily informed him that the letter to Hunter was not under "her Majesty's Royal Sign Manual or under the Seal of" the Privy Council and that it was "not sufficient Warrant for repealing an Act of Assembly." The posture of the council had changed little in ten years. Private interest—in the members' minds the same as the colony's— remained the guiding principle.[41]

Lieutenant Governor Alexander Spotswood arrived in Virginia on June 10, 1710, accompanied by his "niece," Katherine Russell, "a pretty woman"; his friend and personal physician William Cocke; and his secretary, his valet, and a coachman. Spotswood, just thirty-three years old, was an imposing figure. He had served honorably and well in the army for sixteen years, rising to the rank of lieutenant colonel. But disillusioned about his future prospects, he had resigned his commission and then was chosen to serve as lieutenant governor of Virginia under George Hamilton, the earl of Orkney. Orkney had a distinguished military career under the duke of Marlborough and was one of his most reliable subordinates. Appointed governor of Virginia in 1709, he never came to the colony, but he did keep abreast of Virginia affairs and on occasion interjected himself. The governor was later to support an embattled Spotswood and played a crucial role in the appointment of subsequent lieutenants. Orkney retained his position until his death in 1737. As was usual, he received one-half of the governor's salary.[42]

Spotswood spent his first night in Virginia at Green Spring, the home of Philip Ludwell II. An "abundance of company" met him there, including William Byrd, who reported that the governor seemed "a very good man and a very courteous one." The next day, escorted by a large group, he proceeded to Williamsburg where he took the oath of office. Councillors Edmund Jenings, Dudley Digges, James Blair, Philip Ludwell, Henry Duke, John Smith, John Lewis, and Byrd were then sworn in. The swearing in of Robert Carter and William Churchill, who were not present, had to await the first meeting of the council on July 5. It was not until October 19 that a full council met, and by that time John Custis and Benjamin Harrison II, two of the oldest members of the council, had taken their oaths of office.[43]

These were experienced, seasoned men, and by Virginia standards they were quite wealthy. Most of them had served in the House of Burgesses, and at least eight were Virginia born. Blair, Carter, Harrison, and Ludwell had played central roles in the removal of Nicholson. Harrison died in 1713, but his son Nathaniel was appointed to the council in 1714. These four, who were supported by Byrd in England for most of the time, along with Edmund Jenings, remained in office through Spotswood's administration. They were the core group, the most influential members. They knew each other intimately, for the group from which councillors were drawn was made up of no more than forty or so families who were closely related. When the council met in Williamsburg, they lodged, ate, and socialized together. Most of them lived within a thirty-mile radius of Williamsburg, and a good bit of their social life, when not in the capital, involved visiting one another. There were few secrets. One does not get the sense that they were personally close, or if they were, it was only in the way that family members are close. They were self-centered and ambitious. Private interest was predominant. And because their wealth and status were relatively new—even the oldest families went back only fifty or sixty years—they were not entirely secure in their place at the top of Virginia society. They spent much of their time seeking appointment to the council or one of the "places of profit." A council post gave them policy-setting, legislative, and legal influence, which could be used to solidify their position. Which of them had precedence on the council was a point of great contention, for at some point, in the absence of a governor, they might be in the position to become president. William Bassett would not agree to reappointment unless he could retain his "former Rank and precedency"; Edmund Berkeley delayed taking his place on the council for nearly two years because he believed that two other gentlemen had been illegally sworn in before him. Most of them had family in England whom they frequently called on for help. They also sought support from powerful patrons: peers of the realm, members of Parliament, and influential merchants. They did not hesitate to travel to England to take care of family business or to seek and/ or secure a council post or a profitable place. William Byrd spent ten years in England between 1704 and 1726, and in that period he attained a council seat as well as the post of receiver general. He twice sought the governorship of Virginia and on one occasion that of Maryland.[44]

This was the small group of men that Alexander Spotswood was going to have to deal with most closely. They periodically came together in Williamsburg for meetings of the General Court and the assembly and when the governor needed advice and consent. Williamsburg was a tiny place, still unformed. The Capitol had been completed, and there was a jail, but the college had burned in 1706 and was still being rebuilt, and the governor's "palace" was only a shell. The town had a church, at least four ordinaries, a few "gentlemen's" houses, and perhaps a store or two. When councillors met to do their business, there was no escaping one another in this little "hothouse."[45]

Spotswood was younger than all of the council members, and apart from military service, he had no administrative experience. But he was an intelligent, organized, and efficient person who possessed great presence and a good feel for the colonial world where he found himself. And unlike Nicholson he had good control of his emotions. His goals, though, were little different from those of his irascible predecessor. He was to maintain the crown's prerogative while serving the needs of the empire first and those of Virginia second.[46]

The governor's administration began smoothly. He was gracious, considerate, and hospitable. He conveyed messages from councillors' friends and acquaintances in England, and he was careful to seek out and treat with care Jenings, Dudley Digges, and Byrd, the secretary, the deputy auditor, and the receiver general, members of the council who held places of profit. He needed the support of these men "who have the same interest and Obligations to promote" the queen's service. When Digges died early in 1711, he quickly replaced him with Philip Ludwell II, a man of "Capacity" and "Circumstances" who lived nearby. Spotswood reminded Auditor General William Blathwayt of the influence such a man had "over a great many in the country," which "is no small Argument with a Governor." And he appears to have been especially solicitous of Byrd, whom he wined and dined, confided in, gave gifts, and appointed escheator for the region south of the James River. The governor also regularly entertained the remainder of the council, to the extent that some members began to sneak off at the end of the business day to avoid an invitation to dine. Wives were also given much attention. At the conclusion of the first ball of his administration, held at the Capitol on a rainy evening, he gallantly carried "the ladies into the coaches." Virginians responded warmly, even the difficult John Custis IV, who asked Spotswood to be his son's godfather.[47]

At the same time the governor took positions and exhibited attitudes that could lead to trouble. He was perhaps too quick to assert the crown's prerogative, and it was reported that he was "obstinate" and difficult to reason with. He was contemptuous of many of the burgesses, describing them as "persons of mean figure and character" who were elected because of "a defect in the Constitution which allows to everyone, tho' but just out of the condition of Serv't . . . an equal vote with the man of the best Estate in the Country." Even with councillors he was not so sensitive as he might have been, removing from new legislation a clause setting their "Sallary . . . because it is . . . more agreeable" that they should depend on the crown and be reminded that they "owe their Support as well as their promotion, Entirely to her Majesties Bounty, and not to claim it by a law here."[48]

For a while Spotswood's relations with the council were good, and his accomplishments in the first years of his administration were remarkable. There were problems with the House of Burgesses, especially where money needs were concerned, and he complained of its "parsimonious temper" and "mean understandings." But even here, through skillful management and the council's help, he eventually got cooperation. Early on he began to develop plans, "schemes" he called them, to enhance revenues while improving the economy. By the end of 1714, two major pieces of legislation had been passed, and adjustments had been made in regulations governing quitrent collection and the patenting of land. As Alan Williams has said, Spotswood "sought to work within the existing framework of Virginia institutions." He did so by recognizing that any new source of income would have to come without increasing taxes, that whatever he did should not "violate . . . imperial policy" or "Virginia tradition," and "that those who benefited most directly from his program" would "identify themselves with him politically."[49]

Virginia's economy was dependent on tobacco, and in these years its price was low, resulting in, as Spotswood phrased it, "unhappy circumstances" in "the country." Contributing to the problem was overproduction of the weed and the fact that the people were paying their debts, both public and private, with low-grade or "trash" tobacco. The governor's remedy was a tobacco inspection act which required that all tobacco used for the payment of debts or taxes or to be exported had to be inspected by publicly appointed agents, at newly constructed warehouses, where they would certify it to "be good, Sound, well conditioned" and "clear from all manner of Trash." This plan would reduce the amount of marketable tobacco and ensure that only "good" leaf would be exported. Further, for tobacco that was certified good, the owner would receive "tobacco notes" that could circulate as legal tender. The bill, of which Spotswood said he was the "Sole Author," was passed after a "great struggle" with the help of the "whole Council and all the Sensible Members of the lower House." He was justifiably proud. This one piece of legislation, he believed, would raise the price of tobacco, increase the public revenue, and provide a reliable medium of exchange. It would also provide the governor with some "forty Agencys," patronage positions, worth, he said, "nigh 250 pounds P. ann. each," that he could "dispose of among the most considerable men of the Colony, and principally to gratify with a Place all the members of the Assembly who were for the bill." By this means he could create a governor's "party" which would support him in the House of Burgesses and allow him to carry "any reasonable point."[50]

The governor also wanted to develop an Indian policy that would ensure peace on the colony's southern and western frontiers. He had been arranging treaties with neighboring tribes whom he hoped would serve as buffers against more distant and hostile ones. But his policy was hindered by the fact that some Virginia Indian traders took advantage of the natives through "fraudulent practices," which not only endangered the peace of the colony but interrupted a "beneficial and Advantagious" commerce. To solve the problem he proposed the creation of a joint-stock company with a monopoly on all the trade with "tributary" Indians on the south side of the James River as well as all foreign tribes. The company was to be open to anyone who would subscribe from £50 to £100. All trade with neighboring tribes was to be carried on at a company-maintained fort in Prince George County. The company also was to build a schoolhouse at the fort for Indian education and a powder magazine in Williamsburg. Such a company would regularize and encourage trade, develop better relations through an educational program, and contribute to frontier defense. A bill, so designed, was easily passed.[51]

Spotswood also, despite the failures of his predecessors, continued to try to bring some order and efficiency to the patenting of land and the collection of quitrents. Early on he was able to get a clause inserted in related legislation that would require forfeiture of land which had not been improved or for which taxes had not been paid for three years. These provisions were reinforced in 1713. He then inaugurated, with the council's agreement, a more efficient system for the collection of quitrents, requiring, among other things, better record keeping on the part of the deputy auditor and the receiver general.[52]

The governor was an excellent administrator, which accounts for part of his success. But he also used his considerable influence over appointments to gain support for his programs. He courted and rewarded Philip Ludwell and William Byrd. Nathaniel Harrison, of the powerful Harrison clan, was appointed naval officer, as was Christopher Robinson. When Edmund Jenings departed for England for an extended period, Spotswood was able to get his friend and physician William Cocke appointed secretary, but only after a deal was struck assuring Jenings half of the income from the post. Subsequently Cocke was added to the council. Gradually, as the opportunity presented itself, he began to get his own men appointed to the council, a process that was made difficult by death, arguments over precedence, and the fact that so many qualified men were related. But, in addition to Cocke, by 1715 William Bassett, Nathaniel Harrison, and Mann Page were his appointees. He also followed through on his promise to reward his supporters in the House of Burgesses. Twenty-four of the fifty-one burgesses were appointed tobacco agents, as were some of their relatives and Councillor John Smith. Spotswood was leaving nothing to chance. The council seemed supportive, and he had built a majority in the lower house. The future appeared promising, but then Queen Anne died, and new elections had to be called. From this point on there was little but trouble for one the ablest men ever to serve as Virginia's governor.[53]

The council had been accommodating during Spotswood's first four years, but increasingly there were indications that long-term accord would be difficult. The governor had made it clear from the beginning that he intended to uphold the authority of the crown, and he was not an easy man to reason with. He had little patience with "antient Custome," laws that ran counter to his instructions or that lessened dependence on the crown. He was persistent in trying to apply the minimal standards concerning the patenting of land that the Board of Trade had finally agreed to. "I tried to soften" the governor "concerning the land bill," reported William Byrd, "but in vain." Like Nicholson, he often had difficulty securing a quorum of councillors. The problem was especially pressing when the council met in its judicial capacity. So many of them were related that on occasion several would have to recuse themselves from cases that came before the General Court and oyer and terminer courts. The Board of Trade had instructed him in 1710 to establish "Courts of Oyer and Terminer for the more speedy trial" of criminal cases, which meant that the council would have to meet two additional times a year. These circumstances led to the first real conflict between the governor and the council. In December 1712, when Spotswood found that he could only get four councillors to attend such a court to hear the case of a man to "be try'd for his Life," he added the Speaker and two other "Eminent Members" of the House of Burgesses. Soon seven councillors—John Custis, John Lewis, William Byrd, Robert Carter, Philip Ludwell, Henry Duke, and John Smith—protested the action. They asserted that he had assured them that only councillors would serve on these courts. He should consider "How much the Gen'll Court will be divested of its Jurisdiction" founded on the "late Law" and "constant usage." Even if he had the right to appoint other judges, to do so would be unwise, for men's lives should not "be try'd by more inferior Judges than their Fortunes, of which the last Resort in this Country is in the Gen'll Court." They intended no reflection on him, but someday there might be a "passionate and resentful Governor" who would make "dangerous use of Precedent" and threaten "men's Lives and Libertys." If Spotswood held firm in his decision to appoint "other persons," then "we humbly beg you will have the goodness to dispence with our attendance on such occasions." The Board of Trade ultimately supported Spotswood but urged him to appoint other persons only on "extraordinary Occasions." The issue remained an irritant for five years, ultimately becoming a part of a more extended criticism of Spotswood by the council and others.[54]

The governor and his advisers also quarreled over the handling of quitrent income. The tobacco trade was languishing, and the council wanted the money to be used to make up "difficencys" in the public revenue and to cover "extraordinary expenses" rather than following the recent practice of remitting it directly to "the Exchequer of England." This measure would direct quitrents, councillors argued, "back into their old Channell." To Spotswood's chagrin the council cooperated with the House of Burgesses in framing an address to the king to approve this proposal. The governor said that the council was having difficulty separating its legislative function from its executive one and that this was just another attempt to encroach on the king's prerogative.[55]

Hard on the heels of this issue, Spotswood incurred the ire of two powerful councillors, William Byrd and Philip Ludwell. He initiated a plan in 1714 for the more efficient collection of quitrents, anticipating that it would increase the crown's revenue and provide "a just rent roll." His proposal would require better record keeping and, in general, more work for Receiver General Byrd and Deputy Auditor Ludwell. Most of the council approved of the new procedures, and the governor suggested that those who were opposed state their reasons in writing. Only Byrd did so, arguing that the measures would decrease his income; that the sheriffs, who were to be the chief collectors, would also receive less; and that the workload would be substantially increased. Byrd, a considerable Indian trader, also was opposed to the creation of the Indian Company. He was not happy with the governor as he departed for England on family business in the spring of 1715.[56]

Ludwell said he would not respond to the governor for he was an "unequal adversarry." Instead he wrote the Board of Trade while doing everything that he could to disrupt Spotswood's plans and support in Virginia. He adamantly refused to adhere to the new procedures and "loudly" argued in public "before many Bystanders that no man needed to comply" with orders "for obtaining an exact Rent Roll" within the colony. In council he assumed an obstructionist role, and he began to side with the opposition in the House of Burgesses that had emerged from discontent in the small-planter community with the tobacco inspection law. To make matters worse, Ludwell had stirred "up the humours of the people before the last election" in 1715, which aided in the governor's losing his working majority in the lower house. He went so far, Spotswood said, as to keep "mutinous" burgesses informed of what was going on in the council. Ludwell, following the example of his father, seemed to thrive on controversy. The fight against Nicholson had sharpened his skills, and now he became even bolder, boasting of his "Interest at home," accusing the governor of "hectoring and Browbeating the King's subjects," and treating him "with more rudeness and ill manners than . . . any Governor was ever treated." Ludwell also precipitated a lawsuit over crown land that he claimed as his own. Spotswood had had enough. In May 1716 he suspended Ludwell from the office of deputy auditor. He also would have liked to suspend him from the council, but to do so required a majority vote which was "impossible" to gain because seven of Ludwell's "Relations" held council seats.[57]

As the difficulties with Ludwell and Byrd escalated, the governor also came to a parting of the ways with the House of Burgesses. In the elections of 1715, only one burgess who was also a tobacco agent was returned. Most of his supporters were gone. Peter Beverley, on whom he could rely, was replaced as Speaker and lost his seat when it was ruled that the College of William and Mary was not entitled to representation. Suddenly Spotswood was unable to get desired legislation passed, attempts were made to repeal the Tobacco Inspection Act, and he began to hear rumblings protesting the Indian Company. His messages and the response of the house became heated, so much so that the council felt forced to censure the "disrespectfull behaviour of several members of the House of Burgesses towards his Majesties Lieut Governor." A frustrated Spotswood finally dissolved the assembly, lashing out in an intemperate speech in which he attributed the "Miscarriages to the Peoples Mistaken Choice of a

Set of Representatives, whom Heaven has not generally endowed with the Ordinary Qualifications requisite to Legislators; for whom I observe that the Grand ruling Party in your House has not furnished Chairmen of two of your Standing Committees who can spell English or Write Common Sense." The committees were Claims and Elections and Privileges, chaired by George Marable and Gawin Corbin, whom Spotswood had earlier removed from the post of naval officer for forging documents.[58]

Things now got nasty. In February 1716 an anonymous set of complaints against the governor was sent to the Board of Trade. Most of them appear to have been designed to make trouble rather than from any belief that they could be substantiated. He was, for example, charged with using public funds to protect and further two "private interests," the Indian Company and his Germanna settlement and ironworks. He was able to answer such charges effectively. But one charge, clearly intended to raise questions about his personal life, was especially disturbing. When he and a "Strong Guard of Men" traveled to negotiate with the southern Indians, the charge declared, it was merely a pretense for developing trade for the Indian Company, which he headed and in which "the greatest Stock" was "in the name of Cath. Russell." Katherine Russell had accompanied Spotswood to Virginia and had been introduced as his niece. She was the bachelor governor's housekeeper-hostess and his mistress. She had generated much gossip among the elite community; Byrd intimated at one point that Mrs. Russell was pregnant and went to Pennsylvania to have the child. The governor believed that "Secret Enemys" also had begun a whispering campaign in England, attacking his reputation with "malicious storys of" his "private behaviour" that caused his half brother, who had intended to leave him "his whole estate at his death," worth £20,000, to marry and "get a son." With "God" as his "witness," William Byrd, who was in England working for the repeal for the Indian Company and tobacco inspection acts, denied that either he or Ludwell had done such a "heinous" thing as to write Spotswood's brother. Byrd also said that he had not seen the anonymous "articles" until "Col. Blakiston shew'd me a copy." One suspects Commissary James Blair. The governor was to say later that his opponents had "Mr Blair for a staunch Achitophel in all conspiracies against Governors who will take upon him the whole drudgery of forming letters" and "memorials" and would be none too scrupulous in "swearing to them." This was a suitably biblical epithet for the Reverend Mr. Blair: Achitophel (Ahitophel) was David's treacherous counselor who joined Absalom in revolt. The lines were being drawn, and there would be little peace between Spotswood and the council for the remainder of his administration.[59]

The news of Spotswood's troubles with his council spread quickly. From North Carolina in July 1716 came the report that the governor had "gained . . . the ill will of most of the leading men in Virginia" by dissolving "the Assembly" in "a very unusual manner" and "by suspending Coll. Ludwell." Ludwell, the writer commented, "is one of the Council and most of the Council are related to him." Indeed, six of the twelve councillors—Bassett, Berkeley, Blair, Byrd, Harrison, and Ludwell—were all related, although the connection was sometimes slight; William Bassett, for example, was married to Ludwell's half niece. Family relationships, however distant, were important in Virginia. Equally important was the fact that nine of the councillors were Virginia born: William Bassett, Edmund Berkeley, William Byrd, Robert Carter, Nathaniel Harrison, John Lewis, Philip Ludwell, Mann Page, and John Smith. (Blair was born in Scotland and Cocke and Jenings in England.) Spotswood called them "ungrateful Creolians" who, in the final analysis, always supported what they believed to be the interests of Virginia as opposed to those of the mother country. Most of the councillors also believed that the governor was breaking "thro' Laws and Charters" and altering "all the ancient usage and foundations of the Government." This action was, in their mind, more important than the crown's prerogative. The main issues were the governor's firm stand on his right to appoint judges to oyer and terminer courts and the measures involving the more efficient collection of quitrents. Spotswood also had a sharp tongue and argued effectively, and as tensions mounted he offended the sensibilities of proud men.[60]

The governor was not without supporters. Most of his Indian Company associates, a number of his tobacco agent appointees, those men who accompanied him across the Blue Ridge Mountains in August and September 1716, and the signers of two extremely supportive grand jury addresses in 1716 and 1719 were all men of substance. A number of the grand jury members were also members of the Indian Company: John Baylor, Charles Chiswell, William Dandridge, Cole Digges, Thomas Jones, and Thomas Nelson. Two of Spotswood's eight companions on his trip across the mountains, Jeremiah Clowder and George Mason, were also grand jurors. But they were dispersed around the colony, and most of them were from families still on the way up the ladder of success. There were exceptions, to be sure—Digges, Peter and Robert Beverley, Philip Lightfoot, young Thomas Lee, Mann Page—but far more common were people like Baylor, Dandridge, Chiswell, Mason, and Nelson.

They were up against wealthier, better-connected, and more seasoned political operators who already had waged successful battles against earlier governors and who had a working majority on the council. This majority met regularly and could easily organize their strategies in opposition to Spotswood. Blair and Ludwell were the leaders, but in the background was the quieter— Spotswood said "haughty"—Carter. They could always count on the support of John Smith and John Lewis and usually that of William Bassett, Nathaniel Harrison, and Edmund Berkeley. Edmund Jenings and Mann Page were unreliable, especially Jenings, whom Byrd called that "mear sychophant Col. Heartless" who was "a worm to be trod upon, a spaniel to be beat into compliance." Dr. William Cocke, who owed everything to the governor, was the only councillor on whom he could always rely. The opposition also had Byrd in England representing their views. The master of Westover was smart and persistent. He had spent many years in England, had access to a wide range of important people, and knew which buttons to push to get results.[61]

Spotswood believed that these men were motivated by more than their concern for "Ancient Rights and Privileges"; he was sure that greed was also a factor. The secret, he charged, was that they were trying to "procure a sallary of £100 per annum" for "each Councillor." Their earlier petition to the king to allow the use of quitrents to cover extraordinary expenses and shortfalls in the public revenue was really the first step toward attaining the salary. The failure to attain this goal, he said, "unlocks all the cause of their . . . behaviour about quitt rents" and was part of the reason he had incurred their displeasure. Further, these men were intractable. They were resolved, because of their "success in removing former Governors," that "no one ever shall sitt easy here" who did not "submitt to their dictates" and "be governed by their maxims and interests." He believed that they would stop at nothing to attain "the measures they happen to be bent upon," even "another Rebellion as Bacons."[62]

The governor's estimate of his opponents was not without some reason. He dismissed Ludwell as deputy auditor only to see Ludwell's son-in-law John Grymes appointed in his place. Grymes, who represented Gloucester County in the House of Burgesses, emerged as one of his fiercest opponents. Byrd played a major role in gaining the disallowance of two of his proudest accomplishments, the tobacco inspection and Indian Company laws. The majority of the council refused to go to his house to discuss reconciliation over a "bowl of arrack punch." To add insult to injury, they declined his invitation to a "public entertainment" to celebrate the king's birthday, and they did not attend "the play which was acted on that occasion." Instead, they held their own celebration in the chambers of the House of Burgesses and invited the "mobb of the town to a bonfire," liberally supplying them with "liquor to drink the same healths without as their masters drank within" and "without any more notice of their

Governor than if there had been none upon the place." At least one of his opponents' wives was forbidden to visit Mrs. Russell, whom she liked, at his house. The wife may have been Hannah Ludwell, and in fact, Ludwell's dislike of the governor was such that he wrote his old enemy Francis Nicholson that he might have to leave Virginia and if it "be my future to see England again I shall be sure to do myself the honor to wait on you." Ludwell's house in town, which was in sight of Spotswood's, became a "rendezvous" for Blair and "disaffected Burgesses" when the assembly met in the spring of 1718. The governor was aware of this and was convinced that they were plotting against him.[63]

News had not yet reached Virginia in April that the Board of Trade approved of the various reforms Spotswood had made to increase the crown revenue "arising from the sale of land" and that the attorney general had confirmed his right to appoint judges to courts of oyer and terminer. The opposition councillors, emboldened by their success in getting major laws repealed, now moved to make more trouble for the governor and ultimately get him removed through the aegis of the House of Burgesses. Spotswood watched the comings and goings of his opponents as they met at Ludwell's house. He knew that "papers" had been circulated in most of the counties stating that the only reason an assembly had been called was to authorize payment of "great sums" to the Indian Company for expenses incurred as a result of its public services and to dispute the governor's right to appoint judges to oyer and terminer courts. Both of these documents were "creditably" reported to have been drafted by council members. Nevertheless, Spotswood's opening address was moderate in tone. The colony's economy was flourishing, and although there were some warning signs, relations with the Indians were good. The people's representatives had "abundant reason to be easye in your Countrys peacefull State, to be cheerfull under your Thriving Circumstances and to be Joyfull for his . . . Majesties Auspicious Raign," all of which would provide "a better foundation for Harmony."[64]

But there was to be no harmony. Spotswood mentioned the king's instruction of the previous fall ordering that no act concerning trade or shipping was to be passed unless it included a clause delaying its application "until it be approved and confirmed by his Majesty." He also pointed to the repeal of the Indian Company law and the king's recommendation that the company be reimbursed for its "reasonable" expenses in the public's behalf. The company had been the cornerstone of Spotswood's efforts to protect the frontiers and improve relations with Native Americans. He believed that, in addition to the better regulation of trade, the company's construction of Fort Christanna south of the James River and a powder magazine in the capital, as well as the Indian school it maintained at the fort, had led to peace on the southern and western frontiers, and he hoped that in some way they could be continued. Problems also were developing with northern tribes who had given some indication of hostile intent and of breaking a 1685 treaty. Spotswood already had traveled to New York to prevent "Evil Consequences," and he might have to go again if a new "Treaty be Sett on foot." All of these efforts were expensive, as were other "fatigueing Expeditions" he had undertaken since 1711 "purely in the Country's Service," and he indicated that he should be reimbursed for these expenses.[65]

The governor's agenda included other items, but it was around these matters that controversy swirled. The House of Burgesses examined his address minutely, primed, he said, by the council. It raised issues and added articles to legislation that were certain to provoke him. He claimed that he was verbally abused and insulted by some of the burgesses. The house composed an address to the king requesting that the instruction concerning trade and shipping legislation be recalled because it was often necessary to make "needful Laws" that could go into effect "immediately." It also requested reversal of the confirmation of the governor's power to appoint "whatever Judges he pleases" to oyer and terminer courts on the grounds that this placed "dangerous power" in his hands. William Byrd was appointed agent for the House of Burgesses to make sure these matters were properly presented, and a bill was forwarded authorizing payment to him for his services. The council considered the bill for two days but finally rejected it. In a blatant show of independence, the house resolved to pay him, something it could not actually do but which was a further affront to the governor. The Indian Company expenses received special attention. But in the end the house bluntly stated that the only reimbursement the company should receive was £100 for building the powder magazine. The Indian school, the repair of Fort Christiana, and the maintenance of guards there were not things that benefited the colony. There was no need to regulate trade with the Indians. And hostages kept at the fort in order to assure that peace would prevail were to be sent back, albeit, in a slight concession, at public expense. The house sidestepped funding for a new treaty with northern tribes, saying it knew of no threats to Virginia and was sure that the governor and the council would take the necessary steps to preserve their friendship. The final insult came in response to the governor's request for reimbursement for 5,020 miles of travel on public business. The governor included the expenses for his expedition across the Blue Ridge, for which the Indian Company evidently had paid. Such "fatigueing Journeys . . . convince us of your great diligence," the house stated, and "we hope this will give you the Satisfaction of reflecting that you have deserved the Sallary allowed by his Majesty."[66]

Great difficulty arose over two major pieces of legislation: a bill setting the fees that public officers could charge and another for the establishment of a crown-operated post office. The house forwarded the first to the council with a clause shifting the authority for appointing county clerks from the secretary of the colony to the council. Spotswood refused to sign the bill with this clause, and in this instance he prevailed. The clause was removed, and William Cocke, the governor's friend and handpicked secretary, retained control of this important patronage post. The post office bill ran into difficulty because the house argued that government-established postal rates were taxes and that Parliament could not "Levy any Tax . . . without the consent" of the General Assembly. A bill finally passed both houses, but the governor refused to sign it because it was so amended that it could never be "put in Execution."[67]

A further irritation to the embattled governor revolved around a substantial surplus in the public treasury. A bill was introduced authorizing the treasurer to place £4,000 at 4 percent interest and allowing him to keep half of the income. Archibald Blair, brother of the commissary and member of the house, was to be assigned another £4,000 under a similar arrangement. Spotswood could not accept this. The two Blairs and Ludwell, he said, were partners in one of the "most considerable Trading Stores in this Country," and once money was so placed by "Act of Assembly," it could be removed only in the same manner. That would not happen because of the majority these "gentlemen and their relations held on the Council." The action was so transparent that at the last minute the bill was withdrawn. A bill placing £10,000 in the hands of the treasurer to invest at 4 percent was finally passed in December.[68]

The amount of money that was being expended on the completion of the "Governor's house" was another issue raised by the house. Spotswood had lavished great attention on completing and furnishing the building. The Burgesses now asked him if the house was finished, and if not, how much more it was going to cost. He brusquely replied that "it is not finisht and I don't know how much it will take." But the house pressed on, appointing a committee to visit him to find out what remained to be done. In an obvious attempt to insult him, the committee included two of his bitterest enemies, Nicholas Meriwether and Archibald Blair. In 1714 Spotswood had removed Meriwether as a justice of the peace in New Kent County because of "Seditious Speeches & misrepresentations" concerning the Tobacco Inspection Act. Blair, one of the "the most violent men in the house," was working hand in glove with his brother, Spotswood said. He refused to meet with the committee because it included those who were "accustomed to Speak very irreverently of the Kings Governours" and "should I enter into conversation with them may . . . forget what House they are in and be apt to speak to me in their usual rude termes." The house then proceeded to pass a bill limiting further expenditure to £250. Spotswood refused to sign the bill. The result of all this wrangling was that apart from the fee bill, a bill authorizing £1,000 for scholarships at the college, and several private bills, no other legislation was passed in the spring session of 1718. Not even a bill changing the meeting days for the Northampton County court went through, because the council, Spotswood averred, objected to a clause confirming "the right of the King to alter" such days on application from justices of the peace to the governor.[69]

At the end of May, the irked Spotswood adjourned the assembly until July 10, hoping that in the interim the council might prevail on the House of Burgesses to support the expense of renewing the treaty with the northern Indians. But the council refused to back such a measure unless the Indians were openly hostile. He then decided to prorogue the assembly, but in what was certainly an act of further provocation, the council advised him that he could not prorogue an adjourned assembly; he would have to wait until it reassembled on July 10 to do so. The governor grudgingly followed the advice while requesting an opinion from the Board of Trade as to his authority in such a case.[70]

Disaffected councillors kept the pressure on. Commissary Blair and Ludwell now challenged the governor's right to collate and induct ministers (making appointment permanent), citing "the Practice of the Country to be of more force than the Power of the Crown." Encouraged by them, the vestry in James City Parish had installed a minister of its own choosing. Spotswood raised the issue with the council and on a 4-to-2 vote received support for his right "to supply Vacant benefices." Edmund Jenings, John Lewis, William Cocke, and Mann Page were the majority. The defection of Lewis in this instance suggests that Ludwell and Blair could not always count on the backing of the original complainants against the governor. Undeterred, they convinced the vestry to retain the "ablest Lawyer" to argue the case against the governor in an appeal to England. In this case the governor prevailed, but the controversy was to continue.[71]

By the summer of 1718, Spotswood had concluded that the only way he could function effectively was to convince the Board of Trade and the earl of Orkney to remove some of the "most turbulent spirits (vizt. Blair, Ludwell, Smith and Byrd)" from the Council and replace them with Peter Beverley, Cole Digges, John Robinson, and Edward Hill, who had "more peaceable and loyal principles."

He had tried everything, even offering to appoint no other judges to oyer and terminer courts if the council acknowledged that the crown had the power to do so and if it "acquiesced" in the judgments of the Board of Trade and the attorney general concerning this matter. He also asked that the councillors behave toward him "with decent good manners." He recruited the moderate councillors Nathaniel Harrison and Mann Page, along with the clerk of the council, William Robertson, to negotiate with the opposition. But it was all to no avail. They were "startled" at his recent "conduct . . . particularly at the meeting of the Governors of the Colledge" and his "exposing" the "late officers of Revenue in Council." They would do nothing, Page reported, until the governor's attempts to change the "Constitution" stopped and their privileges were "preserved." In despair, the governor said, "I cannot but take them for unfaithful Councillors"; as long as he was "staunch for H.M. rights they will think me a Governor not for their purpose" and would "strive to blast my credit." The governor had a strong case for Byrd's removal because he had been absent for over three years, a good bit of the time without permission, and he was a real problem. Byrd, using his influence with the Treasury, had sold his post as receiver general, leaving him free "to oppose every design that may seem to be arbitrary or unjust." He had worked diligently and effectively representing the views of dissident councillors to crown authorities, and now he was agent for what appeared to be an angry House of Burgesses. To get Byrd out of the way and replace him with his own man would be an important step in constructing a more malleable council. Byrd, on the other hand, told one of his fellow councillors that he did not intend to be the "governor's dog or his ass."[72]

But before any of the governor's strategies could be applied, a political storm erupted in the fall 1718 meeting of the assembly. The session was expected to be a quiet one, for there appeared to be no pressing business. The usual preliminaries took place: the appointment of committees and consideration of petitions from the counties. The house responded positively to a message from the governor and the council proposing ways to deal with pirates led by Blackbeard (Edward Teach), who were threatening trade and shipping in coastal waters. But there were signs that all was not well. The house rejected out of hand petitions from the frontier counties of Hanover and New Kent, forwarded by the governor and council, requesting guards to protect them from Indians. It approved a resolution proposing that Byrd be paid £300 for his work as agent. Then on Thursday, November 20, Nicholas Meriwether, Spotswood's old nemesis from New Kent County and member of the Committee for Propositions and Grievances, chaired by Gawin Corbin, another enemy, presented an address to the king that Spotswood said had been drafted by the commissary. It stated that the Burgesses had considered "several Attempts" of the lieutenant governor to subvert "the Constitution of our Government" as well as "many hardships which he daily exercises" on the king's "good Subjects." It was the house's duty to present its grievances, and it asked the king to receive them from "the Honble William Byrd Esqr" on "behalf of your oppressed Subjects." Byrd was instructed to lay the address and grievances before the king and to "endeavour" to "the utmost" of his power to gain Spotswood's removal. Attendance was poor—it was reported that some members had gone home while others were at a horse race—and the address was approved 22 to 14. But when the list of grievances was considered, the debate was "adjourned" until Friday morning. The absent members, alerted by the governor's supporters to the charges against him, were now in their seats, and as the debate began it was clear that the "Party Managers" were going to have difficulty carrying the day. One by one fourteen instructions, which included eleven specific grievances, were considered. Before the debate was concluded, only five remained. Spotswood's removal was no longer requested, and he was only charged with having misconstrued the laws concerning land patents and the payment of quitrents, lavishing "away the Countrys money" on "the Governors house," trying to keep the counties from levying taxes for the payment of "Burgesses Salary," and abusing the House by "provoking Speeches & messages" and having "thrown undeserved Reflections" upon its members. Byrd was directed to point out that the only way the house could express its grievances was through an agent, because the governor would not forward them, and to obtain an instruction approving the payment of his expenses as agent. Spotswood claimed that his supporters agreed to allow these instructions to pass "purely to expose the weakness and malice of my accusers." According to him, his leading opponents, Blair and Ludwell in the council and Meriwether, Corbin, John Grymes, and Archibald Blair in the house, could not "conceal their Indignation and Resentment." The governor was so confident that he had nothing to fear from English authorities that in a bravado address to the house, he said he would wager £1,000 that none of the charges would be accepted. It was unjust that the country "should be burdened with the private Quarrells of Prejudiced men" and that "Yor Governor should have no recompense for the injury done his Reputation."[73]

The governor exuded confidence, but he left nothing to chance. He immediately sent full letters explaining what had transpired in the assembly, with all of the relevant documents, to the Board of Trade and the earl of Orkney. He made clear that his problems rested with a "sett of men" who for many years had sought to gain "the whole power of government." Efforts were underway, he told Orkney, even "for the removal of your Lordship." This may have been the case, for earlier Byrd had written Ludwell that Orkney was "unalterable in his support" of Spotswood and all they could do was proceed with their efforts because "he can't be more our adversary than he is already." The governor's account was reasonably accurate. Memorials supporting him were coming in from the counties; by May 1719, twenty-one of the twenty-five counties had testified in his behalf. He said these testimonials were "Voluntary and deliberate," while his opponents charged that "they were pressed with all the Interest and artifices of the Governour and his friends"; certainly Spotswood did not discourage such support. Orkney said that Spotswood had failed to bring about reconciliation and asked the board to solve the problem. He was clearly supportive of Spotswood, but he indicated that he believed the only solution was to remove either his lieutenant or the council.[74]

Relations between Spotswood and his foes did not improve. Distrust prevailed, and both sides believed that their mail was being opened. Cracks now began to appear in the solid front of the disaffected councillors, for developments in both England and Virginia were causing concern. Byrd had learned of Spotswood's recommendation that he and other councillors be removed, and in December he requested an audience with the Board of Trade. In March 1719 he became aware that the solicitor general had confirmed the governor's right to induct and collate ministers and that he was sympathetic with Spotswood's problem concerning proroguing of an assembly from an adjournment. All of this made Byrd uneasy, and he informed the board that he was "sincerely inclined to peace" and offered his services in bringing about reconciliation between the governor and his council. He had been working on a peace plan since early March and had presented it to the earl of Orkney, who had "received" him "coldly." In April the board recommended Byrd's removal from the council because of his long absence and proposed that Peter Beverley replace him. Byrd contested this action. Next, the board informed the secretary of state that the House of Burgesses had acted improperly in appointing an agent and that the complaints against Spotswood resulted only from his carrying out the king's instructions.[75]

The spring of 1719 was a busy time as controversy over the collation of ministers continued. For a while the situation brightened for the governor. Many of the clergy, dissatisfied with Blair's neglect of duties, supported Spotswood. They also questioned whether Blair had been episcopally ordained, which placed the commissary on the defensive. (It is now known that Blair was properly ordained.) And when the General Court met in April, the grand jury, composed of many Spotswood supporters, requested that he forward an address to the king describing him as a "a good . . . just and wise . . . Governor." All of this gave the governor's opponents pause.[76]

The dissident councillors responded, and with Blair involved in his own problems,[77] Ludwell led the way. He wrote letters to English correspondents explaining the situation and asking for help. Two formal responses, one of which was printed in Philadelphia, were circulated. Cracks began to appear in the solid phalanx of the opposition. Nathaniel Harrison, a moderate among Spotswood's foes, distrusted William Byrd and feared that he might be appointed governor. Indeed, although Harrison could not have known, Byrd had begun new efforts to gain the governorship in April. Harrison suggested that since Byrd's chances of coming "in that status" were good, it might not be "amiss" to pay him for his services. Others objected to strong statements in the second formal response. Clearly council opponents of the governor were feeling the heat. They went so far as to accuse him of being the author of the grand jury's address, for the "style is more like him and is more tolerable in a person of his high station and is used the Dictators Style, than it is like the style of private men."[78]

The councillors were angry, and they were alarmed. The Board of Trade wrote Spotswood in June that he had done "very well" on a variety of matters, that he should not worry about assembly complaints for nobody "has apply'd on that subject," and that he could depend on "all countenance and support we can give you which we think you deserv'd." Byrd was on the scene, and he knew what was going on. He boasted that he had "interest enough" to retain his council seat, but because it was clear that there was little sympathy in England for the opposition to the governor, Byrd scrambled to smooth over the difficulties. Virginia's agent, Nathaniel Blakiston, wrote Ludwell in May that Byrd was sending a copy "of his proposal for being a pacifick mediator." By early September, Byrd had decided that he must return to Virginia. His "affairs" needed attention after his long absence, and he appears to have made up his mind to bring an end to what had become destructive political warfare. He spent much time in September and October working on the problem, consulting Blakiston and even the hostile earl of Orkney. Byrd, Blakiston, and Micajah Perry visited Orkney, whom they "found on a high rope." But after much negotiation he agreed "to write a letter" to Virginia concerning "the proposed plan for peace" despite the fact that Byrd had "treated him indifferently." Byrd's correspondence to and from Virginia increased markedly. He recruited John Campbell, duke of Argyll, Byrd's patron and a powerful member of the king's household, to "interpose" his "good offices" with Spotswood because "I expect no peace unless your Grace will" do so. Byrd continued to work on retaining his council seat, and this problem was not resolved in his favor until shortly before his departure from Dover for Virginia on December 13.[79]

Spotswood, in the meantime, had confronted the council with the Board of Trade's supportive letter, which included the earlier opinions of the solicitor general and Richard West, counsel to the board, affirming his power of "Collating Ecclesiastical Benefices," as well as the favorable judgment concerning the proroguing of assemblies that had been adjourned. It was at this point that Blair and Ludwell may have presented an opposing opinion of Attorney General Richard Raymond concerning collation and induction. Nevertheless, Spotswood appeared to be in a strong position with support from the Board of Trade and, apparently, broad backing in Virginia. Soon Peter Beverley, Cole Digges, and John Robinson, all the governor's men, would be added to the council.[80]

The situation did not look promising in Virginia for the master of Westover when he came ashore on February 4, 1720, with a painful case of the "piles." He stayed four days with "Captain Smith," probably York County burgess Lawrence Smith, where he was treated by Dr. Archibald Blair and visited by John Smith and Philip Lightfoot, who told him "all the news." Then it was on to Williamsburg, in Lightfoot's "chariot," and his brother-in-law John Custis's home. For two days he received a steady stream of visitors—Philip Ludwell, Commissary Blair, Receiver General James Roscow, Benjamin Harrison, soon-to-be Speaker of the House of Burgesses John Holloway, Clerk of the House John Randolph, and others—with much talk of "public affairs." He also wrote Spotswood, probably about his plan for reconciliation. The governor's response, delivered by Randolph, "put an end to all" of his "thoughts of peace." Over dinner with Custis, Blair, Holloway, and Randolph, the problems with Spotswood were the topic of conversation. Byrd was told that "several gentlemen" had not visited him "for fear of the governor." From Williamsburg he went to Ludwell's Green Spring, with more visitors, and finally home to Westover on February 17. Over the next two months, many other friends and relations came to pay their respects and hash over the troubled politics of the Old Dominion. Rumor was rampant. Nathaniel Harrison wrote that the duke of Argyll had been appointed governor and that Byrd "was made his lieutenant," something that Byrd did not credit. It was clear that Spotswood was not in a conciliatory mood. Councillor John Smith died in March, and the governor urged that he be replaced by a man of "Loyalty, sound principals, good sense and peaceable disposition," unlike the "sett of men" who did nothing but "pursue their private designs."[81]

Byrd learned in April that orders had arrived for restoring him to the council. He journeyed to Williamsburg on the twenty-fifth and went to the Capitol, where the General Court was meeting. He presented his orders to Spotswood, telling the governor that he would have waited on him at "his house but that the messages I had received from him" in February had suggested that he would not be welcome. Spotswood grudgingly responded that he would "obey the King's order" but then proceeded to "rail" at Byrd "most violently before all the people." Byrd felt that he had responded "without fear . . . and came off with credit." He then "loitered about till the court was up," certainly to Spotswood's irritation, and had dinner with his councillor friends. The next day he was sworn in and resumed his seat.[82]

The next few days saw much discussion and planning. One evening Byrd, Robert Carter, and Philip Ludwell sat up until 10:00 p.m. discussing "treasonable matters." On the night of the twenty-eighth, six of the council worked late on a "complaint to be made against the Governor." The next day, in council, the long-simmering animosity boiled over, and there were "hard words spoken" about Ludwell and Blair's past actions. The confrontation went on for an exhausting two hours when suddenly, as Byrd reported, "the clouds cleared away and we began to be perfectly good friends and agreed on terms of lasting reconciliation, to the great surprise of ourselves and everybody else." Another report stated that Spotswood "began to play his old game of dissimulation and when they least thought of it he melted them with the most humble desire for peace and friendship." The terms of reconciliation, as the governor explained them, were simple. The question of his power to appoint judges to courts of oyer and terminer had already been settled in his favor. It was agreed that the differences concerning his right to supply "Vacant Benefices" should be settled "in a judicial way with an appeal to his Maj'ty in Council." There would be no "seperate complaints" over disagreements that might arise in the future. A "fair and impartial" statement, which would be signed by both sides, would be forwarded to the Board of Trade for its decision. If the disagreement concerned "a point of law . . . their Lordships" would be requested to "take the opinion" of the attorney general and solicitor general. Past controversies were to be "buried in Obliviion." Spotswood's account of the "behaviour" of Blair and Ludwell would not be sent to the board, and "Words" spoken by Ludwell as well as "some other indecent Expressions" which the governor had thought "fit to take notice of" were removed from the "rough Journals" of the council.[83]

The response to the settlement of differences was immediate. Spotswood invited the council to dinner, and as the word spread great joy was expressed by the firing of guns and "illuminations" all over town. The evening ended with a "concert of music at the Governor's," and Spotswood, as Byrd recounted, "kissed us all . . . and gave me a kiss more than other people." Early the next morning, before Byrd could pay his respects to Spotswood, the governor came to his lodging, was "exceedingly courteous," and remained for half an hour. Never modest, Byrd said that he had a "great share in this happy resolution" in which "the people's grievances" were redressed and that he certainly had "some claim to the reward that is promis'd peace-makers." John Percival, his English friend and patron, congratulated him on his "good success" in "your struggle in behalf of publick liberty." All of this was overdrawn; private grievance and self-interest had dominated the conflict. But the dissident councillors did believe, as Robert Carter said, that they had been fighting the good fight "to redress ourselves from some oppressions we thought we had reason to complain under."

How can the seemingly quick resolution to the long contest be explained? Clearly the governor had gained the upper hand. He had received virtually unqualified support from the Board of Trade, and his opponents were disheartened "with the great discouragements from home." As time wore on, it became more difficult for them to remain united. Only Blair and Ludwell appear to have been intransigent. Too many, as Carter said, were "ready to sacrifice all that's dear to us, provided they have a small share in that honor and the profit and swim glib in the tide of favor." Byrd recognized that there was no benefit in continuing the struggle, and his intervention was important. But in the end the canny Spotswood brought it to a conclusion. His support appeared solid, and the constant bickering was focusing too much of the Board of Trade's attention on his administration. He was willing to let the courts decide the clergy issue; after all, judicial decisions had gone his way in the past. In fact, the dispute concerning collation and induction was never resolved. Public money was appropriated to pursue the matter through the General Court with appeal to England, but after Spotswood's removal nothing was done. He may have also decided by this time that his long-term future was in Virginia and it was in his interest to mend his fences. In his opening address to the House of Burgesses in November 1720, he asked it "to consider the stake I have among you and the free choice I have made to fix it under this government." Spotswood took the initiative and proposed "reconciliation and friendship," and his opponents, on the defensive, were more than happy to accept the offer.[84]

For a while it appeared that, as Robert Carter said, "all things . . . carry the face of peace." Elections for the November assembly created some division. Both Spotswood and Byrd were accused of electioneering. Byrd had been present at the election in his own county, Charles City, as well as those in Henrico and

Middlesex, causing talk of his being "busy at elections" working against the governor. He was forced to defend himself to the governor "from that calumny." Spotswood probably was not convinced of Byrd's innocence, for he certainly knew of his travels and that he had visited Gawin Corbin and John Grymes during the Middlesex elections in which they were both returned to office. He also had visited Robert Carter at Corotoman, and Blair was with him most of the time. That the governor still did not trust his adversaries became evident when his friend Dr. William Cocke died of a stroke during the General Court meeting in October. Spotswood immediately wrote to his superiors in England recommending the reappointment of Edmund Jenings as secretary and suggesting that John Robinson of Middlesex County be chosen to fill Cocke's council seat. He did not want anyone appointed who was "akin to the greater part of the present Council." Predictably, the council faction wanted someone of their own persuasion in these places. Within days of Cocke's death, Byrd wrote the duke of Argyll requesting his help in getting the secretary's post for Carter's eldest son, John. Byrd had seen a good deal of Carter since his return to Virginia and was much taken with "his fine daughters." Carter himself wrote that rumor had it that Jenings would be appointed, but he hoped "that some other person may be able to come in for a share in the favors of the crown." Reconciliation did not involve altruism, nor had it dampened ambition.[85]

The assembly that convened on November 2 was a more amenable one. "Both Parties" did seem to want to get along, but old wounds remained, as did distrust. In his generally conciliatory address to the house, the governor noted that some still spoke of "the Countrys and the Governours friends" and warned that this might "prove a poison to your proceedings." He was certainly distressed by the election of John Holloway, a man he distrusted, as Speaker of the House and the reversal in the house of the election of supporter Thomas Lee of Westmoreland County on the grounds that Lee's brother Henry, the sheriff, had made a "false return." The expense of completing the governor's house, although finally resolved, remained an irritant. Indian Company expenses in the public interest came up again and despite his best efforts remained unpaid. A council committee, chaired by Blair, recommended, and the council agreed, that the matter should be referred to the next meeting of the assembly, and the House in turn refused to act. A payment of £237 to the Indian Company was finally authorized in May 1722. The lower body finally did agree with the council that measures, requiring help from the mother country, should be taken to settle and defend frontier areas against "savage" Indians and the French. It would be necessary to have someone present the case to the home government. Speaker

Holloway broke a 21-to-21 tie by voting in favor of resolves recommending the appointment of a person to perform this task. Then, in what must have been similarly close votes, William Byrd, who had announced his intention to return to England, was selected, and £400 in expense money was authorized. But Spotswood was wary of Byrd and proposed that his instructions be amended to the effect that he "enter into Bond to the Governour not to meddle in Great Britain with any other affair of this Government than what shall be contained in his . . . Instructions." The house knew that Byrd would not accept such a condition and responded that the instructions were clear: he was not authorized "to go beyond" them. The council approved the resolves with, evidently, only minor changes. Byrd told the governor that he "absolutely" refused to "give such bond," but Spotswood persisted, and two days before Christmas he tried to persuade the Burgesses to accept his amendment only to fail again. Byrd was outraged, but he bade Spotswood a civil farewell. Later in the day he had second thoughts and went to the Capitol to tell the governor that "I had rather my tongue . . . be cut out than it should be tied up from doing my country service." Despite all this Spotswood prorogued the assembly with "Satisfaction" because in other areas it had "agreed on several considerable matters."[86]

Legislation creating two new counties, Brunswick and Spotsylvania, had been passed. Quitrents and public levies were to be remitted for a period of ten years in these counties, thus encouraging settlement. The ostensible purpose of this legislation was to create a frontier buffer zone against the incursion of hostile Indians. But it also made the acquisition of land in these counties attractive. The governor held alone and in partnership 35,000 acres in Spotsylvania County, and within the next year and a half he added another 55,000 acres, some of it before the Board of Trade had time to review the legislation. Spotswood himself ultimately held 86,650 acres in Spotsylvania County. The traditional explanation of this land grab is that he had decided to remain in Virginia and therefore it was better to join than fight the "natives." His reconciliation with the council in the spring of 1720, as well as his opening address to the assembly in the fall, would suggest this to be true. But in fact he may have made the decision to remain in Virginia much earlier, and his acquisition of land from 1714 on was part of an evolving process. In a self-serving letter to Deputy Auditor Nathaniel Harrison, he explained that he was not driven by the desire to acquire "a mighty landed estate" but by "motives of charity," or by "notions of securing the frontiers," or "by a publick spirit in promoting Naval Stores," or, finally, that he had "been drawn in by some incidents or cogent circumstances to engage myself further in those matters" than he had initially intended. "Profit and pleasure" were not involved, he averred. It does appear that before December 1720 he only gradually, and occasionally inadvertently, became more and more attracted by Virginia's potential. In 1714, he took over the failing project of Baron Christoph von Graffenreid to settle German Protestants in Virginia and had placed them on some 6,000 acres in what was to be Spotsylvania County. Then in 1717 the governor became involved with Sir Richard Blakmore to develop "iron works." When Blakmore withdrew from the scheme because of age and health, Spotswood joined with "several Gentlemen here . . . to carry on the project," and this group acquired 15,000 acres in 1719 for a "mine tract." At about the same time he became a partner with Robert Beverley and others in a plan to settle other Germans on land that Beverley had surveyed earlier. It was this land that was expanded to 40,000 acres in December 1720. Finally, in the summer of 1722, after he certainly knew of his removal as governor, he consolidated and added land, some 28,000 acres, for the purpose of producing naval stores. Thus Spotswood had been heavily involved in development projects before the creation of new counties and the implementation of favorable terms for settlement. His encouragement of this legislation was, perhaps, a final indication of a commitment he had already made to cast his lot in Virginia. On the evening of December 23, 1720, after the bills were signed and the assembly was prorogued, Spotswood signed land grants amounting to 91,000 acres in Spotsylvania County, 20,000 of it to his surrogates. The remaining 71,000 acres were granted to both friends and foes, including Peter Beverley and Cole Digges, as well as Robert Carter and Gawin Corbin. So by December 1720, sixteen months before he was replaced, the governor joined, mentally at least, the Virginia elite.[87]

Blair and Ludwell were not involved in this speculative activity, nor was William Byrd. And although they were not now openly critical of the governor, there is little reason to believe that their opposition to his stewardship had diminished. Nor did Spotswood anticipate being removed from office. He continued to build support among the political leadership "by conferring Offices either of Profit or honour on the most popular men in their respective Countys." These men, and other "Favorites," formed an intelligence network by "which means he knows" the most minute "things." His "fixation on Germanna (which his enemys call a monopoly)" did not allay the differences, for those opposing him "Envy the fair view he has of making himself a very great man." All of the talk about securing "Passes threw the mountains" was merely a smokescreen, obscuring the fact that he was improving that part of Virginia where he has "so great an Estate."[88]

In a little over a year the situation changed. Both Blair and Byrd departed for England in the early summer of 1721. The estate of Byrd's father-in-law, Daniel Parke, required further attention, and he probably wanted to continue his search for a rich wife after his first wife had died of smallpox in 1716. John Custis wrote that Blair's trip involved his attaining "just right," presumably in the dispute over the desire of the vestry of Bruton Parish to induct Blair, which Spotswood had blocked, and the withholding of his salary as president of the college since 1706. There is, of course, no reason to believe that either man planned to help the governor in any way, despite Blair's offer to do "him any service." When in April 1722 Spotswood was replaced by Major Hugh Drysdale, the public perception was that Blair had done it again. This view was reinforced by the fact that Blair returned to Virginia on the same vessel as the new lieutenant governor. But it is not likely that either Blair or Byrd had much influence on the decision to replace Spotswood. The governor had served the crown well for twelve years, but the latter part of his administration had seen continual friction and dispute between him and many of the colony's leaders. Such discord was probably made inevitable by the policy that was designed for the crown to play a strong role in colonial affairs. But this policy changed with the return of Robert Walpole to power as the king's chief minister in 1721. He was not too concerned about internal colonial affairs so long as England's colonies continued to fuel the nation's economic growth. Further, he wanted his own men in place as governors, and it was his decision to replace Spotswood with Drysdale. The Board of Trade, as well as the earl of Orkney, having spent many hours dealing with the governor's difficulties with his council, must have agreed that it was time for a change. Drysdale, who had served well under Orkney and the duke of Marlborough, received his commission on April 3, 1722, and presented it to the board on April 22. A new era in the Old Dominion began.[89]

Spotswood was out of office, and the dissident councillors could rest easier. But what was at the bottom of their long and bitter struggle with three governors, and what had been gained? The fight had begun in the 1690s. Then the council's power had been preeminent, but even as England began to attempt to strengthen its control over its colonies, through the agency of strong governors, that power was gradually diminished. The councillors were denied places of profit, they lost immunity from prosecution, and they witnessed government attempts to more closely monitor and control their duties as public officers. Beginning with Nicholson, the fight became personalized and bitter, constantly fueled by Commissary Blair, for whom everything seems to have been personal.

The final insult and attack on the council's authority appear to have revolved around the creation of courts of oyer and terminer and Spotswood's efforts to add men who were not councillors to these courts. In its judicial capacity the council was the court of last resort in Virginia, giving the councillors great power; to have that power diluted was the final straw. These men looked back a few years and remembered when they and their predecessors stood alone as the most powerful individuals in the colony, when they had functioned with little restriction. That situation had changed, and in their struggle they increasingly relied on the help of the popularly elected House of Burgesses. Gradually the power and authority of the lower body began to exceed those of the council. New men began to carve out satisfying public careers in the house, and perquisites began to be spread more broadly. Some of this, perhaps all of it, was inevitable. For example, as the colony grew, the demands on the councillors as judges increased; they had less time for their legislative duties. But still, through the aegis of the House of Burgesses, more people played important roles. Power was being distributed more broadly, and the "great men" were less secure in their place atop Virginia society.[90]

There were gains. The crown had been unable to apply a more restrictive land policy, and in general, the colony gained more control over its internal affairs. These developments were the result of Walpole's more relaxed policy and the fact that though governors had powers, they had little power. William Byrd explained this succinctly. In Virginia, he said, there are no "publick robbers" because governors might "have an inclination to plunder, but want . . . power, and tho' they may be tyrants in their nature, yet they are tyrants without guards, which makes them as harmless as a scold would be without a tongue."[91]

The appointment of Hugh Drysdale as governor in 1722 marked a watershed in the political life of the colony. For the next thirty years calm and usually amicable relations were the rule. That change was taking place may not have been evident to the political leadership. Much remained the same. Search for place and profit continued. Some families became more influential while others declined, seen dramatically in the 1720s in the rise of Robert Carter's influence and the rapid loss of that of Edmund Jenings.

Spotswood said in 1722 that Robert Carter had "the most considerable estate of any man in the country." By then he had reacquired the agency for the Northern Neck Proprietary from the Fairfax family, a plum that brought in large fees from land sales and rents. He replaced Jenings, whom he was just behind in seniority on the council. A substantial merchant, Carter possessed thousands of acres of land and hundreds of slaves, and he was just completing a large new home at Corotoman in Lancaster County where his family had resided since the 1650s. Carter by now had increased his landholdings to at least 25,000 to 30,000 acres, and he had acquired an additional 8,695 acres for two of his younger sons, Robert Jr. and Charles. More discreet and less demonstrative than Blair and Ludwell, he had been a strong opponent of both Nicholson and Spotswood. Carter now emerged as the most powerful councillor.[92]

The first open indication of this change came at the end of Spotswood's administration when the council voted 6 to 3, with the governor's concurrence, that Carter's eldest son, John, be appointed solicitor for Virginia affairs rather than William Byrd. John Carter, "a Gentleman of bright parts," had been educated at Trinity College, Cambridge, and the Inns of Court and was then "a Barrister in Law in the Middle Temple." Two days before the council's vote, John Carter received his commission, for life, as secretary of Virginia to replace William Cocke. Spotswood had recommended Edmund Jenings. Robert Carter paid £1,500 to gain this position for his son, and he also bore the cost of "his Pattent" and "his Equipage." The young man returned to Virginia and soon resigned his position as solicitor. A little over a year later, Governor Drysdale recommended that John Carter replace the deceased William Bassett on the council, a recommendation that was approved by King in Council on June 24, 1724. Robert Carter had said that it would be "an Injustice" if his son was not appointed, but obviously his influence and that of Drysdale were sufficient. At this point the two Carters were, arguably, the most powerful men in Virginia. This concentration of power concerned Drysdale. Not long before his death, he pointed out that John Carter held the office of secretary "during life" and that in addition to his record-keeping duties,

he has at his absolute disposal . . . no less than 28 clerkshipps of counties, and all of 'em places of considerable profitt, and held only during his pleasure: whenever then a person in this station shal have a mind to thwart the King's service, or carry on any private design of his own, he has itt in his power to gett each of the clerks return'd one of the Burgesses for the severall counties or to gain one Burgess in each county by the gift of the Clerkshipp, and so to have one half of the lower House of Assembly entirely in his interest, and ready to vote as he directs, for which services they have the encouragement of his support during his continuance in office . . . as long as he lives.

Drysdale emphasized that he was not suggesting that Carter had acted in this manner but he was concerned about how "the growing power of this officer" could be "made to HM interest and service."[93]

Drysdale was by then probably more realistic about how things worked in Virginia. Earlier the Board of Trade had reminded him of disputes between his "predecessors" and the colony's political leadership and warned him to "take care that there be no innovations made on H.M. Prerogative." He responded that he saw no problems and that "there is a universall sign of contentment on the change made in the Government here, and that my administration meets with approbation of all ranks of people." And well might the people be pleased, because the new governor, perhaps in an overreaction to the problems of the past, was too solicitous and accommodating. He urged the Board of Trade to press the "remittance" of quitrents in the new frontier counties of Spotsylvania and Brunswick and not to limit the amount of land that one could patent. He also approved a tax on liquor and slaves and an act limiting the amount of tobacco that could be planted—a response to poor revenues and low tobacco prices—that were sure to be opposed in England. One native reported that the first would cause "opposition" by "the African Company and the other by the Ministry's unwillingness to suffer such a Seeming abatement of the Revenue." Robert Carter commented that Drysdale had "Enhanct his value with the Generally of the People" and was "Of a Mild Temperate and courteous disposition."[94]

Drysdale's popularity in Virginia was high and remained so. He did not rock the boat and seems to have had good relations with most of the political leadership. It was only against Alexander Spotswood that he demonstrated any animosity. Primed by some of the former governor's enemies, Receiver General John Grymes, and probably Commissary Blair, Drysdale tried to make trouble for him. Spotswood complained that "my successor, Mr. Drysdale," who was influenced by his "adversaries," "seems to aim at nothing less than the ruin of my character and the defeating of all . . . my undertakings." Drysdale, he charged, had selected a "base drunken infamous fellow of the county" to serve as an informer and to infuse "into the people's heads that the best way to obtain anything of the new Governor is to do something to affront or prejudice the old one." Drysdale reported that Spotswood had developed an ironworks of such "perfection" that he was selling at "public auction" in Williamsburg "backs and frames for chymnies, potts, doggs, frying, stewing and baking panns," ignoring, he implied, the spirit of British economic regulation. Further, he asked the Board of Trade's guidance with respect to the way his predecessor had "parcelled out" land in the new counties in a manner "inconsistent" with government policy. He also charged that Spotswood had demonstrated "great regard to his private interest" in acquiring large tracts "under borrow'd n[ames?]." Drysdale did this even while asking the board to intercede with the king to remove any "ristriction" on the quantity of land that could be taken up in the new counties.[95]

Drysdale may have been seeking the favorable attention of the councillors who had fought Spotswood. But most of these men do not appear to have been interested in causing the former governor any further trouble. Spotswood traveled to England in 1724 and while there effectively protected his landed estate. When he returned in 1730, he appears to have been accepted back into Virginia society. The council by then was not so powerful as it had been in the 1690s, but in part because of its efforts the colony had much more control over its internal affairs. In the milder political climate, the councillors turned their attention to their estates and acquiring more land. Further, the long years of acrimony had left them with little stomach for political infighting. And those who had led the fight were, for the time, an aging group. In 1725 Blair was seventy years old, Carter sixty-two, Ludwell fifty-three, Byrd fifty-one, and Nathaniel Harrison forty-eight. Both Ludwell and Harrison died in 1727. Others like Edmund Jenings, sixty-seven, and Peter Beverley, sixty-two, were in the throes of senility. Compared with earlier times, the council was a much quieter body.[96]

Drysdale's careful approach contributed to the political peace. Part of his cautiousness may also have been the result of illness. He admitted as much when he spoke of the difficulty of recommending replacements for council vacancies. There was a scarcity of qualified people, but his poor health had hindered his knowledge "of many Gentm. . . . that live remote." It was reported in the early fall of 1725 that he had been in an "ill stait of health for a great while." By the next spring he decided to return to England to recover his health, and this immediately raised the question of who would serve as president during his absence. Edmund Jenings, the senior member of the council, normally would have assumed this responsibility, but he had become senile; Robert Carter reported as early as 1723 that Jenings was "so debilitated . . . that he doth not know what he says or does." The council began to discuss the problem formally in early June 1726. It noted that Jenings had not attended council meetings for two years and generally agreed that he was so far "decayed . . . to be unfit to" to serve as president. The issue was to be resolved on June 24, and Clerk of the Council William Robertson was dispatched to nearby Ripon Hall to inform the old man. Robertson reported that when Jenings heard the news, he "fell to crying" for a "considerable time" and that he was unable to get an adequate response although Jenings had promised to write a letter to Drysdale. Attorney General John Randolph was immediately sent to try again, and after more emotional outbursts Jenings finally said "he thought himself capable to exercise the power of the President with the assistance of the Council." Randolph reported that he did not think Jenings competent, a view supported by Robertson and Speaker John Holloway. The latter two had been managing Jenings's legal affairs for several years, and Holloway stated that for at least two years Jenings had not been able to give a "rational answer" on any subject related to "his law business," "his borrowing of money," and dealing with his debts. The council deliberated all day on June 25 and into the night. It finally agreed that Jenings was "incapable of Administering the Government," and the governor declared him suspended. Robert Carter stood next in line.[97]

The long meeting on June 25 and a partially legible comment in Robert Carter's diary suggest that Drysdale and some of the council were concerned about Carter's assuming the presidency. When the governor proposed that his own "half year salary" and that for "Ld Orkney" be approved, a dispute arose. Normally the president would have signed such an approval, but Carter's appointment to that post had not been confirmed in England. It was suggested alternatively that the approval be "don by Order of Council," but there was opposition. Carter offered a compromise that Drysdale rejected, swearing "that he was not gon yet he would stay," and the debate continued until after midnight with nothing resolved. Later that morning, Sunday the twenty-sixth, with his coach waiting, Carter made preparations to depart. But then Receiver General John Grymes, who had just been elevated to the council, rushed up and reported that the governor was calling a meeting for Monday morning "to take off Jennings Suspension." Carter could not abide Grymes, and they immediately "had a mighty dispute," but eventually he took his coach to the governor's, where "we soon came to a reconciliation of the terms," and the summons for Monday's meeting was rescinded. Drysdale was not happy. He wrote the Board of Trade that his health had improved and he had decided not to make the long trip home. There was now no need to suspend Jenings despite "his infirmities." Certainly he was worried about the amount of power that could be wielded by Robert and John Carter. But the matter was out of his hands. The board had received his request to return home, and had queried Spotswood about Jenings, confirming what was already known in Virginia. The earl of Orkney told the board that Jenings had "turned perfectly dos'd and childish." He also reported that he had been told that Carter was "very capable." On July 20, 1726, the king signed the warrant appointing Carter to serve as president during Drysdale's absence. Two days later the governor died of "a Pleurisie."[98]

The suspension of Edmund Jenings, who died the following year, marks the changes that were taking place in Virginia's political world. James, duke of York, when recommending Jenings to Governor Effingham, had said that Jenings's "father and his friends" hoped that "he will behave himselfe" and be able to continue in the "said Employment." Indeed, once he moved to the colony, Jenings was successful. He married well, acquired a large estate, and held at various times most of the important public offices. But late in Spotswood's administration things began to fall apart for him. He was not a good manager, fell heavily into debt, and lost his position as the Fairfax agent for the Northern Neck Proprietary to Robert Carter. Drysdale spoke of the "low condition" of his estate and "the great debts in which he is involved," accompanied by his physical and mental deterioration. In contrast, Carter was Virginia born. He had inherited a substantial estate and had increased it manyfold. By 1726 he was the wealthiest man in Virginia. He too held major public offices, and his eldest son was following in his footsteps. Carter had never thought highly of Jenings, and he must have been outraged when Catherine Fairfax replaced him as agent in 1712 with Jenings, who was then in England, and Thomas Lee. But Jenings had managed proprietary affairs badly, and when Carter reassumed the agency in 1719, Jenings was in debt not only to the Fairfaxes, for uncollected rents, but to Carter himself. By 1723 Carter was saying, "Tis reckoned he is more Engaged than his estate is worth." In 1728 Carter acquired the Ripon Hall part of Jenings's estate as a result of a foreclosed mortgage.[99]

Robert Carter was now acting governor, the second native Virginian to hold that post, but he claimed that he was not excited by the prospect. Philip Ludwell sent an express with the news of Drysdale's death, but Carter informed Ludwell that it was impossible for him to be in Williamsburg for the funeral and to tell Commissary Blair and Speaker Holloway to proceed without him. "The Carter [a tobacco ship] now lies before my Door her business done, ready to depart. My letters unfinished, my Bills of Lading not taken, those things must be settled before I leave my home."[100]

But they did wait, for a week. Carter was in Williamsburg by August 1, when he took the oath of office and was sworn in. Afterwards he provided the council with dinner, sent condolences to Mrs. Drysdale, and made final arrangements for the funeral. The following afternoon the council gathered at the governor's mansion at three o'clock. In somber attire, including mourning gloves, rings, and scarves, they held the pall over the coffin as it was moved from the house to the

hearse and walked after it "thro the militia" to the church. There the chaplain of
the House of Burgesses, William Le Neve, "preached the sermon" from Isaiah
57:1, "The righteous perisheth, and no man layeth it to heart, and merciful men
are taken away, none considering that the righteous is taken away from the evil
to come." Hugh Drysdale, "so good a Governor," as Carter put it, was properly
dispatched to his reward.[101]

Carter did not tarry long in Williamsburg. He paid his respects to Mrs.
Drysdale and was on his way home by August 6. Nor did he spend much time
in the capital over the next year, for he was ill and by late December he knew
that a new governor had been appointed. There was, of course, much discussion
about who the new executive would be. Commissary Blair had again gone to
England on college business, but it was hoped that he would use his influence,
said John Custis, "with the Lord Orkney to send us a man of good principles,"
for Blair had, after all, already provided Virginia with "two good Governors."
William Byrd continued to hope for the post, but it was "his misfortune to have
been born on the wrong side of the Tweed," and he had heard that Walpole had
reserved it for a friend, information that proved to be correct. "William Gooch,
Esqr.," who was very well connected and had also served with Marlborough and
Orkney, was the new lieutenant governor.[102]

The council did little in the interim. There was the usual scrambling to fill
council vacancies. John Custis, who had sought a council appointment for years,
hoped to fill Philip Ludwell's place and sought the help of Mrs. Drysdale, despite the fact that he expected that one of "Coll Carters relations" would succeed, "he presiding over us at present." But Custis finally got his wish. He replaced Edmund Jenings, and William Dandridge filled Ludwell's spot. Carter
in the meantime appointed his second son, Robert, as naval officer and receiver
of Virginia duties for the Rappahannock River. He proposed the appointment
in a March 1 council meeting. "I let them know," he said, that "our chief business
was to appoint a N.O. and I named my Son R & and hoped there would be no
objections." John Grymes had approached Carter before the meeting suggesting, it appears, that someone else be appointed, and in return he would appoint
Robert Jr. to "an Equivalent . . . Place" that "would soon be his Gift." Carter
"scornd any such thing." Grymes in the meeting then argued that Robert Jr. did
not live close enough to fulfill his duties satisfactorily, but Carter "told him he
lived very convenient & when he did not twoud be time to make that Objection. All the Council declared their opinion of the Qualifications of my son so
he was appointed." He was sworn in on March 3, 1727, the elder Carter reported
in his diary, noting also that "I paid for the Dinr" for the council "all 3 days."[103]

Major William Gooch arrived in Virginia in early September 1727, after a voyage of eight weeks, with his wife, son, and sister-in-law. Gooch was forty-six years old and had long service in the army behind him. He was to prove to be Virginia's most effective governor, remaining in office for twenty-two years. He impressed the councillors immediately. William Byrd described him as "a very worthy man" who "has a reasonable share of good sense, good nature and good breeding." Even Robert Carter spoke of his "noble Qualitys"; he was a man "whose temperate & Gentlemanly behaviour" makes him "a fit Pattern for us all . . . who have the honour to be frequently in his company." Gooch was ever the diplomat, but his mild manner masked a sharp intelligence and a sensitive understanding of human nature. Commissary Blair returned to Virginia on the same vessel as the governor, and he entertained the Gooches while the "Pallace" was being prepared for them. The long voyage and Blair's hospitality allowed the governor to size up the old man quickly: despite the fact that Blair was "courteous and kind," Gooch decided that "I can't think him sincere." Within a few months he reported that Blair was "an unaccountable spark" and "a very vile old fellow" who "when he can't advise nor direct" is "inclined to perplex." Blair was not aware of this view, and Gooch wrote his brother that he hoped to keep it that way, "being still in appearance good friends; the best Policy will be to kill him with kindness." The fact that he was able to survive the next sixteen years of the commissary's life and not fall out with him is a tribute to Gooch's political and interpersonal skills. These skills were enhanced by the fact that the governor was very well connected. Not only had he served under Marlborough and Orkney, but he hailed from Norfolk, the home county of Sir Robert Walpole and his brother Horatio, the auditor general of plantation revenues. Peter Leheup, Virginia's agent as well as a Treasury clerk, was related by marriage to Horatio Walpole. Gooch's brother Thomas was an influential clergyman and master of Gonville and Caius College, Cambridge. He had been extremely helpful in his brother's obtaining the governorship. Later he was, successively, bishop of Bristol, Norwich, and Ely. These connections provided Gooch a variety of avenues through which he could pursue his goals and when coupled with his substantial abilities account for his success.[104]

The governor's tenure began on a high note. Carter, Blair, and Byrd, the senior members of the council, swore him into office. He in turn swore in the councillors and other officers. Then a procession led by "Pack the herald," with Gooch and Carter in the "first Coach," moved down Duke of Gloucester Street. At the Capitol, the marketplace, and the college green, George II was proclaimed the new king, and guns were fired at each stop. The assembled dignitaries pro-

ceeded to the "Pallace" for dinner followed by drinking "the social health" at
"three Tables" of "Rack Punch." The governor drank "all the healths" at each
table with guns fired after every toast. The celebration continued until midnight
and included "the town and all the neighbors around." Gooch reported he was
told that his reception "'twas greater than has always been practiced," but he
grumbled that the festivities cost him £50. And the expenses continued: £100
to celebrate the new king's birthday as well as £20 for that of the heir, Prince
Frederick. But it all got Gooch off to a good start, and he continued to entertain on royal birthdays and on other occasions. He was overwhelmed with company. At first, he said, "respect brought them," but then "in October came the
General Court, in December the Court of Oyer & Terminer" and, before long,
the meetings of the General Assembly. He lamented that it was his misfortune
"to be so well respected."[105]

The council that Gooch had to work with was not complacent, and the core
of the old leadership remained. Carter, Blair, and Byrd had served for years and
remained active. Newer members like John Carter, John Robinson, and John
Grymes were men of ability. The equally able William Dandridge, John Custis,
and William Randolph joined them. They did not rest on their laurels. Council members vigorously pursued their interests, and in the first session of the
assembly of 1727–34, four pieces of legislation originated in the council, but
thereafter the number declined. The major fights were over; they were dealing
with a governor who understood not only the crown's interests but also those of
Virginia, and as time wore on their duties increased. The council was involved
in almost everything the governor did in his official capacity: four yearly meetings of the General Court and the court of oyer and terminer, the meetings of
the General Assembly, and the numerous other times the councillors were called
to provide advice and consent. Judicial responsibilities became especially demanding as the colony expanded and its population grew. These chores coupled
with the fact that the House of Burgesses was playing an ever more powerful
role explain why the council was less visible than it had been earlier.[106]

Gooch's skill in dealing with the council can be seen early on when Councillor and Deputy Auditor Nathaniel Harrison died. Places of honor and profit
were scarce. As John Custis predicted, there was a great struggle for the auditor's
position. Robert Carter told the earl of Orkney that he was going to remain a
"Spectator," but he became involved, although on whose behalf it is not clear.
Gooch informed the Board of Trade that support had arisen for Henry Harrison,
brother to Nathaniel, and John Blair, the commissary's nephew. He remained
neutral but gave firm support for either Harrison or William Randolph for the

council post. Gooch had sized up the situation, and he was not going to offend either the commissary or the powerful Harrison clan. Further, Horatio Walpole, the auditor general, would have the most powerful voice in the decision. Carter was admiring: "The Govr. has taken the most prudent way in respect to the Auditors place to disoblige none." Blair and Randolph were selected. Custis, who had supported Blair and had sought Mrs. Drysdale's and Micajah Perry's help, remarked that "the commissary got the Auditors place for his nephew, by engaging Mr Walpole many years before." After several years of effort, Gooch was able to get Harrison appointed to the council in 1731. A delicate situation had been handled successfully.[107]

The governor was determined to get along with powerful men and families. Orkney's instructions were clear. Councillors were to be "men of good Life and well affected to Our Govvernmt: and of good Estate and Abilities, and not neccessitous persons." Gooch was punctilious in following these orders, repeating them to the Board of Trade when making nominations. When two persons appeared equal, he preferred "him who has the most Plentiful Fortune." This requirement severely limited the pool of individuals from which he could choose. In his first year ten of the twelve councillors were from the twenty-one elite families. Nine were in the House of Burgesses, and two of them chaired two of the three major committees. If the next twenty families are included, sixteen were in the House of Burgesses, and members of the expanded group made up all of the council and chaired all of the major house committees. From 1734 until the end of the colonial era, the Speaker of the House was, successively, Sir John Randolph, John Robinson, and Peyton Randolph.[108]

The council also wanted good relations with Gooch. It granted him £300 to cover his travel expenses from England, and the House of Burgesses followed with £500 in Virginia currency. His instructions forbade him to accept such awards, but it appears that he ultimately was allowed to keep them.[109]

The competition for places of honor and profit was stiff. Despite a lower profile the ambitions of the councilor families remained high. Robert Carter's continued search for profitable and honorable posts for his sons provides a good example. In December 1727 he wrote the earl of Orkney explaining that Gooch had renewed his son Robert's commission as naval officer for the Rappahannock River but that soon he would move to his "Patrimony" on the Potomac and would have to resign his post. Carter wanted to procure the position for his son Charles and requested that Orkney write the governor in his behalf. He concluded in, for him, an obsequious manner. "I have a very large family to provide for [and] am grown a very crasy [infirm] man. I have no merit to plead only that

I have served the Governmt. in the station I am in almost eight & Twenty years & my receivings from it have not answered my Expenses." Orkney complied, and several months later Carter asked him to write Gooch a second time; he enclosed Orkney's portion of the salary for the period that Carter was acting governor. There was opposition from Surveyor General and Councillor Richard Fitzwilliam. Carter asked London merchant William Dawkins to use his influence with customs officials. Charles Grymes, brother of Receiver General John Grymes, was the chief competition, and there may have been others because Carter spoke of "vigilant and pressing enemys" when writing his son-in-law Mann Page, who was managing the details of the quest. He told Page that Robert would not resign the position until Charles's appointment was certain. He did not think the governor was a problem despite the fact that Gooch had initially promised Grymes the post. But he wrote Gooch reminding him that he had already provided Grymes with a customs officer's "place" and that it would be inconsistent for Grymes to hold both positions. The matter remained unresolved because the Commissioners of the Customs had not approved Grymes's appointment. When that was done, Carter told Orkney, Gooch would be off the hook. The governor had given "his respected word that he will not turn out my son Robert but that the place shall remain in my family as long as it shall lye in his power to Continue it." Carter hoped Orkney would "continue to concern himself," and the earl did. By August it was done. Two of Carter's son-in-laws, Mann Page and George Nicholas, were Charles's securities in Virginia, and Dawkins was the security with the Commissioners of the Customs. Charles Carter was sworn into office on November 21, 1729. This was not an exceptional case, although the intensity with which the appointment was pursued may have been. Plans for children were made far in advance of any vacancy. John Custis wrote Micajah and Philip Perry in 1730 thanking them for "assuring me that you would be glad to serve my son." He realized that there was no opening "at present but I thought it fit to desire early your favor in case any thing should happen."[110]

But for Gooch these difficulties were minor. The economy was not good. Tobacco prices had declined beginning in 1725, and, in fact, the whole decade had seen problems, caused in part by the South Sea Bubble affair in England. Good tobacco prices from 1713 to 1725 had encouraged increased production, which was fueled by the large importation of slaves and vigorous population growth, almost doubling in the first thirty years of the century. Legislation curtailing tobacco production had proved unsuccessful, and attempts to limit the labor supply by taxing slave imports had been rejected in England. Virginians understood what was going on. Even Robert Carter, who William Byrd said was "born to be rich," bemoaned the times and talked of the need for diversity. Planters needed to "find some Other ways to employ our people," he wrote in 1729, or "in a few years" all would "become beggars."[111]

Gooch decided to revive Spotswood's short-lived tobacco inspection system of 1713. He consulted a wide variety of people, "merchants, inhabitants and others." The only solution, he concluded, was to require the "strict examination" of tobacco before it was shipped, destroying all that was bad. He skillfully explained the problem to the Board of Trade in June 1729. The price of the "weed" was so low that planters were discouraged from "making tobacco" and might turn "to making their own cloathing." Smuggling was rampant, and much "trash" tobacco was being shipped, so that the market for good tobacco was "damp'd by the . . . importation of the bad." All of this discouraged the "fair trader" and "honest and industrious planter." Gooch realized the risk he would run "by this good work of Reformation," for a majority of the House of Burgesses was opposed. But he was determined to go ahead, especially because he had the support of "the Trading Men" and the "most judicious Planters." He asked the Board of Trade to let him know its "Sentiments," but none were forthcoming. Finally, after several prorogations and the assurance of Micajah Perry that London merchants had no objections, he called for a May 1730 meeting of the assembly.[112]

The governor expected "great opposition the Planters having been so long in a very wrong method," and he came to the May 21 meeting well prepared. His speech to the assembly was respectful of the people's representatives, and it was persuasive. He pointed to the "miserable circumstances your Staple is reduc'd to" and the threat presented to "your own Fortunes and Estates as well as those of your Constituents." Something had to be done, and he laid before them a "Scheme" which he believed would solve the problem. Certainly "your better observations and Practical Knowledge" could improve it. He would not comment on the "wretched Condition" of the tobacco trade or "the flourishing state that must Evidently follow from such a Law, because by the one I might be Censur'd for blaming what Experience can only best Correct, and the other would look like limiting your Judgements in Favor of this Formulary and both together but a needless Subserviency to Introduce a Scheme to Gentlemen so Capable of Judging for themselves." But be assured, he continued, that his proposal "has been already approv'd at home": the mercantile community would put up no opposition. And his only interest was "for the general Prosperity of the Colony." Gooch was off to a good start, and he was persistent but flexible.

The bill, which a house committee presented on June 3, required his "chief attention," costing him "a great deal of pains and application." John Custis reported that there "never was more pains taken to give it [breath?] and such methods I never saw before." The debate was intense, and a key vote came on June 15 when it was proposed that a clause be added requiring that all public tobacco (tobacco paid for taxes) "Shall pass inspection before it be paid Collectors thereof." The vote was tied 23 to 23, and Speaker Holloway broke the tie by voting "yea." The bill proceeded quickly thereafter and was passed 46 to 5 on June 19.[113]

The action then moved to the upper house, where it appears Gooch had carefully prepared the way. He had managed to get the support of the two Carters, Cole Digges, John Robinson, William Dandridge, and William Randolph, the governor's "judicious planters." Blair, Grymes, Custis, and Richard Fitzwilliam, surveyor general of customs, were opposed. The debates were "warm," but after Gooch had quashed a clause proposed by Grymes, that the bill not go into effect until "his Majesty's pleasure is known," the opposition subsided. Blair, for example, only opposed it "in private." And councillors were actively involved in the process of improving the legislation, offering a number of amendments, most of which were agreed to by the house. Final agreement came on July 4, and Gooch signed the "Act for Amending the Staple of Tobacco" on July 9. John Custis spoke for the opposition: "May it travell to England and like that air so well that it may never return to Virginia."[114]

The act was very similar to the ill-fated one of 1713 but with several important exceptions. Tobacco inspectors were to be appointed by the governor and the council. They were also to be salaried rather than paid a fee for each hogshead of tobacco they inspected. And separate legislation specified that inspectors, among others who held places of profit, could not serve in the House of Burgesses, thus avoiding the possibility of the creation of a governor's party. Gooch did not like this legislation because it prevented "men of capacity and integrity," who did not "abound," from serving in the legislature. But the fondness of the burgesses for the bill "and my desire to keep them in good humour, while matters of greater moment were under deliberation, prevailed with me to assent to it." Clearly he felt that the inspection act would have failed passage had he not agreed to this legislation.[115]

Gooch happily forwarded the legislation to England, telling his brother that he expected the tobacco merchants to make him a "Present of a piece of Plate." But Micajah Perry had dissembled, and both he and others in the London mercantile community opposed the act. Perry himself persuaded the Commissioners of the Customs to recommend disallowance. The governor responded vigorously and used his political connections effectively. Peter Leheup, Virginia's agent, was a key player and despite the powerful opposition was able to get the Board of Trade to recommend that the act "lye by probationary" until its effects could be determined. So the legislation survived despite rioting and the burning of inspection warehouses in the Northern Neck in the spring and summer of 1732 and small-planter protest in peripheral areas over the next four years. There was uneasiness among the councillors. Robert Carter's feelings were mixed. The act would cause an "abundance of trouble" and be expensive, but by the fall of 1731 he could already see benefits because "all people" and especially overseers were more careful in the "handling of tobacco." Because they were now "throwing away abundance of what they used to get good money for," the tobacco being shipped would be "the neatest & best handled that ever you saw." He continued to complain about the extraordinary trouble the law caused but spoke of the "great hopes the country entertains" for it: "Pray God grant we find the good effects of it from the tryal to relieve us out of the dismal circumstances we are at present under." John Custis remained opposed and said that revisions to the law in 1732 did not solve the problems it created. To him it was not worth the cost, and he blamed it on the "tedious chargeable assembly." Still, Gooch retained majority support in the council and was able to beat back a serious attempt at repeal in 1736.[116]

The passage and survival of the inspection act were a great triumph for Gooch, but Virginians did not consider it a cure-all, and it came as relations between tobacco planters and British merchants worsened. Planters agreed that merchants regularly took advantage of them, and this belief was reinforced by Parliament's passage of the Colonial Debts Act of 1732, which made it easier for British merchants to collect money owed them in the colonies. Especially disturbing to Virginians was a clause allowing the seizure of real estate and slaves for debts, even though they were not secured by bond. John Custis declared this provision "contrary to the Laws of the Mother Country"; the colonists were not being treated as if they were British subjects. Robert Carter reported that it caused a "general . . . fury in the Assembly." The legislation made Virginia's leadership more favorable to an excise scheme devised by the Walpole administration to increase revenues. Virginians liked the plan because no duties would be paid on tobacco until it was sold to a retailer in Britain or exported to the Continent. British merchants disliked it because it would cut their commission earnings. They charged a commission on the sale of the full amount of tobacco imported, whereas under the proposed legislation they would lose their commission on "two thirds or more of" reexported tobacco. Walpole, hoping to avoid protest from interested parties in England, attempted to make it appear that the idea had originated in Virginia. Gooch had presented it to the council in December 1731 with positive results. Further discussion probably occurred the following April when there was a full council. And when the "furious" assembly met in May, it agreed to petition the king, with the help of the Lords Commissioners of the Treasury, concerning the "miserable State of the Tobacco Trade" as well as to support the effort "to put Tobacco under an Excise." The council and the house agreed to appoint John Randolph, Esq., clerk of the House of Burgesses, as agent for the colony to present the petition and work for the excise legislation. As Virginia's special agent in 1729, Randolph had been successful in gaining repeal of a law prohibiting the importation into Britain of tobacco stripped from the stalk. And he was, as Robert Carter remarked, "one of our Eminentest Lawyers."[117]

The assembly appropriated £2,200 to support Randolph in his efforts, but despite such largesse the mission was a failure. Well-orchestrated protests by the mercantile community caused Walpole to withdraw the bill in the spring of 1733. Further, though the assembly and Randolph were not dupes, in the larger scheme of things it is clear that Walpole and his associates used them to the fullest. Randolph, for example, was knighted not long after he got off the boat in London, presumably for presenting the assembly's petition to the king, as well as for voicing the colony's support for the excise plan. No doubt this honor had been planned well ahead of time to suggest the Virginia origins of the plan and perhaps to give Randolph more creditability as he worked hard both in and out of Parliament. The petition to the king was published in pamphlet form early in 1733 as *The Case of the Planters of Tobacco in Virginia as Represented by Themselves, Signed by the President of the Council and Speaker of the House of Burgesses.* Later, when the excise scheme had been attacked, he published a larger pamphlet adding arguments to the assembly's petition. He also seems to have worked closely with Walpole on the excise bill, and he testified before a committee of the House of Commons, but all to no avail.[118]

Sir John Randolph returned to home in the summer of 1733 as the only Virginian to have been honored with a knighthood. He took full advantage of this circumstance. Educated at the College of William and Mary and Gray's Inn, Randolph was known as Virginia's finest lawyer. He had served as the clerk of the House of Burgesses since 1718 and twice had represented the colony with distinction in England. His time had come for a position of wider influence. Within a year Randolph not only was elected to the House of Burgesses but was its Speaker and treasurer. Two circumstances, apart from his fame, made this possible. Dr. George Nicholas, who represented the College of William and Mary in the House, died in the spring of 1734. When the assembly convened on August 22, Randolph resigned his position as clerk. That same day the college corporation, with only "six or eight" voting members, selected Randolph, who lived in Williamsburg, to replace Nicholas. Two days later Speaker John Holloway resigned, citing ill health. John Clayton, the attorney general, immediately recommended "Sir John Randolph . . . a Person Equal to, and eminently qualified" to succeed Holloway, and he was "unanimously" elected. Randolph, conveniently, had an acceptance speech ready and delivered it within minutes thereafter. The entire process was swift, smooth, and clearly engineered. Holloway, who was old and "suffering from the infirmity and weakness of his body and memory" and whose accounts as treasurer were short £1,850, may well have been pressured to resign. A relieved Gooch responded to Randolph's election by stating that the Burgesses "could not have voted to your Chair a Person more agreeable to me, nor one that will do greater Honour and service to the Country."[119]

The acceptance speech that Randolph delivered on August 22 and a second one given on the occasion of his reelection in 1736 were considered so remarkable that for the first time the addresses of a Speaker were printed in full in the journals. They suggest, perhaps, what Randolph hoped would be the distinguishing features of Virginia politics rather than what the reality was. They also mark a turning point in Virginia's political history. Randolph knew that over the past three decades the legislative role and, in fact, the power of the House of Burgesses had increased while those of the council had declined. And his response to Gooch on the occasion of his second election was a history lecture. He had been working on a constitutional history of Virginia for several years, and he proceeded to describe the emergence and development of representative government in the colony. Government under the London Company, he explained, was carried out "without consent of the People," who had been "miserably harrassed." But in 1621 the company, to prevent "Injustice and Oppression," ordered that there be two "Supreme Councils": a Council of State composed of a governor and certain councillors and another composed of the "Council of State and Two Burgesses to be chosen by the Inhabitants of every Town, Hundred or other Plantation," which would be called the General Assembly. This assembly would have the power to deal with all matters "concerning the Public Weal," guided by the "Laws, Customs, Manner of Trial, and Other Administration of Justice" followed in England. Further, "no Orders of their General Court should bind the Colony, unless ratified in the General Assemblies." James I confirmed the original of "our Constitution," as did all subsequent crowned

"Heads of England and Great Britain successively on the Appointment of every new Governor, with very little alteration. Under it we are grown to whatever we now have to boast of." As a result, the House of Burgesses had long enjoyed diverse "Privileges," and its members "claim as their undoubted Right" freedom of speech, exemption from arrest, protection of their estates, power over their own members, and a "sole Right of determining all Questions concerning their own Elections." Sir John prefaced these remarks with a reminder that the house was "no more than the Representative Body of a Colony dependant on the Mother Kingdom." Its authority was circumscribed, its influence of "small extent," and the members should understand that "All we pretend to, is to be of some importance to those who send us hither, and to have some Share in their Protection, and the Security of their Lives, Liberties and Properties." He was, in responding to the governor, being properly deferential, and he was certainly no radical; Robert Carter had described him earlier as a "rank Tory." But Randolph's remarks clearly suggest that he believed the influence of the House of Burgesses to be more than of "small extent."[120]

What he could not know, but perhaps sensed, was that during the next thirty years the House of Burgesses was to become the dominant body and its Speaker the most powerful man in Virginia. Randolph was, arguably, at that point Virginia's most notable son. Yet, despite the fact that he had been the beneficiary of patronage from Spotswood, Robert Walpole, and Gooch, he never appeared on any list of those recommended for appointment to the Council of State. Unlike, for example, his contemporary Thomas Lee, he appears not to have sought a council seat. Perhaps Randolph recognized that to get things done, he needed to make the lower house his stage. Council seats were limited, and its multiple roles, especially the increasingly demanding judicial responsibilities, inevitably muted the voices of its members. His speeches provide insight to where Virginia was politically by the mid-1730s and by implication where it might expect to go.[121]

Sir John's 1734 acceptance speech began with no pretense, no feigned expression of unworthiness or incapacity. He wanted the job, and to represent himself as "incapable" would be either "false . . . modesty" or a "bland compliance with a Custom." Such an assertion would be "An Abuse of Words" and totally insincere, something he considered "useless" and vicious." So he embraced the opportunity "with a particular Pleasure" to "employ my small Talents," which "appear to you in a better Light than they deserve." Time would tell if he was up to the job. But his long service as clerk had prepared him well, and he would use what he had learned to advance "your Reputation and the Public Good." His vision would not be clouded by the "Pageantry and Formalitie" of the office. Whatever "Honors" that came to him would be the result of his "Labor and Diligence and to prevent any imposition upon your Proceedings and Resolutions." He did hope that whatever "happens amiss here" would not reflect unduly on him, while understanding that his own "failings will lie wholly on myself."

He reminded the Burgesses that it was not easy "to hold temper" in public debate and "to place what is done" there "justly and laudably in such a View as will be acceptable to every Body." The prejudices with which "we imbibe all our own Opinions, which are generally, impressed upon us too hastily, are often the Occasion of great Injustice." People have difficulty approving "what is done by those" who do not agree "with all of their sentiments" and are apt to charge their opponents "with Ignorance, Obstinancy or perhaps Corruption." They tend to be overly impressed with the "imaginary Excellence of their own Modes of Thinking." Randolph hoped he would be exempt from "such unkind censures" not only because of "the candor of this House towards me" but because of "the happiness which seems almost peculiar to ourselves." There were no "Factions and Parties" or "Footsteps of Corruption among" them. So the burgesses should look upon "Differences" as proceeding from the doubts concerning "Expedients that shall be proposed for the Common Good." The minority should "calmly and cheerfully" submit to the will of the majority "'til Time and Experience shall either convince, or furnish the more Forcible arguments Against it."

The burgesses should hear each other "patiently," he admonished, and "put the weight of everyman's reason in balance against our own," ultimately forming "a judgment which if not the wisest, still results from the "Integrity of our own Principles" and would be "honest and commendable." Avoid "Resentments and Impatience" with being "outvoted." Avoid considering "Men more than Matter" for if these things were not put aside "we must lose all Advantages of Reasoning and Argument." For "a Variety of Opinions is not only . . . necessary to our Natures, but is likewise of all Things the most useful." If "all men were of one Mind there would be no Need of Councils; no Subject for Learning and Eloquence; the mind would want its proper Exercise, and without it, like the Body" would atrophy "from a Habit of Sloth and Idleness. Truth itself will receive an Addition of Strength, by being opposed, and can never be in Danger of Suffering by the Test of Argument." These "notions" should guide the burgesses as they proceeded in their work of "discharging the Trust the People have reposed in us." Establish these notions "in our Practice" and "then obtain the true Dignity of our Representation." The Speaker assured the house that he would do his best to follow his own advice and would not make the established rules "of your proceedings subservient to my own Fancies and Humours or Interests"; he would not be restless and impatient with "Points carried against my Sentiments; or . . . pretend to any Authority of swaying any Member in his Opinion." And if his efforts proved successful, he would "expect no other praise than that of not having deceived the Expectations of so many worthy Gentlemen, who have continued to heap upon me such a Series of Favors, which so long as I retain Memory of anything, I must look upon as the chief Foundation of the Credit and Reputation of my Life."[122]

The Speaker was strongly suggesting that "the Happiness which seems almost peculiar to ourselves" was the result of following such practices in recent years, however imperfectly. Earlier there had been too much "Heat and Intemperance" in house debates. Moderation, coolness, and the ability to doubt one's own views and always to consider the public good were appropriate precepts for a magistrate to follow. Two years later, in a slap at Spotswood, he pointed to another factor that had cooled tempers and smoothed the legislative process: good leadership. William Gooch had mastered "the Art of Governing Well." He had "extirpated all Factions from among us by discountenancing Public Animosities, and plainly prov'd that none can arise, or be lasting, but from the Countenance and Encouragement of a Governor. *Hinc illae Artes* [That's where these skills come from]."[123]

It was Gooch and Randolph who paved the way for the stability that was to characterize Virginia politics over the next three decades. And despite the fact that the sons of many of the leading families continued to seek council seats, the House of Burgesses was where most of them served. Randolph died in 1737, and by that time Nicholson's "little factious party" was no more. The same families were represented on the council, but their political role had changed markedly.[124]

3 The Economy

He that measures his expenses by his seven Last years getting
in Virginia may Seven years hence have little [to] Spend.
—ROBERT CARTER, 1702

The mystery[s] in trade are as great as those in religion.
—WILLIAM BYRD, 1735

WHEN SIR JOHN RANDOLPH DIED in 1737, the same twenty-one families
remained dominant in Virginia society. From their ranks came ten of the eleven
members of the Council of State: William Byrd, John Carter, John Custis, Cole
Digges, John Grymes, Thomas Lee, Philip Lightfoot, William Randolph, John
Robinson, and John Tayloe. Commissary James Blair, from the second group
of families, was the senior member of that august body. John Robinson Jr. succeeded Randolph as Speaker of the House of Burgesses, where nine others from
the notable families joined him. These ten men controlled the standing committees of the house. Robinson, for example, chaired the most important committee, the eighteen-member Committee on Propositions and Grievances, on
which the remaining nine also served. Their political power is evident at all
levels of Virginia society, including the county courts and a wide variety of other
appointive offices.

The basis of this power was wealth. All of the eleven councillors were very
wealthy. Landholding provides an idea of their affluence. Reasonable estimates
are available for eight of the eleven: together they held at least 325,000 acres.
William Byrd owned 181,299, but his colleagues were no pikers. John Carter
possessed at least 41,000 acres, followed by William Randolph, Thomas Lee,
and John Grymes with 28,829, 20,659, and 18,296 acres. John Custis, who may

have been the wealthiest and probably the most solvent, owned 14,989 acres. John Tayloe owned between 13,000 and 14,000 acres. John Robinson Sr. was at the bottom of the list with an estimated 11,000 acres. Philip Lightfoot, who held unspecified amounts of land in seven counties, left £10,000 sterling to his three sons. Commissary Blair left an estate valued at £10,000. Little is known of the wealth of Cole Digges, for few of his family papers remain.[1]

Nine of the ten councillors were either second- or third-generation Virginians; only John Custis IV represented the fourth generation in the colony. All of them had learned the lessons necessary for survival and growth in Virginia. John Carter is an example from the third generation. Educated at Trinity College, Cambridge, and the Middle Temple, by 1736 he had been secretary of state for fourteen years and a member of the council for twelve. He possessed two large estates, Corotoman in Lancaster County and, through marriage, Shirley in Charles City County. All of this had been made possible as a result of the accomplishments of his remarkable father, Robert.[2]

Born at Corotoman in 1663, Robert Carter's career provides insight into how wealth was accumulated, protected, and dispersed. When he died in 1732, he was almost certainly the wealthiest man in the Old Dominion. His obituary may have exaggerated the size of his estate when it indicated that "he has left among his children 300,000 acres of Land, and above 1,000 negroes, besides 10,000 Pounds in Cash"—but not by much. It can be established that he possessed and distributed among his children and grandchildren at least 218,000 acres of land and 734 slaves. But these figures do not include the Ripon Hall estate in York County or what he may have given his children before his death.[3]

Robert Carter was "born to be rich," William Byrd remarked. He illustrates what it was possible to achieve in the Virginia of the late seventeenth and early eighteenth centuries, but his success was not foreordained. Carter was a younger son, and he received only a small portion of his father's estate and, probably in the 1670s, an English grammar school education. By 1690, when his older brother, John, died, Robert already had at least 1,000 acres of land and around ninety-five slaves and indentured servants. Slaves did not become real estate in Virginia until 1705, so it appears that all of John Carter II's slaves went to his widow, who married Christopher Wormeley, and his daughter, who married Col. William Lloyd. However, by the mid-1690s all the family real estate was Robert's, including between 6,000 and 10,000 acres of land and a gristmill. At the age of thirty, he was a man of substance and standing in the colony. Elected to the House of Burgesses in 1691, he was recommended as eligible for the Council of State two years later and attained the post in 1700.[4]

At his death in 1732, Robert Carter's wealth had been multiplied many times. He was exceptional, but the process by which all attained wealth and status was the same. Tobacco was, of course, a part of almost everything they did. Virginia, someone remarked, was a "colony founded on smoke"; its importance cannot be denied. But for Carter and his peers, production of "the weed" was only one of the ways they made their fortunes. They operated stores, loaned money, served as agents and factors for English firms in both the tobacco and slave trades, managed estates for absentee owners, rented land, owned parts of vessels in the Atlantic trade, operated ferries and ironworks, and held a variety of remunerative public positions.

Robert Carter was involved in most of these activities. For him, as for all of these men, the connection between economic and public life was close. Carter became a member of the Lancaster County court in 1691. In 1698 his fellow justices selected him to be the "undertaker" to construct a new courthouse and jail, for which he was to receive 45,000 pounds of tobacco. Later he built public warehouses on his own land and received an annual rent of 2,400 pounds of tobacco. Beginning in 1701 he was chosen to operate the ferry across the Corotoman River. The court was to pay him 1,400 pounds of tobacco annually, and he continued to run the ferry for the remainder of his life. In the 1690s he also served as naval officer and collector of Virginia duties for the Rappahannock River. His elevation to the Council of State excluded him from these posts but provided him with the opportunity to have great influence over economic legislation and land grants, not to mention appointments to "places of profit," something that benefited his immediate family. Councillors were also the judges, with the governor, of the General Court, the court of last appeal in the colony. The court's records did not survive the nineteenth century, but this position gave one great power over a variety of matters governing the economic lives of Virginians. Carter also served a three-year term as treasurer of the colony, administering taxes on the importation of liquors, servants, and slaves. And for two long periods, 1702–12 and 1719–32, he held the highly remunerative office as agent for the proprietors of the Northern Neck, a post that one bought and that provided substantial returns from a portion of the rents collected and gave an entrée to the acquisition of the best lands.[5]

In private life Carter can best be described as a businessman. Virtually all business activity in the colony involved, in one way or another, tobacco. He grew large amounts on his extensive holdings. In the 1720s he was producing at least 110 hogsheads annually, and he was immensely proud of his crops. But his own tobacco was only a portion of that which he handled. It is reasonable to suggest that he annually exported between 800 and 1,000 hogsheads, much of it from his wharves on Carter's Creek on the Rappahannock River. Part of this tobacco had been collected in payment of proprietary quitrents, part from the rent on lands he leased to tenants. Some of it represented income from his Corotoman store, and some of it was from estates he managed for absentee owners like London merchant Micajah Perry. From time to time he acted as an agent for English firms, collecting debts and providing other services, which brought in more tobacco income. And he regularly handled the sale of crops from the estates of his deceased son-in-laws, Nathaniel Burwell and Mann Page. Carter also loaned money and frequently received payment in tobacco.[6]

Tobacco grown on Carter's lands, and those of his peers, was the product of slave labor, and Carter not only bought slaves, but he sold them. As early as 1700 he was part owner of a vessel that brought 12 blacks into the Rappahannock from Barbados. On one occasion 467 slaves were consigned to him and a partner for sale. More frequently he agreed to sell slaves brought in by traders, for which he received 10 percent of the sale price. Throughout the 1720s he was involved in the sale of between 900 and 1,000 slaves, roughly 7 percent of the total number imported into Virginia between 1719 and 1729.[7]

Additional income came from whatever grain and other food products remained after Carter's large slave and servant population was fed. Food production was substantial. He also operated three gristmills, and a year before he died, he began operating a fourth mill at Ripon Hall in York County. Cloth was also produced at Corotoman. In September 1722 he reported that 500 yards of "Virg[ini]a Cloth" had been "scoured." Carter also held part interest in a tobacco ship that served only the Rappahannock River. When the *Carter* became obsolete, he proposed building "a new ship of 5 or 600 hhds" to be called "after my name" and "to be a Standing Ship for this River"; "I will hold an Eighth on her." Late in life he tried his hand at copper mining.[8]

Rarely if ever in debt, Robert Carter managed the profits from his multiple activities wisely. He reminded Micajah Perry in 1724 that he had run a favorable balance with the London merchant "for many years past" of not less than "3 thousand pounds . . . sometime 4 & I may say Sometimes 5 M." In the letterbook copy the figure for the current year was left out, but it is clear that it was at least a thousand pounds. Perry was only one of a number of merchants in London, Bristol, Liverpool, Whitehaven, Weymouth, and Lyme with whom he dealt. Carter invested his money not only in land but in government annuities and bank stock. Occasionally he also left balances with merchants if they would pay an acceptable rate of interest.[9] The wealthy Virginian's trade was not limited to Britain. The extent of his involvement in the provision trade with the West Indies is not clear, but he bought sugar, molasses, and rum from Antigua, Barbados, and Jamaica that he sold at his Corotoman store.[10]

Carter's varied economic activities represent large-scale business, involving many employees as well as servants and slaves. There were overseers on each of his forty-eight plantation quarters, and on thirty-one of these units, nineteen in Richmond and Westmoreland counties and twelve in King George, Stafford, Spotsylvania, and Prince William, there were two head overseers or farm managers. Rent collectors had to be employed for both proprietary lands and his own. Mills, of course, required millers, the store a storekeeper, and his vessels—three sloops, a pinnace, a yawl, three flats, and a barge—had a "skipper" and seamen, plus a ship carpenter. Slaves and servants needed medical attention, so there was always a doctor on retainer and a barber surgeon. The list could go on: coopers, carpenters, blacksmiths, butchers, sawyers, tailors, and more. All of this activity required management and record keeping, and Carter employed at least one head clerk or manager as well as clerks and bookkeepers.[11]

Robert Carter managed all of his multifarious concerns from the mouth of Carter's Creek on the Rappahannock River about fifteen miles from the Chesapeake Bay. The Carters had been at this spot since the 1650s, and here were located docks, storehouses, an office, at least one shop, and four stores. Nearby were slave quarters and two dwellings; a third that faced the Rappahannock River, built in the early 1720s, burned in 1729. The scene must have resembled a small and bustling village.[12]

Robert Carter presided over all of this with a certain equanimity and constant attention. He may not have been a micromanager, but no detail escaped him. For example, February 17, 1726, was a fine day with the wind from the west, and the "Geese flocked together mightily, very noisy." He began the day by sending 6½ gallons of rum and 6 pounds of sugar to his storekeeper, Captain Thomas Carter, and giving his slave Tom Gumby several "Chissels to frost." Carter's miller at the "Little Mill" had recently died, so he proceeded there to measure 17 barrels of "Indian Corn" and 3 pecks of wheat. Returning home, he found that servant Tom Connor had not completed the prizing of a hogshead of tobacco and observed that the next hogshead would have to be filled with seconds. Quarters in Lancaster and Northumberland counties appear to have had no general overseer, and on April 6 he visited five of his six quarters in Lancaster; when he returned home "after sun sett," he did not feel well. But the next day he inspected three of four quarters in Northumberland County. He gave detailed written instructions to his more distant general overseers in a brusque and businesslike manner. When these managers did not perform as he expected, he informed them specifically of their shortcomings and threatened them with dismissal. He told Robert Jones, who was responsible for quarters in King George, Spotsylvania, Prince William, and Stafford counties, that his performance was unsatisfactory. Because Jones had a large family, Carter was influenced "by the streights you would be under" if he dismissed him. He wrote Jones that in view of "his huge promises," he would "adventure to make a tryal of you one year longer." But Jones must perform the conditions "of last years agreement."[13]

The scale of Robert Carter's operations was so large that one wonders how he managed to keep up with it all. No slothful planter living a life of ease was he. By a recent estimate of what revenue a field hand could produce in the period 1680 to 1740, Carter's gross income from his plantations alone would have been £3,915, a figure that excludes the production of specialized workers—sawyers, coopers, carpenters, etc.—and some twenty-six indentured servants, not to mention salaried employees such as millers.[14]

Robert Carter loomed large in both the public and private worlds of the Virginia elite in the first third of the eighteenth century. But he was not alone. John Tayloe, a colleague of Carter's son John on the council, provides another example. Born in 1687, Tayloe inherited at least 3,000 acres in Richmond County from his father in 1710, some of which he began to lease to tenants. At about this time he began to function as a factor, or mercantile agent, for the Bristol firm of James and Lyonel Lyde. Tayloe replaced the Lydes' brother Stephen, who died in 1710. Two years later he married Lyde's widow, Ann Gwyn Lyde. Soon Tayloe was managing a plantation owned by the Lydes on the Potomac River. As a business representative he made sure the Lydes were consigned tobacco, collected money owed them, and managed two of their local stores. He served the Bristol firm of Thomas Crofts & Company in similar ways and probably others as well. By 1716 he was shipping between 80 and 100 hogsheads of his own tobacco. As early as 1717 he was significantly involved in the slave trade, part of the time with John Baylor, whom Robert Carter called the "great negro seller." Tayloe also seems to have carried on a substantial internal trade, especially with and through the Norfolk area, in shingles, tar, salt, and West India goods such as rum, sugar, and molasses. Like Carter he held part interest in a tobacco ship, which bore his name, and operated at least one sloop. In the late 1720s he was a partner-manager, with British investors, in an ironworks in King George County where pig iron was produced. Then in 1737 he founded his own ironworks in Prince William County. By this time he was also operating three gristmills. At the age of forty, Tayloe was among those in the colony whom Governor Gooch described as having the "best character and capacity, joyned with a good Estate." He was elevated to the council in 1732, having served six years in the House of Burgesses.[15] John Tayloe's business pursuits were not so extensive as Carter's, but before he died in 1747, he had combined the roles of merchant, planter, producer of pig iron, builder of flats and ships, some of which supplied the ironworks, and operator of gristmills. Diversification was a key component in both achieving and maintaining wealth. His son, John Tayloe II, inherited it all, including 20,000 acres and 327 slaves.[16]

William Beverley, the only child of Robert Beverley II and Ursula Byrd Beverley, was born in 1696. English educated, he was for twenty-eight years clerk of the Essex County court, a post he probably combined with the practice of law. He inherited a large landed estate at the death of his father in 1722. By 1745 he was producing fifty-seven hogsheads of tobacco. His income from tobacco was probably exceeded by that from tenants, for in the same year he was receiving rent from 119 tenants, all, it appears, located in counties east of the mountains, primarily Caroline, Orange (Culpeper in 1749), and King and Queen counties. He received additional income from the sale of land in the Shenandoah Valley. In 1736 Beverley patented 118,941 acres of land in what was to become Augusta County, and he began immediately to sell this land. He enlisted the help of James Patton, an Ulster ship captain, to recruit Irish and Scots-Irish immigrants. By 1744 Beverley had sold 42,119 acres, and by the time of his death in 1756, he had disposed of 80,455 acres, for which he had received £2,647.5.5. Beverley also sought a grant of 20,000 acres on the Shenandoah River and the South Fork of the Potomac in the Northern Neck from Lord Fairfax in 1743, on which he was proposing to seat tenants and raise horses and cattle. In 1745 he was involved in more speculative activity when he was associated with the two John Robinsons and others in acquiring 100,000 acres of land on the Greenbrier River in Augusta County. Beverley also operated an ordinary at Caroline Court House and was involved in the West Indian trade. "I am very conveniently situated for the sale of Negroes, rum, sugar & Mollasses," he told a potential Barbados correspondent in 1739. Later he sold Barbados salt in Virginia and shipped corn to the island for sale. But tobacco planting and tenants appear to have been his main source of income. A partial inventory of his estate in 1745 reveals sixty-one slaves on four quarters and numerous cattle, hogs, sheep, and horses. His son Robert reported in 1763 that the estate produced "about £1800 Currency, all plantation expenses deducted." A prominent member of the House of Burgesses from 1736 to 1749, William Beverley replaced John Custis IV on the Council of State in 1750.[17]

Thomas Nelson, unlike Carter, Tayloe, and Beverley, was not Virginia born. The son of a cloth merchant in Penrith in Cumberland, England, he went to Whitehaven on the Irish Sea in 1695 when just eighteen. He made three trips to Virginia, finally settling in Yorktown in 1705, where he established a successful mercantile business. And a merchant he remained for the rest of his life. Nelson did gradually acquire some land—ultimately some 6,500 acres—but land and planting were not his first priorities. He focused on building his mercantile concern, and he was immensely successful. Measures of his success include the £500 he invested in 1715 in Spotswood's Indian Company and the enlargement of his wharf and warehouse facilities on the York River in 1728. Tobacco was, of course, central to his business. Either buying it on the local market or receiving it in payment for store goods, he shipped the cured leaf to England, obtaining credit for the purchase of products salable in Virginia. His volume of business was substantial. Williamsburg planter-merchant Thomas Jones, for example, ran up bills of over £6,600 with Nelson between 1730 and 1738. The provision trade with the West Indies supplemented the tobacco business, and as early as 1720 Nelson owned a one-third interest in the sloop *Martha,* which carried Virginia pork and corn to Barbados. The slave trade also produced income. The York River received the majority of the over 47,000 slaves imported into Virginia between 1700 and 1745, and Nelson was clearly a significant player. He also owned a gristmill, operated the ferry between Yorktown and Tindall's Point, held half interest in a tavern, and in the early 1730s invested £500 in an iron mine. At his death in 1745, his obituary described him as "an eminent merchant." Thomas Nelson never served in public office above that of the county court. He was on the eligible list for the council in 1738, a post he does not appear to have sought vigorously. But both of his English-educated sons, William and Thomas, became councillors in the 1740s, and Thomas was also appointed to the powerful and lucrative post of deputy secretary. In his will Nelson left cash bequests of more than £10,000, an amount that includes nothing of what the eldest son, William, who inherited the bulk of the estate, received. The Nelsons, in a comparatively short period of time, were firmly established as members of the Virginia elite. Economic success could quickly move one up the social ladder.[18]

The substantial estates that these men and their peers built were almost always entailed, and entail, "once invoked, enforced primogeniture and prevented all other transfer of designated land and slaves forever." These estates, the results of hard work and a modicum of good fortune, represented wealth and status. Once they had acquired this property, these men, following English practice, made sure that it remained in their families. Thomas Nelson put it this way in his will: "All my Lands, Tenaments, slaves, and real estate whatsoever I give and Devise to my son William Nelson, and his heirs forever" as well as "all residue of my goods, chattels, and other personal estate of what kind soever it be, after my just Debts and Legacies herein before mentioned are fully satisfied and paid." This was the model usually followed, varying only when "heirs male" were specifically designated. It has been convincingly argued recently that "entail and primogeniture were feudal institutions critical to the growth and perpetuation of aristocracy and slavery in the South." These institutions appear to have been "vigorously enforced" and difficult to evade in Virginia.[19] Entail could also be a burden, especially if business success was not achieved and debts mounted. The problems associated with a one-crop economy and the desire on the part of many, as Robert Carter put it, to live a life that was "too extravagant" were evident early on. When men died heavily indebted an obvious solution was to sell property, but if that property was entailed, and among the elite most was, the only solution, after 1705, was "a private act of the legislature . . . to break" the entail, a process that was lengthy and expensive.[20]

The cases of Ralph Wormeley II and Mann Page I are good examples. Wormeley died in 1701, and to the amazement of his peers, he was heavily in debt to English merchants, even though he had inherited a "Large . . . fortune" and "held "great places of profitt . . . for near Thirty yea[rs]." The debts of the father descended to his two sons. When the second son, John Wormeley, died in 1727, the estate remained heavily encumbered; eleven years later John's son Ralph III was still trying to pay the debts and legacies designated in his grandfather's will. The lands Ralph inherited were entailed, so he initiated a private act in the legislature which, when passed, allowed him to sell 3,000 acres for the "paiment and discharge of the debts" as well as "the several legacies and portions." Mann Page I, Robert Carter's son-in-law and fellow councillor, died in 1732 "considerably indebted to several persons in Great Britain" and in Virginia, owing "more than the value of his slaves and personal estate." His "books," Carter said, had been "kept in a very confused and negligent manner." Mann Page II, the surviving heir, tried unsuccessfully to pay the debts and legacies and in 1744 initiated legislation that would allow him to sell 30,797 acres of land as well as all but seventy-five slaves to meet these obligations. The process was not easy, and in Page's case it was not until 1747 that the act had been approved in England and he could proceed with the sales.[21] Despite the advantages that entail provided in protecting estates and the access to the centers of power that status and money allowed, the management of complicated business affairs was difficult, and not all had the skill and persistence to maintain and build on their inheritance. Cases like those of Wormeley and Page were more often the rule than the exception.

Part of the problem related to the dependence on tobacco and the mercantile system that required the sale of the staple in Great Britain. Virginia planters were prisoners of the system and subject to a price per pound of the weed over which they had little or no control. The first decade of the eighteenth century saw very low prices, but about 1715 began a gradual rise, punctuated by sharp ups and downs, that continued until the Revolution. It hovered between 1 and 1.5 pence until about 1750, when the price exceed, barely, 2 pence a pound. Such prices required large and improved production for the elite to make a profit, and it was best if this production was tied to the sale of store goods to smaller planters. Men like Robert Carter and John Tayloe were able to deal in large amounts of tobacco not only because of their own crops but also because of what they received in rental payments from tenants and from the sale of British goods to tenants and neighbors. It was a situation that could be compared to the company store of a later era. Tenants remained, but challenges to stores run by the elite emerged rather early in the century. Scottish traders, largely from Glasgow, played an increasingly large role in the tobacco trade, buying great amounts of the leaf at prices that Virginians and English merchants could not meet. They also began to operate stores with resident storekeepers, catering to the small and "middling" planters who increasingly produced most of the tobacco. Their resident factors bought tobacco in advance and gained permanent customers who exchanged tobacco for store goods. When their ships arrived, they could load them quickly and thus reduce the turnaround time and freight costs. The route they took, north of Ireland, to the Chesapeake was also shorter. When this cost reduction was coupled with the rapid sale in bulk to Continental customers, it allowed them to offer better prices. English merchants who sent vessels to Virginia to seek consignments could not compete with this system, nor could Virginia merchant-planters. The consignment process was slow, and their ships frequently returned home with partial loads. By midcentury Scottish traders controlled over one-half of Chesapeake tobacco exports.[22]

Merchant-planters had trouble understanding how Glasgow traders could pay such "extravagant prices." Both Robert Carter and William Byrd believed that the Scots were "running away with the trade here" because of "frauds," that is, because they were able to avoid paying customs duties, or as Byrd put it, they "have found some new invention to ease themselves in paying duties on tobacco." Much later Yorktown merchant William Nelson understood better what was going on. He explained that they sailed "their ships so much cheaper . . . & by having Factors here, who are always buying against the Arrival of their ships, they make two voyages a year." But even Nelson believed they suppressed manifests, reporting 400 hogsheads when in fact they were shipping 500 and then unloading part in "small boats at the Isle of Skye."[23]

The growth of the Scots in the tobacco trade meant that the planter-merchant operating on the Carter or Tayloe model was not so profitable as his predecessors had been. Most of the families continued to sell some store goods at their home plantations, but storekeeping was not so important. Indigenous Virginia merchants like the Nelsons remained, but it was Scots stores that began to dominate the landscape, especially after 1730 as the population grew and expanded westward. They located, primarily, inland along the fall line where most of tobacco was beginning to be grown. William Cunninghame, for example, had fourteen stores in Virginia, almost all of which were located along the fall line from Falmouth in the north to Mecklenburg County in the south. What had been a profitable business for many of Virginia's elite had become marginalized.[24]

This change was taking place as elite Virginians were beginning to experience additional pressure from the mother country. Indebtedness to British creditors grew as the population and tobacco production increased. British merchants who faced difficulties in collecting money owed them began to pressure the government to enact legislation that would facilitate debt collection. Such efforts had begun in Spotswood's administration and were given emphasis by the highly visible case of Colonel William Randolph, who at his death in 1711 owed Micajah Perry & Company £3,259.15. His heirs had reduced the debt to £2,465 by 1717, but thereafter only interest was being paid. In 1722 the Perrys sued in the Virginia General Court, and in the trial that followed, the jury ruled in favor of the Randolphs by disallowing all interest and insurance costs on the debt; they owed the Perrys only £80.8.1. The decision was appealed, and ultimately in 1725 four London merchants arbitrated the case, and the Privy Council reversed the decision. This caused quite a furor in Virginia, and President Robert Carter wrote a protest on behalf of the Virginia General Assembly. Carter explained that the debt went back to before 1687, and that in ruling for the Perrys, the Lords Justices in Council ignored "Custom and Usage": interest upon interest had never been charged on "Open running accounts" (book debts). Further, in such cases the plaintiff "by Laws & Customs of England" must accept the jury's verdict, and the only recourse was a new trial. There had been no new trial, and the merchants who had been consulted were not under oath and "are

ever inclined to favor one another." If such practice prevailed, Carter argued,
Virginians would be subject to whatever debts factors and correspondents in
England "think fit to load them" with, to the great discouragement of trade and
industry. He hoped that Virginians "may still enjoy the benefit of Trial according to the Laws and Customs of England under which this Colony was happily
planted." The protest was ignored. The "custom of merchants" prevailed, not
what Virginians considered customary practice. Virginians were still complaining of interest being charged on "common accounts" as late as 1783.[25]

Government actions, as well as those of the merchants, over the next few
years did nothing to allay the feelings of elite Virginians that they were being ill
used. Merchant efforts to defeat the Tobacco Inspection Act, their instigation
of the Colonial Debts Act of 1732, and the failure of Walpole's excise scheme
supported such a view. The debt issue was especially sensitive. The mercantile
community had pressured the government for years, with some success, to make
debt collection easier. Governor Gooch had been instructed to propose a law
for making the Virginia estates of "Bankrupts" liable to the "satisfaction" of their
British creditors. When he argued that such a law was unnecessary because English creditors had "great advantages," he was told that his reasoning was not sufficient. But a bankruptcy law was not forthcoming from the assembly, nor did
the merchant community deem other legislation appropriate. The result was the
debt act of 1732. The "general fury" that Robert Carter reported in the assembly
related in part to the fact that Virginians believed they were not being accorded
the same rights as Englishmen. Carter had argued this in the Randolph case.
Gooch in a letter to the Board of Trade opposing the bankruptcy law made a
similar point. Real estate in America was liable to the claims of British creditors,
but Virginia creditors were not afforded this right with respect to the lands of
British debtors. Commenting on "that cruel and unjust act," John Custis wrote
Bristol merchant Lyonel Lyde that "I must call it so because it does not give us
the liberty of our fellow brittish subjects," for "subjecting our Lands for book
debts is contrary to the Laws of our Mother Country; wch cannot touch real
[estate?] without A specialty ["a Bond, or Bill, or such like Instrument" (*OED*)]
and as we are brittish subjects wee might reasonably expect British liberty." Indeed, he wrote, "wee desire nothing else than to be subject to the Laws of the
Mother Country but wee have good reason to think that you aim at our possessions who have got most of your possessions by us." Custis explained that he
could not be charged with "self interest" because he did not owe anyone in England "a farthing"; his reaction was "purely the result of my thoughts." And he
warned that the English merchant had "so incensed the Country that you will

force them as soon as convenient to have nothing to do with you." John Custis was prescient; it took forty years, but the political implications of merchant and government action were already clear.[26]

Most of Virginia's elite in the eighteenth century did not sell their tobacco on the local market; they consigned it to London and outport merchants. These merchants arranged for the sale of the tobacco and charged a commission for their services, usually 2.5 percent, which included a ½ percent added in the 1720s for assuming the risk when a tobacconist or dealer to whom the tobacco had been sold went bankrupt. The planter assumed all the risks up until the sale of his crop and paid freight, insurance, duties, etc. More often than not, he requested that the merchant in return ship him specified finished goods from other tradesmen, for which a commission was also charged. Ideally the planter would be paying for these goods with the proceeds from the sale of his tobacco. Frequently he would order when he had no balance of funds with the merchant, hoping that his new crop would cover the costs, or just as frequently the orders exceeded the balance in his account. The merchant invariably extended credit, for it was a competitive business, and charged interest.[27] The system was far from perfect. Planter and merchant were doing business far removed from one another. Mutual trust was an important ingredient; there was no contract, and the merchant was nearly as dependent on the planter as the planter was on him. Doing business at a distance of 3,000 miles, when an Atlantic voyage took six to eight weeks or more, made relationships difficult and open to misunderstanding, distrust, and anger.

Robert Carter made his expectations clear to merchant Edward Athawes, who was seeking his business. The most important thing, Carter said, was to send "me good accots of my Tobo upon which the Sinews of my livelihood depend. . . . Another considerable article is the well buying of our goods both as to their Price and goodness." But the planter was frequently disappointed in the price he received for his tobacco as well as in the cost and quality of the goods he ordered. Carter, expressing the feeling of many, said that it was difficult if not impossible to satisfy the merchant and "if we must follow yor directions to make such Tobo as you will think fitt to give a Character twill do little more than pay the Queen her Customs and the Merchts their commissions." Prices were rarely adequate as far as the elite were concerned. John Custis IV "was startled to see such a crop of tobacco given away" and asserted that various people got better prices including "one James Shelton, a carpenter and a man just free." Carter could not understand why "Mr Pratt should get more for his miscellaneous stuff . . . than I do for mine that is made with my own people." Later he was to complain that "miserable are our circumstances" because of poor sales. Items that merchants shipped were frequently just as displeasing. William Byrd asserted that "tradesmen . . . send all the refuse of their shops to Virginia," while John Custis complained that he had never had goods delivered in such miserable condition, "6 rugs entirely rotten and the rest . . . wett and damnified." The ironmonger, on another occasion, sent the wrong "hand mills," for which Custis was "exorbinantly charged," as he was for "my daughters gear" which came from "Mrs Wright" the "Millener." He did not pretend to be a judge of "such things . . . but Mad: Ludwell . . . tells me I am very much imposed on." Later Custis complained about goods sent that he did not order, including a "machine" which he was unable to identify until "the Governors sister told me it was a French device to powder A beau Periwig; I am very sorry that I should be thought such an insipid part of Creation as A beau." Occasionally a planter was charged for goods he ordered but did not receive, and much correspondence and irritation ensued. The merchant, of course, wanted to avoid ill feeling, but his lot, as a purchaser of goods for distant customers, was not easy. Liverpool merchant Charles Goore explained to Mrs. Priscilla Lewis that he had "packd up" her "former order and cleard out the Shipp long before your last order came to hand wch is compleated in the best manner the time woud allow but I cannot say all the goods" were the best "as I was obliged to go to the shops for several Manchester articles I could not get in time and the shipp being cleard out you lose the Bounty on some Linnen & Bottles. . . . Whenever you order goods pray do it in time."[28]

Planters did not always understand the details of the sale of their tobacco. Better grades of the leaf were often sold on the English market while those of lower quality were reexported to the Continent. Customs duties for the latter, which usually sold for a lesser price, were returned. Duties had to be paid on tobacco sold on the home market, but that tobacco, which sold more slowly, brought a better return. To cover the bond on customs duties, merchants borrowed money at 5 percent so they could pay the bonds early and receive the 7 percent annual discount allowed by the government. Robert Carter, who understood more than most people, wanted the benefit from the discount on fifty-one hogsheads of tobacco that the Perry firm had sold "to Inland Customers." He warned that unless the Perrys gave him credit "for the Discounts," he did not intend to give them "any more trouble of my Tobo." He felt strongly about this matter especially because he had a positive balance in the Perrys' hands for which he was receiving no interest. Merchant John Starke, on another occasion, charged Carter "with all the duty and then" discharged "it all on the Credit side which is bulk'd up to a large sum by the dutys making your commission twice as much." Starke replied that all merchants did so, but Carter reminded Starke that "you bond it and none of the money is Ever out of your hands"; for this "I want Satisfaction." Most of the elite were not so solvent or savvy. As William Byrd said, they viewed much of the details of trade as a "mystery." Accounts of sales often were not sent promptly, keeping the planter in the dark as to his debits and credits. Many tobacco hogsheads were damaged by "the carelessness of those Rascalls that carry it from the Tob house to the ship." And those who unloaded the tobacco in England were paid so little that they "make up the wages by pilfering," which may have accounted for the difference in the weight of hogsheads between Virginia and England, of which John Custis complained.[29]

The production and sale of tobacco were a difficult business that required skill and constant attention on both sides of the Atlantic. Debt was always problem. Robert Carter explained the matter succinctly: "Too many among us, when a good market offers for their tobacco, will lay it out in stores and leave their old debts unpaid." The debt act was an expression of merchant concern, as a Glasgow merchant explained in 1731 when he told his brother, "By all means . . . Endeavour to make it your Business to leave as few Debts in the Country as you can or rather none at all, for you know that when at Home what Immense Difficulty there is of Raising them when at such a Distance."[30]

Indebtedness to British merchants grew as Virginia society expanded and became more stable and as a dominant, clearly defined elite emerged. That elite began to demonstrate their position in visible ways. They built grand houses and furnished them with expensive rugs, draperies, furniture, china, and silver. This development coincided with the emergence of what has been called the consumer revolution in England. More items of increased variety became available, and the wealthy, both in Britain and America, fueled this trend with increased buying. For elite Virginians such expenditures frequently translated into more debt than was desirable. Debt, of course, had always been present; it is a given in an agricultural economy and especially one that relies on distant markets. But for many of the wealthy, debt became an increasingly nagging and often serious matter after about 1730.[31]

Increased purchases of slaves, upon whose labor the production of tobacco depended, added to the problem of debt and were among the early indications that all was not well. John Custis in 1721 complained of the difficulty of getting "our debts in, people will buy nigros wn at the same time owe mony to other people." Importation figures suggest what was going on. In the 1720s over 13,808 slaves were imported, and another 15,346 were added in the 1730s. Between 1740 and the outbreak of war in 1754, 16,526 were brought in. "So many Negros" were coming in that William Byrd remarked that "I fear this colony . . . will be confirmed by the name New Guinea." Members of the Virginia elite were both buyers and sellers, some significantly so. Robert Carter's son Secretary John Carter sold, either by himself or with others, especially Thomas Lee, at least 1,027 slaves between 1735 and 1739, a time of heavy importation. In 1738 Carter commented on the "many Negro-ships in this [James River] & York River." William and Thomas Nelson advertised the sale of 607 blacks in this period. They sold 317 and forwarded the remainder to Maryland for sale. The Beverley, Digges, Harrison, Lewis, Randolph, Robinson, and Tayloe families were also involved in the slave trade, as were the Baylor, Braxton, Churchill, and Willis families from the second list of twenty. William Byrd II, whose father had been deeply involved in the trade, said that a "few ravenous traders . . . woud freely sell their fathers, their elder brothers & even the wives of their bosoms, if they coud black their faces and get anything by them."

All of those who sold significant numbers marketed these slaves on consignment from English firms based primarily in Liverpool and Bristol and to a lesser extent London. It was a highly competitive business that was fraught with difficulties. John Carter and his brothers Charles and Landon wrote in 1736 from the Northern Neck that "So many ships have Crowded upon us with slaves that we have been Obliged to give more and longer Credits." They went on to advise that while one of these ships, the *Liverpool Merchant,* was being repaired, they would be trying to get tobacco for her return voyage. Out of another shipment field hands were selling for "£18 a head," but sales were slow, and "many" were "stuck on hand" for over a year. A crowded market led to low prices. Sometimes the "sort of slaves" consigned did not please buyers. One shipment included a "large number of Children and some Men and Women, all but a Few past their prime." Some of "the children were in such a Miserable State that it was impossible to conceel it," and John Carter accepted any reasonable offer. But sales were so slow that "Some that seem'd to ail not much, would dye the Day following." He could not describe "the Wretched Condition these slaves were in." When the ship left Africa, 290 slaves had been on board, but by the time it arrived in Virginia, 106 had died. Carter managed to sell 45 of the slaves, for about £10 each, "A Very Melancholy Account," he lamented.

It is impossible to know the profit and loss in what Byrd II called this "unchristian traffick of making merchandize of our fellow creatures," but by the time the war came in 1754, most of the elite families were not involved in the trade. What had been a good business for Robert Carter and Thomas Nelson

does not appear to have been something their sons and grandsons could profitably pursue. Richard Randolph II, a grandson of William Randolph of Turkey
Island, was consigned, with John Wayles, a cargo of slaves that arrived in the
James River in September 1772. The ship carried 400 slaves as it left the coast
of Africa, but only 280 survived the voyage. Wayles died shortly thereafter, and
although the slaves were sold, little or no money was ever collected. Randolph,
who had massive debts, died in 1786 owing Bristol merchants Farrell & Jones
£6,770 not including interest.[32]

Robert Carter and his peers had been involved in diverse activities, but as
time wore on their descendants found it difficult to maintain that diversity.
Large landholdings remained on which tobacco growing continued, as did the
leasing of land to tenants. Some began to try to lessen their dependence on tobacco by growing more grains, especially wheat. And not a few explored land
speculation, a seemingly attractive option. The colony grew from thirty counties and a population of 114,000 in 1730 to fifty counties with a population of
231,000 in 1750. Much of the good land east of the mountains had been taken
up, but this was not the case farther to the west and southwest. To Virginians
of an entrepreneurial bent, the possibility of benefiting from this situation appeared obvious. The internal population was growing, and there was substantial
in-migration to the western piedmont and the Shenandoah Valley. A more liberal land policy gave further encouragement. This policy allowed rights to large
tracts if they were able to settle one family for each 1,000 acres within two years
from the time of the grant. The policy had emerged in 1720 with the creation
of Spotsylvania and Brunswick counties and the desire to protect the frontiers
from the Indians and the French. Settlement was encouraged by allowing inhabitants to be free of "publick levies for ten years." And despite the order of the
Privy Council to limit grants to 1,000 acres, the council and the governor found
ways to avoid this stricture. They controlled the granting of any parcel over 400
acres, and as Manning Voorhis pointed out, "Who was there to protest?" The
House of Burgesses did not see the governor's instructions, and it had no legal
authority in the matter. Further, many of its members were large landholders.
English authorities were concerned, but they were 3,000 miles away, communication was slow, and by the time they were on top of the situation, vast amounts
of land had been granted.[33]

Alexander Spotswood's exploratory trip across the mountains in 1716 and
his subsequent acquisition of large amounts of land in the new county of Spotsylvania had turned the eyes of wealthy Virginians westward. Robert Beverley
and Thomas Lee, among others, had been involved with Spotswood, and it was

Beverley's son William who in the 1720s and early 1730s began aggressively to explore the possibility of acquiring land west of the mountains. Time was of an essence because "northern men" were busily taking up land and bringing in settlers from Pennsylvania and elsewhere. Beverley and some associates, the "first discoverers," had trouble getting their land surveyed, but in early 1732 the survey had been finished, and they "sold the Land to a pensilvania man for 3 lbs of their money pr hundred." This had been done without obtaining grants for the land, and Beverley wrote on April 30 to what appears to have been a member of the council requesting that he obtain an order for 15,000 acres "at the first Council held after you receive this." The rights were granted on May 5; he was in the clear, providing that "the same do not interfere with any of the Tracts already granted in that part of the Colony."

But the land had already been granted to Jacob Stover, "a native of Switzerland," and he had settled people on it who petitioned the council to set aside Beverley's effort to shut out Stover. The council, after hearing all the evidence, confirmed the grant to Stover. Beverley persevered, and in 1734 in association with Thomas Lee and John Tayloe, both members of the council, he was granted the right to survey 60,000 acres "on the River Sherando & Branches thereof." Tayloe and Lee then withdrew and were replaced by Sir John Randolph, Richard Randolph, and John Robinson. In 1736 Beverley, with these men, patented 118,491 acres. Council minutes reported that the surveyor "by some mistake . . . had included a far greater quantity than the said Sixty thousand Acres," but the council was not concerned. By the time of the patent, Beverley had seated some sixty-seven families on this land "beyond the Great Mountains on Sherando Riv[er]." Soon Beverley controlled the entire tract, now called the Beverley Manor, and he quickly began to sell the land. By 1750 nearly 80,000 acres had been disposed of at an initial price of seven pence an acre and after 1744 eight pence. Hard on the heels of this acquisition, he received an order in council for an additional 30,000 acres in the same area. To James Patton, a Scots-Irish ship captain who was to play a major role in the settlement of the Shenandoah Valley, Beverley wrote that he was prepared for Patton to hold one-quarter of land if he would be responsible for his share of "the charges & doing your utmost endeavour to procure families to come in & settle it." He planned to "hold it undivided & to sell out & make the most of it." The order was in the name of Edward Barradall, a lawyer who represented Lord Fairfax in his negotiations with the colony to determine the extent of his Northern Neck Proprietary. Barradall was soon to be attorney general and was fronting for Beverley, who may have been concerned because he had just received another large grant. Beverley assured Patton that Barradall's name on the order "signifies nothing for he will convey his right to me when we have got a pattent." Lee and Tayloe seem to have functioned similarly in connection with the Manor grant. This arrangement with Lee and Tayloe did not work out, but William Beverley had seen the possibilities beyond "the blew Ridge of Mountains" early on and pursued them relentlessly. He was a man on a mission; profit was his goal, and profit he did. Wealthy Virginians remained interested in acquiring land as a sound investment and as security for the future. William Beverley's son Robert wrote in 1773 that he was thinking of acquiring "Land" on the "Frontier, for I sincerely believe Population will flourish . . . in a most Extraordinary Manner, & I do imagine 20 years hence our Sons would think a Tract of Fertile Land on the waters of the Ohio no contemptible Possession."[34]

William Byrd had also turned westward. In the 1730s he began to explore and acquire land to the southwest, where he had surveyed the line between Virginia and North Carolina. In 1733 he acquired 20,000 acres in North Carolina on the Dan River. Soon thereafter he acquired rights to 100,000 acres nearby in what was then Brunswick County, Virginia. His plan was to settle the land with a group of immigrants, one family for every 1,000 acres. But the vessel with "250 Switzers and Germans on bord" sank off the Virginia coast in 1738, and only 90 persons survived. A subsequent plan to sell the land to "200 Highlanders with their lairds" seems to have failed. Finding that he could "not depend on the importation of families," he was given permission to survey and buy the land, which was accomplished in 1742. Byrd died in 1744, and his son does not appear to have been able to manage this portion of the estate profitably. But Beverley and Byrd set a pattern for their fellow Virginians to follow.[35]

During the 1730s and 1740s a wide spectrum of Virginians sought out land for speculative purposes, and elite families were in the forefront. Eighteen of the twenty-one leading families were involved, some substantially so. The period from the death of William Byrd II in 1744 to the outbreak of the war with France ten years later was marked by intense activity. Unlike Byrd and Beverley, those that followed them were involved in more problematic undertakings. They organized in groups and, of necessity, sought out lands farther to the west and southwest. New provisions "allowed four years Time to survey and pay rights" and return plans, probably about bringing in settlers, to the "Secretarys office." The time frame was attractive, and the costs of such an enterprise would be spread among a large group of investors. Everyone hoped, of course, that the returns would be large. Beverley, after all, was gaining good income from the sale of his Manor lands. The elite families were well positioned to benefit for they held a majority of council seats. Power was in their hands, and they used it to their advantage.[36]

John Robinson of the council and his son John, Speaker of the House of Burgesses, led the first of these groups, which came to be called the Green Brier Company. Secretary Thomas Nelson and William Beverley were also members, as were eight others. The council gave these men permission on April 26, 1745, to survey 100,000 acres just west of the Allegheny Mountains on the Greenbrier River. At the same time it also made grants for 200,000 acres to three other groups, one of which included John Tayloe Jr. The following November, in one day, another 217,000 acres were doled out. To the west of the Fairfax proprietary, 100,000 acres were granted to John Blair Sr. and Jr. and sixteen others. Another 60,000 acres went to an all-Randolph group, nine of them, led by Richard Randolph I and II. The land was to the southwest in Brunswick County on the Staunton and Otter rivers "at the Great Mountains."[37]

Two years later Thomas Lee and eleven others, among them Secretary Thomas Nelson, requested 200,000 acres on the north and south sides of the Allegheny River. Secretary Nelson appears to have been included to strengthen the petition; he soon resigned and later was to be a member of the Loyal Company. Lee may have begun to think about such an acquisition in 1744 when he and William Beverley represented Virginia in negotiations with the Iroquois resulting in the Treaty of Lancaster in which the Indians relinquished land claimed by Virginia in that area. Gooch and the council—John Grymes, John Custis, William Fairfax, John Blair, William Nelson, and William Dawson— postponed a decision on the proposal. It is possible that having granted so much land west of the mountains, Gooch delayed until he could check with home authorities. Politics also may have been involved. Lee and his colleagues, with the exception of Nelson, were from the Northern Neck, while Councillors John Robinson and John Blair, who had already received large grants, were associated with men living south of the Rappahannock River. In any case, Gooch's letter to the Board of Trade gave a positive view of the request and emphasized "National Advantages": trade with the Indians and the creation of a buffer zone against French expansion. Lee, at about the same time, brought in London merchant John Hanbury as a partner, and Hanbury petitioned the king on behalf of the group, now identified as the Ohio Company. The request was acted on positively on March 18, 1749, and on July 12 the governor and council agreed to allow the company to "take up and survey" 200,000 acres free of payment for "Rights" and of "Quitrents" for the "Space of Ten years." The company was required to erect and garrison a fort and seat one hundred families on the land within seven years. As soon as these requirements were met, it could acquire an additional 300,000 acres. That same day a large partnership, to be called the Loyal Company and headed by Councillor John Lewis, obtained 800,000 acres to the southwest on the North Carolina border, extending into what was to become Kentucky. This grant, like that to the Green Brier group, specified only that the land be surveyed, rights paid for, and a plan drawn with four years. Proximity to the French may have been one reason that only the Ohio Company had to build a fort and put settlers on the land; Lee and his associates suspected politics was a factor and complained that "1,350,000 acres . . . were granted by the governor and council to borrowed names and private land mongers." Indeed, on July 12, excluding the grant to the Ohio Company, permission was granted to others to take up and survey 1,150,000 acres. Whatever their differences, the governor and the council possessed the power to grant land, and John Robinson, Thomas Lee, Thomas Nelson, and John Lewis amply provided for themselves and their peers. And when those outside of the circle of power challenged grants to their members, they proved themselves flexible and savvy. Zachary Lewis, for example, entered a caveat against the elder John Robinson and others for a grant they received in 1743. The council responded by getting Lewis to agree to dismiss the caveat in return for being allowed to take up 30,000 acres elsewhere that "did not interfere with any prior Order or Entry."[38]

Over the next few years substantial grants were made to others, including 220,000 acres to a group headed by Richard Corbin with members from the Carter, Harrison, Burwell, Randolph, Page, Fitzhugh, and Grymes families. But the Ohio, Loyal, and Green Brier companies appear to have been the most viable, and even they brought few returns to their investors in the eighteenth century. The outbreak of war in 1754; changing British policies, which restricted settlement beyond the mountains in the 1760s; and the Revolution itself all delayed and disrupted the best of plans. But these things did not dampen the desire of "Speculative Gentlemen" for western lands. The appetite was so great that as George Washington reported in 1757, the Ohio Company, which included "many Gentlemen that had a share in Government," for too long ignored the French menace. Even Washington was "hunting out good lands" in the late 1760s; he asserted that "I can never look upon" the Proclamation Line limiting western settlement "in any other light (but say this between ourselves) than a temporary expedien[t]." One other group, led by William and Thomas Nelson and including Washington, sought out land to the southeast in Norfolk and Nansemond counties known as the Great Dismal Swamp. They hoped that the swamp could be drained, rich land reclaimed, and large crops grown close to the

port of Norfolk. The Dismal Swamp Land Company did substantial reclama-
tion work before the Revolution, but again, its efforts brought no early significant returns. Land speculation was no substitute for the business activities in
which elite families were no longer, or only marginally, involved. The failure of
land speculation to provide significant income was one indication that what had
been an important, even dominant, role in economic affairs for these families
was diminishing.[39]

Speculative activities aside, the economy of the Old Dominion in the twenty-
five years before the Revolution was good despite the war with France, some bad
crop years in the late 1760s, and the credit crisis of 1772. The tobacco trade
tripled between the 1720s and the 1770s. Population, land values, and income
increased. And the elite families seem to have generally benefited from these circumstances. But growth in wealth was accompanied by increased debt. British
merchants extended more credit because, as Jacob Price has explained, planters
appeared to be better credit risks than they had been. "One would naturally
be prepared to advance much more to a man worth £10,000 than one worth
£1,000." Price quoted Thomas Jefferson's father-in-law, John Wayles, who wrote
in 1766 that

> within these 25 years £1,000 due to a Merch[an]t was looked upon as a
> sum immense and never to be got over. Ten times that sum is now spoke
> of with Indifference & thought no great burthen on some Estates. In-
> deed in that series of Time Property has become more valuable & many
> Estates have increased more than ten fold. But then Luxury & expensive
> living have gone hand in hand with the increase in wealth. In 1740 I don't
> remember to have seen such a thing as a turkey carpet in the Country
> except a small thing in a bed chamber, Now nothing are so common as
> Turkey or Wilton Carpets, the whole Furniture of the Roome Elegant
> and every appearance of Opulence. All this is in great Measure owing to
> the cred[i]t which the Planters have had from England & which enabled
> them to Improve their Estates to the pitch they are arrived at, tho many
> are ignorant of the true cause. In 1740, no man on this [James] River
> made 100 hhds of tobacco; now not less than six exceed that number.[40]

John Wayles understood what had been taking place; increased income and
wealth brought increased credit, and that in turn produced increased debt.
This indebtedness was especially visible among the elite families. Because they
had more money, they spent more, and for many their spending exceeded their

income. Part of their spending, as Wayles pointed out, was on luxury items, but this is not the whole story. Not a few appear to have been worse managers and businessmen than their fathers and grandfathers, or they simply were not willing to devote the necessary time to running complicated agricultural enterprises. There were few Robert Carters among the post-1750 Virginia elite. None of his surviving sons, for example, were able to obtain his level of success. John, the eldest, did well but he did not match his father. Charles of Cleve and Landon, younger sons, present a mixed picture. Charles died heavily in debt while Landon maintained the estate he inherited. Of his grandsons, Robert of Nomini Hall and Charles of Shirley were very successful men, but they were in the minority.[41]

Generational decline also can be seen in the Harrison family. Benjamin Harrison V (c. 1726?–1791)—whom John Adams was to later describe as "an indolent, luxurious, Gentleman" who was also "obscene, profane, impious"—was, in the words of an early biographer, a man whose "talent" was "rather useful than brilliant." He had inherited a "very large fortune" and had "twice succeeded to considerable property under the . . . law of primogeniture." Harrison's enterprises, like those of his peers, were diversified. In addition to producing and selling tobacco, he operated a store, mills, and a shipyard. In all of these things, he was, reportedly, "very unsuccessful." He was deeply in debt by the 1750s and apparently was unable to reduce it. Edmund Jenings III, a grandson of Councillor Jenings who had been born in Maryland and was now a London attorney, was one of his creditors. In 1758 Richard Corbin was informing Jenings that despite "many promises" the expectation of payment "seems further removed than it was sometime ago." Corbin feared he would have to use "compulsory methods," which it appears he did in 1760. The Bristol firm of Farrell & Jones was also a substantial creditor. John Wayles reported that he did not think the firm would lose its money but commented that the Harrison family "is somhow so connected with your other Friends, that, where the debt is not in danger, indulgences are unavoidable. They require more than other People, & therefore on that Score are less desirable correspondents." Believing that "his misfortunes proceeded from a want of mercantile skill," Harrison determined that his son Benjamin (1749?–1799) should receive a business education. He sent the young man to be trained in the Philadelphia firm of Thomas Willing and Robert Morris in the hope that he could "retrieve the fortunes of the family." Benjamin Harrison VI also attended the Philadelphia Academy where his classmates included Tench Coxe and William Tilghman, and sometime between 1770 and 1773 he traveled on the Continent and England. He played a significant role in the pre-

Revolutionary protest movement and was deputy paymaster general in Virginia during the war. He also operated a mercantile firm in Richmond during the war and until the late 1780s. A supporter of the Constitution, he saw his business suffer in the 1780s, and his fortunes were not helped by a $45,000 loan to Robert Morris in the 1790s. Unable to regain the family's wealth, Benjamin Harrison VI died in 1799, and creditors were unsuccessfully pursuing payment of old debts into the 1820s.[42]

The Randolphs, the descendants of William Randolph I of Turkey Island, are another family that did not prosper as the century wore on. By the end of the century, most members of this family, which then numbered at least 248, found themselves in straitened circumstances. There were exceptions. Peyton Randolph (1721–1775) managed his inheritance better than most, but even he left substantial debts that burdened his nephew Edmund Randolph (1753–1813) until his death. More typical were two members of the third generation, Peter Randolph (1717–1769), son of William Randolph II, and Ryland Randolph (1734–1784), son of Richard Randolph of Curles. John Wayles reported to Peter Randolph's creditors, Farrell & Jones, that at his death Randolph owed £14,000. This circumstance, Wayles wrote, "excites the amazement of many as well as yourselves but when it is considered that he was the most expensive Man in every article of Life And his Estate was under but indifft management for he never went to a plantation himself the wonder ceases." The debt was actually £18,772, and this for a man who possessed nearly 20,000 acres of land and 250 slaves. His cousin Ryland held over 21,000 acres, and his debts amounted to nearly £6,000 as the result of an "indifference to business matters" and "personal extravagances." By 1774 he owed London merchant Osgood Hanbury £3,000, yet he requested extension of "my credit so far as immediately to order me a Pipe of Wine from Madeira, & to purchase me a State Lottery Ticket." The wine, he asserted, "is to me an essential necessary of life," and he ordered more in 1783, a year before his death at the age of fifty. Before the Revolution six of William I's grandsons owed a total of almost £60,000.[43]

The Randolphs represent the situation in which many elite families found themselves on the eve of the Revolution. William Byrd III is an extreme example among this group. He had inherited an estate that included over 179,000 acres and at least 1,000 slaves, plus mills, fisheries, vessels, warehouses, and a store. But by the time he was twenty-seven, he was in dire financial straits, and in 1756 he conveyed his estate to trustees who over the next few years sold £40,000 in land and slaves. Even this sum was not sufficient to pay his debts. In 1767 he resorted to a lottery, the prizes to come from the bulk of his estate at the falls of the James

River, which was valued at £56,796. He hoped to raise at least £40,000 from the sale of tickets in Virginia and England, but this effort proved unsuccessful. Byrd sold additional lands and then mortgaged slaves, all of the Westover silver, and finally his English estate, which he had inherited from his mother, for £15,000. He still could not cover his debts, some of which dragged on well into the next century. Byrd's lifestyle was lavish—he denied himself and his family nothing—and he was an inveterate gambler. He was the epitome of elite excess, but it does not appear that Byrd was idle or that he was unconcerned about his estate. An indulged son, he acquired wealth and responsibility too soon, fled to the army to escape a bad marriage, and when he finally settled down, it was too late. John Wayles wrote an English creditor of Byrd's in 1772 that "Col Byrd's trustees have just advertised the sale of 100 slaves on two years Credit which I believe are nearly all he has, except those contained in your mortgage. John Tabb has made an offer of £10,000 Currt. for the Falls Land 'Tis worth £12,000, but if no other bidder offers he must have it.—By this you'll observe Col. Byrds Affairs are coming to conclusion."[44]

By 1776, fourteen of the twenty-one families were in serious financial trouble. It is unclear what the status of three others was, while the remaining four appear to have been solvent (table 3). Some did very well. Nathaniel Burwell II of Carter's Grove was quickly establishing himself as a wealthy man, and Robert Carter of Nomini Hall was rich, as was his cousin Charles Carter of Shirley. Richard Corbin, who died in 1790, was a man of means, but he was Loyalist in persuasion, and one of his sons served in the British army. None of his children seem to have attained his great wealth, but the family appears to have remained prosperous well into the nineteenth century.

The Revolution, of course, did not help matters. Key members of the families were deeply involved in politics and/or the military, which took them away from the management of their estates and businesses. But these activities were usually accompanied by decreased ability and, on occasion, interest. Benjamin Harrison V was one example, and William Nelson's eldest son, Thomas Nelson Jr., provides another. William Nelson died in 1772, and Thomas and his brother Hugh took over the prosperous Yorktown mercantile firm. Very quickly they proved not up to the task, and they brought in Augustine Moore, who had worked for their father, to help manage the business. Further, the firm had £30,000 in outstanding debts in Virginia, and the war appears to have ruined the chances of collecting most of them. These circumstances coupled with Thomas Nelson Jr.'s heavy involvement in politics and his expensive lifestyle resulted in none of the family's earlier wealth being carried over into the next century. The

Table 3   FAMILY SOLVENCY, C. 1775

Solvent	Unclear	In question
Beverley	Digges*	Burwell*
Corbin	Lewis	Byrd
Fitzhugh	Lightfoot	Carter*
Tayloe		Custis
		Grymes
		Harrison
		Jenings*
		Lee
		Ludwell*
		Nelson
		Page
		Randolph
		Robinson
		Wormeley

* At least one member of the Burwell family and two members of the Carter family were solvent. Edmund Jenings's son moved to Maryland and ultimately to England. Philip Ludwell III moved to England in 1760. The Digges family's wealth was not maintained after the death of Cole Digges in 1744; they are not among the sixteen elite families that appear in Main's list of "The 100," nor do the Robinsons after the death of John Robinson in 1766.

Sources: DVB, s.v. "Beverley III, Robert," "Burwell, Nathaniel," "Byrd III, William," "Carter (1732–1806), Charles," "Corbin, Richard," "Custis, John Parke"; Louis Morton, *Robert Carter of Nomini Hall: A Virginia Tobacco Planter of the Eighteenth Century* (rept. Charlottesville, VA, 1964); Richard B. Davis, *William Fitzhugh and His Chesapeake World, 1676–1701* (Chapel Hill, NC, 1963), 54–55; *VMHB* 7 (1899–1900): 317–19, 8 (1900–1901): 91–95; Benjamin Harrison V in John Sanderson, *Biography of the Signers of the Declaration of Independence* (9 vols., Philadelphia, 1820–27), 8:127–72; Benjamin Harrison Jr. to Charles Herries & Company, April 10, 1786, Feb. 10, 1791, March 10 and 22, 1791, to David Buchanan, Nov. 17, 1790, Brock Collection, Huntington Library, San Marino, CA; Paul Nagel, *The Lees of Virginia: Seven Generations of an American Family* (New York, 1990); Emory G. Evans, *Thomas Nelson of Yorktown: Revolutionary Virginian* (Charlottesville, VA, 1975); John Page to John Norton, June 28, 1770, Norton Papers, CW; Page to Duncan Campbell, June 14, 1773, American Loyalist Claims, PRO, T 79/12; Philip Hamilton, *The Making and Unmaking Revolutionary Family: The Tuckers of Virginia, 1752–1830* (Charlottesville, VA, 2003), 78, 107; Gerald S. Cowden, "The Randolphs of Turkey Island: A Prosopography of the First Three Generations, 1650–1806" (Ph.D. diss., College of William and Mary, 1977); Laura C. Kamoie, "Three Generations of Planter Businessmen: The Tayloes, Slave Labor, and Entrepreneurialism in Virginia, 1710–1830" (Ph.D. diss., College of William and Mary, 2000); Ralph Wormeley Letter Book, 1783–1800, UVA.

same is true of the Lee family. Thomas Lee's descendants were a mixed bag. Among his five sons, Philip Ludwell, Richard Henry, Francis Lightfoot, Arthur, and William, only William Lee was an able businessman. He married a woman of great wealth, Hannah Ludwell, but his surviving son died in 1803, and the estate dwindled away. The fortunes of the Leesylvania line of the family, represented by Richard Bland Lee and Henry "Light Horse Harry" Lee, ran aground on their speculative activities after the war.

The list can go on, but the nineteenth-century generation did not wield the great economic power of their forebears. Among the solvent families, the Beverleys and the Tayloes retreated from politics, as did Robert Carter of Nomini Hall. Only the Fitzhughs remained both politically active and economically successful up until the Civil War. The second group of twenty families also saw their fortunes decline. An exception is George Mason, who protected his fortune while politically active and whose two sons were equally successful.[45]

The twenty-five years before the Revolution were the period in which the economic problems of most of the families increased. It was a stressful time of war and political differences, but it was also a time in which money could be made. An English commentator in the late 1760s or early 1770s said that it was wrong to attribute the difficulties in which Virginians found themselves to the fact that "their husbandry is not profitable." Their problems had little "reference to their culture, but to the general luxury and extravagant living which obtains among" them. He argued that Virginians enjoyed "advantages which would make any set of men rich, but instead of applying their money in making use of these advantages," they spent "it on temporal enjoyments of living, dress and equipages." A Virginia planter, in "most articles of life," he asserted, "lives more luxuriously than a country gentleman in England." William Nelson told London merchant Samuel Athawes that he expected the colony would produce 80,000 hogsheads of tobacco in 1770. This large crop would reduce prices for two or three years, but a big crop "is always of good Quality" and would inevitably make "its way to new Markets, that are yet unknown to us, as has been the case for near 40 years." In 1731 tobacco had sold for about 1.4 pence a pound, but "now We make more than double the Quantity and it is worth" 2.7 pence a pound. He believed that "the greater part of Europe are still strangers to the Virtues of fine Virginia Tobo" and when they tasted it "at a modest Price, they will be coveting to have it." Virginia lands were not "too much worn and impoverished," as Athawes had suggested, because "We make more & I trust as good Tobo as we formerly did." A "skillful Planter can make fine from any land, it being his part and interest to improve any he finds worn or wearing out."

So if money could be made, why were so many of the leading families in trouble? Close observers, like the English commentator, attributed the difficulties to an extravagant lifestyle. Athawes explained that Virginia "gentlemen" in general "over value their income, & live up to their suppositions without providing against Calamitous accidents." He said that "many good Familys have been reduced to this unthinking conduct" and wished "when it is too late" that they had been more prudent. Some argued that what led to this extravagance was the large emission of paper money—£440,000 during the war with the French—which encouraged people to believe they possessed more money than was the case. Richard Corbin explained that the large amount of currency in circulation had "two bad effects": it "banished Gold & Silver from amongst us & introduced a Train of Luxury & extravagance. Debts were wantonly contracted, when they could be so easily paid in this fictitious representation of money." Governor Francis Fauquier said there was a more "fundamental Cause," that is, "the Increase of Imports, to such a Height that crops of Tobacco will not pay for them, so that the Colony is so far from having Money to draw for in England; that they are greatly Debt . . . which is daily increasing."

Many planters, perhaps most, blamed British merchants for what Robert Beverley said was the disposal "of our Commodities on such wretched terms," making it "impossible" to "keep the Balance of Trade in our favour." Beverley explained that the relationship between planter and merchant should be one of "a mutual Intercourse of good offices, conducted with Honor & Candor." But such a relationship, if it ever existed, appears to have been short-lived. Even William Nelson, perhaps Virginia's most respected merchant, often complained of the prices he received for his tobacco. To Edward Hunt & Son he asserted that they sold his "town" tobacco "at last years Prices; when others were selling it much better." Charles Carter of Corotoman and Shirley, another prudent man, said that "with all the frugality nay even parsimony, I cannot keep out [of] Debt—owing to the extreme mean price of Tobo." He told Robert Cary & Company that for this reason he was seriously thinking of doing no more business with them.[46]

One other factor must be taken into consideration. Over the years elite Virginians developed a sense of entitlement with respect to their business relations with British merchants. They came to believe that it was their right to draw on merchants for credit no matter what the balance was in their accounts. Further, they were extremely sensitive when their ability to pay was questioned. Not infrequently they would threaten to stop doing business with the doubting merchant. Robert Beverley told merchant John Bland that he found his friend

"Mumford very displeased with you on account of a protest to one of his Drafts, w[hic]h, you promised should meet honor, and at that time seem'd fully determined to break off all connexions with you." William Nelson told merchant Edward Hunt that perhaps he was right to be cautious in "advancing a little Money for a correspondent," but "it hurts me to have your ship go out without being fully loaded." Local merchant James Dean warned his London supplier about "how ready they are to goe to every new man that will advance them money even when they leave large Ballances unpaid with their old friends." But in their own minds wealthy planters were honorable men, and the fact that they were committed to ship their tobacco to specific traders entitled them to be, as they would have phrased it, "a little in advance." Robert Carter Nicholas told merchant John Norton that the "Losses I have sustained in my slaves, and my Inclination to enlarge my Plantations added to the considerable Sum I laid out last year in purchasing tobacco, have left me pretty bare of Cash; so that I may be obliged to avail myself of yr Friendship by several Draughts." Norton could be assured that "I will not suffer you to be long, if at all, in advance for me." Charles Carter complained to Steward & Campbell about the price he received for his tobacco while conceding that his lands were producing reduced yields, but at the same time he expected them to lend him £3,248 sterling to purchase an "Estate upon York River." John Baylor, who was already indebted to Edward Athawes, told Bristol merchant Lyonel Lyde he was shipping him twelve hogsheads of tobacco "on which I [h]ave made bold to draw £7 pr hhd." He had purchased some "fine slaves for my own use which obliges me to draw," and he promised to send Lyde one-half of the next year's crop, which he expected to be "extremely good." Moreover, if good land became available, he hoped it would not be "disagreeable to draw moderately on my Tobo." Surely the quantity and quality of tobacco he shipped Lyde was such "that a few score or even hundreds on either side will not be so regarded." He concluded the letter by ordering, among other things, a young "redd bull," a young ram, and a "Ewe."

Part of the problem was that British merchants had extended credit for many years. Then, especially after 1770, when Virginia indebtedness had grown to alarming proportions, they became less willing to do so and began to press for prompt payment of old debts. In response Virginians expressed hurt and anger. Earlier, in 1764, when John Norton insisted on payment, John Baylor told him that he "took the word Insist . . . extremely unkind." In another case, when Norton questioned a planter's ability to pay, he was told that he should have more confidence in his "Friends" and that his suspicions "will ever have a bad effect and will always injure the person you meant to serve." Robert Beverley told

Samuel Athawes, "Yr Suspicions and apprehensions sometimes appear so great that they become a reflection upon your correspondents here, & betray such want of confidence & Esteem, as I think ought not to subsist between People in our way." When pressed for payment, Thomas Jones told a London merchant that "I must say . . . you did not treat me genteely" and "I assure you that my feelings are as delicate as any Mans living." On occasion the Virginians expressed a certain arrogance. Thomas Nelson Jr. told Thomas and Rowland Hunt, when they were hesitant to supply him store goods, that "I tell you freely that unless a Mercht will upon occasion advance 3 or 4,000 he is not the man for me."[47]

There is no way to know what the longer-term economic condition of the twenty-one families would have been had there been no Revolution, but as 1776 approached they were not in good shape. Samuel Athawes said in 1773 that he was advancing money only to "approved Friends" who "are oeconomical & attentive to their affairs" because of "the great ex[cha]nge of Property which has taken Effect in Virginia" in recent years. Richard Randolph told Farrell & Jones that he would like to ship them all of his tobacco, but he had to pay "old London debts," and to be free of them he needed a loan of about £3,000. Money was difficult to collect and scarce. Only about £80,000 was in circulation in an economy that required "near five hundred thousand pounds to support a proper medium."

The combination of large crops of tobacco after 1770 and a financial crisis in 1772 resulted in lower tobacco prices and difficult times. Not a few planters had tried for a number of years to produce less tobacco and more grains, especially wheat. Some hoped that hemp would be a viable alternative. By 1793 Robert Beverley was able to say that the "agriculture of this country has undergone a surprising revolution . . . tobo is scarcely a secondary object—wheat is so in universal demand." But in 1775 tobacco was still dominant, and most of the elite families were so deeply in debt that there was not time, before relations broke off with Britain, to reestablish themselves on a firmer footing. Thomas Adams wrote from Williamsburg that it was disagreeable to be there at any time "but made moreso at this Time by the distress of Numbers of Worthy People which dont know which way to turn for want of Money to pay their just debts." Thomas Nelson Jr. spoke of the "unhappy state" of things and declared that he did not know when things would be better. He told Thomas and Rowland Hunt, to whom he had written so arrogantly earlier, that he had "burnt" his fingers "so much by purchasing" tobacco that he had "given that over & my Debtors chose rather to let other people have what little they have made than myself." The amount he owed the Hunts was "still large & I have it not in my power to wipe it off at this time." Robert Beverley said that if the difficulties could be resolved, "this Colony alone could remit in Tobo, Wheat, Corn, Lumber & provisions upwards to one Million & one half sterling. A sum more than sufficient to liquidate all its Debts." But when "the Tempest shall subside . . . I am afraid is an Æra vastly distant."[48]

William Fitzhugh (1651–1701), John Hesselius's copy of a seventeenth-century portrait, oil on canvas, 1751. (Virginia Historical Society, Richmond)

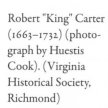

Robert "King" Carter (1663–1732) (photograph by Huestis Cook). (Virginia Historical Society, Richmond)

Sir John Randolph (1693–1737) (photograph by Huestis Cook). (Virginia Historical Society, Richmond)

John "Tulip" Custis IV (1678–1749), at age forty-eight, c. 1740. (Washington-Custis-Lee Collection, Washington and Lee University, Lexington, Virginia)

Mann Page II (1718–1778), by John Wollaston, oil on canvas, 1750s. (Virginia Historical Society, Richmond)

John Tayloe I (1687–1747) (photograph by J. E. H. Post). (Virginia Historical Society, Richmond)

Landon Carter (1710–1778) (photograph by Huestis Cook). (Virginia Historical Society, Richmond)

John Robinson (1704–
1766), c. 1885 copy, in oil,
of an original portrait
owned by Mrs. Benjamin
Robinson. (Collection of
The Library of Virginia)

Richard Henry Lee (1732–
1794), by Charles Will-
son Peale, oil on canvas,
c. 1795–1805. (National
Portrait Gallery, Smith-
sonian Institution; gift of
Duncan Lee and his son,
Gavin Dunbar Lee)

William Byrd III (1728–1777), oil painting, c. 1748–60. (Collection of The Library of Virginia; gift of Mrs. Maria Byrd Hopkins Wright, 1920)

4 Society, 1700–1776

Our Gentry have such proud spirits, that nothing will go down,
but equipages of the nicest & newest fashions.
—FRANCIS JERDONE, 1755

Indeed to be people of consequence is vastly clever.
—ANNE BLAIR, 1768

The world without refinements might as well not exist at all.
—ROBERT BEVERLEY III, 1783

LOVE, COURTSHIP, MARRIAGE, FAMILY

When Governor Francis Nicholson complained in 1701 of the difficulty that
recent arrivals had in attracting mates, the elite by then were predominantly
creole. Although ties with the mother country remained strong, a distinctly Virginia identity was emerging. They continued to travel back and forth across the
Atlantic with some regularity, but this contact appears merely to have strengthened their view that they were valued only for their economic contribution to
the emerging empire and would never attain the status of English gentry. Even
William Byrd II, who spent much of his life in England, felt this way; he had,
after all, failed to get the governmental posts he thought he deserved. In England with his Virginia-born wife in 1716, he wrote John Custis IV that "tho my
person is here my heart is in Virginia."[1]

Nicholson's futile courtship of Lucy Burwell confirmed his observation that
the elite married within their group. Few sought mates outside the one hundred
upper-class families. The process that had begun in the late seventeenth century
continued. For example, Robert Carter's sons married a Hill, a Churchill, two
Byrds, a Walker, a Taliaferro, a Wormeley, and a Beale; as the result of deaths,
two of his sons, Landon and Charles, were married three times. His daughters

married a Burwell, a Page, a Harrison, a Braxton, and a Fitzhugh. Another good example is the Wormeley family of Middlesex County, who were related to ten of the twenty-one families. To the south William Randolph of Turkey Island's four sons who remained in Virginia married two Beverleys, a Fleming, and a Bolling, while two of his daughters married a Stith and a Bland. Of William Byrd II's four children by his second wife, two daughters married Carters, another married a Page, and his son also married a Carter. An example, later on, of how interrelated families became can be seen with one of Robert Carter's great-grandchildren, Thomas Nelson Jr. Five of Nelson's children married into the family of John Page of Rosewell. Of the remainder, two married into another branch of the Page family, while another married a Nelson cousin, and the last a Carter. Someone has remarked that trying to sort out family relations among Virginia's eighteenth-century elite is like trying to separate a box of fishhooks: it was one extended cousinry. A 1775 poem makes the point:

> Apply to Mrs. M.C. a daughter of LW
> My husband's my uncle, my father's my brother,
> I am sister and aunt to a brother called John,
> To whom wit and good nature combin'd doth belong.
> This paradox, strange as it may be to you,
> Any day that you please I can prove it to be true.
> N.B. The marriage is lawful[2]

One did not marry beneath oneself. The preamble of "An act for the prevention of clandestine Marriages" of 1696 warned of clandestine and "secret marriages" that created "great and grievous mischeifes" and resulted in "the utter ruin of many heirs and heiresses, and to the great greif of all their relations." Thomas Lee was reported to have said "that the fall & ruin of familys and estate were mostly occasioned by imprudent matches to imbeggar familys & to beget a race of beggars." William Byrd II, commenting on the elopement of Mrs. Fleming's daughter with "her uncle's overseer," said that "the man has not one visible qualification except impudence to recommend him. . . . But there is sometimes such a charm in that Hibernian endowment that frail women can't withstand it. . . . Had she run away with a gentleman or a pretty fellow there might have been some excuse for her, though he were of inferior fortune, but to stoop to a dirty plebeian without any kind of merit is the lowest prostitution."

But the process of gaining an appropriate mate was not an easy one, especially for men. Their choices were limited to a relatively small number of families, and in the first third of the century the ratio of men to women was high. Even when the male-female ratio began to even out, it was difficult to find a suitable mate. Anne Blair wrote in 1769 about the numerous suitors who were "Dancing and Coopeeing" around her sister that "nay they scrape all skin off their Shins steping over Benches at the Church, in endeavouring who should be the first to Hand her in the Chariot." The *coopee* or *coupee* was "a dance step where the dancer rests on one foot and passes the other forward and backward, making a sort of salutation, hence sometimes used for a bow made while advancing" (*OED*). Suitors not only had to be nimble but frequently had to travel long distances in search of a wife, virtually camping out in their homes.

Some fathers allowed their daughters free choice in choosing a mate, as Francis Nicholson discovered. Lewis Burwell told Nicholson that "I left my daughter to make her own choice as to a husband"; he would never "be guilty of such a horrible piece of Cruelty (for the gain a Kingdom) as to force my daughter to marry ag[ains]t her will the best man alive." When Charles Carter of Cleve sought the hand of the orphaned Miss Howell, John Lewis, who managed "her affairs," told Carter that she had a mind of her own, was of age, and would "choose for herself." If she had "settled her affections another way I believe it will be a hard matter to remove them. I take her to be a girl of resolution." Failing in this pursuit, Carter soon joined his brother Landon at Westover where they were successful with the two young daughters of William Byrd II. Thomas Lee was engaged in 1717 to "the great fortune Jenny Willson." Orphaned, she was living with her aunt, whose son, James Roscow, close at hand, persuaded his first cousin "to choose him for a guardian and immediately marrys her," much to the disappointment of "poor Tom Lee." Lewis Burwell (1710–1756), "labouring under the paroxism of an ill fated love," wrote in 1734 that he was "not so desirous . . . to change the single for the matrimonial State," but within two years he was married, even though he found Virginia women less "fair" than English ones. In 1759 young Bryan Fairfax, twice refused "in his love addresses," ran away from home to join the "No[rth]en Regulars" only to be arrested in Annapolis with "no pass" and thrown into jail under the name of William Fisher. His father arranged his release, and a year later Bryan was still trying to find "some fair Nymph" in order to "reconcile the Toying, Triffling, Billing Sports of Love." Robert Beverley III traveled to Philadelphia seeking a bride, and "tho it was an Affair w[hic]h I most earnestly wished," he was disappointed. But within three months he married Landon Carter's daughter Maria.[3]

There was an almost desperate quality about the need to marry. William Byrd reported in 1728 that matrimony "thrives so excellently among us so that an old maid or an old batchelour are as rare among us . . . as a blazing star." Older men were not content to remain single. Speaker John Holloway, three years earlier, wanted to marry the young widow Elizabeth Cocke Pratt, but when that hope failed, he married her widowed mother. Charles Carter of Cleve, who had lost two wives by the age of fifty-one, was reportedly "very gay & says he has attacked the widow Custis." Unsuccessful there, he continued his search "in his new chariot & six," only to be rebuffed by Miss Hamilton. Three years later, in 1761, shortly before his death, he married Lucy Taliaferro, "abt 16 or 17 years old," "whose face is not the most beautiful" but who possessed a fine "shape" and "carriage" and the "sweetest temper." Speaker John Robinson, soon after the death of his second wife in 1755, married Miss Sukey Chiswell, the daughter of his business partner, John Chiswell; he was fifty-four years old. Elite Virginians, then, considered marriage the preferred, even necessary condition. Thomas Nelson Jr., writing a London merchant friend in 1774, asserted that "you old Bachelors are strange beings why don't you get a Wife. The many solitary Howers you must pass. I should detest the thought of going to bed alone so often as you do. Prithee look out for some pretty Lady . . . that make you pass the waves of this troublesome world with joy and satisfaction." In 1786 Englishman Robert Hunter said that it seemed that "courtship" was "the principal business in Virginia."[4]

Fathers, of course, played a crucial role. Their permission to marry was required of all those under the age of twenty-one, although some were more flexible than others. Marriage settlements were almost always involved and sometimes were used to influence children's decisions. William Byrd II threatened to disinherit his daughter Evelyn if she married an English baronet. Byrd also sent Paul Johnson away "with a gentle denial" when he made a proposal "about Annie," his second daughter. John Custis delayed the marriage of his son for years; Daniel Parke Custis was thirty-nine when he finally married Martha Dandridge in 1749. In a witnessed statement, Edmund Berkeley, who wanted his son to marry Miss Judith Randolph, promised to give young Edmund large amounts of property in land and slaves and to build him a "convenient dwelling House" if he did so. Soon thereafter he married Judith. Negotiations frequently continued for long periods. Benjamin Harrison IV, whose father was dead, asked William Byrd in 1721 to intercede on his behalf with Robert Carter, whose daughter Anne he wished to court. Byrd reported that after some discussion he "at last obtained leave for him to wait on the Colonel at Rappahannock." The trip to visit Carter and his daughter was over a hundred miles, across two large rivers, but over a year later they were married. Anne's marriage portion included land

and slaves. William Beverley and Edmund Jenings II provide other examples of fathers who granted marriage portions. Beverley's daughters, Elizabeth and Ursula, who married James Mills and William Fitzhugh, each received £1,000 sterling or its equivalent. Jenings's daughter, who married John Randolph, also received £1,000.[5]

Such a marriage portion was intended to enable the couple to get a better start in life. Whatever property the woman brought to the union became part of the husband's estate, over which she had little influence. The importance of marriage portions is seen in wedding announcements in the *Virginia Gazette*. Invariably the wealth of the bride is emphasized. Betty Tayloe, who married Richard Corbin in 1737, was reported to be a young "Lady of great Beauty and Fortune," and Betty Lightfoot, who married Beverley Randolph the same year, was said to have "a Fortune of upwards of £5,000." The theme was repeated time and time again: the bride had "great Merit and Fortune," or "considerable Fortune," or "handsome Fortune." There are examples of premarital contracts that allowed the bride to control such property but none among the twenty-one elite families. Jane Swann alluded to one such contract in a letter to Elizabeth Jones in 1757, remarking that she could not but say "you acted prudently in having a provision made for you out of the fortune you brought him [Thomas Jones] to secure you in case of misfortunes which you might no ways occasion."[6]

Economic arrangements were almost always involved in the proceedings surrounding elite marriages. But such arrangements did not preclude romance. Historians differ as to how much romance entered into the decision to marry in the seventeenth century, but all agree that by early in the eighteenth century, mutual attraction was a important factor. A piece in the *Virginia Gazette* in 1738 explained that when "Money . . . is married instead of the Person," the result was an unhappy marriage. If there was not love, then "they will certainly love where they do not marry, and love without Ends has no End." There is substantial evidence of mutual attraction, affection, and love. William Byrd II told his "Fidelia" (Lucy Parke) that he loved her better "than any pamperd priest can love himself"; never was "a man created that loved with more tenderness and sincerity than I do." Robert Bolling, half a century later, spoke of the "pleasing passion" he felt in Anne Miller's presence, which became "as much a Necessity with me as Hunger, Thirst, or any other involuntary Inclination." Bolling's passion was, in part, the result of "the great Intimacy between Relations in this Colony, permitting many Freedoms." In this rural society courtship took place not only in the young woman's home but in the homes of others, and the visits often were extended ones, stretching over several days. Bolling reported that his

Nancy was frequently "on a Bed with me" where he had "sufficient Opportunity to represent the violence of my Passion."[7]

Thomas Jones's courtship of Elizabeth Cocke Pratt in 1725 is somewhat different in that they both lived in Williamsburg and she was a recent, albeit young, widow with two small children under the age of five. The courtship involved visits and extended correspondence. Williamsburg was a small town, and they knew that there would be gossip or, as she phrased it, "slandrous toungs." He wrote that my "late visits to you have not passed without observation." He was uncertain how to "proceed for fear of incurring your displeasure," but "there is so much Beauty in your gentle repulses & soft reproofs that they leave Stronger impressions than the rest of your Sex could doe were all their Powers united in any one person besides yourself." He would always "confine" his conduct to her "prescription," but she was not to be surprised if "you see me in the Garden this Evening about eight or nine a clock." The correspondence began in early September and continued unabated for several months. In December he wrote that "you are belov'd with a most ardent affection"; if she would return his "profession for" her, he would not exchange his "condition for the greatest Monarchy in the universe." And finally in January he asserted, "The longer I think the more I love the longer absent the greater my pain." Elizabeth Pratt, for her part, agonized. She was not surprised that he noticed how little she relished "the things that amuse other people of my age and quality." His "partiality for" her "makes you fancy that my indifference is the result of good understanding and that the force of my judgment" has subdued "my passions but alas how are you mistaken: my melancholy proceeds from the irregularity of my Affections Love, Vanity, distrust and repentance conspire to rack me." She feared that "destructive passion" alone motivated her, and she hoped that "reason would prevail" and "calm" the "wild disorders" of her "breast," that she would no longer "feel Love['s] cruel fire." Perhaps through "the grace of . . . God" she could "cull" her "passions." But Jones prevailed, and by February they were married. Ten years and several children later, Jones's feelings for "my Dearest Life" had not abated. She was away, and he wrote that he had read her letter "about twenty times" not only "with regard as a truly kind and tender husband, but with the pleasure of a passionate lover that flatters himself with hopes sometime or other of being possessed with his Mistress's Charms."[8]

Elite women, through the first three-quarters of the century, were usually married in their late teens or early twenties, although some were as young as sixteen and others as old as twenty-five. Men were usually in their early to mid twenties when married, but some were in their early thirties. William Byrd

II was thirty-two and Lucy Parke eighteen; their daughters Maria and Anne were fifteen and seventeen when they married Landon Carter, thirty-two (second wife) and Charles Carter of Cleve, thirty-five (second wife). Charles and Landon were twenty-one and twenty-two, respectively, when they married the first time. Robert Beverley III was twenty-three and Maria Carter eighteen; Richard Corbin was twenty-three and Elizabeth Tayloe sixteen; Thomas Lee was thirty-two and Hannah Ludwell twenty-one; Sir John Randolph and Susanna Beverley were both twenty-five; Peyton Randolph was twenty-five and Elizabeth Harrison twenty-three; John Randolph was twenty-four and Ariana Jenings twenty-one; Ralph Wormeley IV was twenty-seven and Eleanor Tayloe seventeen.

The law required a marriage license or the publication of banns on three consecutive Sundays, but these requirements were not always observed. William Byrd II writing Daniel Parke Custis in 1742 reported that the marriage of his daughter Maria to Landon Carter was "solemnized . . . yesterday." He continued that "nothing ever fell out more suddenly than this affair, none of us thought anything about it at ten in the morning, and by three the Gordian knot was tyed." The wedding most often took place in the home of the bride. Friends and relations who attended the ceremony visited for a few days thereafter, and there was frequently much conviviality: eating, drinking, and dancing. Guests were, of necessity, accommodated in the home, sometimes in crowded circumstances. When the newlyweds attended church for the first time after the wedding, the minister might deliver a sermon recognizing the union, as was the case in November 1771 for William Nelson and his bride. The scripture was from Genesis: "And Jacob served seven years for Rachel, and they seemed unto him but a few days for the love he had for her." He "touched on the Tender Passion of Love, as a necessary Requisite in Courtship and Marriage. The Duty of Husband and Wife, with Respect to acquiring and preserving domestick Happiness; concluding with some very pertinent Animadversions on the Conduct of Parties in Regard to the disposition of children in Marriage, and how far the Duty between both ought to be reciprocal."[9]

Once married, the new husband took control over all property the wife brought to the union. He could not sell or mortgage the real property without her consent, but that was about the extent of her influence; she was the lesser partner and could not institute any legal action on her own. Premarital agreements did allow for separate estates, but they were rare and were used more often when widows married. Further, women were not only the lesser partners, but they were considered the weaker "vessel" who should submit to the will of the husband. Phrases such as "woman's weakness" were common. After the death of one husband "who was a sot" and who had used his wife "ill on all Occasions," her brother commented that "yet she always behaved herself towards him . . . as a good & dutiful wife ought to." "H.C.," writing in the *Virginia Gazette*, advised wives to "banish the least thought of managing your husband"; they should not "impose on his understanding nor make him uneasy" for those that "lord it over their husbands are odious to mankind." And wives were advised not to overlook the "Word Obey."[10]

How elite couples related to one another is an interesting and difficult question. William Byrd's diaries provide some insight, from his perspective, on his marriage and on that of his brother-in-law John Custis IV. They married the Parke sisters, Lucy and Frances, both of whom were strong-willed and intelligent women who did not fit the mold of a complaisant wife. The relationship of Frances and John was especially difficult. She exercised her full rights, as a result of her grandfather's will, concerning the transfer of inherited property to William Byrd and delayed the transaction, much to the outrage of her husband. The relationship became a troubled and unhappy one. Byrd thought that despite Frances's charge that Custis was unkind, the problem was, in part, due to the fact that her "humor" was "none the best." The situation deteriorated to the point that the Custises drew up a marriage agreement. Frances agreed not to "run him into debt without his consent" and not to "call him . . . any vile names or give him any ill language." She was also not to "intermeddle in his affairs." John, similarly, was to avoid verbal ill usage and not to interfere in her "domestique affairs" as well as to settle all the debts "due to the estate" she had brought to the marriage. He was also to provide one-half of the income, after expenses, from the estate to Frances for her personal needs, those of their children, and "all things necessary for housekeeping . . . soe long as the sd Frances shall live" peaceably and "quietly with him." Other arrangements provided for household servants. Both were also to keep "true and perfect" accounts and to "live lovingly together and to behave as a good husband & wife ought to doe." Frances died of smallpox less than a year later, so the efficacy of this agreement was untested.

The marriage of William Byrd and Lucy Parke was more normal. She was high-spirited and quick to anger, but the marriage appears to have met the assumption of the male-dominated culture that a woman was the subordinate partner who should be guided by her husband's wishes. At least, so it appeared to Byrd, who was fourteen years older than his wife. Typical of his comments were "my wife & I disagreed about employing a gardner" and in the evening "my wife and I continued very cool." When he reproached Lucy for ordering old beef kept and fresh beef used "contrary to good management," it made her "very angry" and put him out of humor, but in the evening she apologized and "we were friends again." Most disagreements ended in "her submission," although occasionally he "made the first advance." When reflecting on their relationship after an evening walk with Lucy, he expressed relief that she "has not quarrelled with me in a great while." Despite the one-sided perspective, the marriage appears a loving one. At one point Lucy joined him in Williamsburg where they dined, visited, and at 10:00 went to bed "where I lay in my wife's arms." When Lucy joined him in London and died soon thereafter of smallpox, he wrote John Custis that "no stranger ever met with more respect in a strange country than she had done here, from many persons of distinction, who all pronounced her an honor to Virginia. Alas! how proud I was of her, and how severely am I punished for it. But I can no longer dwell on so afflicting a subject, much less think of anything else."[11]

Custis was an extremely difficult, cantankerous man who made a fortune and kept it. He never remarried and fathered a son by one of his slaves, something that he freely acknowledged, for whom he provided handsomely in his will. Byrd was a gifted and multitalented man who spent twenty-eight of his first forty-two years in England. He was not only well read but a good business-man who inherited a fortune and ultimately increased it. The fact that he kept a diary that reveals a great deal about himself, including his sexual activity, should be considered in light of the "ethical reaction to the perceived excesses of the Restoration" and the "kind of supervision of one's daily actions a diary might encourage." Take the case of the Jones family, not on the list of fifty or so top families but certainly among the elite. Elizabeth Jones had two children quickly after her marriage. Then, to restore her health, she departed for England and remained nearly two years, visiting in London and taking the waters at Bath. Thomas Jones was left to care for her daughter by her first marriage and the two babies. She took her young son, William Pratt, with her. Jones, perhaps influenced by his strong-willed wife, ordered in his will that his sons and daughters should receive equal shares of his estate.

Beyond examples such as these, information concerning marital relations is scarce. Some wives fled difficult marriages, if only temporarily. English-born and Cambridge-educated Isaac W. Giberne, reputedly the nephew of the bishop of Durham, was the pastor of Lunenburg Parish in Richmond County, ministering to and socializing with the elite of Lancaster County. He confided to Landon Carter that "what rendered the *Circumstances* of my present Disorder worse was the *Elopement* [adultery] of my *Wife*, who I am credibly Informed keeps company Every *Night* with some *strolling Players!*" Despite this conduct the marriage survived, perhaps because divorce was not possible in Virginia. Abused wives could seek separate maintenance, which the courts occasionally granted. Tradition has it that Richard Corbin (1715–1790) and his wife Elizabeth dealt with their marital problems by living in separate wings of their 250-foot-long Laneville mansion in King and Queen County. William Byrd III's solution was to desert his wife in 1756; she died, a probable suicide, in 1760. He returned to Westover in 1762 with a new wife. That there were unhappy couples in Virginia is no surprise, and that some women were sensitive to and not happy with their situation is clear. A poem in the *Virginia Gazette* titled "The Lady's Complaint" was to the point:

> Custom, alas! doth partial prove,
> Nor gives us equal measure;
> A Pain for us it is to Love,
> But is to Man a pleasure.
> They plainly can their Thoughts disclose,
> Whilst ours must burn within:
> We have got Tongues and Eyes, in Vain,
> And Truth from us is Sin.
> Men new to Joys and Conquests fly,
> And yet no hazard run:
> Poor are left, if we deny
> And if we yield, undone.
> Then Equal laws let Custom find,
> And neither sex oppress;
> More Freedom give to Womankind,
> And give to Mankind less.[12]

Replying with tongue in cheek to the admonition of "H.C." that women should not forget the "Word Obey," "Andromache" noted that because "it so happens that most of us are illiterate it is certainly the greatest Piece of Friendship to give us seasonable Instruction." But she could not "forbear thinking it hard we should be attacked with a Weapon we are unacquainted with (I mean the Pen)." She did not need to be reminded that angry wives should not desert the marital bed. She referred to his "Simile of the Moon" in which he declared that the "further" the moon is from the sun, the brighter it shines, "and the nearer the more obscurely." "Bad Wives" dealt with their husbands "by being hearty and gay in their Absence; but when they appear, become sorrowful, and pensive," while the good wife, he advised, "never visits or receives any that may make her husband uneasy." To "Andromache" this advice was far-fetched, inverted, and not altogether accessible to "common understandings," but because "he seems to soar in on a Superior Orb to us Sublunary Folks, I don't know that it may be proper enough." She would not pretend to try to match the work "of so masterly a Pen (Causa qua supra [in the aforementioned case])," but because he seemed to be speaking in general, she was pleased that he allowed "our Sex to have a greater Share of Sense," assuming, for example, "that we are able to impose on the Understanding of a Husband, which is indeed a matter of some Consolation to us." Finally, she informed him that several ladies of her acquaintance had read the *Spectator* on this subject and for the most part thought his observations better. "I'm inclined," she said, "to pitty poor Mr. *Addison* and *Steel,* when I observe a Genius so much exceeding theirs." She hoped to hear more from the gentleman. In any case, what the norm was for marital relations in eighteenth-century Virginia cannot be accurately defined. After a visit to Virginia in 1765, Lord Adam Gordon reported that "the women make excellent wives, & are in general great Breeders. It is much the fashion to marry young & what is remarkable in a stay I have made of near a month in the province I have not heard of one unhappy couple."[13]

If the husband was the eldest son, a newly married couple usually moved into his parents' home. New houses sometimes were built for younger sons, or property was provided on which they built. William Byrd II, whose parents were dead, was living at Westover when he married Lucy Parke. After John Carter, the eldest son of Robert Carter, married Elizabeth Hill, they probably lived at the plantation she inherited, Shirley, close to his responsibilities as secretary of the colony and a member of the council. When his father died, he inherited Corotoman. Robert Carter built Nomini Hall for his second son, Robert, who lived at Corotoman while the house was being completed. The two younger sons, Charles and Landon, were to build homes on inherited land. Thomas Nelson Jr. and Lucy Grymes, who married in 1762, lived with his father, William, in Yorktown for five years until they moved into his grandfather's house after the death of his grandmother.

Children came quickly, and families were usually large. Some attributed this prolificacy to the women. William Byrd II, in a half-humorous letter to his sister-in-law, said of his wife that he knew "nothing but a rabit that breeds faster" and that it "woud [be] ungallant in a husband to dissuade her." She "was delivered of a huge boy in September last and is so unconscionable as to be breeding again."

Later in the century Landon Carter asserted, "I do believe women have nothing in general view, but breedg contests at home. It began with poor Eve and ever since this has been so much the devil in Women." Some women prolonged the breastfeeding of their children in an attempt to delay their next conception. Byrd suggested that the only way to solve the problem was for him "to make a trip to England sometimes." Elizabeth Jones, after having four children in seven years, did depart for England for an extended stay for her health, leaving three of her four children with her husband. When she returned, she went on to have eight more children. The average number of children among the twenty-one leading families in the eighteenth century was roughly seven, but there were wide differences. Elizabeth Bland and William Beverley had five children, while their son Robert Beverley III and his spouse, Maria Carter Beverley, had fifteen. Three generations of Ludwells had two, five, and three children, respectively, while in the Nelson family it was four, six, and twelve. John Page (1744–1808) had seventeen, but this was with two wives, as was the case of William Byrd III, who had fifteen. Robert Carter of Nomini Hall and his wife Frances led the group with seventeen children in thirty-seven years. There does not seem to have been much, if any, decline in the number of children as the century wore on, and the age at marriage remained about the same.[14]

Children were born at home and delivered with the assistance, most often, of a midwife, frequently white and sometimes black. Robert Beverley III, for example, reported that his wife was recently delivered "of a daughter." He had sent for an "operatrix," but she did not arrive on time, and "we were obliged to depend upon the Skill of one of my Negroes." Earlier in the century Robert Carter gave "a Pistol" to "Mrs. Falconer" for assisting in the birth of his grand-daughter. Miscarriage, stillbirth, and early death were not infrequent, but if the children survived, they were often breastfed by slave wet nurses. The children grew up in households that included housekeepers; tutors, male and female; servants, slave and indentured; and often grandparents as well as brothers and sisters, some with their own families. The children did not lack for attention, and in their early years they appear to have grown up in a warm and affection-ate environment. While his wife Elizabeth was in England, Thomas Jones de-scribed the progress of the three children she left behind. Her eldest daughter "is as Sturdy as Ever" and "Grand Ma-Ma and her Grand Pa-pa are extremely indulgent of her." Tom "was a little out of Order with his Teeth" but now "runs about the House, hollows & makes Noise all day long." Dolley was healthy and thriving "& a fine child I think as was ever born"; she "is a most engaging Chit."

William Byrd II devoted much attention to his only son, the "little governor." He not only played billiards and cards and bowled with the child but at the age of sixty-six "ran" with him. Clearly an indulgent parent, Byrd seems to have catered to his heir's every wish.[15]

Robert Carter of Nomini Hall and his wife Frances, later on, were also indulgent but kept their children "in perfect subjection to themselves and never pass over an occasion of reproof." This discipline had a negative effect on one of the children. Robert Bladen Carter, the second son, was a disappointment to his parents. Robert Carter, it seems, was not sensitive to his son's nature and was perhaps distant. Years later, after repeated failures and temporary escape to London, the younger Carter begged his father for employment. Not able to face the stern parent because he was always "afraid when before you," he wrote and promised that if he was given work, "I shall feel that lively joy which I have been a stranger to since my birth." Robert Carter complied, but again the son did not succeed; he eventually died in London in 1792 after a coffee house fight.[16]

But disciplining children in large family situations was difficult at best, especially if grandparents were present. Robert Wormeley Carter, the eldest son of Landon Carter, lived at Sabine Hall with his wife Winifred and their nine-year-old son, Landon Carter III. Landon senior's two daughters reported that young Landon was "impudent" to his mother, something he denied. The elder Carter asked him what he had said and when he refused to answer "shook him," much to the outrage of the boy's father. The next day the child would not come to breakfast despite having been called three times. Landon then struck his grandson across the arm with his whip, which caused the child's mother to rise "like a bedlamite that her child should be struck . . . and up came her Knight Errant to his father with some heavy God dammings." Winifred Carter raved "like a Madwoman" and talked of leaving, which caused the grandfather to suggest that because "the child is thus encouraged to insult me" and because he had "been at great expense . . . in maintaining him," he would do it "no more." He, of course, did not cut off support, and the parents, and ultimately Landon himself, continued to indulge the boy. Young Landon did not live up to his parents' hopes and expectations, which the grandfather attributed to his indulgent parents. But perhaps Philip Lee expressed the general view when he wrote his brother Henry, who was to take care of his daughter Sarah "for whom I have great value. She is a girl of Excellent Genius but has had her own way rather too Much." He asked Henry to use the "Gentle method with her by which I hope she will be persuad[e]d to know and Practice her Duty."[17]

EDUCATION

The education of their children was a major concern of upper-class Virginians throughout the eighteenth century. This concern, predictably, came as the emerging native-born elite rose to dominance, and it was especially true of the twenty-one families who were at the very apex of society. Aware of their removed situation, they worked hard to see that their children would have the necessary intellectual and cultural underpinnings appropriate for their class, status, and role in society. A good education, one son was advised, "will preserve you in the same Class & Rank" in which "Divine Providence has placed your parents." William Fitzhugh, writing in 1687, for whom it was "better" to "be never born than ill bred," unhappily declared that "Good Education is almost impossible" in Virginia. Robert Carter spoke of the "Thick Cloud of Ignorance" under which "the Country . . . does at this time Labour" and hoped that the next generation would be "better Polsht patriotts." Attempts to remedy the situation began in the 1690s with the establishment of the College of William and Mary, but for the first third of the eighteenth century, it was little more than a grammar school. An English education, for not a few, was the solution. This experience, of course, set them apart from most of the remainder of society.[18]

Before the trip to England could be taken, education began under a tutor, male or female, employed by a family for their children or in one of the small public or private schools usually run by a minister. Robert Carter was hoping in 1720 to get a "suitable woman" from England "for the education of my younger children." He desired a grave woman "of about 40 years of age, that hath been well bred and is of good reputation." Carter appears to have settled for a "schoolmaster" who may have been an indentured servant. Ministers frequently added to their income by running schools. Jonathan Boucher kept a "very respectable school" in Caroline County in the 1760s which Charles Carter of Cleve's son Landon attended along with the children of "first Gentlemen" in the "neighbouring counties." This was presumably a "public school," which all could attend who could afford it. Just as common were private schools that sometime were located at particular plantations, such as the one at Westover, the Byrd home, which William Beverley's eldest son attended in the early 1740s. Female tutors sometimes had long and close relationships with particular families, such as Mrs. Anne Walter who "servd Mrs [Mann] Page as a School mistress many years" and was paid "fourty or fifty pounds" annually. John Tayloe II in his will left Margaret Garrett £20 above her annual wages for the tender care of his children "during their education under her." Male tutors became more numerous as the century wore on. They were often Scotsmen such as John Harrower, who served the Daingerfield family in Spotsylvania County, or John Warden, who was retained by the Jones family in Westmoreland County in the 1760s and 1770s. Philip Vickers Fithian, a Princeton graduate, tutored the children of Robert Carter of Nomini Hall in the same period. On occasion, if there was no good alternative, children were placed in "New Light" schools, as was the case of Walter Jones, who in 1758 attended a school probably run by Samuel Davies. His mother did so with trepidation "because they are a subtle crue and when they find he has quick parts a good memory and glib Tongue, which are all necessary qualifications for an Itenerant preacher, they will leave no stone unturn'd to bring him over." Whatever the religious affiliation of the school or the particular bent of the tutor, children were supposed to learn to write well, to master "Arithmetick," and to "translate Latin into English." Fithian explained the educational level of each of his eight pupils at Nomini Hall: "The eldest Son is reading Salust; Gramatical Exercises, and latin Grammar—The second Son is reading english Grammar Reading English: Writing and Cyphering in Subtraction—The Nephew is Reading and Writing as above; and Cyphering in Reduction—The eldest daughter is reading the Spectator; Writing and beginning to Cypher—The second is reading in the Spelling-Book, beginning to write—The next is reading in the Spelling-Book and The fourth is Spelling in the beginning of the Spelling-Book—And the last is beginning her letters."[19]

Robert Carter emphasized the importance of a good education when he said, "The health of my sons and their improvement in learning and manners is one of the greatest blessings I can meet with." Nathaniel Burwell in 1718 worried about his half brother Lewis's lack of progress, fearing that he would be unable to manage "his own affairs" and "unfit for any Gentleman's conversation & therefore a Scandalous person & a Shame to his Relations." To prevent such a fate, the education of children began early. After being tutored at home, George Carter, Robert Carter's youngest son, was sent to William and Mary at the age of eight. All of his four brothers were sent to England when they were only slightly older. Early in the century an educational sojourn in England was the norm even for younger sons. Daughters were almost never sent, although there were a few exceptions. Robert Beverley III was ten when he began a public school education in Yorkshire at Wakefield, and Thomas Nelson Jr. was fourteen when he entered a private school in the London suburb of Hackney. If a university education followed, as was usual for eldest sons, the young men were often away from home for as long as ten years. Despite the assumed advantage of an English education, the psychic impact of such a long absence from home could not have been all positive.[20]

The pattern was for young men to be placed in the overall care of an English merchant who paid their expenses and kept track of their progress. Initially they would be placed in a public school such as Eton or Wakefield or a private one, frequently located near London. The latter were often preferred because it was felt that they were better able to nurture a child's individual genius and because public schools were considered to be "hotbeds of vice and brutality." After a time at public or private school, elder sons would go on to Oxford or Cambridge, followed, on occasion, by a period reading law at one of the Inns of Court. This was the route followed by John Carter, Robert Carter's eldest son, who attended Mile End School and then Trinity College, Cambridge, and the Middle Temple. John Randolph, his contemporary who was later knighted, was a younger son who attended William and Mary, followed sometime later by a trip to London and attendance at Gray's Inn to study law. Younger sons who had completed their school education sometimes were placed with a merchant to explore the mysteries of trade and commerce. By the third quarter of the century, the advantages of a educational stay in England became less attractive. William Nelson, who had sent his eldest son, Thomas, to England in 1752, had changed his mind by 1768. He decided that his second son, Hugh, would not go because "the Temptations to Expense & Dissipation of Money & Time are too great for our estates here; especially as the Improvements of our youth are Seldom answerable to such great Expenses as they often Incurr." This view was seconded by Landon Carter, who remarked that "everybody begins to laugh at English education the general importers of it nowadays bring back only a stiff priggishness with little good manners as possible." The College of William and Mary improved, and as the century wore on a majority of upper-class children attended that institution. But the 1750s and 1760s were also years of turmoil for the college, and some fathers continued to send their sons across the Atlantic.[21]

There was always a certain tension concerning what an education was designed to accomplish. Certainly young men were supposed to emerge as accomplished and cultured gentlemen. Presumably a classical education in England or its equivalent at William and Mary would accomplish this. The progress "in Learning" of one young Virginian in England, as described by his teacher, set forth what was involved. He had "greatly improved in French, Latin, Greek, Writing & Arithmetick; Music, Drawing, Fencing he has learn't as far as was thought necessary for a Gentlemen, & Still continues Dancing under a very good Master." If the student went on to one of the universities, he might continue in mathematics, music, astronomy, logic, rhetoric, and Greek and Latin literature. But for some it was also necessary to become acquainted with and knowledgeable about commerce and business. Richard Ambler wrote his sons in 1749 that "I do not mean to confine you to any particular branch of Learning but am willing to be at the expence of your attaining a degree of all or any branch of learning that suits your genious or inclination, but Latin, French, Writing and Accounts especially the latter, must by no means be omitted, as it is likely it may fall to one or both of your Lots to be concern'd in Trade and Commerce."[22]

In the late seventeenth and early eighteenth centuries, the commercial aspect appears to have been an important complement to a classical education. William Byrd II, for example, was sent to Felsted Grammar School in Essex to receive "a thorough grounding in Latin, Greek and probably Hebrew." He then spent four years in Holland with Rotterdam merchant Jacob Senserff and went on to London for two more years with the firm of Perry & Lane. In 1692 he entered the Middle Temple, and he was called to the bar in 1695. Thus Byrd was prepared for what his father considered would be the responsibilities he would face when he returned to Virginia. The Felsted School provided the classical education that was the underpinning for his role in upper-class society. His apprenticeship with the merchant firms gave him the experience needed to manage complicated mercantile and planting affairs. And the legal education supplied the necessary tools for his expected duties on the Council of State, a position William Byrd I held. Both Robert Carter and John Custis had similar educations, although it is not known if they read law.[23]

But as time wore on, the emphasis on the practical seems to have declined among the leading families. As the Scots came to dominate the store trade, the need for mercantile training declined. The families perhaps also were more aware of their standing in Virginia society and influenced by what they considered to be the English upper-class model. Most lived more expensively than their fathers and grandfathers and as a group were not as good managers of their estates. They believed it important to attain all the trappings of an English gentleman, so they usually attended a public or private school and then went on to Oxford or Cambridge, where most did not take a degree. Robert Carter did not have a university education, but he told his grandson Lewis Burwell III that the goal was "to make you a Scholar and a Gentleman." It was Carter's "prayer" that Lewis absorb the "Learning & Knowledge and wisdom and virtue that makes a valuable man." "Good learning as well as good breeding" was the end that was sought. When Gawin Corbin, the eldest son of Richard Corbin of

Laneville, was sent to England in the 1750s, he was not intended "for any particular profession" but to "be qualified to discharge the Duties of a good Citizen, a polite Gentleman and a benevolent friend." To accomplish this, he was
to attend Cambridge for two or three years, "reside some time at the Temple to
gain" some knowledge of the law, "and if convenient . . . to go to foreign parts."
Robert Beverley III wanted his son William, who went to England in 1781, to
be a "polite well bred man" and hoped that his studies would prepare him for
a large public role. Initially he desired that Billy be placed for three years with
some "able clergyman" who would provide him with a knowledge of "the Latin
language, of history and geography and any other accomplishments requisite
to form a man of the World." The "Latin Classicks" were especially important
for they provided the "Foundation for correctness, ease & Elegance in Diction
and Style." "Geography, History & Mathematicks" also deserved "the utmost attention." He was then to move to Geneva to become acquainted with "modern
Languages," to be followed by a period of time at Trinity College, Cambridge,
interspersed with further travel on the Continent. Robert Beverley's desire that
William return home and become a leader in the new nation was not fulfilled;
after two years back in Virginia, his son returned permanently to England and
met an unhappy end. But the goal of the old elite for their sons, especially the
eldest, remained, as Ralph Wormeley IV said of his ward John Tayloe III, that
he emerge "purged from every Species of prejudice, to have the pride of honor
and virtue, and a disdain of the littleness of vanity—to be liberal noble minded,
and highly cultivated." "I am fully sensible," one mother said, commenting on
her son, "how Essencial a Liberal [English] Education is for [the] Sex and the
indifferent figure they make in the world with out it."[24]

   Eventually William and Mary became the school of choice for most elite
Virginians. One Virginian described his father's education: when young he pursued classical studies "under the direction of an old Scotch Tutor by the name of
Gordon . . . who was still considered as a most admirable tutor." After grammar
school, where he finished "his study of the dead languages, he was placed . . . at
the College of William and Mary . . . where he completed his collegiate studies."
He then studied law with his uncle in Williamsburg and obtained a "license to
practice." There was much complaint about the college in the decade of the
1750s and after. It was the victim of weak presidents, an aggressive governing
body made up of strong-minded political leaders, an improving and vocal faculty, and the emerging imperial crisis. The faculty was largely Anglican clergymen who tended to support imperial policies, which, of course, did not sit well
with the political leadership. Criticism tended to revolve around the fact that

the faculty appeared to do little to control what was considered bad conduct on the part of the student body. Rector Dudley Digges explained in 1767 that the "Education of our Youth has been strangely neglected; instead of improving their Morals, and growing in Virtuous Principles at the College, it is to be lamented, as a sad truth—that both have often been corrupted for want of strict Attention to their Behaviour." He went on to say that there were many "Irregularities and Immoralities" among "Collegians."

But at the same time those students who were serious about their studies, and there were a number, appear to have received a good education. Francis Fauquier, the governor from 1758 to 1768, was an intellectual who periodically invited the best students to the Governor's Palace for talk and music and to demonstrate their skills. Thomas Jefferson was one student who benefited from Fauquier's hospitality. Walter Jones, who was at the college at about the same time and went on to Edinburgh to attain a medical degree, was another of those invited. He wrote his brother in 1762 requesting money for "new Cloths" because "I am to repeat at the Governours." The presence of several distinguished lawyers in Williamsburg, like Benjamin Waller and George Wythe, buttressed the intellectual experience. Wythe was a frequent visitor at the Governor's Palace. The fact that the period after 1750 was one in which relations with the mother country worsened also provided something of a political education for students at the college. Some of the sons of elite families, such as Jefferson's schoolmate John Page, emerged as important leaders in the protest movement.[25]

Some parents continued to send their sons to England in this period and even after. If a medical education was desired, one had to go to Edinburgh, as did Arthur Lee, a younger son. Some parents were disturbed by faculty turnover and student turmoil at William and Mary. Others felt it was not possible to get a good education in Virginia. Early on some like William Nelson and William Byrd II appear to have been concerned about the constant contact their sons had with black children. But more important was the continuing belief that an English education was the only way sons could attain the learning and polish appropriate to their rank and status. So, among the twenty-one families, some Beverleys, Burwells, Byrds, Corbins, Fitzhughs, Grymes, Lees, Randolphs, Tayloes, Wormeleys, and a few others continued to send their sons across the Atlantic for their education. Concerns remained about the impact of the long stay in England with all of its temptations. William Nelson urged his English friends to let him know if his son Thomas showed "a disposition to idleness and pleasure." And, in fact, all of his remaining four sons attended the College of William and Mary. The moral climate in England was not the only concern, for as Thomas

Nelson was to say later, of the nine or ten young Virginians who were in England with him for their education, he was the only one not to return a Tory. This may have been an exaggeration, but among the twenty-one families at least four—the Byrd, Corbin, Grymes, and Wormeley families—had members who were of Loyalist persuasion. The Randolph family was split, with Peyton emerging as a leader of the protest movement while his brother John was a Loyalist. All of these individuals were English educated. And of the English-educated man among the elite families, only Richard Henry Lee, Thomas Nelson, and Peyton Randolph were leaders in the protest movement. More typical were new men like Patrick Henry, Thomas Jefferson, and James Madison who had not crossed the Atlantic.[26]

From early on then the pattern was to send the eldest son to Oxford or Cambridge and/or the Inns of Court. Younger sons would attend a public or private school and might then be placed with a mercantile firm to become better acquainted with trade and commerce. But as the College of William and Mary improved, more sons were sent there. It does not appear, for example, that any member of the Harrison family received an English education in the eighteenth century, while eight attended William and Mary. Further, emphasis on mercantile training declined. Some continued to send their sons across the Atlantic. They were among the dominant elite, and such an education was one of the necessary components for preparing these young men to assume the place in society that their families had attained. This experience would produce "polite and well bred" men who were "liberal noble minded and highly cultivated," men who would stand apart from the mass of society. It was a goal that remained for some well into the nineteenth century. John Baylor Jr. (1750–1807), who had attended Cambridge, stated in his will that if his sons, John and George, had sons, he desired that the eldest be sent to England for their education. They should first go to Eton, Westminster, Harrow, or Winchester and then on to Cambridge: one to Caius and Gonville, the other to Trinity or St. Johns. By then the old elite were no longer dominant, but their social standing had diminished little, and the desire to be clearly defined remained.[27]

MASTERS AND SLAVES, SERVANTS, AND DAILY LIFE

Once their formal education was completed, most young Virginians of the landed class returned to manage their estates. Their success depended upon the services and labor of numerous black slaves, a situation with which they were familiar and, for the most part, comfortable. Some had been born with the aid of black midwives, and many were nursed and cared for by black women. Slaves were everywhere, and on the plantations to which the young masters returned, they were the majority of the population. There were cooks, maids, and butlers as well as coachmen, artisans, and gardeners, in addition to the field hands. George Washington said that "the common mode of disposing of the children of opulent families" was to send them to England for their education, "for such as were brought up at home were in danger of becoming indolent & helpless from the usual indulgence giving a horse & a servant to attend them . . . ; if not imperious & dissipated from the habit of commanding slaves & living in a measure without controul." This sort of life, as William Byrd II remarked, served to "blow up the pride, & ruin the industry of white people."[28]

Among the responsibilities of these young men was the disciplining of their black labor force, and punishment, frequently severe, was common. Slaves had few legal rights, the state having yielded near total control over slave property to the owner. Whipping by masters and overseers was an everyday occurrence as punishment for even minor infractions. Thomas Jones reported to his wife that because of repeated trouble with Juliet, "I Cheer'd her with thirty lashes a Saturday last and as many more on Tuesday again." Robert Wormeley Carter's overseer pursued "a wench" who had gone from Ripon Hall to Williamsburg to see her husband without informing him. When he apprehended her in town, "he turned up her cloaths and whipt her Breech." Carter evidently disapproved of the public "mode of correction, and I made the matter up between them." Incidents of this nature made one Virginian despair about raising his children in a country "where they must make whipping Negroes their chief employ." And no matter how forcefully planters pressed themselves on their slaves, slaves resisted. For persistent runaways a county court could allow a master to mutilate and dismember the offender. In 1708 Robert Carter asked the Lancaster County court for permission "to dismember by cutting off" the toes of "two Incorrible Negroes of his named Barbara Harry & Dinah . . . for the better reclaiming the sd negroes & deterring others." His request was granted.

Slaves were tried for capital offenses—burglary, robbery, theft of expensive items, arson, manslaughter, murder, poisoning, rape—by special courts of oyer and terminer (criminal courts) usually composed of county justices of the peace; there was no jury trial. Whipping, branding, and hanging were among the punishments prescribed. Daniel was convicted of raping a white woman in Henrico County in 1701. He was sentenced to death by hanging. It was further ordered that the "head of Daniel . . . be seperated from his body" and be "placed upon a pole to be Erected for that purpose by the River Side" near the "ferry Landing to

Deter Negroes . . . from Comitting the Like Crymes and offences." The state in
the person of the governor and the courts supported the masters in their efforts
to control the slave population, but occasionally the interests of the governor
and the courts varied from those of the masters, which complicated their position atop the plantation order. In 1732, at the instigation of Governor William
Gooch, some amelioration was provided by allowing slaves to plead "benefit of
clergy" and thus avoid execution for some capital crimes, although not manslaughter, burglary at night, or burglary in the day if the stolen items were valued
at five shillings sterling. The law emerged from a case involving a felony by Mary
Aggie, a Christian slave. Gooch apparently felt that she should have the right to
plead benefit of clergy, but the council was divided, so the matter was referred
to the solicitor and attorney general through the Board of Trade. The ruling
was that "Christian or not," slaves were "entitled to the privilege of the statutes
of England concerning Clergy."[29]

Gooch's desire to extend to Mary Aggie the rights given all criminals perhaps
spoke to his image of himself as that of a patriarch who while possessing absolute power had humane concern for his "family." Often slaveholders shared his
feelings. "Like one of the patriarchs," William Byrd II wrote the earl of Orrery,
"I have my flocks, and my herds and my bond-men, and my bond-women" who
were "free . . . in comparison of the slaves who till your ungenerous soil; at least
if slavery consists in security, and hard work." His concern for his "family" or his
"people," as he referred to them, is seen especially in his care of the sick. "More
sick people," he reported in December 1710 and January 1711; "these poor people
suffer for my sins, God forgive me . . . and restore them to their health." He personally ministered to them: "I spent most of the time looking after the sick,"
he wrote on January 4. John Custis IV exhibited a similar approach thirty-two
years later. He said that he had "diligently studied Phisick more than 40 years"
and had "large experience having not less than 200 young and old in my several
familys" whom he treated, not to mention "all poor people that have not money
to employ a doctor." He had paid such close attention to them that he contracted
a "Negro distemper" as a result of his "endeavouring to care [for] them."

The fact that slaves married and had children also led some masters to make
adjustments concerning separation of families. Slave weddings were usually
informal affairs, although some ministers married Christian slaves. John Gar-
zia, minister of Northfarnham Parish in Richmond County, reported that in
March 1724 he had baptized 341 blacks and married one couple. Sanctified or
not, the unions appear to have been long-term, and the desire to keep productive workers happy resulted in efforts to keep families together. When Robert

Carter transferred twenty-one slaves to his recently acquired Ripon Hall estate in York County, they included "Tom and Jenny his wife; Lambo, Judy his wife and two children"; and "Joe his wife Hannah and three children." His eldest son, John, ten years later explained that he was keeping a family together because the husband was a valuable slave and "some misfortune might have been the consequence if" he "had been separated from his wife." If separation did occur, arrangements occasionally were made for visitation. Joseph Ball arranged for Black Jo to have a horse at Little Falls, so that "once a month" he could ride down to "Taliaferro's Mount" to visit his wife. His slave was not to make the trip more frequently; "if his wife & he are so fond of one another she must come at other times." More frequently economic factors out weighed such considerations. Frederick Jones told his brother Thomas in 1762, when the family estate was up for sale, that he hoped that the "Negroes" would not be sold because of his "concern to see them separated and squandered about the Country," but seventy-nine were ultimately sold.[30]

The rights of mastership, grand houses, fine clothes, and fast horses, along with the privileges that attended a white skin, separated the planters from their slaves; but physical propinquity and the necessities of the plantation routine brought them together, often in intimate ways. The joining of planter and slave was often denied, sometimes recognized, and it always complicated life. Some young elite Virginia men had their first sexual experience with slave women. It was reported, for example, that the eldest son of Robert Carter of Nomini Hall had taken "Sukey . . . a young likely Negro Girl into" the stable, where they "for a considerable time lock'd" themselves "together." Not only the young took advantage of the circumstances; in some cases relationships were long-term and appear to have involved an element of affection or more. Councillor John Custis IV freed a "boy Christened John otherwise called Jack born of the body of my Slave Alice." He gave him 250 acres in York County as well as his mother and her other children and four "likely negro boys of his choice." Jack was to live with Daniel Parke Custis, John's legitimate son, until he was twenty years old and "be handsomely maintained out of the profits of my estate given him" Until that time a "handsome strong convenient house" was to be built for Jack and furnished with "Russian leather" chairs and couches, walnut tables, feather beds, etc. He was also to receive a riding horse, two "able" workhorses, hogs, cattle, sheep, and Indian corn, not to mention a variety of clothes and six "Ells of Ozenbrigs." The boy died in 1751, two years after the death of Custis. There does not appear to have been any extraordinary comment on this relationship. As John Blair wrote in his diary, "Col. Custis's Favourite Boy Jack died in abt 21 hours illness . . . from a Pain in the back of his neck for wch he was blooded." Ryland Randolph, a lifelong bachelor, in his will freed his house servant Aggy and her infant son and daughter, for all of whom he expressed great affection. They were to receive most of his household furniture as well as "Gold & Silver." He also provided for their passage to England and established a trust fund for them of £3,000. But when Randolph died in 1784, he was heavily in debt, especially to his brother Richard, who kept the slaves in bondage. He too soon died and left a will providing for the eventual freedom of Aggy's children so long as they made no claims against the estate. What happened to Aggy is not known. It is reasonable to assume that Custis was Jack's father and that Ryland Randolph was the father of Aggy's children. The support these men provided may have been exceptional, but to have sexual relations with one's slaves was not uncommon, for Virginia had the largest mulatto population of all of the southern colonies.[31]

Some few of the elite were critical of the impact of the institution on Virginians "brought up from their Cradles, in Idleness, Luxury & Extravagance, depending on their Myriads of Slaves, that Bane (if not curse) of this Country." William Byrd II bemoaned the importation of "so many Negros." Having to control this black population made even "a good natured man have recourse to foul means"; here was no in-between for a master of slaves could "be either a fool or a fury." Parliament should put an end to this "unchristian traffic of making merchandize of our fellow creatures." John Custis IV agreed but said the slave trade was "so sweet" to the traders "and so much concerns the trade of Navigation of great Britain, that it will be next to impossible to break the neck of it." Robert Beverley III, on his return from studying in England in 1761, spoke of his "aversion to Slavery; 'tis something so very contradictory to Humanity . . . if ever I bid adieu to Virginia it will be from that cause alone." But the English did not stop the slave trade, and in Virginia there were only isolated incidences of freeing individual slaves before the Revolution. Even those who criticized the trade did nothing. As Patrick Henry said, "I cannot justify" owning slaves, but "I am drawn along by the general inconvenience of Living without them."[32]

These elite families were so dependent on their slaves and the relationship was so intimate and pervasive that before the Revolution little attention was given to addressing the problems of chattel slavery. Concern about the increasing slave population and attempts to decrease importation by heavy taxation, almost always blocked by the mother country, marked the extent of their thought. Contradictions were everywhere evident. Trusted slaves were given major responsibilities. Some functioned as plantation surgeons and physicians, while others operated ferries and provided skilled labor as blacksmiths, carpenters, wheelwrights, etc. Others were sent on long trips to deliver messages, even money. Yet as chattel, if they "misbehaved," they were whipped, in some cases worse than one would whip a horse or an ox. By the middle of the eighteenth century, the institution had a long history in Virginia, but even so, the incongruity of much that went on could not have escaped notice. Joseph Ball, George Washington's uncle, left the colony permanently for England in 1743, taking with him several slaves, including Martha, Aron, and Pat—all young. In 1754 he decided to send them back to Virginia. They were all to be well provided for, but the case of Aron is of special interest. Ball informed his cousin Joseph Chinn, who was managing his estate in Lancaster County, that Aron, to whom he had given the surname Jameson, was returning with "his Things," which filled a

> Large Harness Barrell as big as an Eighty Gallon Cask, a Small Chest, & a box, Containing a Seabed, a Large Mattress Stuffed with flocks and Stitched with Tufts, and a bolster filled with feathers . . . ; and two New Coverlets, and other Old Bedcloths, and three suits of wearing cloths (One New) and Two pair of New Shoes; and several pair of Stockings a pair of boots, and twelve Shirts Eight of which are New, a Small Iron pot & hooks and Rack to hang it on, an Iron Skillet, a Copper Sauce pan, an old Bridle & Saddle, a Cheese a Narrow ax, a tin pint pot, Three hats, Twelve Neck-cloths, Two Handerchiefs, one Violin and some spare Strings, a Small Spit, an old pewter basin, Two pair of Sheets, and several other things which Aron very well knows of.

Aron was to be "used kindly Especially this year." He was to work at the hoe "but not Constantly . . . for perhaps he may not be able to bear it, not having been used to hard Labor," but next year he was to be "put in for a full Share." Chinn was instructed to have one of Ball's "old Bedsteads Cut Short" to fit Aron's mattress and as soon as possible a "framed House Twelve foot Long, and ten foot wide built for him." It was to be "Lathed and filled" and "underpinned with brick or Stone five inches above the ground." He was also to have a lock for the door, which was to be wide enough to "take in his Great Harness barrell." Aron was to have all of "his Household Goods in his own Little House." The young black man was also to have "his own Meat to himself in a good little powdering Tub" and "his own fat & Milk to himself and be allowed to raise fowl." Finally he was "to have the Liberty of a Horse to Ride to Church" and wherever else Chinn thought "Convenient . . . but not to be too nice about it he must have one of the Worst." Aron was better off, in material things, than many free Virginians. But he was a slave who had been "very Saucy" to Ball in England and "Resisted" him twice. There was to be no more of that, Ball wrote Aron, for if he "offered to Strike" his overseer "or to be unruly, you must be tyed and Slasht Severely and pickled," and if he ran away, he was to "wear an Iron Pot Hook about your Neck, and if that won't tame you, you must wear Iron Spaniels till you Submit, for as you are my Slave you must and Shall be obedient." If he behaved himself, Ball would send him "Some of my best old cloths" and "other things. Take warning and don't Ruin yourself by your folly. I recd. yr Letr. If you will be good I shall be yr Loving Master." The following year Ball told Chinn that Aron was to have "a Quart of Brandy Every month and advise him to put some Snake root in it." Three years later Ball sent some old clothes, which included a pair of "Breeches for Aaron." And that is all that is known of Aron Jameson.[33]

The households in which the slaves worked also included white servants. Almost all had a housekeeper. Some had a nurse who cared for small children. There were male tutors and occasionally a "school mistress" or governess who taught the "young ladies." William Byrd I's wife had a secretary. Usually it was the wife that presided over household affairs, but there were exceptions. Charles Carter of Cleve was married three times. His first two wives died young. Sometime after the death of his first wife, her sister was retained to manage the household and remained in this capacity until well after his death. Young wives needed help, and Carter's second wife, Anne Byrd Carter, was seventeen when they married. Frequent childbearing and keeping complicated households running smoothly made such assistance a necessity. And when there was no longer a wife, as was the case of Robert Carter in the 1720s, the full responsibility rested with the housekeeper. Mrs. Young, who served Carter in this role, told him when "her time was up" that "the troubles of the house was so great she could not please everybody." She had, for example, "a great quarell" with him earlier "abt the wenches clearing their doors and paths." But he told "her little jarrs would arise in such a family." Mrs. Young agreed to stay on for another year. Her annual pay was "12£ sterling, 6£ current money."[34]

The daily routine was a busy one. Philip Fithian reported that at first light the "Boy" knocked at the door to make the fire. He then rose and dressed, and the children arrived at the schoolroom, where he heard one lesson. Breakfast was with the family at 8:30, and at 9:30 he returned to teach until noon. Dinner, the main meal of the day, was at 2:00 or 2:30. Lessons began again at 3:30 and continued until 5:00. Supper was a light meal, at 8:30 or 9:00, and on a normal day everyone was in bed by 10:00. These school days were interspersed with instruction by dancing and music masters who traveled from plantation to plantation. The routine for the older members of the household was similar. William Byrd II was usually up by 5:00 a.m. and read Greek and Hebrew until breakfast. He dealt with plantation and business affairs until dinner, and after eating he frequently walked around the plantation checking on work in progress and/or took care of more business. Various commentators spoke of the indolent nature of Virginia planters, but this was not true of successful ones like William Byrd II and Robert Carter of Nomini Hall, nor was it the case with their wives.[35]

SOCIAL INTERCOURSE AND LEISURE ACTIVITY

Most of these gentry families lived in isolated areas throughout eastern Virginia, but despite their removed situations their leisure time, which few others had, was also active. There was much visiting with neighbors within a fifteen-mile radius of their homes. And family and other visitors from afar appear always to have been welcome. Robert Beverley wrote early in the century that a "Stranger has no more to do, but to inquire upon the Road where any . . . Gentlemen lives and there may depend on being received with Hospitality." One could "ride in where two Chimbls [chimneys] shew & there is a Spare bed & Lady welcome," an English visitor wrote in 1732. Visitors brought social contact and news to these isolated areas. "Mr Bland came," wrote William Byrd in May 1709, "and told us an abundance of news." Especially welcome were family and friends. For example, Robert Carter reported on January 10, 1723, that his daughter Judith and her husband, Mann Page, arrived at Corotoman from Gloucester County for a six-day visit. Five days later his daughter Elizabeth Burwell arrived with John Wormeley and Jo Ring Whiteside. Whiteside remained for two days, but Elizabeth and Wormeley stayed on until January 25 when they crossed the Rappahannock to his home, Rosegill, where Elizabeth visited for the day. Four days later Carter's eldest son, John, arrived "in company of Col. Page," and the next day Wormeley was back, this time with Armistead Churchill. The following year on August 30 "came here Whiteside Jas Read & Captn Ben they dined here I eat a whole squirell drank plentifully of Cyder & six glasses of wine." The dance master, Mr. Stagg, was teaching the children, and he remained overnight. A few days later "Mr Stepto &c here played at cards till 3 clock in the morning." The next day, September 5, Carter went "to the Race" with "Collo Ball," who came home with him and "stayd with me next day." Six days after this he "brot home" from the meeting of the Lancaster County court "Major Smith Captn Everard Captn Whiteside they drank two boles rack [punch]." Similar examples can be found earlier in William Byrd II's diaries and later in Fithian's journal of his year at the home of Carter's grandson Robert Carter of Nomini Hall.[36]

Churchgoing provided another form of visiting. Fithian explained that before the "Service gentlemen" gave and received "letters of business," read "Advertisements," and consulted about "the prices of Tobacco, Grain &c & settling either lineages, Age, or qualities of favorite horses." They remained outside until the service was beginning, when "they enter as a Body." The service was always brief, and when it was over, gentlemen again waited and exited "en masse." Once outside, "three quarters of an hour was spent strolling around Church among the crowd." Conversation frequently involved "Balls, the Fish-Feasts, the Dancing-Schools, the Christenings, the Cock fights, the horses," and the gentry would invite friends and visitors "home with them to dinner."[37]

Dance was extremely important to the gentry, and the ability to perform a variety of dances well was another of their distinguishing characteristics. It was also entertainment, and when they got together, more often than not dancing was included in the day's activities. Dance was an integral part of children's education. Dance masters provided training in Williamsburg and throughout eastern Virginia. Charles and Mary Stagg taught dance in Williamsburg in the 1720s and 1730s, and Charles Stagg regularly traveled to the Northern Neck where he taught Robert Carter's children and those of other gentry. Sometimes children from various families would gather at one plantation to be instructed, as they did at Corotoman in August 1723. Fifty years later three of the children of Carter's grandson Robert Carter of Nomini Hall went in the "Chariot to Stratford [Hall] to attend the Dancing-School." This training paid off, and Governor Gooch reported that the "Gentm and Ladies here are perfectly well bred, not an ill Dancer in my Govmt." An English cleric wrote in 1759 that Virginians "are immoderately fond of dancing," and Fithian asserted that they "are of genuine Blood—they will dance or die." So they danced in small groups, at private homes, at larger "Balls" held on particular plantations, and at ordinaries. Landon Carter grumbled in March 1772 that his daughter Lucy went to "the ordinary keepers hop" at Westmoreland Court House "where ... there was not a pain to the windows and the Very ballroom" was "covered with snow." He asserted that "many ladies," evidently including Lucy, "sat up at a Perishing fire all night." Squire Richard Lee held a "splendid Ball" at Lee Hall in Westmoreland County in 1774 which was to last "four or five days" and to which "upwards" of seventy attended. After an "Elegant" dinner, dancing began "about 7," and they danced minuets, jigs, reels, and "Country-Dances" to the music of a French horn and two violins. In Williamsburg during the meeting of the General Assembly and/

or the General Court there were balls and assemblies, some of which required an admission fee. An "Assembly" was more often than not held at the Capitol and included not only dancing but other entertainment. Madame Barbara De-Graffenriedt, for example, who came on the scene after the death of Charles Stagg, regularly held assemblies, and at one a "likely young Negro woman, fit for House Business and her child" were to be raffled for. Balls were frequently held at the dancing master's home. Private balls were also held in Williamsburg. George Braxton, it was reported in 1751, "has made a ball & invited all the Girls in town to it, young and old." And anyone among the privileged, as the leading families were, would be invited to the Governor's Palace on special occasions. The king's birthday, which was celebrated annually, provided an opportunity for Governor Gooch to hold, in November 1737, an "elegant entertainment and Ball for the Gentlemen and Ladies, who made a very handsome Appearance."[38]

Music, like dance, was frequently a part of home entertainment. In Williamsburg, John Blair heard fine harpsichord and violin music at home and when he dined with Dr. Gilmer and Colonel Hunter in July and September 1751. The capital also possessed "the modern Orpheus—the inimitable [Peter] Pelham," who, in addition to being the town jailor, was the organist at Bruton Parish Church and taught harpsichord and spinet. When the steeple was being added to the church in 1769, John Blair's daughter Anne reported that its doors were open and residents could hear Pelham playing "[William] Felton's, Handel's, Vi-vallys [Vivaldi] &c, &c, &c, &c." Later, in 1785, Robert Hunter spent several evenings in Tappahannock playing the violin and harpsichord with Catherine McCall and others. Fithian said that Robert Carter of Nomini Hall owned a harpsichord, fortepiano, harmonica, guitar, violins, German flutes, and a "good Organ." His children were taught by Mr. Stadley, a "good German" musician. His neighbor John Tayloe II advertised a little earlier in London for a "Music master," which serves to emphasize the importance some of the gentry placed on musical training. And they sang at Colonel Lee's "Ball" in 1774. In Williamsburg one evening after guests had left, Anne Blair and some friends sat on the front steps and sang a "few songs," which inadvertently entertained the governor, Norborne Berkeley, fourth Baron Botetourt, who was out for a walk. His predecessor, Francis Fauquier, was a devoted musician and possessed two violins, a viola, and two violoncellos. He often brought in town residents and William and Mary students to play chamber music.[39]

Musical training and entertainment were not so universally a part of home leisure activity as was dance, but almost everyone seems to have played cards. To be able to play card games was important and fashionable. It was something in which women could and did participate, and it was an easy way to socialize, especially when conversation dragged. Piquet and whist appear to have been most popular. The former was a two-handed game, while the latter required four players. Whist, the ancestor of modern bridge, became especially popular after 1742 when Edmund Hoyle's *Short Treatise on the Game of Whist* appeared, "the first scientific study of a card game." William Byrd II's sister-in-law wrote him about this time that a "game upon cards call'd whisk" was "much in vogue" in England and that it "engaged men of all ages to keep company with women more than they ever had before." William Byrd III owned an expanded version, *Mr. Hoyle's Games of Whist, Quadrille, Chess and Back-gammon Complete* (1760).[40]

And not only did they play cards, but they wagered, usually small amounts, on these games, for elite Virginians, men and women, loved to gamble. They bet not only on cards but on billiards, dice (hazard), and various other games. By the time Governor Gooch arrived in 1727, gambling was perceived to be a general problem, and an act for preventing "excessive and deceitful gaming" was passed. Any "promise, agreement, conveyance, or securities" for "money, or other valuable things, won by gaming, or playing cards, dice, tables, tennis, bowles or other game or games" were forbidden. The law was strengthened in 1744 and 1748, and in the latter year "horse racing, cockfighting or any sport or pastime" were added. Gambling at "an ordinary, race field, or any other public place" was prohibited, but wagers on "billiards, bowls, backgammon, chess or draughts" were excepted. The 1748 law remained in force until the Revolution when it was again revised, but the elite seems to have largely ignored it. Gentlemen appear to have believed that it did not apply to them, although there are instances of enforcement. That they openly gambled, and sometimes excessively so, is not in question. William Byrd III and Robert Wormeley Carter, Landon Carter's eldest son, were among those who gambled heavily. A visitor in 1777 observed that despite "a severe Act of Assembly against Gaming," members of "the House are as much addicted to it as other men and frequently transgress the law: I have known one of them to bett 30 dollars upon an odd trick of Whist. Gaming is amazingly prevalent in Williamsburg." The situation had not improved as the war drew to a close. A Virginia doctor remarked that "gaming is carried to a higher pitch ... than ever ... it was before," even in Richmond "under the eye of the Assembly," many of whose members gambled. T. H. Breen has argued that gambling in Virginia was a "ritual activity" and the "wager whether over cards or horses, brought together in a single, focused act the great planters' competitiveness, independence and materialism," which were major "strands" of gentry culture. He also has asserted that by gambling the gentry "openly expressed their extreme competitiveness, winning temporary emblematic victories over their rivals without . . . threatening the social tranquility of Virginia." Gaming relationships were "also one of several ways by which the planters" perhaps "unconsciously preserved class cohesion."[41]

Horse racing, and gambling on it, had special significance for the elite. Breen has explained that horse racing strengthened the gentry's cultural dominance. He saw this trend as emerging in the last quarter of the seventeenth century, but it appears to have happened after about 1730. Before then, quarter-horse racing, a straight race over a one-quarter-mile path, predominated. This race was one in which a broad segment of society participated. It is true that the York County court ruled in 1674 that it was "contrary to Law for a Labourer to make a race, being a sport for Gentlemen." And in 1713 a law was passed prohibiting landless men from keeping or breeding a "stoned horse or unspaid mare." Overseers who did not own land in the county where they resided or any servants were forbidden from keeping "an unspaid mare" or "horse, mare or colt" without a license, in writing, from their "master and mistress." But these restrictions left room for a substantial segment of society to be involved. In the 1730s the situation changed. The wealthy began to import blooded horses, run stud farms, and produce stock of Arabian descent that were distance racers. Races began to be run on circular tracks a mile in length, and they were funded by subscription from "Gentlemen of Honour." Gradually jockeys replaced owners as riders, formal rules of competition were established, and purses grew in size. Quarter-horse racing continued at the county level, but subscription racing, limited to the tidewater, was a sport of gentlemen. It had developed into one of those things that defined Virginia's upper class.[42]

Horses and horse racing became a major preoccupation for many of the elite. William Byrd II and Robert Carter had regularly attended quarter-horse races and bet on them. But now gentlemen became enthusiastic horsemen, and the topic often dominated conversation. Philip Fithian noted on one social occasion that all other talk was drowned out by "Loud disputes" about "the Excellence of each others Colts—Concerning their Fathers, Mothers (for so they call the Dams), Brothers, Sisters, Uncles, Aunts, Nephews. Nieces and Cousins to the fourth Degree!" One advertisement announced that John Willis's Fearnought was to "cover Mares" at five pounds "the season" or forty shillings "the leap" and noted that "Fearnought was got by old Fearnought, upon an imported mare belonging to Colonel Thomas Nelson, called Blossom. Blossom was got by old Sloe, a Famous King's Plate Horse, her dam was a mare belonging to *Lord Rockingham*, that won the King's Plate of a hundred guineas for five years old mares at Hambleton, in Yorkshire, and was got by Regulus the sire of Fearnought." In a 1771 letter to John Baylor, John Tayloe II discussed Baylor's financial problems but commented that he was "pleased to find that you can still write letters in this world and still think of *Sport*." Tayloe then devoted two pages to horses, especially those that Fearnought had sired, the Port Royal race, and his desire to "exhibit Camille there." Three years later he told George William Fairfax that his young son was "fond of horses to distraction" and that his father "is foolishly so." He went on to describe how his "old horse Yorick," who was thirteen years old and had been at stud for six years, had won a race over a horse of Dr. Flood's. The race had been arranged by some of the "young Fauntelroys . . . for £500 a side." Yorick was unable to train because of "bad feet," but he won the five-mile race "easy" in 12 minutes 27 seconds. Tayloe thought that some of Fairfax's "sporting acquaintances" might find his account amusing. Fithian attended this race and commented on the "purse of 500 pounds besides small betts enumerable." He was surprised that the "assembly was remarkably numerous . . . and exceeding polite in general." Quarter-horse races, which were now found chiefly in the Southside and the backcountry, were frequently raucous affairs attended by a diverse audience; a purse of £500 was unheard of there. Thus Virginia's gentry, through all of the activity associated with horses and racing, more clearly defined themselves in the four decades before the American Revolution.[43]

Elite Virginians also participated in more vigorous recreations than watching a horse race. Early in the century Robert Beverley reported "that for their Recreation, the Plantations, Orchards, and Gardens constantly afford 'em frequent and delightful Walk. In their Woods and Fields they have an unknown variety of Vegetables, and other rarities of Nature to discover and observe. They have Hunting, Fishing, and Fowling, with which they entertain themselves in a hundred ways." In Beverley's day most of the hunting was on foot for deer with "Mongrells or swift Dogs" and for rabbits, "Racoons, Opposums, and Foxes" with "small Dogs" but "in the night." They had "many pretty devices besides the Gun, to take Wild Turkeys," and in season they hunted other wild fowl. Angling was also popular because fish were so plentiful. Beverley said, "I have set in the shade, at the Heads of the Rivers Angling, and spent as much time in taking the Fish off the Hook, as in waiting for their taking it." These activities continued throughout the century, but again, after 1730 or so the way some of them were pursued changed. John Clayton Jr., the botanist, wrote in 1739 "that some hunt the foxes w'th hounds as you do in England." Later William Nelson told an English friend that his brother Thomas, who "learnt to shoot Wood-cocks under" Captain Simpson, "is now as fond of the diversion as ever, and goes after them almost every Day in the Season, and all this he does in spite of the Gout, for he shoots chiefly off his horse." His "eldest son . . . is fonder of Fox hunting. I partake now & then sparingly of both these diversions." The change is most demonstrable in foxhunting. Land was increasingly cleared, and the fox could be hunted, as in England, from horseback. Landon Carter commented frequently on how often his grandson was out foxhunting "as soon as light." Many others pursued the sport avidly. In 1768 George Washington hunted foxes forty-one times with the Fairfaxes and other Northern Neck friends. And as in the case of horses, wealthy Virginians imported hunting hounds from England in the middle years of the century. Some like John Custis IV, his brother-in-law William Byrd, Attorney General John Randolph (1727–1784), and others were inveterate gardeners. Byrd also took frequent walks, swam in the James River, fenced, played cricket and ninepins, and on occasion his wife and his sister-in-law "went romping," and he and his brother-in-law "romped" with them. In cold weather some of the leading families skated on their millponds.[44]

Most of the elite spent some time in Williamsburg, usually when the General Assembly was in session and when the General Court was meeting. Some had homes in the capital. The town provided a wide variety of ways to occupy leisure time. There were plays, musical events, and public ceremonies such as those held on the arrival of a new governor, the king's birthday, or an English military victory. During legislative sessions there were always balls and assemblies, where fine clothes could be displayed. Fairs were held in April and December with all sorts of buying, selling, entertainment, and competitions. One could also shop at a variety of stores. And in season all had easy access to horse racing at a nearby course. There was a theater on the Palace Green from 1718 on, but performances were intermittent at best. Things picked up in the 1730s when the "young Gentlemen of the College," a self-styled amateur group, began to present performances that included Joseph Addison's *Cato* and *The Drummer* and George Farquhar's *The Recruiting Officer* and *The Beaux' Stratagem*. The theater was moved in 1745, and ultimately a "New Theatre" was built behind the Capitol. It opened in 1751 with *Richard III* and for the next twenty years hosted performances by professional companies during court and assembly meetings. Landon Carter was dragged by his brother Charles and Peyton Randolph to see Farquhar's *The Constant Couple, or A Trip to Jubilee* in April 1751 and reported that he was "surfeited with Stupidity and nonsense delivered from the mouths of Walking Statues." Later, in 1770, his son Robert Wormeley Carter was more enthusiastic when he "saw a Comedy acted better than I have ever seen anything in my life." In the intervening years Virginians could see a varied fare by Shakespeare, Addison, Farquhar, Richard Steele, William Congreve, John Gay, Colley Cibber, David Garrick, and many others. Some Virginians who had spent time in England kept well informed on the London theatrical and musical scene. Edmund Jenings III wrote Philip Ludwell Lee in 1754 that London had all the entertainment "last winter" that was available "when you was here" plus Italian opera performed at Covent Garden. He later complained to Robert Beverley that "Garrick has probably left the Stage and Sing Song & Pantomine supplies the place of Shakespeare." Although he did not like Italian opera, "as it is now [brought?] to great Perfection it is more worth seeing than the . . . poor Imitation & Gross Extravagance of the Theatre Royal." Scots merchant Robert Donald, upon returning home after seventeen years in Virginia, wrote Elizabeth Jones about the delights of London theater, including the Drury Lane performances of David Garrick, "a most surprising fellow as is Spranger Barry at the other house [Covent Garden]." Rather than going on about "a subject that you are much better acquainted with than I am," he sent her "a New play call'd Agis," by John Home, just printed on March 2, 1758, in London, which had a long run of "10 nights." As the Revolution approached, interest in English cultural affairs seems to have declined. Plays do not seem to have been presented by professionals in Williamsburg after 1771, although the American Company performed in Annapolis as late as 1773. However, college students did continue performances after the war.[45]

Leisure time was a luxury that few Virginians possessed, and as time wore on, critics began to suggest that some gentlemen were spending too much time in nonproductive activity. But these distractions may have had some beneficial effects. Some have suggested that horse racing and gambling on it, as well as cards and other games, provided an outlet for the competitive nature of Virginians. Indeed, there are no known duels among the leading families. They appear to have gone to court to settle disputes as Robert Carter of Nomini Hall threatened in 1772 when Ralph Wormeley reneged on a wager. But elite recreation must be seen in proper context: it was primarily entertainment.[46]

THINGS MATERIAL: HOUSES, FURNISHINGS, DRESS

Just as horse racing, hunting, and other recreations changed in the 1720s and 1730s, so did the homes in which many of the elite lived, as they began to build larger and more impressive houses. There were some imposing mansions before this: William Berkeley's Green Spring, the Custis family home on the Eastern Shore known as Arlington, Lewis Burwell's Fairfield in Gloucester County, William Fitzhugh's thirteen-room Eagle's Nest in the Northern Neck, and a few others. But most of the early elite homes, including Fitzhugh's, were of frame construction rather than brick, and some were even earthfast-post buildings. One would have noted, viewing the seventeenth-century Virginia landscape, that almost all houses were one- or two-room affairs, with a loft, on posts set directly in the ground. Some elite continued to build frame homes in the eighteenth century, albeit more substantial ones. Thomas Randolph's Tuckahoe, built after 1713, was "probably a modest wood-framed-structure of but one full story in height." His son William replaced it in 1730s with a "two-story wood-framed five-bay house with weatherboard siding and details inspired by classical precedents." But increasingly the homes of the elite were impressive brick structures, while the vast majority of Virginians continued to live in small frame homes. Yorktown provides a good example of this point. Hugh Grove, an English visitor, explained in 1732 that the town had about thirty houses, ten of them "good, not above 4 of brick, the most of Timber, viz. Pine Planks Covered with shingles of Cypress." Merchant Thomas Nelson's home was among the four brick houses. It was built between 1711 and 1720, and it still stands, "broad, substantial and masculine." It is a "sturdy house, which is not quite as large as it looks because of its excellent detail, large scale and great chimney stacks" with molded brick caps, among "the finest in Virginia." This home was an early statement by the emerging eighteenth-century elite of their place and status in Virginia society, and others soon joined it.[47]

Robert Carter had built a home at Corotoman in Lancaster County about 1690. Thirty years later he began to build an impressive 90-by-40-foot two-story "mansion dwelling" nearby which faced the Rappahannock River. Completed about 1725, it had a "gallery, running the length of a single pile plan." The central hall was paved with white marble. There were end pavilions, a central porch pavilion, and a large arcade below the gallery. A spate of Carter family building followed. His son-in-law Benjamin Harrison built Berkeley in Charles City County in 1726, and about the same time Mann Page, another son-in-law, began Rosewell in Gloucester County, a mansion that Hugh Grove said was "reputed" to be "the best house in Virginia." In 1726 Carter himself began building Nomini Hall in Westmoreland County for his second son, Robert. Philip Fithian described it years later as a large, elegant two-story brick house, 76 by 44 feet, that sat on high ground and could be seen "at a Distance of six miles." In the 1730s Carter's sons John, Charles, and Landon built Shirley in Charles City County,

Cleve in King George County, and Sabine Hall in Richmond County—equally impressive houses. John Carter's Shirley was completed about 1738, a 48-foot-square mansion flanked by two 60-by-24-foot dependencies, with a kitchen, laundry, icehouse, and granary in the rear. The complex, viewed from the James River, "must have been grandiose," impressing those who saw it as "an appropriate home" for the rich and powerful. William Byrd II had lived in the frame dwelling that his father had completed in 1691 at Westover, just downriver from Shirley and Berkeley. But he said in 1729 that he intended to build "a very good house," and he appears to have done so in the 1730s. There was a fire at Westover in 1749, and his son either rebuilt or built (I believe the former) what has been described as the "nation's premier example of an 18th-century Georgian domestic complex." The main house, as it appears now, is "one of the most imposing of surviving Virginia plantation mansions." Thomas Lee, his contemporary, was building Stratford Hall in Westmoreland County on an H-plan. Its raised main floor includes a great hall 29½ feet square. There is "abundant space" in the remainder of the house including the ground floor where there were areas for wet and dry storage, a "counting house," and housekeeping activities.[48]

Other imposing houses followed. Carter Burwell, Robert Carter's grandson, built Carter's Grove in James City County in the 1750s, while in King William County, Richard Corbin constructed "Laneville," a two-story 52-by-27-foot main building with 71-foot wings. John Tayloe II was also building Mount Airy in Richmond County, a five-part Palladian country house whose walls are of local sandstone. Soon thereafter, across the Rappahannock River in Essex County, Blandfield was rising, another five-part Palladian mansion that was the home of Robert Beverley III.

Mann Page's Rosewell stands out among them all. Looking over the York River, it loomed three stories high above an English basement, surmounted by a flat roof with two cupolas. It was said to have had forty rooms, and on either side of this edifice stood dependencies. Rosewell burned in 1916 after years of mistreatment and neglect, and only its walls remain. But today, as it did in the eighteenth century, the house suggests how far removed this small group of elite were from the remainder of Virginia society. Architectural historian Camille Wells has explained that in 1773 in Robert Carter's Lancaster County, 73 percent of the 289 landholders lived on tracts of 200 acres or less, and "beneath them was the landless majority, tenants, craftsmen, overseers, indentured servants, free and enslaved blacks, as well as most women and children." To make her point more explicit, she described Verville, "one of Lancaster County's surviving eighteenth-century houses, . . . a story and a half brick structure with a central passage two room plan." Merchant James Gordon built the house in the 1740s on a parcel of 460 acres. Elsewhere in the county he was to acquire another 1,050 acres. These tracts placed Gordon among the thirty-four, or 11.2 percent, of the county's landholders who held 400 acres or more. When Gordon "is positioned among his contemporaries according to the total 1,510 acres he was able to bequeath in his will, he and his brick house become representative of less than 2% of the landholding population in Lancaster County." It is easy to imagine how Rosewell and the other great houses appeared to the mass of the Old Dominion's population.[49]

"Tho rich," Robert Beverley Jr., it was reported in 1715, had "nothing in and about his house but just what is necessary." The beds at Beverley Park were "good," but there were "no curtains and instead of cane chairs he hath stools made of wood." But Beverley was not typical, whereas his contemporary Nathaniel Harrison, who died in 1728, probably was. In the main hall, which invariably served as a sitting room in eighteenth-century Virginia houses, Wakefield, Harrison's nine-room home in Surry County, had two oval tables, eighteen leather chairs, two armchairs, a couch, and a desk. Sideboards held, among other things, four china punch bowls, one china teapot and five stone ones, forty china teacups, three milk "Potts," two tea canisters, a case with twelve silver teaspoons, a "skimmer" and tongs, seven glass decanters, forty wineglasses, and a "Desert Case" with a dozen knives and forks and a dozen silver spoons. Among the pieces in the parlor were six cane chairs and two armchairs, all with cushions. There was a "Dutch" table and a tea table, a chest of drawers, a corner cupboard, and a desk, not to mention a bed and a trundle bed, both with "Furniture" and a mirror. The dining room had three tables and appropriate cane chairs, a cabinet, a corner cabinet, and a sideboard. There were candlesticks, three silver tankards, two silver "canns," and two silver salvers, as well as silver spoons, a tumbler, and two small silver cups. A pepper mill, a coffee mill, a coffeepot, and a chocolate pot accompanied by thirty-four coffee cups also graced the room, as did numerous earthenware dishes, bowls, and plates. All of the five bedrooms were similarly well equipped, with dressing tables in two of the rooms and mirrors in three. The study held "Books of several sizes and sorts[,] writing papers etc." as well as leather chairs and a table. One passage in the house held six leather chairs, a writing desk, a small oval table, and a mirror along with a "Speaking Trumpet," a violin, and two guns. In another was a "Linen Press" which held, among other things, thirty-three pairs of "fine sheets," tablecloths, napkins, towels, quilts, and bed and window curtains. Nathaniel Harrison had been a member of the Council of State, but his contemporary, Thomas Jones, a merchant-planter who lived in Williamsburg and served briefly in the House of Burgesses, had a home that was just as well furnished. The contents of their houses set both men apart from the rest of Virginia society. In the last quarter of the seventeenth century, elite homes were not so elaborately furnished, but even then the distinction was clear. Display of silver plate was an early manifestation of this difference. William Fitzhugh began in the 1680s to acquire "an hansom Cupboard of plate," which he considered a good investment as well as something that would impress visitors. He thanked Nicholas Hayward in 1690 for "sending me my plate." It had arrived safely just before he "had the honour of the Governor's [Francis Nicholson] company at my House . . . who first hansell'd [used] it. Curtains with valances, all sorts of furniture, carpets and tapestries, fireplace equipment, and a wide variety of linens marked the homes of the gentlemen and their families. All of this, and much more, came from England.[50]

The elite also began to display prominently on the walls of their homes portraits of themselves, their children, other family members, and on occasion English notables, another manifestation of their wealth and status. Most of these portraits were done in Virginia, and although the names of early painters are unknown, their presence is clear. In 1698 William Fitzhugh ordered "40 or 50 shillings of colours for painting wt. pencils Walnut Oyle Lynseed Oyle proportionable together with half a doz: 3 quarter clothes to set up a painter." These supplies presumably resulted in a portrait of Fitzhugh which no longer exists but which was copied by John Hesselius in 1751. Another unknown artist painted several Virginians in the 1720s and before, including Robert Carter and his two wives. Charles Bridges was the first known painter to spend substantial time in Virginia. Arriving in the colony in 1735 with a recommendation from Governor Gooch's brother Thomas, the master of Gonville and Caius College, Cambridge, Bridges did a portrait of the governor as a way to introduce "his Art" to the Virginia gentry. Within months he had "drawn" William Byrd II's children "and several others in the neighbourhood." Byrd then recommended him to Alexander Spotswood, whose portrait he also did. Bridges had arrived in Virginia in financial difficulty at the age of sixty-five, and over the next seven years he went on to produce portraits of at least thirty-five of the Virginia elite, including members of the Page, Blair, Ludwell, and Grymes families. And there were others, including William Dering in the late 1740s, John Hesselius and John Wollaston in the 1750s, John Durand in the 1760s and 1770s, and Charles Willson Peale in the early 1770s. Some of the elite were painted elsewhere in the colonies. Robert Feke painted William and Elizabeth Burwell Nelson, probably in the 1740s in Philadelphia. Others had their portraits done in England while on a visit or during their education. Thomas Hudson in London painted Robert Carter of Nomini Hall in 1753. The next year Mason Chamberlin did a portrait of the sixteen-year-old Thomas Nelson, the son of William and Elizabeth, who was in England for schooling. Similarly Robert Edge Pine did a portrait of Ralph Wormeley in 1753, long before Pine came to America. These portraits were not only a statement about the status and wealth of elite families, but they were also a prominently displayed generational record. By the end of the century, the walls of Westover, the Byrd family home, were filled with portraits of four generations of Byrds, as well as relatives and friends, not to mention at least twelve of William Byrd II's English acquaintances. They were a constant reminder of the family's long and distinguished history.[51]

It has been argued that colonial Americans invested only in portraiture at the expense of other forms of painting. But prints were readily available, and elite Virginians acquired them in large numbers, mostly through merchant correspondents. Americans expressed their interest in visual representations by ordering these prints, which included engravings of old and modern masters, as well as a wide range of other subjects. William Byrd II was a collector, as was, later, Robert Carter of Nomini Hall. They appear to have kept them in their libraries, which suggests they were preserving fine art prints. Byrd's brother-in-law John Custis IV leaned toward "comicall diverting prints to hang in the passage," but he also bought prints by subscription, the nature of which is not clear. Humorous prints and those of famous personages were popular, including "the fattest man in England," the "oldest man Since the Flood," the king of Prussia, and the Corsican patriot Pasquale Paoli. Hogarth's prints were also in demand, as were "Prints of the best Engravers from most eminent Masters." Some few did have fine paintings. William Byrd II evidently owned a Titian and a Rubens, and William Nelson owned a landscape by John Collet (1725–1780). Nelson asked merchant Samuel Athawes to acquire other Collet paintings, authorizing him to pay as much as "25 guineas." Even though Virginians of the upper class possessed and displayed a variety of art, the portrait dominated. Edmund Berkeley, who died in 1718, left portraits of himself and his wife as well as "Eleven house pictures" and ones of King William and Queen Mary.[52]

Wealthy Virginians also set themselves apart by their dress. In the seventeenth century the dress of the English upper classes tended toward the ostentatious. But as economic opportunity became more widespread and members of the rising middle class began to demonstrate their upward mobility by their dress, it became difficult to distinguish between who was a gentleman and who was not. The elite then turned to "habits of restraint" and "refinement" in their dress. Apart from gold and silver buckles, they wore little or no jewelry, and rather than "rich and garish costumes," they emphasized "rich fabrics," "fine tailoring," and more conservative colors. Historian Karen Calvert has explained that a "gentleman wore a white linen shirt, breeches, stockings and shoes, a coat, and waistcoat, and cravat. The breeches, coat, and waistcoat could be en suite of a single cloth, or of different fabrics and colors." Perhaps the most distinguishing characteristic was the change to wearing wigs, which were expensive and required extensive grooming that "was a tedious and messy process." After about 1750 clothing became even more restrained. According to Calvert, the "full bodied wig, huge big sleeves, and coats with voluminous full skirts gave way to a darker slimmer ideal." Proportions "shrank, requiring less material but better tailoring," and the "light queue wig" or simply powdered hair became more common. Women's dress also became simpler over time and the arrangement of their hair more natural.[53]

Upper-class Virginians were much influenced by English fashion, and how one dressed was important. Commenting on a ball held at the Capitol in 1711, William Byrd II said that "the President," Edmund Jenings, "had the worst clothes of anybody there." The following year Byrd reported that Benjamin Harrison had come to Westover "yesterday" in his "worst" clothes and, obviously embarrassed, appeared the next day in his "best clothes." John Carter, who was in England, complained to his father that John Randolph, now in Virginia, had done some "disservice" to his character. Robert Carter denied this and said that as "for his wearing finer linen or finer clothes than you, he never appeared in such here that I have seen." This focus on dress was not isolated. Much later Robert Wormeley Carter wrote his father, then in Williamsburg, that "your cloaths" have just "arrived" and are "vastly genteel" especially the "velvet waistcoat and Breeches, to be sure you will be very fine." A few years later he wrote from Williamsburg that "I turned out yesterday in my new cloathes, & they were universally allowed to be the handsomest that had been seen"; "other cloaths of the same sort appeared in a mean light when compared with mine." Philip Fithian, who was impressed with how people dressed, men and women, commented that Joseph F. Lane of Loudoun County, an old acquaintance from Princeton days, left Nomini Hall "dresst in black superfine Broadcloth; gold Laced hat; laced ruffles; black silk stockings & to his Broach on his Bosom he wore a Masons Badge inscribed Virtute and Silentio cut in Golden Medal! Certainly he was fine!"[54]

Early on most clothing came from England, and those who had spent time there had tailors and shoemakers they could call on. Robert Carter and William

Byrd II used the same London tailor, and many of the subsequent generations continued to buy most of their clothes in London. As late as 1773 Robert Beverley III wrote to his London tailor that he would "never more have anything made in this Country in the apparel way." Occasionally those who visited the mother country procured clothes for their friends. Mary Stith asked Elizabeth Jones, then in England, to get her a "Suit of pinners fashbly. dress'd with a Cross knot Role or whatever the fashn. requires, fashbl. ruffles & hankerchief." This cap had "two long flaps, one on each side, pinned or hanging down and sometimes fastened at the breast" (*OED*). She wanted the lace to be "of some breadth, and a beautiful pattern" but not "superfine Costly." She also wanted Jones to choose a "genteel fan" and hoped she could do all of this while shopping for herself. Earlier Thomas Lee bought Henry Fitzhugh a coat of "Satton Drugget the kind with Silver buttons . . . made by my Taylor & I hope will fit" and be "fashionable." Among men "plain" but "fashionable" seem to have been the guiding principles. Robert Carter ordered "a fashionable suit of broadcloth for myself . . . of a grave colour, lined with shaloon." Edward Athawes wrote to the executors of Robert Carter Jr.'s estate that he hoped the clothes ordered for Carter's young son that were "made by Mr Guest" would not give offense because of the "Lace put on them since it is done with no other intent but to please" his mother. Although sober clothes appear to have been favored, some bright colors were used. Crimson or red were popular. Charles Carter of Cleve ordered a "Scarlett Duffle riding coat" in 1731, and John Baylor specified a "redd Duffle great Coat with a velvet cape" in 1749. Much later, when Carter was a widower seeking another wife, he requested that London tailor John Priestman make him new clothes. These included a "Rich Black Paddusoy Cord. full dress suit," a "Duroy french frock suit" and a "Sup fine Blue cloth french frock suit," a "Second pair Blue Cloth Breeches with Gilt garters," and "a pair of Rich Crimson Silk Stockings & Breeches." The cost was £31. Robert Beverley III, who was also courting, ordered from Mr. Scot "the Taylor" a "scarlet Hair Shag Frock Coat superfine green cloth waistcoat & Breeches, with plain buttons." He also wanted "a Pair of the best Doe Skin Breeches of Jones in James Street." A few months later he requested that Scot make him "a crimson . . . silk French Waistcoat & Breeches & Line with Silk of the same colour" with embroidered buttonholes. In addition he desired a suit of light-colored silk and four pairs of "Nankeen Breeches."

Through the first half of the century, attire of this sort was almost invariably topped off with a wig. Wigs were sometimes acquired in England, but by the 1720s they were readily available in Williamsburg. Men shaved their heads to accommodate wigs that they wore in public. At home a "soft" cap was often worn.

Robert Beverley III ordered "black velvet caps . . . with Silver Tassels" for this purpose. A wide variety of wigs were available, and they were expensive. Over four years in the 1750s, Charles Carter of Cleve spent £17.2.8 for wigs of various sorts, including a "Can Wig," "cutt Brown wig," "Sarach Wig," and a "Grizel Dress Wig" priced at between £1.12.6 and £3.18 each. These wigs required constant attention, for they had to be powdered and pomaded before wearing and frequently were sent to a barber-surgeon for dressing, bobbing, and altering. Thomas Jones paid a barber-surgeon ten shillings for dressing his "son's Wiggs [for] one year." Gentlemen also cared for their own wigs, and Robert Carter ordered "half a dozen pounds of powder" and "one quart of perfumed oyle" for this purpose. The wearing of wigs declined gradually after midcentury as men began to wear their own hair, powdered, or a "light queue wig," but many gentlemen continued to wear full wigs until the Revolution.

Finally, the belted sword was frequently a part of men's attire when away from home. And in all cases clothes and related accoutrements were worn for a long time and passed down from father to son. Robert Carter instructed in his will that his wearing apparel, wigs, swords, canes, and pistols be divided among his three eldest sons. This bequest reflects the importance of dress among Virginia's elite.[55]

Things of Mind and Spirit: Books and Religion

Most elite, perhaps all, had libraries. Despite John Clayton's comment in 1684 that Virginians "for want of books . . . read men the more," even then some elite Virginians had substantial libraries. William Fitzhugh, William Byrd I, John Carter II, and especially Ralph Wormeley II all had libraries of several hundred volumes, with Wormeley's of about 700 being the largest. Between 1700 and 1776 there is evidence, in some cases inventories, that at least eighteen members of the twenty-one leading families had collections from 100 or so volumes to the over 3,500 that William Byrd II possessed. Other than Byrd, the Carters left the best record, beginning with Robert and including his sons John and Landon and later his grandson Robert Carter of Nomini Hall, who had between 1,500 and 2,000 volumes. Richard Lee II had a large library, as did Henry Fitzhugh, son of William Fitzhugh. The same can be said of Sir John Randolph and his son Peyton and three generations of Beverleys: Robert II, William, and Robert III. John Custis IV and his son, Daniel Parke Custis, should also be mentioned.[56]

They acquired their books most often from English and Scottish booksellers. But after printer William Parks moved to Williamsburg in 1730–31, it was possible to acquire titles from him. William Hunter and others succeeded him after 1750. Parks advertised in 1745 that he had imported a "considerable Quantity" and "great variety" of books on divinity, history, physic, philosophy, and mathematics, as well as schoolbooks "in Latin and Greek among which are some very neat Classicks." He also had available a number of "large Church and Family Bibles and Common Prayer Books, Sermons, Plays etc. too tedious to mention." As Scots stores were established in the piedmont, they also began to carry books; many were religious in nature, but they also included history, memoirs, and poetry. The elite continued to acquire most of their books from Britain, especially London, Glasgow, and Edinburgh. Wealthy families regularly read English newspapers, reviews, and magazines, from which they kept up with the latest publications. William Nelson wrote merchant John Norton that he wanted three copies of Robert Dodsley's poems, one copy of "Gordon's Young Man's Companion and one copy of Boyer's New Pantheon all of which are mentioned at the end of the London Magazine for April last." Robert Carter Nicholas wanted "by the first Opportunity Sir James Stewart's *Political Economy* a book much celebrated by the Reviewers." And although they did not often deal directly with booksellers, having merchant correspondents doing the buying for them, they knew who the dealers were and where they were located. Nelson complained to Norton that "Mr Rivington your bookseller" had not sent him all the volumes of "Lord Littleton's Harry" and that he also wanted "Boswell's *History of Corsica,* poor Paoli, Sir James Stewart's *Political Oeconomy* and *The Art of drawing without a Master* printed for Corrington Bowles No. 69 & Wm. Harris No. 70 no side of St. Paul's Churchyard." The *London Magazine* was in many libraries and provided much information about books, as did the *Imperial Magazine* and the *Universal Magazine.* The elite also subscribed to English newspapers like the *Evening Post,* the *London Mercury,* and the *London Chronicle,* which included notices of the latest books. Landon Carter frequently ordered books soon after publication, as did others. Robert Carter of Nomini Hall began purchasing William Blackstone's *Commentaries on the Laws of England* (4 vols., 1765–69) in 1767, and others followed suit. In 1769 Walter Jones wrote his brother from London "that the last volume is just published" but he might wait a few months when "a complete Irish edition will be published, less than half the Price in English Quarto." In the late seventeenth century Ralph Wormeley II was acquiring John Rushworth's *Historical Collections* (7 vols., 1659–1701) as each volume came out. Similarly, William Byrd I purchased "the 2d part" of Thomas Burnet's *Theory of the Earth* (1684) in 1689. Years later, in 1744, Byrd's grandson William Beverley informed London merchant Charles

Smyth, "By the public papers I find that there are subscriptions to be taken for a new Edition in folio . . . of Salmons present State of all nations and I desire you will subscribe one Sett for me." He also ordered the *London Magazine* for 1744 and 1745.[57]

Religious works and sermons composed a large portion of every library, and most included history, some classics, belles lettres, and usually instructional books. The owner's interests and tastes, of course, influenced the focus of a library, but because all of the twenty-one families had at least one member on the Council of State, a body with judicial and legislative functions, and because many other members served on the county courts, legal works were always present, frequently in large numbers. One-third of Robert Carter's library of over 500 volumes was law books. William Byrd had 298 legal titles, and Carter's grandson Robert Carter of Nomini Hall also had a large collection. The scarcity of doctors and the state of medical knowledge dictated that libraries also include works on medicine and anatomy. Books on husbandry and gardening were also present among these works of an occupational nature. Religious works loomed large in Virginia libraries. Almost every library included Richard Allestree's *The Whole Duty of Man,* a manual of Christian morality. The collected sermons of John Tillotson were also popular. The presence of belles lettres grew as the century wore on. Poetry led the list; the poems of Robert Dodsley were much liked, as were the novels of Henry Fielding. The buying and reading habits of elite Virginians tended to mirror what was going on in England. From about 1700 on, the availability of books increased. Religious works, especially sermons, were among the most available, but close behind came books on politics, literature, history, and geography. It also appears that the elite not only bought books but they read and shared them with their friends. In rural Virginia leisure activities were limited, and reading was one of them. Landon Carter described Robert Burwell, a widower at fifty-two, as an "unhappy man." He "has never been given to much reading," Carter remarked, "and as he grows older he must be miserable; for without books or a desire to read how can the aged enjoy themselves." Their libraries set the leading families apart from the commonality, even from most of the rising middle class. Merchant Roger Atkinson perhaps expressed the views of the majority when he ordered the *Middlesex Journal,* "[Lays?] Weekly Paper," a pamphlet titled "Thoughts on the Cause of the present Discontents," and "anything else you judge clever—For I never read anything Else hardly but such papers—Except an Almanack, a Prayer Book & a Bible."[58]

The presence of large numbers of religious books in elite libraries is not surprising, for they were, in most cases, deeply religious people. They have been described, in contrast with Puritan New England, as not having deep faith and instead preferring a bland moralism, but nothing can be further from the truth. Religious practice in Virginia was influenced by the fact that ministers were frequently in short supply and churches were often far removed and not easy to reach. As Edward Bond has pointed out, devotional life was not restricted to the parish church, and great emphasis was placed on private devotions. Bond stressed that Anglicanism was concerned primarily with "the spiritual care and guidance of individuals rather than with theological polemic" or "intellectual debate" difficult for the average individual to comprehend. The theology was orthodox Christian, but it "typically contained rationalism, moralism and piety. Within limits the world was comprehensible." It was then an "orthodoxy adjusted to a Newtonian universe." The emphasis was on faith and God's grace. "You shall be saved by your faith, not for your works," John Page I told his son, "but for such faith as is without works you shall never be saved." So their religion was a part of their daily activity. "Religion," as Bond has emphasized, "was less something individuals believed than something they did, a practice rather than a set of propositions." The moral person was the good Christian, and this meant that through daily devotions people were constantly reminded of their religious duty, their conformance to God's laws. Thus the Sunday service was no more important than the practice of piety on a regular basis at home. This does not mean that they did not place emphasis on Sunday worship, for, comparatively speaking, church attendance was good, especially among the gentry. And the socializing before and after the church service, which is frequently noted as confirming the lack of piety among Virginians, has to be understood in relation to the colony's rural character. Church services, like court days, were among the few times people came together, and it is understandable that visiting would take place.[59]

William Byrd II's religious beliefs were similar to those of most of Virginia's eighteenth-century elite. Pierre Marambaud has described them clearly: "Byrd . . . expressed belief in the Fall of Man, in Christ's mission to redeem Man, and in a future Resurrection when every man shall be given his due." Byrd entered his creed in his diary in 1709; and later in the 1720s, after having read William Wollaston's *The Religion of Nature Delineated* (London, 1724), he explained his belief in "natural religion," that part of religious belief that people could discover for themselves through reason. We "may not plead ignorance," he wrote, for God "has endued us with Reason, which if duly attended to will be our Sufficient Direction. Upon this Foundation all natural religion is built . . . and the light by which any Person of common understanding may clearly discern the distinction betwixt moral Good & Evil." Complete understanding was not possible without revelation, but "natural religion" was "complementary to revelation" and reinforced the view that the "foundations of Christian belief are reasonable." Byrd's religion, as the editors of his commonplace book have explained, "is no where theoretical or metaphysical; it deals with the practical day-to-day challenges of existence. These challenges are faced with faith that God will supply grace that allows reason to moderate passions and resist the downward pull of vice." Robert Carter expressed his views more succinctly when speaking of the education of his sons: "As I am of the Church of England, so I desire they should be. But high flown up top notions and the great stress that is laid upon ceremonies, any farther than decency and conformity, are what I cannot come into reason of. Practical godliness is the substance—these are but the shell."[60]

Even Sir John Randolph, described by Governor Gooch as the leader of "free thinkers" and by Commissary Blair as holding "Scarceley Christian opinions," was close to Byrd and Carter in his belief. Having been called a "Deist, Heretic and Schismatic," he felt it necessary to preface his will with a statement of his faith. Randolph said that he adored the "Supreme Being the first cause of all things whose infinite power and wisdom is manifested through all his works." Further, "Jesus was the Messiah who came into the world to give light to mankind," who were lost and "wandering in Miserable Darkness" and "ignorance of the true religion." His mission was to destroy "factions and parties" and to "persuade us to love one another which comprehends the whole moral law as the only way to eternal life and establish peace and liberty among nations." And Randolph believed "that the dead shall rise at God's appointed time" and would not be judged "for errors or mistakes, in matters of speculation," but by the immorality of their lives "and above all, for that Fierceness with which Mankind is inspired in Religious Disputes, Despising, Reviling and Hating one another about trifling and insignificant opinions." He was convinced that people would be rewarded according "to the degree of virtue" they "practiced in this life." This he learned "from the gospel" and believed it to be "truely Christian" and suited "to the weak capacities of Men." It was easy to "understand" and needed none of the explanations of "learned Doctors" who did not have the strength or courage to establish "a true, uniform, consistent System of their own." They tried to make the "Religion of Christ, a Science of mighty Difficulty and Mystery," and all they had done was make their followers "more fierce and obstinate, fixing irreconcilable animosities among them about unintelligible Propositions and senseless Doctrines." They did not influence people's minds "to ammend their lives" but weakened the obligation for morality and destroyed Christian unity, "which cannot be founded but in strict Obedience to the Precepts of the Gospel." So he believed that the "ways and means publicly established for the reformation of our lives . . . is quite worn out."[61]

John Custis IV may have had views similar to Randolph's, but neither Byrd nor Carter would have gone so far as to question the utility of the established church. They would, though, have agreed with his statement of faith and his criticism of theological nit-picking. Landon Carter, much later, also would have agreed. Carter was not much interested in formal theology, as Jack Greene has pointed out. "Parsons," Carter wrote in his diary, "can almost anathematize their Parishioners when they want them to act against Nature, and pretend it to be a duty." He believed that there was "more true religion in the real sensibility of men who knowing his human machine endeavors by his reason to counteract it so far as never to give it an opportunity of resenting injury." Carter was having a disagreement with Parson Isaac Giberne, who had written him, "Your Religion is very different from what I am ordained to teach." Carter appended a note to the letter protesting that he was only applying "common sense" to the scriptures.[62]

Despite occasional disagreements with the clergy, Carter and most Virginia gentry were deeply religious, good churchmen, served on the vestry, and attended church regularly. Theirs was a moderate religion in the mold of John Tillotson, archbishop of Canterbury in the 1690s, who was a leading Latitudinarian, a proponent of doctrinal flexibility and ecclesiastical broadmindedness. They were also, as a group, tolerant of other faiths. Robert Carter told an English correspondent that although "I go different ways to pay worship to the Author of our beings, and I dare say I shall never change my old mode to get into yours in my way to Eternity, yet I am not so uncharitable to think but that honesty is to be found in your persuasion as well as my own." His son Landon was of similar persuasion, favoring toleration and even going so far as to oppose burdening non-Anglicans with support of the established church. In fact, it appears that most of the elite families were tolerant of dissenters and did not feel threatened by them; the concern and criticism came from Anglican clergy. Up until the Revolution most Virginians attended established churches where all were welcome. Fithian reported that on an Easter Sunday in 1774, "all the parish seem'd to meet together. High, Low, black, white all came out," but he hastened to add that only "communicants" were admitted to the "Sacrament." He could also have noted that as people entered the church, they were seated differently, for the vestry allocated seats according to class and rank and occasionally on the basis of gender, separating men from women. "Personal social standing and official title" were frequently taken into account when assigning pews, so leading families received the best seating, and the poor and slaves usually were assigned to the periphery or to balconies. William Byrd II made a point of the fact that the "vestry . . . gave me the best pew in church." Seats were free of charge, but once a pew was assigned, families considered it theirs. If their circumstances changed, they sometimes sold their pews. Benjamin Waller noted that Thomas Jones and his family were leaving Williamsburg, and he wondered if Jones would be willing "to sell yours in the Gallery? And what would you take for it?" When people entered church, they were made immediately aware of their status in Virginia society.[63]

Living beyond Their Means

Clearly Virginia's gentry lived well. Once the twenty-one families began their rise into prominence in the 1680s, the amenities that distinguished them from the rest of society became more evident. From the early eighteenth century on, their acquisition of a wide variety of good things increased. New English marketing techniques began to emerge, appealing to "drives for social emulation and competition." The availability of "new kinds of goods" also grew. The elite continued to buy primarily from England, but many of these items, especially after midcentury, could be acquired locally as stores spread throughout the colony. These developments were part of what has been described as a "consumer revolution" that was taking place in England.[64]

The elite continued to travel across the Atlantic throughout the first seventy-five years of the century for familial, business, and educational reasons, and they became acquainted with the most recent fashions and tastes. This knowledge, coupled with increased availability, resulted in ever more spending on a wider variety of goods. Wealthy Virginians came to perceive that they were importing more products from Great Britain than they could pay for. The balance was in England's favor from 1765 to 1774; from 1757 to 1774 imports into the Chesapeake from England exceeded exports to England in ten of those seventeen years, and most manufactured items, especially luxury ones, came from England. However, if Scotland is added to the import-export figures for the Chesapeake (Maryland included), then imports exceeded exports in only two years after 1740: in 1759 and 1774. But comments about extravagance were by and about the elite, and it does appear that many were living beyond their means, especially from midcentury on. Inventories for estates of the wealthy are scarce, but customs records for the Chesapeake are helpful. The importation of seventeen luxury items into Virginia and Maryland between 1749 and 1774 can be used to test the idea of extravagance: chariots, coaches, books, cabinetware and furniture, carpets Turkey and Irish, silk thrown and wrought, "bandannoes," gold and silver lace, ginghams, "taffeties," romals, imported chinaware, horses, plate, pictures and prints, pepper, and wine. Virginia, a much larger and wealthier colony, certainly imported the bulk of this merchandise. In the 1760s the importation of these articles increased 75 percent over that of the 1750s. The war interrupted the subsequent decade, but in the years 1769 through 1774 there was a continued escalation, and in this five-year period 35 percent more of these articles were imported than in the entire decade of the 1750s. For example, 66 coaches and chariots were imported in the 1750s, 145 in the 1760s, and 99 in the five years beginning in 1769. The pattern with imported china is similar. There was a 34 percent increase in the decade of the 1760s over that of the previous decade, and the amount imported in the five years beginning in 1769 was about equal to that of the 1750s. With wrought silk (cloth) there was a 66 percent increase in the 1760s over that of the 1750s, and from 1769 through 1774, the amount was 48 percent more than from 1750 to 1760. The pattern with imported pepper was similar. The importation of some items remained roughly level, including "bandannoes," which were dyed handkerchiefs of silk, linen, or other fabrics; 3,892 of these came in the 1750s, 4,041 in the 1760s, and from 1769 through 1774, 3,277. The same was true with silk or cotton handkerchiefs called romals. And Chesapeake gentry continued to import blooded horses, ordering ninety-eight in the 1750s, ninety-six in the 1760s, and thirty-eight in the subsequent five years.[65]

Literary evidence suggests that the customs numbers for chariots and coaches may be low. A visitor in 1736 commented that "almost every considerable man keeps an Equipage," and he was struck by "the prodigious numbers of Coaches that crowded the deep sandy Streets" of Williamsburg. Merchant Francis Jerdone told an English correspondent in 1753 that he had been fortunate to be able to sell his "second hand" chariot because "our Gentry have such proud spirits, that nothing will go down, but equipages of the nicest and newest fashions. You'll hardly believe it when I tell you there are sundry chariots now in this country which cost 200 Guineas, and one that cost £260." Further, the vehicles were personalized. When Daniel Parke Custis ordered "A New Neat hansom two wheeled Chair Body & Carriage . . . to carry one person" in 1750, he instructed that it be lined with blue cloth and painted "a pleasant Stone Culler" with "heightened gold Shields Armes & Crest." Later Robert Beverley instructed "Page a Coachmaker in Little Queen Street Lincolns Inn Fields" that his new "neat light post chariot" should be "painted as my Phaeton, a light green upon silver, with three bells heads upon the front & back & one upon each side the lining to be a light colord Cloth." The front was "to be divided into two glasses instead of the usual one," and the inside "must have neat brass rods with green silk curtains" as well as "netting inside to put Ladies hats." Nor were families satisfied with one vehicle. William Nelson bought a chariot in 1766 and Lord Botetourt's "Post Coach" in 1771, "hardly the worse for wear," and two years later his widow ordered a "genteel Chariot with six Harness to be painted of a grave Colour & the Coat of arms of our family." Robert Carter of Nomini Hall possessed a "chair" for his personal use as well as a chariot for the family."[66]

When the gentry traveled in these vehicles, they did so in style, usually with a postilion and driver and often with "waiting men" and a coachman in livery. Even when traveling alone in his "chair," Robert Carter did so "with two waiting men." Charles Carter of Cleve stipulated in his will that his "Coach and Chariot shall be kept with six horses, Coachman & Postillion at the expense of the estate for the use of my daughters." Robert Fairfax, who arrived in Virginia in 1768 to visit his brother Thomas, Lord Fairfax, was impressed with how he was entertained by the gentry and conveyed from Hampton to Greenway Court in the backcountry "by gentlemen with their coaches and Six from one House to another, with the utmost politeness and civility." A visiting Englishman reported somewhat later that at the end of a wedding celebration at Robert Beverley's Blandfield, the guests departed "in their phaetons, chariots, and coaches in four, with two or three footman behind. They live in as high style here, I believe as any part of the world."[67]

It was very expensive to maintain oneself in this manner, and as the century wore on, it became increasingly difficult to do so. Many of the first two generations of the elite families were English educated and/or had family or business connections in England. Despite the fact that they were of middle-class origin, they were well aware of what was required to be a gentleman. By the 1730s and 1740s all had acquired those perquisites that Lawrence Stone has explained were the minimum to be a member of the squirearchy: "great power (at some point in the family's history), participation in local administration, substantial landed wealth, broad but not deep education, a generous lifestyle, and high status." Virginia's leading families had reached this position rather quickly, and they felt some pressure to maintain a genteel lifestyle that was comparable to that of the English upper class. It has been argued that this pressure created insecurity because they had to be constantly vigilant to maintain "complete gentility" on the

English model. There may be some evidence of this feeling, but in general, most of the families did not exhibit such an attitude. It is clear that they did everything they could to demonstrate their status in Virginia society and that others noted their lifestyle. For example, Sir John Randolph's obituary reported that "his parts were bright and strong, his Learning extensive and useful. If he was liable to any Censure . . . it was for too great a Luxury and Abundance." Their economic success had been based on commercial activity combined with planting, but by midcentury most of them had been forced out of the mercantile business by the onslaught of Scottish "chain stores," and speculation in western lands between 1730 and 1760 did not serve as an adequate replacement. If they were going to maintain their lifestyle and status, they would have to do so through planting alone. At the same time the model of the country gentleman was gaining favor in Virginia and was replacing that of the successful businessman as exemplified by Robert "King" Carter. The country gentleman was not involved in trade. His landed wealth was to provide the independence necessary to "be a fully enfranchised citizen and only landed wealth was associated with virtue." Some few were able to maintain their wealth as planters—Robert Beverley III and Charles Carter of Corotoman and Shirley, for example—but most did not. A few also continued their involvement in business, the most successful being Robert Carter of Nomini Hall. But most insisted on living the life of the country gentleman, which drove many into heavy debt. Insecurity then came with the knowledge that their independence was compromised by the failure to maintain the family's wealth. If a man's fortune was lost, he would not meet with "as great respect" as was formerly the case, Philip Fithian noted. Some attempted to mend their ways, and he was "best esteemed . . . who attends to business with the greatest diligence." The "People of fortune," "who are the pattern of all behaviour here," he asserted, were beginning "to be frugal and moderate." It was possible to operate a plantation profitably. As one merchant's representative explained, £5,000 "prudently laid out in a Virginia estate" would bring more return than in England, but to do so it "must have care & frugality in management." And despite Fithian's observation, only a few had these qualities. What some have referred to as the Golden Age might also be called the Age of Excess.[68]

As debt grew, there also came increased sensitivity to criticism and the questioning of one's ability to pay. Robert Beverley wrote English merchant John Bland that on his arrival in Virginia, he found his "Friend Munford very much displeased" because Bland had protested "one of his Drafts, which you had promised should meet honor" and that he was "determined to break off all connexions with you." James Dean, a merchant's representative, commented to London merchant James Buchanan that William and Peter Randolph had the most influence in "these upper parts" but "at the same time . . . there are none more ticklish & sooner disobliged." William Randolph was angry because he had been charged a "Commission on his Chariot that he said he bought himself and only drew an order on you to pay it." Both Randolphs were heavily in debt. Robert Carter of Nomini Hall told Samuel Athawes, who was evidently questioning his ability to pay, that "there was a time of life when my gratifications exceeded my yearly income: will such a fault create a rogue? will complaining up[on] some parts of the liturgy used by the church of england create an atheist? he that steals my fortune steals trash, but he that takes from me my good name, makes me poor indeed." William Nelson agreed that Athawes was the "best Judge" as to whether or not he had been correct "in not sending Mrs. Lightfoot Sen. all the goods" she had ordered, but Nelson was sorry that the letters the merchant wrote her were "uncivil" and gave her "much uneasiness, & Disgust to some others for it was much the subject of conversation, as well as what you wrote to Mr Jaquelin About his Goods." And when Athawes criticized Hugh Nelson's tobacco, Hugh's father told him that "I fear it has made a difference in his consignment" for as "I told you once before that it is as great an offence to a Virginia Planter to find fault with his Tobacco as with his Mistress."[69]

CLASS AND STATUS

Despite the decline in wealth among most of the twenty families, they do not appear to have lost any social status. There was marked decline in their economic position and arguably in their political influence, but not in their position at the top of Virginia society. An English observer commented in the early 1770s that he found "the best families and fortunes" were liberally educated and had an enlightened understanding and knowledge of the world which gave them "an ease and freedom of manners and conversation, highly to their advantage in exterior, which no vicissitude of fortune or place can divest them." They demonstrated this position not only in their houses, dress, and other possessions but also in the way they related to others in Virginia society. From early on they were addressed in terms of respect. St. John Shropshire, in a letter to Robert Carter, made so "bold" as to recommend "to your . . . honour" a man who wanted to rent one of the deceased Ralph Wormeley II's plantations. Throughout the letter he referred to Carter in respectful terms—"Your honour pleases"; "if your honour thinks fit"—and closed by giving his "humble respects to your honour and & good Lady." Later when the tobacco ship *Carter* arrived "before" his house, Carter went aboard and received a 28-gun salute. On occasion they were haughty. When Councillor William Churchill was asked to deal with a lawsuit involving the absence of a will, he was reported to have refused "to concern himself" for he was "so great as to be Employed." Recent arrivals in the colony had even more difficulty. George Fisher, who migrated to Virginia in 1750, rented a house in Williamsburg the next year. Soon thereafter "a strange mortal" came "into my house in the garb or habit of one of our Common Soldiers." He had "an arrogant, haughty carriage" and demanded that Fisher exchange houses with him because he did not like the one he was in. When Fisher demurred, he left "very much offended." Later Fisher learned that the person was Colonel Philip Ludwell Lee, "an heir to the late President of the Council." During a bad crop year John Carter expressed concern to his brother Landon for "Poor People" who could expect little "from their cornfields." He was prepared to help as best he could and was surprised that Landon, who said he was applied to by many, had told him "the only Charity you can do is recommend them to such as have the Bowels of Compassion to be moved." He could not believe that Landon intended to "shut up your own [tenants?]" when "your Barns must be much better filled than mine."[70]

Even among the gentry there was a pecking order. Elizabeth Jones sold a "Negro fellow" named Freddy to Susanna Randolph, the widow of Sir John. Freddy proved to be a problem, and Jones agreed to take him back. But Randolph's "Son Johnny" then told her that he must be returned "to your Quarter," which Jones "supposed to be a mistake." She allowed Freddy to go to church, and he did not return. Randolph's "Negro Fellow Blenheim" told her that Freddy was at the Randolphs' home. Jones said that she would have had no objection to his going back if "Your Ladyship . . . had given me notice." She wanted to do what was "most obliging to you," and "without giving your Ladyship or myself any further trouble," she would be content to be paid for him. But Jones added that she did not deserve "to be contemtuously used." Elizabeth Cocke Pratt Jones was a cultured and able woman. She had spent time in England, "taken the waters" at Bath, and attended plays in London. Her father, William Cocke, had come to Virginia as Alexander Spotswood's physician and later was secretary of the colony and a member of the council. But Jones's husband, Thomas, briefly a member of the House of Burgesses, had fallen on hard times and was heavily in debt. Clearly Susanna Beverley Randolph did not consider Elizabeth Jones her equal. Henry Lee, who was not of second rank, wrote his brother Richard that "my fellow Harry and Colonel Tayloes Gawin are condemn'd for attempting to Poyson my Wife," but because Tayloe was anxious to have a pardon granted to Gawin, "who appeared the greatest villain of the two," he supposed it would be done "as he belongs to a Great Man." The Randolphs and the Tayloes, with a few others, were at the top of the pyramid. Governor Gooch gave support to this estimate when he wrote his brother Thomas at Cambridge requesting that he treat William Stith, "Nephew of the Randolphs," well for it would "be taken kindly by them on my account." But generally respect for those below them on the social scale was the rule. William Byrd II had problems with Richard Fitzwilliam, surveyor general of customs and a member to the commission to establish a Virginia–North Carolina boundary line. Byrd told Governor Gooch that "the men" had not been "uncivil" to Fitzwilliam and "if a man be never so great, if he looks for extraordinary respect from his inferiors, it will be just to give them good words. Those I think are due even slaves." Much later St. George Tucker remembered that the "rich rode in coaches, chariots, or on fine horses, but they never failed to pull off their hats to a poor man whom they met, & generally appear'd to me to shake hands with every man in a Courtyard, or Church-yard, and as far as I could judge the planter who owned half a dozen negroes, felt himself perfectly on the level with his neighbor who owned a hundred."

Whether or not Virginia society seemed level, the gentry were readily identifiable, and by midcentury Charles Hansford, a blacksmith-poet, saw fit to recognize them in verse.

> The Nelsons, Digges, Carters, Burwells, Pages
> The Grymes and Robinsons engages
> Respect, and reverence to those names be paid!
> Blairs, Ludwells, Byrds in the same scale are laid.
> Randolphs and Wallers, Harrisons likewise—
> These all contend for honors, noble prize.
> Willises, Wormeleys, Lewises do run
> In honor's path, as loath to be outdone.
> The Spotswoods, Berkeleys, Armisteads thither bend
> Their steps and for the lively prize contend.
> I hope Virginia hath many more
> To me unknown—might lengthen out the score.
> As stars of the first magnitude these shine
> And in their several stations, do condone
> The great support and ornament to be
> Of Britain's first and ancient colony.

Hansford was not blind to problems and singled out gambling, horse racing, and cockfighting. And he worried about the influence of gentlemen.

> A gentleman is placed so that he
> In his example cannot neuter be:
> He's always doing good or doing harm
> And would not this a thinking man alarm?
> If he lives ill, the vulgar will him trace;
> They fancy his example theirs will grace.

But when gentry lived well:

> Their bright example is a spell
> Which does insensibly attract the crowd
> To follow them on virtue's pleasant road.
> In such a way, who would not delight
> To see gentry and commons both unite?
> This would true honor to our gentry bring,
> And happiness to all will flow and spring.
> We find example is a greater force
> Than the most famous clergyman's discourse.
> None will deny the assertion to be true:
> Example always precept will outdo.[71]

It has been argued that as the Revolution approached the "gentry and commons" did unite, if not exactly in the way that Hansford hoped for. To a degree this is true. But there probably had always been an undercurrent of antagonism toward the gentry, not only because of their "Haughtiness," which Fithian said was "a Common foible here," but also because of the way they treated others and/or expressed themselves toward those whom some of them referred to as "the vulgar." Owen Griffith, an indentured servant, charged that Landon Carter was a "Boisterous Tyrant" who considered him a "fool." John Dixon wrote Robert Carter of Nomini Hall that he was surprised that Carter had ordered a suit to be "commenced on my Brother's Bond for which I am security. . . . The Rattle-Snake is want to give Warning before he strikes! I own it would have been difficult to make me believe (otherwise than by Experience) that the benevolent, the Generous, the Honorable Rich Mr Carter, should be the first to fall on a distressed Widdow & eight Children." He asked Carter to recall his "Hasty

Mandate," for all are "liable to misfortune and misery" and it might not be long before "Your Children are Orphans." After a meeting at Farnham in the wake of the Boston Tea Party and the British response, Walter Jones told Landon Carter that not a few "People . . . came there with [an?] opinion, too common among the vulgar the Law [about?] Tea alone did not concern them" because they "used none of it" and "let the *Gentlemen* look to it." Later, when Governor-Dunmore was raiding in the Chesapeake Bay, Carter reported that one "G.R." refused "to lend his firelock to go against" a British naval tender and expressed the opinion that those who did were "fools to go to protect Gentlemen's houses on the River side; he thought it would be better if they were burnt down." Some gentry expressed themselves too freely, as did Attorney General John Randolph when he remarked that the "Ignorant Vulgar are as unfit to judge of the modes as they are unable to manage the Reins of Government." And when queried about the views of "the people" concerning Dunmore's seizure of and removal of powder from Williamsburg, Randolph replied that he knew little of their "designs . . . not mixing much with them." So as the Revolution approached, the role of Virginia's old political elite was problematic.[72]

Epilogue

I find myself as much at loss & perhaps more so than I should at Constantinople so much has the late accursed war altered both men and things.[1]

—WILLIAM LEE ON HIS RETURN TO VIRGINIA IN 1783

FROM THE ELECTION OF JOHN ROBINSON JR. as Speaker of the House of Burgesses in 1738 until the Declaration of Independence, the elite families controlled Virginia politics. Robinson and Peyton Randolph, who succeeded him, made sure that members of these families dominated the major working committees of that body. Charles Carter of Cleve, Landon Carter, Benjamin Harrison V, and Richard Henry Lee emerged as important leaders. Not far behind came William Digges, Thomas Nelson Jr., John Page, and William Randolph. All told, members of twenty-one families held leadership positions, and for eight sessions of the assembly, from 1751 to 1775, an average of nineteen members of the families were serving.[1]

The rise in influence of the House of Burgesses does not mean that the Council of State lost power and authority. The same families also dominated that body: twenty-one of the twenty-seven who served came from their ranks. It is true that less legislation originated in the upper house, especially after 1750. Not only had the General Court docket become increasingly heavy: Governor Gooch reported in 1748 that it had grown to "1,000 causes" as opposed to 300, and thirty years later a chancery case might take eight years to be resolved. But equally important, over time the council tended to be in agreement with the House of Burgesses.[2]

The increased agreement of the two houses came as a result of two factors. First, the Board of Trade, "the only body sufficiently informed . . . to deal with colonial matters," began exercising more authority over the colony's internal affairs. Laws, some of them important ones, were disallowed, and increasingly a suspending clause was attached to most legislative acts specifying that they could not go into effect until the king had signed them, which made it unclear what act could become law, even necessary temporary ones. And second, war with France began in 1754. The conflict placed heavy military and financial demands on the colony.[3]

The end of the war in 1763 brought more problems. Faced with increased debt, the mother country tried to shift the expense of colonial administration and defense to the colonies. In the hope that problems with Native Americans could be defused, migration was forbidden beyond the Appalachian Mountains, despite the fact that many settlers were already there. New laws imposing taxes were passed, including the Stamp Act of 1765 and the Townshend Acts of 1767. Colonial response was so strong that most of these taxes were removed, save one on tea. But by 1770–71 things had gone too far as colonies began to operate in extralegal ways to boycott the importation of many British products.[4]

Tensions ran high in Virginia. The situation was not helped by the fact that when Speaker John Robinson, the most powerful political figure in Virginia, died in 1766, it was learned that as treasurer, rather than burning paper currency emitted to pay for the war when it came in as payment for taxes, he had loaned over £100,000 of the paper back out to "particular friends." William Byrd III had been loaned the most: £14,921. The list of others included Burwells, Carters, Grymeses, Randolphs, Wormeleys, and ten members of the Speaker's extended family. This revelation served to emphasize the problem of debt in Virginia society, especially among the elite, accompanied by the slow decline in their power and influence over the years to come.[5]

The decline did not happen immediately. The 1760s saw sixty-one new members elected to the House of Burgesses, some of whom Governor Francis Fauquier described as "Young, hot, and Giddy." The "cool old members," he said, had lost the "Lead" they "formerly had." But by the 1766–69 assembly the young and old were closer together, and the elite families continued to play a major role, serving on and chairing major committees. Richard Henry Lee, whom Fauquier described as one "who had been most remarkable in opposing all measures of government," led a vocal contingent from the Northern Neck including three other Lees and three Carters. Landon Carter, one of them, had already written a series of essays protesting the Stamp Act that expressed the view of many. He asserted that the attempt to "govern the colonies by laws made without the consideration or consent of the inhabitants, or their representatives" was "in the end to enslave them."[6]

Shortly after the passage of the Townshend Acts, William Nelson, the most powerful member of the council, privately expressed what was probably the position of a majority of that body. The people of England "pride themselves on being the freest People on Earth & that they are govern'd by laws of their own making, that is by their Representatives," but in fact "half the members are imposed upon them [by] some Great Lord or rich commoner and are bought and sold whole boroughs at once." A "member who buys in this Way" had "a right to sell, and if he sells them into slavery," they should have "little right to complain since they first set themselves to sale." "Poor old England, she seems to have passed the summit of her Power & Grandeur & to be verging fast to her decline," he wrote. "Who knows but where they have left their Liberty, they may come and hide themselves in this western Part of the World as many brave Men did during the Usurpation of the Last Century. They struggled against Tyranny & lawless power: and deserving of the divine Protection found here in the Wilderness, Enjoyed Liberty & Ease & laid the Foundation of what may in future ages become a mighty Empire: But what will the Present Race deserve from their Posterity; after having . . . sold their Birthrights & laid the Foundation of slavery and Ruin." The "Fall of Kingdoms," he concluded, had "generally been preceeded, if not occasioned by Venality and Corruption." Later he asserted the "Constitutional Right" of a "freeman" to dispose "of his Property, by himself or Representative." If "any Man or set of Men have a Right to take from me any Part of my Property without consent, that Right extends to the whole of it, and then what am I but a slave?" He hoped that "hateful Name . . . will never be branded on the Forehead of the Poor Americans." They had "humbly submitted to every Act imposing Duties for the Regulation of Trade" in order to give "a necessary advantage and Power to Great Britain, to enable her to extend her Protection to her Colonies, who, labour for the support of the Glory & Aggrandizement of the Parent Country." He was certain that whenever the "Connexion of Protection & support shall be broken we shall all fall into a Common Ruin." He apologized for dwelling "on the subject: But my heart is Full." Sometimes he had to "find a Vent for Reflections that are so interesting to every Thing that is near and dear to me, My Fortune, my children, & their children to the latest Posterity; maybe the Cause of Humanity, all depend upon this Grand Question, Are Americans to be slaves or Freemen."[7]

The answer to this question was to come over the next nine years. Associations were formed up and down the eastern seaboard to boycott the importation of British goods, and in Virginia county committees were formed to pressure adherence to the regulations. The mother country responded by removing all new taxes except that on tea. And for a while, there was not much support for the boycott among the wider public. The importation of British products grew. Imports of luxury goods into the Chesapeake in 1770–71 increased a phenomenal 60 percent. But by 1773 conditions quickly worsened.[8]

In the spring of 1773, the royal revenue cutter *Gaspee* was seized and burned off Rhode Island, and a royal commission was appointed with the authority to send any of those involved to England for trial. This development coupled with the Tea Act giving the nearly bankrupt East India Company a virtual monopoly on the sale of tea in the American colonies resulted in 362 casks of tea being thrown into Boston Harbor in December. By the time the assembly met in Williamsburg in May 1774, news had arrived that the port of Boston would soon be closed. Thomas Jefferson remembered that he, Patrick Henry, Richard Henry Lee, Francis Lightfoot Lee, and "3 or 4 other members" proposed a resolution calling for "a day of prayer and fasting" on June 1, the day the port was to be closed and kept shut by "armed force." It was passed with only one dissent, from Attorney General John Randolph, and on May 24 the governor, John Murray, fourth earl of Dunmore, dissolved the assembly.[9]

Events now moved rapidly. Three days later, eighty-nine members of the late House of Burgesses met at Raleigh Tavern and agreed not to import tea and other East India commodities. They also agreed that the Committee of Correspondence, formed a year earlier, should contact the other colonies on the "expediency of appointing delegates" to meet annually in a "general congress" to consider measures that the "united interests of America may . . . require." Subsequently, with only twenty-five members present, it was agreed to inform the other colonies that the Virginia General Assembly had been dissolved and to suggest that a nonimportation agreement was desirable and at some point one against nonexportation. They also announced that the "late representatives" would meet in Williamsburg on August 1. Thirteen members of the leading families signed the May 27 Association: four Lees, three Carters, two Burwells, a Randolph, a Nelson, a Page, and a Harrison. Seven were present at the meeting that followed, and all signed. Two Randolphs, a Corbin, and a Digges did not sign either document, suggesting the beginning of a division in the ranks.[10]

The dissolution of the General Assembly meant that needed legislation had expired, including a fee bill that provided perquisites for county officers— clerks, sheriffs, coroners—and closure of the courts resulted. The council urged Dunmore to call for the election of a new assembly. He was dubious but issued writs for a new election. When the results came in, he found that the new House of Burgesses resembled the old; he prorogued it and continued to do so. It did not meet again until June 1775. There was division in the colony concerning court closure and the nonpayment of debts. But as James Parker bluntly stated, "I believe the whole continent is against taxes without consent." Councillor John Tayloe, no radical, wrote merchant Duncan Campbell that although "I do not sign associations I certainly concur in such measures and I think conducive to the preservation of my country in Liberty & Freedom and judge nonimportation and non-exportation to be materially so considering the Revenue Tobo. brings the crown."[11]

Through June and July freeholders in the counties met to choose and instruct delegates to the August 1 convention. All agreed that taxation without representation was unconstitutional, and most favored nonimportation of British products. If that did not achieve redress within a year, nonexportation should go into effect. One of the addresses made by moderators at the county meetings has survived, that of Thomas Nelson Jr. in York County. Nelson was among the group of younger leaders who had been a "burr" in the side of governors for the past ten years. His remarks were eloquent. Parliament had attacked "what is dearer to Americans than their Lives, their Liberties"; what had taken place in New England was only a prelude "to designs of Parliament upon every Part of this wide extended continent." His audience knew what it was to be a "*Freeman;* you know the blessed Privilege of doing what you will with your own, and you can guess at the misery of those who are deprived of this Right." Which of these conditions "will be your case depends upon your present conduct." Because "Petitions and Remonstrances" had no effect on Parliament, it was time to try "other Expedients" that would make the British "feel the effects of their mistaken and arbitrary Policy." All imports from Britain should be stopped. As for exports, he was doubtful if it was consistent "with Justice, as a People in Debt," to stop them. Stopping imports would be a great inconvenience, but what was inconvenience "when opposed to the loss of Freedom?" Nelson admitted the colonists must "resign the Hope of Making Fortunes," but why should fortunes be made "when they be taken from us at the Pleasure of others?" He and his colleague Dudley Digges joined other delegates in Williamsburg on August 1.[12]

The session lasted six days. The weather was warm, and so were some of the debates. Endorsement of "a general congress of deputies from all the colonies" appears to have caused little or no opposition, nor was there any to the creation of an Association that would attempt to make the mother country overturn "its ill advised Regulations." How this was to be accomplished created a division of opinion. But the delegates finally agreed to nonimportation of "Goods,

Wares or Merchandise . . . Medicines excepted" after November 1. If grievances were not redressed, nonexportation would be imposed on August 10, 1775. Enforcement was to be carried out by county committees. It was also agreed that whatever "Alterations and Additions" the Virginia delegates supported at the General Congress would be "strictly observed." Seven delegates were elected on August 5, and they included old and new leadership. Peyton Randolph, Richard Bland, Benjamin Harrison, and Edmund Pendleton represented the older leaders, while Richard Henry Lee, George Washington, and Patrick Henry were from those who had emerged in the 1760s. Thomas Jefferson and Thomas Nelson Jr. were close runners-up. The Virginians joined delegates from other colonies in Philadelphia in early September.[13]

Randolph, Harrison, and Lee were from the elite families. Some fifteen family members signed the Association, but there was no Beverley, Byrd, Corbin, Custis, Grymes, Jenings, Lewis, Lightfoot, Ludwell, Page, Robinson, Tayloe, or Wormeley among them. Five from the group were council members. Richard Corbin, as early as 1766, opposed taxes levied by Parliament but thought it had the right to do so. John Tayloe was a supporter of the Association, as were John Page and John Page Jr. Secretary Thomas Nelson, the senior member of the council, well may have been in favor of it, but there is no indication that he gave public support, as his nephew Thomas Nelson Jr. was doing. Dunmore was to say later that the older Nelson was one who took "care to giving offense to anyone." But the lines were being drawn. William Byrd III, all of the Corbins, and the Wormeleys supported the government. Attorney General John Randolph, younger brother of Peyton Randolph, was the only member of that family to remain loyal. The Grymes family was divided. Some like Robert Carter of Nomini Hall and John Tayloe ultimately withdrew from politics but did not oppose the colony's leadership. Robert Beverley was in favor of nonimportation but would have to be characterized as neutral. The Lewis family would emerge as patriots but were not among the leadership. The Robinsons had little political influence after the death of Speaker John Robinson, as was the case of the Lightfoots after the death of Philip Lightfoot II in 1748. The same was true of the Custis family after the death of John Custis IV in 1749. The male portion of the Jenings family left the colony in the 1720s. Philip Ludwell III went to England in 1760 and died in London in 1767. So, for various reasons, six of the twenty-one families had little or no political influence. And of the three who did, not counting the attorney general, all were opposed to the activities of the August convention. Of the fifteen that signed the Association, eight were from the Northern Neck: four Lees, three Carters, and a Fitzhugh. And it was the Lees, especially Richard

Henry and Francis Lightfoot, who brought energy to the protest movement. Their brothers William and Arthur, who were in England, kept them informed of developments there and fueled this energy. To the south the leadership was less aggressive except for Thomas Nelson Jr.[14]

Throughout the summer and fall of 1774, support for resistance to British measures appears to have been almost unanimous. Among the leadership there was little dissent except for some division in the council. An indication of the unanimity of Virginians can be found in the functioning of the county committees. Representative from eight of the elite families served on committees in twelve tidewater counties and one county in the piedmont. One demonstration of unanimity occurred in late October when it was learned that London merchant John Norton's ship *The Virginia* included tea in its cargo. A group of York County inhabitants led by Thomas Nelson Jr. boarded the vessel and deposited two half chests of tea into the York River. News of the incident reverberated around the colony. British mercantile firms were advised not to "evade the agreements entered into." Merchant James Russell was warned, "For god sakes don't permit any Tea or other goods to come in any of your ships." Gunpowder would be "winked at."[15]

The First Continental Congress convened in Philadelphia on September 5 and continued in session until October 16. Peyton Randolph, who had been Speaker of the Virginia House of Burgesses for eight years, was elected president. Over the next seven weeks, much was accomplished, including agreement on equal voting rights for each colony and a bill of rights that among other things denied the right of Parliament to legislate with respect to the internal affairs of the colonies. A Continental Association was also approved that resembled that of Virginia. If objectionable legislation was not revoked, nonexportation would begin after September 1, 1775. The Virginia delegation played a significant role in the deliberations.[16]

Dunmore continued to prorogue the assembly, and that made another convention necessary to elect delegates to the Second Continental Congress that was to meet on May 5. Peyton Randolph, moderator of the first convention, called for an election of delegates from "the several counties and corporations" to meet in Richmond on March 20, 1775. It met in Henrico Parish Church, now Saint John's Church in Richmond. Attendance was good, and ultimately 120 delegates were present. Fifteen members of the leading families were there, eight from the Northern Neck and others from counties between the Rappahannock and James rivers, including Peyton Randolph, Benjamin Harrison, and Thomas Nelson Jr. Four members represented the Lee family. Richard Henry

and Francis Lightfoot Lee arrived in Richmond as especially strong supporters of the Association. There were also new faces, as seventeen of the delegates
had never served before, and another twenty-seven had not attended the first
convention. Peyton Randolph was elected president, and the proceedings of
the Continental Congress were endorsed. Then on March 23 a memorial from
Jamaica asserting colonial rights but pledging nonresistance was approved. This,
to many, was too moderate a response, and Patrick Henry proposed a series of
resolves, including one stating "that a well regulated militia . . . is the natural
strength and only security of a free Government." Such militias rendered it unnecessary "for the Mother Country to keep among us . . . any standing Army,"
which was "always subversive of the Quiet, and dangerous to the Liberties of the
People." The governor had not called the assembly, and laws crucial to the "Defence of the Country" had expired or would soon expire. It was necessary "that
the colony be put in a posture of Defence." He then asked that a committee
be appointed "to prepare a plan for embodying, arming and disciplining such
number of men" that might be sufficient to defend the colony.[17]

Debate over the resolves was intense, and there was opposition from some
who thought such action precipitate. Henry again rose and delivered a impas-
sioned address. Accounts vary as to what he said. James Parker reported that he
"called the K[ing] a Tyrant, a fool and a tool of the ministry" and said "he could
not have been more completely scurrilous if he had been possessed of John
Wilkes' Vocabulary." But whether the address was a harangue or an eloquent
oration ending with "Give me liberty or give me death," there was substantial
opposition. Richard Henry Lee, Thomas Jefferson, and Thomas Nelson Jr. came
to Henry's aid. Nelson was especially effective, stating "that if any British troops
should be landed within the county of which he was lieutenant, he would obey
none, which forbid him to summon his militia and repel invaders at the water
edge." Even with their help, the resolves passed by only the slimmest of mar-
gins; few votes would have changed the outcome. Peyton Randolph then appointed a committee that included opponents to the resolves, but Henry was
chairman and Richard Henry Lee, listed second, presumably was vice-chairman.
Plans were approved to strengthen the militia and to recommend that counties
form and train "Volunteer companies of infantry and troops of horse." Also approved were provisions for equipping and supporting the militia and volunteers.
Delegates were also elected to represent the colony at the meeting of the Second Continental Congress, the same group who represented the colony at the
first meeting.[18]

The show of support demonstrated by those who opposed Henry's resolves suggests that a good many Virginians hoped, as one said, to avoid taking up arms "against King & People whom we have been taught from our infancy to respect." But Dunmore's actions soon dashed that hope. He, along with all the other colonial governors, had received two instructions from Lord Dartmouth ordering measures to apprehend any gunpowder "or any sort of Arms, or Ammunition" that might be imported and to prevent elections of delegates to the Second Continental Congress. In the wake of these instructions and the convention's decision to place the colony in a "Posture" of defense, he decided to seize the colony's powder supply stored in the public magazine in Williamsburg. News also was filtering in from the north of the failed British attempt to seize the Massachusetts leaders as well as gunpowder at Lexington and Concord. So when on the early morning of April 21 the governor had marines from a nearby British naval vessel remove fifteen half barrels of powder from the magazine, the response all over the colony was strong.[19]

The situation rapidly deteriorated, and ultimately Patrick Henry with 150 volunteers marched on Williamsburg to force payment for the powder. Receiver General Richard Corbin, a supporter of Dunmore, sent Henry a bill of exchange for £330 that he refused to accept. But he did accept a signed note from Thomas Nelson Jr., and Corbin agreed to reimburse Nelson. Henry then sent the volunteers home. From this point on it was all downhill. The only support Dunmore had was from four council members: Richard Corbin, John Camm, Ralph Wormeley, and William Byrd III. John Page and Philip Ludwell Lee were now dead, and John Tayloe and Robert Burwell had ceased to attend. President Thomas Nelson and John Page Jr. were in opposition. Robert Carter of Nomini Hall, who stayed in Williamsburg through most of June participating in council business, remained quiet but supported the protest movement. The governor now had few he could recommend to fill council vacancies. For the remainder of May, an uneasy calm settled over Virginia, and the governor, extremely uneasy, reported he had shut himself in and made "a garrison of my house, expecting every moment to be attacked."[20]

Dunmore had called for the assembly to meet on August 11, 1774, and it was prorogued until June 1, 1775, to consider Lord North's plan of reconciliation. The proposal promised that Parliament would not tax any colony if it would, through its own assembly, provide funds necessary for defense and administration. Parliament, however, would specify how much was needed. When the assembly convened, seventeen members of the elite families were present. Peyton

Randolph had returned from Philadelphia to assume his role as Speaker of the House. A committee was appointed to prepare a response to the plan. It included four members of the families: Henry Lee, Thomas Nelson Jr., Francis Lightfoot Lee, and Charles Carter of Stafford County. The assembly then proceeded with its regular business, but disturbing events interrupted. On the evening of June 3, several young men broke into the public magazine to obtain arms and were injured by a device allegedly designed by Dunmore. The Burgesses appointed a committee to inspect the magazine, but the governor denied it access. The council then informed the lower house that a detachment of marines and sailors from His Majesty's ship *Fowey,* anchored in the York River, was expected at the Governor's Palace. Dunmore denied that he had requested them but, citing "constant danger," moved himself and his family to the *Fowey.* The assembly rejected the plan of reconciliation, and after the governor refused its requests that he return, the House of Burgesses adjourned on June 14. It would not meet again.[21]

The governor sent his family to England on June 29 while he remained on the *Fowey* in the York River. Only a few among the leadership remained loyal. Richard Corbin worked to bring about reconciliation. The king had offered Dunmore "discretionary" leave to return to England. Unknown to most Virginians was the further provision that if Dunmore accepted, Corbin was to serve as lieutenant governor with full powers. Corbin's eldest son, Richard, already had decided to leave for Great Britain, which he did in August. Gawin Corbin, a younger son, was the last person appointed to the council. Ralph Wormeley Jr., distressed with the activities of the June assembly, left Williamsburg for his home, Rosegill. And William Byrd III, who already was held in ill repute because of his perceived advocacy of "ministerial power," wrote his old commander Sir Jeffrey Amherst in July that he was "ready to serve His Majesty with my life and fortune." Attorney General John Randolph, who in the previous year had written a pamphlet counseling moderation, visited Dunmore in late August in Norfolk. A month later he advertised his estate for sale, and in October he departed with his wife and two daughters for England, never to return. By then his son, Edmund, was serving as an aide to Washington in Boston. Early in the next year, John Randolph Grymes, whose father had been a member of the council, joined Dunmore and later served with Simcoe's Queen's Rangers. He eventually went to England and married his cousin Susanna, the daughter of John Randolph. He was in London as late as 1791 functioning as a merchant but later returned to Virginia. His nephew Benjamin, who remained in Virginia, appears to have shared his views. These were the most conspicuous of those among the elite families who were loyal. If there were others, they remained quiet. Robert Beverley, who denied the right of Parliament to tax Americans, "to remove us from out of our vicinage for Tryal, or . . . burden us with oppressive Laws or Regulations," thought it a mistake to leave the British Empire. He considered himself a "true Patriot" but did not participate in the protest movement or its aftermath.[22]

The Third Virginia Convention met in Richmond on July 17 with seventeen members of the leading families present. Peyton Randolph was elected president. Plans were developed to provide for and equip a regular armed force to defend the colony. Most importantly, in the place of an executive, an eleven-member Committee of Safety was elected to manage military and civilian affairs when the convention was not in session. Edmund Pendleton was elected its president and John Page Jr. vice president. Two other members of the elite families, Dudley Digges and Thomas Ludwell Lee, were also chosen. John Page Jr.'s election suggests a subtle shift away from Pendleton's more conciliatory stance. This movement is also seen in the election of a new delegation to the Continental Congress that included Richard Henry Lee, Thomas Nelson Jr., and Francis Lightfoot Lee. Peyton Randolph died in October, leaving George Wythe and Benjamin Harrison to represent the more moderate bent at this point.[23]

The convention completed its business on August 26, and it would not meet again until December 1. The first steps had been taken that would lead to independence, despite the fact that many hoped that reconciliation was still possible. Dunmore's activities through the following months diminished such hopes. He had moved to Portsmouth where he took and armed two merchant vessels. Two royal naval vessels supported this small fleet, and sixty British regulars from Florida joined him. By late September he shut down the *Virginia Gazette* of Norfolk and began seizing arms and ammunition in the area. The Committee of Safety sent the newly formed Second Virginia Regiment, under Colonel William Woodford, to the Norfolk area where the British were having some success against local militia. Then on November 7 Dunmore decided to declare martial law and ordered all who were able to bear arms "to resort to His Majesty's STANDARD" or be considered "Traitors." He also declared that he would free "all indented Servants, Negroes or others" who joined "His Majesty's Troops." The governor had done what Virginia slave owners had feared, and it sent a shock through the colony. Dunmore, with a force of British regulars, occupied Norfolk on November 25 and began to fortify the city. By this time the Virginia regiment was approaching the city; it was attacked by the British at Great Bridge on the Elizabeth River, but the Virginians repulsed them, killing

fourteen and wounding forty-eight. Dunmore then decided to abandon Norfolk, and Woodford occupied the city on December 14. By early January most
of Norfolk was burned, partly from British activity but largely from that of the
Virginia forces.[24]

In the midst of all this military activity, the Fourth Virginia Convention met
in Richmond on December 1. The elite families were again well represented.
Edmund Pendleton was elected president, and it was decided to reconvene in
Williamsburg on December 5. William Byrd III, who was not a member of the
convention, did an amazing about-face, his mind changed by the governor's
proclamation offering freedom to slaves who would join him. Byrd had com-
manded Virginia forces during the war with France, and he now offered his services to the convention as commander of the Third Virginia Regiment, but he
evidently was not trusted, and his offer was rejected. The convention stayed in
session until January 20, 1776, passing ordinances, not laws, to deal with a wide
variety of needs and problems including providing for additional troops for
the armed forces and their supply. County government was reactivated, as was
the Committee of Safety. Nine of those who served previously on the committee were reelected, but the vote tally was different. Dudley Digges received the
most votes, and John Page Jr. was in second place. Pendleton, who earlier had
received the most votes, was now ranked fourth. This may suggest a shift toward
a more vigorous prosecution of the war. But Pendleton was reelected president
of the committee, and this combined with his reelection as president of the
convention indicates that moderation still had strong appeal. The delegates to
the Continental Congress remained the same. Three of them, Richard Henry
Lee, Thomas Nelson Jr., and Francis Lightfoot Lee, were among those whom
Governor Fauquier had described a decade earlier as "Young, hot, and Giddy
members." Together with Jefferson they formed a group who had moved to a
position in which they thought independence was inevitable. George Wythe
and Benjamin Harrison reached that point by March 1776. The convention had
not gone that far. Edmund Randolph best described its position as it adjourned:
it had closed "without expressing any yearning for independence; and yet they
had ascended an eminence from which independence was visible. . . . An army
had been levied. The regal government had been laid aside; Virginia had exercised the rights of nation, with reference only to the power granted by conventions. Still, if the most influential members of those bodies had in terms moved
for independence, the exceptions would have been few."[25]

The direction of Virginia affairs from January 21 until May 5 was in the
hands of the Committee of Safety. It met almost daily, working to raise troops

and supply them. Dunmore was still present and through Richard Corbin urged that the colony accept the king's offer of amnesty if Virginia's leaders would restore the colony "to its allegiance To the Free Exercise of its Trade & Commerce and to the same protection and Security, as if such province or Colony had never revolted." Pendleton replied to Corbin that the committee "was not authorized, or inclined to intermeddle in the mode of negotiation." That was the role of the Continental Congress. Even by late April, Pendleton and Robert Carter Nicholas thought there was still the possibility of reconciliation. Some like Patrick Henry thought the first step should be an alliance with a foreign power, preferably France or Spain. It was clear that some of the leadership had to be convinced that there was no alternative to declaring independence. And it was three members of the elite families, joined by others like Thomas Jefferson, who worked diligently to convince the hesitant. Francis Lightfoot Lee and Richard Henry Lee with Thomas Nelson Jr., all delegates to the Continental Congress, led the way. Early on Nelson wrote John Page that if "terms should be proposed they will savour so much of despotism that America cannot accept them." Francis Lightfoot Lee told Landon Carter that "Our Late King & his Parliament having declared us rebels & Enemies . . . have effectually decided the question for us, whether or no we shou'd be independent." His brother took on the task of convincing Patrick Henry. He reminded Henry of British actions over the past twelve years. Virginia must take the lead, and others would follow. As for a European alliance, it would come more easily if "we take decisive steps now . . . for the security of America." Nelson added weight to the argument in a letter to a delegate, almost certainly Henry, in which he stated that there was no need to determine the opinions of France and Spain before acting. France would benefit from an American declaration of independence, and fear that a British offer of additional territory might divert it from supporting the colonies was "chimerical and contrary to the settled policy of the court of Louis XVI." The "people," he added, except for a few, "cry out for this declaration." A "man of your excellent discernment need not be told how dangerous it would be to . . . dally with the spirit or disappoint the expectations of the bulk of the people."[26]

On May 6 delegates to the Fifth Virginia Convention gathered in Williamsburg and began deliberations. It was a changed group, for out of the 126 delegates, 46 were new members. Some former members were now in the military, ministers could no longer serve, and some were absent because they had accepted positions that disqualified them. Others chose not to run or were not reelected. Charles Carter of Corotoman had decided to retire from public life, but surprisingly in Richmond County a man whom Landon Carter described as a "worthless though impudent fellow" defeated Francis Lightfoot Lee, and another he thought was a "silly though good natured fool" defeated Robert Wormeley Carter. He worried that "this Present Convention abounds with too many inexperienced creatures" whose understanding of what independence involved was severely limited. And he was not sure that "mode we are in" would "Preserve Justice, Order, Peace and Freedom." The creation of five new western counties since 1770 had brought new faces. In general, the members were a mirror image of those of the soon-to-be-elected lower house of the legislature, whom Roger Atkinson said were "not quite so well dressed, not so politely Educated, nor so highly born" as members of "some Assemblies have formerly been" but they were "full as honest, less intriguing, more sincere." Nevertheless, thirteen representatives of the elite families were reelected, and some were to play important roles in the successful deliberations of this last convention.[27]

The only committee that was appointed was Privileges and Elections with expanded authority. It included five members of the leading families: William Fitzhugh, Richard Henry Lee, Richard Lee, Thomas Ludwell Lee, and Thomas Nelson Jr. Edmund Pendleton was again elected president, and after reminding the convention that it was faced with "subjects of the most important and interesting nature," he urged "calmness Unanimity and diligence." But various matters intervened, and the debate did not begin until May 14. Among the issues that had to be dealt with was what to do about Ralph Wormeley Jr. An intercepted letter had indicated that he would reluctantly join Dunmore if ordered to do so. Wormeley was apprehended, and the Committee of Safety had placed him under a £10,000 bond with an order not to associate with the enemy or leave the colony. But when the convention opened, the delegates ordered that he be brought to Williamsburg. Once there, he pleaded for forgiveness, promising to "conduct himself conformably to the measures and ordinances of this honbl. House." Instead, it was ordered that he be "confined" to his father's estate in Berkeley and Frederick counties until the convention was assured of his "contrition and future good behavior." The delegates were in no mood to tolerate dissent.[28]

The debate on the question of independence began on Tuesday, May 14. Three resolutions were presented; the strongest was from Patrick Henry and was presented by Thomas Nelson Jr. Henry had been hesitant, but he was no political novice, and it was evident that he would lose support if he did not lead the movement. Nelson had been squarely behind independence for months, and Henry asked him to present the resolution "That our delegates in Congress be enjoined in the strongest most positive manner to exert their ability in procuring an immediate, clear and full Declaration of Independency." Edmund Randolph was present, and he described the scene well.

> Nelson affected nothing of oratory, except what ardent Feelings might inspire, and characteristic of himself, he had No fears of his own which to temporize, and supposing That others ought to have none, he passed lightly over the difficulties of procuring military stores and the inexperience of officers and soldiers, but pressed a declaration of independence upon what, with him, were incontrovertible grounds; that we were oppressed; had humbly supplicated a redress of grievances, which had been refused with insult; and to turn from battle against the sovereign with the cordiality of subjects was absurd.

Henry then rose to support the resolution, closing with the prediction that the colonies, like the children of Israel, would reach their goal in "the promised land." Robert Carter Nicholas responded, arguing that the resolutions were premature, but he was in a distinct minority. It was left to Edmund Pendleton to take the three resolutions and compose a compromise acceptable to all. He presented his version the next day. It asserted that the Virginia delegates "in the General Congress be instructed to propose that respectable body to declare the United Colonies free and independent states. Absolved of all allegiance to or dependence upon, the Crown or Parliament of Great Britain." The 112 delegates present unanimously agreed to this statement. Soon thereafter Nelson left for Philadelphia with the resolution in his care. There, on June 7, speaking for the Virginia delegation, Richard Henry Lee moved that the "United Colonies" declare themselves independent from Great Britain.[29]

The Virginia Convention then began to work on a declaration of rights and a plan of government. A committee with thirty-one members was appointed to take on the task. Five members of the leading families—Randolph, Dudley Digges, Henry Lee, Thomas Ludwell Lee, and Mann Page Jr.—were on the committee. One of the group, George Mason, commented that it was "overcharged with useless Members" who would produce "hetrogenious, jarring & unintelligible ingredients" unless prevented "by few Men of Integrity & Abilitys." Edmund Randolph, also a member, agreed, stating there was an "ardor for political notice rather than a ripeness in political wisdom." But Mason, he said, "swallowed up all the rest by fixing the grounds and plan." By May 27 the committee submitted a declaration of rights to the whole convention, and after much debate it was approved on June 12. It was America's first such document asserting individual liberties. By this time Dunmore, who had received no support from the main British army, decided to leave Virginia.[30]

The convention now turned its attention to the completion of a constitution. This was accomplished by June 29. The constitution created a bicameral General Assembly composed of a House of Delegates and a Senate, and it was here the power resided. The House of Delegates, where all legislation was to originate, was the most powerful body, and only it could amend money bills. The Senate could only approve, reject, or amend legislation. Senators were elected from districts that included several counties. Although it became a more representative body than the old Council of State, 60 percent of the senators came from wealthier families. The executive was composed of a governor who was elected annually by the General Assembly, could serve no more than three terms successively, and was assisted by a Council of State elected by the legislature. The governor could not prorogue, adjourn, or dissolve the legislature, but with advice of the council he could call it back into session early. The executive had no veto power. There was also an independent judiciary elected by the General Assembly. It was an amazingly republican form of government. As one contemporary later commented, the representatives in the assembly "are the People's men and the people are in general right." Edmund Randolph was to observe that "the convention gave way to their horror of a powerful chief magistrate." The House of Burgesses had emerged as a powerful force over the preceding twenty-five years. That the House of Delegates was now where the power resided is not surprising; the resentment of the colonial governors can be seen in the new weak executive.[31]

There was, interestingly enough, little reaction to the constitution. Landon Carter was concerned that the legislature would "usurp all the power" and feared that "men of real distinction" would not have sufficient influence. But he much preferred this form of government to the one that preceded it. George Mason, the principal author of the constitution, had similar concerns, and he and Carter probably represented the views of the upper classes. This perspective can be seen in the election of a governor that came immediately after the approval of the constitution. Early in May, Richard Henry Lee had suggested to Edmund Pendleton that Secretary Thomas Nelson would be a good choice for governor because "he possesses knowledge, experience and has already been in a dignified station." But when the voting took place, Patrick Henry received 60 votes to Nelson's 45. Most of Nelson's support probably came from the tidewater where the majority of the elite lived. The old families, though not without continued influence, no longer possessed the political power that they once had.

That they understood this is not clear. They were concerned about the presence of so many new members, not a few from western counties, in the convention and the new House of Delegates, who were, in Landon Carter's words, "inexperienced." And there were fears about their economic status in the years to come, as Thomas Nelson Jr.'s view that they should "resign the Hope of Making Fortunes" suggests. They were still very much present; of the seven Virginia signers of the Declaration of Independence, four were from the elite families: Benjamin Harrison, Richard Henry Lee, Francis Lightfoot Lee, and Thomas Nelson Jr. But the decline did continue. They had lived beyond their means too long, a process that had begun for some before 1730. It gained momentum with the consumer revolution, and by 1783 most of the families had lost the independence they so much valued.[32]

Symbolic of this decline is William Byrd III. He committed suicide on the night of January 1 or early morning of January 2, 1777. Unable to escape an enormous debt and unwilling to give up an extravagant lifestyle, he long since had lost the independence so important to him. He also had found it difficult to decide where his allegiances lay as the Revolution approached. Thinking first that the decision to leave the empire was a mistake, he offered his services to the British forces in America; but when Governor Dunmore freed all slaves who would join him, Byrd changed his mind and made similar offers to Virginia and the Continental Congress. Rejected by both, he saw that his world had collapsed, and he took his life.[33]

Byrd's case, although early and extreme, foreshadowed the ultimate fate of most of the elite families, who, victims of their own improvidence and incompetence, had lost their wealth and power by the end of the eighteenth century. Over the past thirty years, their increasing indebtedness to the British mercantile community threatened their economic status. Most of them had been commercially oriented, but the increasing dominance of British mercantile firms in Virginia eroded that source of income. Land speculation proved to be no substitute. Further, many did not bring to plantation management the necessary attention and hard work, qualities that were more evident in earlier generations. At the same time they had become accustomed to a lifestyle that was difficult to maintain, and the growing availability of goods only made extravagance more tempting. Finally, as the population increased and more counties were formed across the Blue Ridge Mountains and beyond, and as the protest against British actions grew, they felt their political influence declining. The election of Patrick Henry as the state's first governor points to the change that was taking place.

Most of the elite leadership, despite their various concerns, supported independence. William Byrd's friend Robert Munford, who had represented Mecklenburg County in the House of Burgesses from 1765 to 1775, was one of those who were alarmed in the period before independence about "the intemperate warmth displayed by the people" and hoped to avert "the evils of civil war." Munford's lukewarm approach to the protest movement led to his exclusion from Virginia's Revolutionary conventions, and although he ultimately supported the American cause, his concerns about republican government remained. After serving briefly in 1780–81 in the House of Delegates, he voiced worry about the decline of "educated and discerning men" in the new government by writing a play titled *The Patriots*. As Michael McDonnell has explained, its "underlying message . . . was that men like Munford could no longer claim legitimacy for their authority through their connections, wealth, education, or values." He despaired of the fact that "petty and ignorant men" were now in control. As the war came to an end, Munford turned to drink. A justice of the peace, he had to resign his position when his "indecent and disorderly" behavior interfered with the business of the court. His "uncommon intemperance" became habitual; there was no hope "of reclaiming him," and he died in December 1783. But Byrd and Munford were exceptional, for most of the old leadership made their peace, some perhaps grudgingly, with the changing world then emerging.[34]

The political impact on them was not immediately evident. They continued to have significant representation in the House of Delegates in the fourteen years after 1776, roughly equal to what they had in the House of Burgesses from 1770 to 1775. Their numbers ranged from a low of eight in 1776 to a high of fourteen in 1788. They continued to serve as chairmen of important working legislative committees despite the fact that they were dramatically outnumbered as twenty-six new counties were formed to the west between 1750 and 1770 and an additional nineteen counties by 1790. Members of the Carter, Harrison, and Lee families were most prominent, but Burwells, Nelsons, Pages, and Randolphs also were present. A total of forty-nine members of the families served in the lower house; all but seven came from the Northern Neck; the adjacent counties of Spotsylvania, Caroline, and Middlesex; and other tidewater counties to the south. Benjamin Harrison V served as Speaker of the House of Delegates three times and Richard Henry Lee once. In the less powerful Senate, the Lee family was most prominent, followed by Carters, Fitzhughs, Harrisons, Lewises, Nelsons, Pages, and Randolphs. With the exception of Thomas Mann Randolph, who briefly represented a piedmont bloc of counties, all the remainder came from the tidewater or the Northern Neck. Nathaniel Harrison was the only member to serve briefly as Speaker in the Senate. Four of the first six governors came from the elite families: Thomas Nelson Jr., Benjamin Harrison V, Edmund Randolph, and Beverley Randolph. There was also representation on the Council of State—ten members from nine of the families—but other than Beverley Randolph's seven years, service was brief. Five Lees served in the Continental Congress, followed by a Fitzhugh, a Nelson, a Harrison, a Page, and a Randolph. Ten family members served in the Convention of 1788 that ratified the Constitution. Interestingly enough, two of those in attendance were English-educated Francis Corbin and Ralph Wormeley Jr., who came from Loyalist families and represented Middlesex County. They voted to ratify the Constitution, as did all but Benjamin Harrison V and Edmund Custis. Their votes in the House of Delegates in the 1780s and support of ratification suggest their political bent: to defend creditors, abide by the Treaty of Paris with some reservations, take a moderate approach to Loyalists, and despite poor economic conditions, support the collection of taxes. Those who voted most consistently on these matters were Francis Corbin of Middlesex, William Fitzhugh of Stafford, Nathaniel Nelson of York, and Mann Page of Spotsylvania. There was, predictably, some public reaction against these "men of family" who were viewed as hating "republicanism" and considering themselves a "superior species of people; and entitled by virtue of their riches to superior and exclusive advantages." A "Republican" voiced his opposition to Loyalists in poetry.

> Where then is the wretch who'd change Congress for Kings
> And degrade all our friends to pitiful Things
> Let *feathers* and *tar* be that fellow's lot
> Call him *Tory* and let his name be forgot[35]

The continuing important political role that the elite families played did not mask the fact that economic conditions in the state were bad for most of the 1780s. There was a brief resurgence of prosperity in 1783–84 after the ports were opened to British commerce. But by the fall of 1785 the bottom had fallen out of the tobacco market, and Great Britain had banished American trade from its West Indian colonies, resulting in depressed conditions for the remainder of the decade. Debts to British creditors loomed large. Early in the decade Virginians felt that these debts should be repaid, but the failure of the British to return slaves seized during the war and their refusal to remove military posts from the Northwest Territory caused attitudes to harden against payment. Many members of the elite families were heavily indebted. Some data on the amounts owed exist for seventeen (table 4). Reasonably accurate information is available for four Randolphs, Thomas Nelson Jr., and, from the second group of families, Archibald Cary. Most of these people believed that British debts should be repaid, although without interest for the war years. The opposition to debt payment, in 1784, 1785, and 1787, came largely from the region south of the James River. There was some support for reopening the courts for these debt cases, but that did not happen until 1790 after the establishment of the new national government.[36]

Virginians hoped that after the Treaty of Peace was signed, economic conditions would improve. But in addition to low tobacco prices and reduced West Indian trade, heavy debt, high taxes, and shortage of money made for hard times in the Old Dominion. William Lee, after his return home in 1783 from many years abroad as a merchant and diplomat, was shocked to find how much the war had changed the Virginia he remembered. "I find myself," he reported, "as much at loss & perhaps more so than I should at Constantinople so much has the late accursed war altered both men and things." Money was so scarce that there was little demand for the luxury items he had brought from Europe. We "have not only had a revolution in Political Government, but also in many people's private circumstances," merchant William Allason reported to a Glasgow correspondent. Ralph Wormeley Jr. explained that there was

little money in the country, no price for lands, none for Negroes, except on credit, and laws of so little Stability, that every action of political judicature affairs Suspended, until some promise of permanency may be given to ourselves—men who have property and especially wish to pay their debts by parting with some of it cannot at present effect their purposes. So extremely Scarce is money, and so precarious and loose are things that there is little reliance on future payments, property may be dispersed of and nothing gotten.

St. George Tucker agreed with Wormeley's view. There was no money for people to buy land. The lands east of the mountains had been cleared but not improved so that "fresh lands of far inferior quality" were as productive. He estimated that "barely one tidewater planter in twenty" made enough "for the support of himself and his family." Robert Beverley confirmed that the "situation in the Country continues as lamentable as ever" with the scarcity of cash and the lowness "of our commodities intolerable."[37]

These problems were not so much evident when the marquis de Chastellux

Table 4   ESTIMATED DEBT OF SELECTED MEN IN THE 1780S

Debtor	*Debt*
Robert Burwell	£4,000 partial
Lewis Burwell	£7,000 est.
Charles Carter	£1,241 partial
Edward Carter	£5,714 est.
Archibald Cary	£50,000
Philip Grymes estate	£476 partial
Benjamin Harrison Jr.	£541 +
Thomas Nelson Jr.	£35,000
John Page Jr.	£389 partial
Mann Page	£2,027 partial
John Randolph Jr. (Loyalist)	£3,406 partial
John Randolph of Bizarre	£13,450
Peter Randolph	£18,337
Richard Randolph	£8,266
Ryland Randolph	£6,000
William Randolph	£8,513
Ralph Wormeley	Substantial

Sources: List of Foreign Debtors, Norton Papers, CW; American Loyalist Claims, PRO, T 79/12/30/73; U.S. Circuit Court, Ended Cases, 1797, 1798, 1803, LOV; Harrison Family Papers, 1682–1915, MSS 2485a, 31–33, 34–60, VHS; Gerald S. Cowden, "The Randolphs of Turkey Island: A Prosopography of the First Three Generations, 1650–1806" (Ph.D. diss., College of William and Mary, 1977), except for John Randolph Jr.; Richard Hanson's letters that relate to Archibald Cary, Aug. 22, Dec. 20, 1784, Feb. 8, March 30, April 30, 1787, American Loyalist Claims, PRO, T 79/30; List of Creditors of General Nelson, box 11(1)C, Brock Collection, Huntington Library, San Marino, CA; Emory G. Evans, *Thomas Nelson of Yorktown: Revolutionary Virginian* (Charlottesville, VA, 1975), 191 n. 48; Ralph Wormeley Letter Book, 1783–1800, UVA; Jonathan H. Poston, "Ralph Wormeley V of Rosegill: A Deposed Virginia Aristocrat" (M.A. thesis, College of William and Mary, 1979). It should be added that some of these debts were owed in Virginia.

traveled around the state in 1782. He found the government "democratic but the national character . . . will always be aristocratic." Slavery, he believed, nourished "vanity and sloth" among the people. The only benefit of the "indolence" was that it obliged the public "to rely upon a small group of enlightened citizens," who had led them into revolution. He also observed that these "old families"

were seeing "with pain ... new men occupying distinguished situations in the
army and the magistracy." And some dissipated "their fortunes through gaming,
hunting and horse races." Wanting to "speak of the virtues peculiar to Virginians," Chastellux "found only magnificence and hospitality to mention." Generosity he could not add, "for they are so strongly attached to their interests." He
did not see, just after the war's end, a decline in "their great wealth" and made no
comment on their heavy debt to British merchants.[38]

Had he had the opportunity to observe Virginia society more closely, he
might have noted that among the upper class in general there had not been much
enthusiasm for offering their services in support of the war effort. Thomas Nelson Jr. found that they were more interested in "accumulating Money" and that
"Public Virtue & Patriotism were sold down to South Quay and there ship'd
off in Tobacco Hogsheads." In the spring of 1778, he began to raise volunteers
for a corps of light cavalry to join Washington's army and serve at their own
expense, but for the remainder of the year he was disappointed to find that he
had no hope of gaining "one hundred" even though "several of the first young
Gentlemen in the Country" had joined "to set the example for others." Early on
the wealthier Virginians, including some members of the elite families, hired
substitutes to serve in their place. In 1780 a new draft law levied a proportional
tax on property to provide bounty money allowing militia to hire recruits. The
greatest protests about its passage came from the wealthy, for as large property
owners they would pay the heaviest tax. And during the "confused crisis" of
1781, with a British army in the state, there were "frequent Balls" and "gallivant-
ing." William Lee commented that the "religion and piety" that had once distinguished Virginians were now replaced by "dissipation, immorality ... and
vice." Edmund Pendleton noted in May 1783 that several vessels "in our ports"
could not be "admitted to entry" until the Treaty of Peace was signed, "to the
great mortification of some Gentlemen who seem to long for the Flesh Pots
of Egypt, particularly some cheese and Porter in a vessel from Ireland." Once
the ports were opened, they were "filled with British goods and British Factors, which affords every excitement to Luxury," an enthusiasm that appeared to
seize "all ranks of people." Despite their heavy debt not a few found it difficult
to change long-held habits. Archibald Cary's debts were so considerable "that
they can never be paid," and he ignored good business practices and kept "no
books." Charles Carter of Stafford inherited a large estate before the war but
squandered it in "whimsical projects." He died in 1797 a "ruined man," and no
British debts had been paid. Cary and Carter were extreme examples, but even
Richard Henry Lee, a more responsible man, could not forgo fine wines and

"other luxuries." When he served as president of Congress in 1785, his "lavish living" impressed all, including John Quincy Adams.[39]

With ratification of the Constitution and the beginning of the new government, the political service of the old leading families declined dramatically. The aftermath of the war and its resulting problems seem to have finally caught up with them. Their membership in the House of Delegates in the decade of the 1790s was at a high of ten in 1790; thereafter it was never above seven (in 1791 and 1793), with a low of three in 1795 and four and five in the remaining years. Twelve families were represented, with Carters, Corbins, Harrisons, Nelsons, Lees, and Pages appearing most frequently. The Digges family was represented twice, and the Fitzhughs, Lightfoots, Randolphs, Tayloes, and Wormeleys once. Membership in the Senate was similarly limited. The families had no Speakers of the House of Delegates in the decade and only one Speaker of the Senate, Ludwell Lee. Henry Lee was the only governor from the elite families in the period.[40]

The trend was to continue into the nineteenth century. Lorraine E. Holland has estimated, using a larger sample than the twenty-one, that of the wealthy families in 1788, 81 percent held local offices that year but by 1860 they held only 14 percent. Similarly, in 1788 73 percent of the group she examined held state and national office, but in 1860 only 15 percent did so. There were only three members from the twenty-one families in the House of Delegates in 1860, and they produced no governor from Thomas Mann Randolph in 1819–22 until Fitzhugh Lee in 1886–91.[41]

The decline in public service was directly related to debt and economic problems. These resulted in the loss of independence so valued by upper-class Virginians. Of necessity, if they were to survive, many were forced to spend more time "attending to business" leaving little time for public service and forcing them, in the nature of things, to spend more time with their families. Further, as Jan Lewis has argued, in this period of economic decline the family offered a comforting retreat. This withdrawal was accompanied by a search for solace in religion, which in an "unstable and painful world" offered the promise of a better one to come in the next. It was inevitable that public service was not so much valued as in the eighteenth century. Such an attitude affected even those who were not poor. Francis Corbin explained that he was not going to run for public office: "I have determined to remain a private citizen, because I consider the *Post of Honor* to be at this time in the private station."[42]

The decline in wealth was even more immediate. It had begun before the Revolution, and by the 1790s it had become most evident. After Richard Henry

Lee died in 1794, his possessions were auctioned off to pay his debts. John Page's political career continued into the nineteenth century; he served in the House of Delegates and Congress and was governor from 1802 to 1805. But by 1792 his affairs were in the hands of trustees who were selling some of his slaves to pay his debts. He died in 1808 leaving his second wife with still unpaid debts and the necessity of selling his magnificent home, Rosewell. Page's friend Thomas Nelson Jr. died in 1789. Most of his substantial debts were paid in the 1790s, but they were so large that his five daughters, who were to receive cash payments from what was left from the sale of property, received, it appears, little or nothing. His daughter Judith, for example, asked St. George Tucker in 1808 for a loan of £200 to open a boardinghouse in Richmond to help her support "the younger part of my family." Earlier, Nelson's son Thomas was almost begging Micajah Crew, who appears to have been renting land and a mill from him, to provide his mother with pork and flour. He told Crew that if he could see "the distresses . . . of a family you once knew in affluence almost reduced to beggary, your heart would bleed."[43]

The difficulties of the Randolph family can be seen in the life of John Randolph of Bizarre and his two surviving sons, Richard and John. Randolph died in 1775 leaving a debt that exceeded £14,000 which St. George Tucker, who married his widow, Frances Bland Randolph, had to manage during the minority of the sons. The young men believed they could prosper as planters despite the picture of economic distress around them. They wanted to live, as they believed as their parents had, entertaining lavishly and importing foreign goods. When Richard died in 1796, his debts were large, and John was left to deal with the problem liquidating part of the property he inherited, a chore which dragged on into the next century.[44]

The problems of the Lee family have been well described by Paul Nagel, who summed them up by saying that "the story of the Lees from 1640 and 1870 seems at times to be little more than a succession of catastrophes." The family's plight is demonstrated by the careers of Henry "Light Horse Harry" Lee (1756–1818) and his younger brother Richard Bland Lee (1761–1827), two young men who grew to maturity during the Revolution. Harry, a brilliant cavalry officer with a strong personality, had little business sense and was frequently irresponsible. Richard fell under his spell; investments went bad, and they borrowed to keep afloat. Unable to pay their debts, they both died insolvent. Stratford Hall, the magnificent home their great-uncle Thomas Lee had built, was sold by Harry's son Henry in 1822. The remainder of the family did not fare so badly, but only the career of Robert Edward Lee, Harry's youngest son, brought back a measure of renown to this once proud family.[45]

Despite their dramatic economic and political decline, Virginia's eighteenth-century elite did maintain a measure of social status, and as time wore on they began to romanticize their past. John Randolph of Roanoke epitomized this view. St George Tucker tried, with no success, to get him and his brother to pursue legal careers. They "believed that the path to prosperity lay in following traditions of the past. The image of the independent planter who grew tobacco and dominated the household powerfully resonated with them" even while they were already witnessing "the collapse of many tidewater families." Richard died heavily in debt, but John persevered and ultimately was a successful planter in the piedmont, confirming his belief that power should be, as in the past, "in the hands of Substantial landholders." Unfortunately for most the land was gone. Upon visiting his birthplace, he found "desolation & stillness as if of death—the fires of hospitality long since quenched—the hearth cold & the parish church tumbling to pieces, not more from natural decay than sacrilegious violence," declaring it to be a "faithful picture of this state from the falls of the great rivers to the seaboard." The "old gentry" had "disappeared." He looked back to a time when "the Nelsons and Pages and Byrds and Fairfaxes" were "living in their palaces, and driving their coaches and sixes; or the good old Virginia gentlemen in the assembly" were "drinking their twenty and forty bowls of rack punches, and madeira and claret in lieu of a knot of deputy sheriffs and hack attorneys each with his cruet of whiskey before him, and a puddle of tobacco spittle between his legs." Such was Randolph's view of things in 1813–14, and for the gentry at least they were not to improve.[46]

In September 1732 William Byrd II visited former governor Alexander Spotswood's "enchanted castle" on the banks of the Rappahannock River in Spotsylvania County. The house was elegantly furnished, tame deer ran around it, "beautiful walks" led down "a shady lane to the landing," and he drank "from a marble fountain that ran incessantly." Over one hundred years later a visitor found this place that "must have merited its name of the Palace," and it was in ruins. A "huge chimney stack of fine brick rears its head amidst a mass of debris." Only one wall remained, a story high, in which he counted "three doors . . . and a long line of windows that look like the eye sockets of a skull." The "appearance is mournful in the extreme." Spotswood died in 1740 heavily in debt "to persons in Great Britain" and Virginia. His children were minors, and despite the efforts of executors who sold land and managed the estate, the debts were not paid, and neither were bequests and an annuity to his wife. When the eldest son, John, reached his majority, he too was unable to pay anything off. At his death he also left a wife and minor children. The assembly passed an act providing that the profits from the sale of what remained of the estate be applied to the "necessary maintenance and education of the children" and that the residue go toward discharging his debts and those of his father. But John's eldest son, Alexander, "was as worthless as [an] eldest son could be." He "lived a little too much 'like a gentle man' spent all he could lay his hands on." Although he soon was unable to get "anymore advances" from "his money lenders," "he continued to keep his seventy hounds and his three coaches and six." Ultimately his lands, stocks, slaves, and "blooded horses" were sold. He lived to an "extreme old age . . . a threadbare gentleman forced . . . to hide himself and his broken pride on a little 400 acre place which . . . in his folly" he had forgotten to "dispose of." His older son, Alexander, moved to Indiana, and the younger one, William, remained on "the little farm his Father's asylum." The visitor met William, who spoke of "the splendor of his forbears whose extravagance he said was like wood whose burning with bright light reduced it to ashes." As the visitor left the ruins of the "enchanted castle," he kicked a pile of leaves and uncovered "a Black snake of the kind called Racer" and remarked that this "was truly the abomination of desolation."[47]

Notes

Abbreviations and Short Titles

ANB   *American National Biography.* 24 vols. New York, 1999.

Cavaliers   Nell M. Nugent et al., eds. *Cavaliers and Pioneers: Abstracts of Virginia Land*
and Pioneers   *Patents and Grants, 1623–1800.* 7 vols. Richmond, 1934–80.

CSP   *Calendar of State Papers, Colonial North America and the West Indies, 1574–*
     1789. 40 vols. London, 1860–1939.

CW   Colonial Williamsburg Foundation, Williamsburg, VA

DVB   *Dictionary of Virginia Biography.* 3 vols. to date. Richmond, 1998–.

EJC   H. R. McIlwaine et al., eds. *Executive Journals of the Council of Colonial Vir-*
     ginia. 6 vols. Richmond, 1925–66.

FHCC   Foundation for Historic Christ Church, Irvington, VA

Hening,   William Waller Hening, ed. *The Statutes at Large, Being a Collection of All the*
Statutes   *Laws of Virginia from the First Session of the Legislature, in the Year 1619.* 13 vols.
     Richmond et al., 1809–23. Rept. Charlottesville, VA, 1969.

JCTP   *Journals of Commissioners of Trade and Plantations, 1704–1789.* 14 vols. Lon-
     don, 1920–38.

JHB   John Pendleton Kennedy and H. R. McIlwaine, eds. *Journals of the House of*
     Burgesses of Virginia, 1619–1776. 13 vols. Richmond, 1905–15.

JHD   *Journals of the House of Delegates, 1776–1790.* 4 vols. Richmond, 1827–28.

LC   Manuscripts Division of the Library of Congress, Washington, D.C.

LCTP   Lords Commissioners for Trade and Plantations

LJC   H. R. McIlwaine, ed. *Legislative Journals of the Council of Colonial Virginia.* 3
     vols. Richmond, 1918–19. 2d ed., 1979.

LOV   Library of Virginia, Richmond

NYPL   New York Public Library, New York

OED   Compact Edition of *Oxford English Dictionary.* Oxford, 1988.

PRO   Public Record Office, London

RC Diary   Robert Carter Diary, 1722–28, UVA, transcript FHCC

RC Letter   Robert Carter Letter Books, 1723–24, 1727–28, 1728–31, 1731–32, UVA,
Book   transcripts FHCC; July 1723–June 1724, VHS, transcript FHCC; 1728–30,
             transcript VHS. [For recent transcripts, see Edmund Berkeley Jr., ed., "The
             Diary, Correspondence, and Papers of Robert 'King' Carter of Virginia,
             1701–1732," http://etext.virginia.edu]

UVA   University of Virginia Library, Charlottesville

VHS   Virginia Historical Society, Richmond

VMHB   *Virginia Magazine of History and Biography*

WM   Swem Library, College of William and Mary, Williamsburg, VA

WMQ   *William and Mary Quarterly*

INTRODUCTION

1. Louis B. Wright, *The First Gentlemen of Virginia: Intellectual Qualities of the Early Colonial Ruling Class* (rept. Charlottesville, VA, 1964), 2.

2. For example, see Philip Alexander Bruce, *Social Life in Virginia in the Seventeenth Century* (2d ed., Lynchburg, VA, 1927); Thomas Jefferson Wertenbaker, *Patrician or Plebeian: The Origin and Development of Social Classes in the Old Dominion* (Charlottesville, VA, 1910); Bernard Bailyn, "Politics and Social Structure in Virginia," *Seventeenth Century America: Essays in Colonial History,* ed. James M. Smith (Chapel Hill, NC, 1958); Clifford Dowdey, *The Virginia Dynasties: The Emergence of "King" Carter and the Golden Age* (Boston and Toronto, 1969); Carole Shammas, "English Born and Creole Elites in Turn-of-the-Century Virginia," *The Chesapeake in the Seventeenth Century: Essays in Anglo-American Society,* ed. Thad W. Tate and David L. Ammerman (Chapel Hill, NC, 1979); Martin H. Quitt, "Immigrant Origins of the Virginia Gentry: A Study in Cultural Transmission and Innovation," *WMQ* (3), 45 (1988): 629–55.

3. Charles Sydnor, *Gentlemen Freeholders: Political Practices in Washington's Virginia* (Chapel Hill, NC, 1952).

4. Jackson Turner Main, "The One Hundred," *WMQ* (3), 11 (1954): 354–84. For the next twenty families, see chap. 1, n. 1.

5. See Bailyn, "Politics and Social Structure," 106–7; John Rainbolt, "The Alteration in the Relationship between Leadership and Constituents in Virginia, 1660–1720," *WMQ* (3), 27 (1970): 411–34, and "A New Look at Stuart 'Tyranny': The Crown's Attack on the Virginia Assembly, 1676–1689," *VMHB* 75 (1967): 387–406; Warren M. Billings, *Virginia's Viceroy: Their Majesties' Governor General, Francis Howard, Baron Howard of Effingham* (Fairfax, VA, 1991); Warren M. Billings, *A Little Parliament: The Virginia General Assembly in the Seventeenth Century* (Richmond, 2004); Edmund Morgan, *American Slavery, American Freedom: The Ordeal of Colonial Virginia* (New York, 1975), chaps. 14–17.

1. Beginnings

1. David Hackett Fischer, *Albion's Seed: Four British Folkways in America* (New York, 1989), 240–418. The next twenty families are the Armistead, Ballard, Berkeley, Bolling, Bland, Blair, Cary, Churchill, Claiborne, Cocke, Eppes, Farrar, Fauntelroy, Kemp, Mason, Parke, Smith, Scarborough, West, and Willis families. This list results from my own work using Swem, *Virginia Historical Index,* and Bruce, *Social Life in Virginia;* Lyon Gardner Tyler's list of the "F.F.V.s" compiled in 1914–15, in *WMQ* (1), 23 (1915): 277; and lists compiled by Warren Billings in connection with his article "The Growth of Political Institutions in Virginia, 1634–1676," *WMQ* (3), 31 (April 1974): 225–42.

2. Swem, *Virginia Historical Index; Cavaliers and Pioneers,* vol. 1; printed genealogies at VHS and the Library of the Daughters of the American Revolution, Washington, D.C.; Quitt, "Immigrant Origins," esp. 634–39; Gerald S. Cowden, "The Randolphs of Turkey Island: A Prosopography of the First Three Generations, 1650–1806" (Ph.D. diss., College of William and Mary, 1977), chap. 1.

3. Paul C. Nagel, *The Lees of Virginia: Seven Generations of an American Family* (New York, 1990), 8–9; Ludwell Lee Montague, "Richard Lee, the Emigrant, 1613–1664," *VMHB* 62 (1954): 3–49; will of Thomas Stegge, ibid., 48 (1940): 31–34; Marion Tinling, ed., *The Correspondence of the Three William Byrds of Westover, Virginia* (2 vols., Charlottesville, VA, 1977), 3; *DVB,* s.v. "Byrd, William I"; Richard Beale Davis, ed., *William Fitzhugh and His Chesapeake World: Letters and Other Documents* (Chapel Hill, NC, 1963), 7–9, 76n; *VMHB* 28 (1920): 281–83, 29 (1921): 124–25, 244–45, 374–76; Darrett and Anita Rutman, *A Place in Time: Middlesex County, Virginia, 1650–1750* (New York and London, 1984), 50–51.

4. Most of the general data come from Swem, *Virginia Historical Index,* and *Cavaliers and Pioneers.* For Christopher Robinson, see Rutman and Rutman, *Place in Time,* 49–50; *WMQ* (1), 17 (1908–9): 181–88, (2), 1 (1921): 134–36; *VMHB* 3 (1895–96): 2–5n, 7 (1899–1900): 17, 10 (1902–3): 380–82, 16 (1908): 215–17. Maurer Maurer, "Notes on the Honorable Edmund Jenings (1659–1727)," ibid., 52 (1951): 246–61, and "Edmund Jenings and Robert Carter," ibid., 55 (1955): 20–30. For Philip Ludwell, see *WMQ* (1), 19 (1910–11): 199–214; Bruce, *Social Life,* 56; *Cavaliers and Pioneers,* 1:429, 2:63, 185. For Henry Corbin, see Beverley Fleet, *Virginia Colonial Abstracts* (34 vols., rept. Baltimore, 1961), 4:54; Rutman and Rutman, *Place in Time,* 50–51, 243–44; *VMHB* 28 (1918): 281–83, 29 (1919): 124–25, 244–45, 274–78. William Fitzhugh to Oliver Luke, Aug. 15, 1690, Davis, *Fitzhugh,* 279–80.

5. Morgan, *American Slavery, American Freedom,* 336, 404, 407, has the best population figures but see also Wesley Frank Craven, *White, Red, and Black: The Seventeenth-Century Virginian* (Charlottesville, VA, 1971), 25–27, 98–99, and Ben J. Wattenburg, introduction and user's guide, *The Statistical History of the United States from Colonial Times to the Present* (New York, 1976), 1168. For life expectancy, see Gloria Main, *Tobacco Colony: Life in Early Maryland, 1650–1720* (Princeton, NJ, 1982), 13–14; Morgan, *American Slavery, American Freedom,* 158–84. On the character of Virginia society in the seventeenth century, see, for example, ibid., chaps. 8–12; Bailyn, "Politics and Social Structure," 95–96; Richard L. Morton, *Colonial Virginia* (2 vols., Chapel Hill, NC, 1960), vol. 1, chaps. 8–17; Warren Billings, John Selby, and Thad W. Tate, *Colonial Virginia* (White Plains, NY, 1986), chaps. 3–6; Fischer, *Albion's Seed,* 210.

6. Morton, *Colonial Virginia* 1:143; Billings et al., *Colonial Virginia,* 107.

7. John Clayton to Honour'd Doctor, April 24, 1684, Edmund Berkeley and Dorothy Smith Berkeley, eds., *The Reverend John Clayton, a Parson with a Scientific Mind: His Scientific Writings and Other Related Papers* (Charlottesville, VA, 1965), 3–5.

8. Gilbert Chinard, ed., *A Huguenot Exile in Virginia, or Voyages of a Frenchman Exiled for His Religion with a Description of Virginia and Maryland* (New York, 1934), 109–10.

9. William Fitzhugh to Nicholas Hayward, Jan. 30, 1687, June 11, 1688, Davis, *Fitzhugh,* 203–4, 245.

10. Harold Perkin, *The Origins of Modern English Society, 1780–1880* (London, 1969), 18–61; Bruce, *Social Life in Virginia,* chaps. 2–7; Sir William Berkeley, *A Discourse and View of Virginia* [January 1661–62], Warren M. Billings, ed., *The Papers of Sir William Berkeley, 1605–1677* (Richmond, 2007), 161–68. For Nathaniel Bacon's background, see Stephen Saunders Webb, *1676: The End of American Independence* (New York, 1984), 27–28.

11. For council membership, although there are a few errors, see Cynthia Miller Leonard, comp., *The General Assembly of Virginia, July 30, 1619–January 11, 1978: A Bicentennial Register of Members* (Richmond, 1978), xix–xxi.

12. Jon Kukla, *Speakers and Clerks of the Virginia House of Burgesses* (Richmond, 1981), 98–102, 141–43, 144; H. R. McIlwaine, ed., *Members of the Council; and General Court of Colonial Virginia* (2d ed., Richmond, 1979), 200, 224, 250, 257, 272, 312, 336, 383, 411, 503, 504, 516, 518, 523; *EJC* 1:84, 92, 97, 189, 333–34, 364, 511; Maurer, "Notes on the Honorable Edmund Jenings," 241–46; PRO, CO 5/1310, June 8, 1699; Sarah Hughes, *Surveyors and Statesmen: Land Measuring in Colonial Virginia* (Richmond, 1979), chap. 1; Petition of Edmund Jenings to Governor and Council, [1692], Warren Billings, ed., *The Papers of Francis Howard, Baron Howard of Effingham, 1643–1695* (Richmond, 1989), 445–46; Robert Beverley, *The History and Present State of Virginia,* ed. Louis B. Wright (Chapel Hill, NC, 1947), 245–48.

13. Robert Beverley Title Book, MSS 5:9 B4676, VHS; Hening, *Statutes* 3:564–65; *Cavaliers and Pioneers,* vols. 2–3. For Carter and Corbin, see ibid., 1:132, 150, 256, 326, 369, 288, 392, 409, 504, 518, 536, 2:21, 32, 33, 37, 73, 128, 189. Davis, *Fitzhugh,* 373–85; Pierre Marambaud, *William Byrd of Westover, 1674–1744* (Charlottesville, VA, 1971), 25; Martin H. Quitt, *The Virginia House of Burgesses: The Social and Economic Basis of Political Power* (New York, 1989), 64. Quitt confused John Custis II with his father, John Custis I; the latter came with his son to Virginia about 1650 and evidently died before the end of that decade. See Ralph Whitelaw, *Virginia's Eastern Shore* (2 vols., Richmond, 1951), 107–17, 287–89, and *Cavaliers and Pioneers* 1:264, 346, 353. Further, Custis II died Jan. 29, 1696, not in 1695; see *WMQ* (1), 3 (1894–95): 257. W. Stitt Robinson, *Mother Earth: Land Grants in Virginia, 1607–1699* (Charlottesville, VA, 1957), 17–47, esp. 30–40.

14. Col. Nicholas Spencer to Brother Spencer, June 13, 1672, *WMQ* (2), 3 (1923): 134–36; Tinling, *Byrd Correspondence,* 71n; William Byrd to William Blathwayt, Dec. 30, 1687, June 21, 1688, June 12, Oct. 22, 1689, June 9, 1691, Nov. 4, 1692, Feb. 20, 1693, Byrd to Perry & Lane, July 30, 1688, June 10, 1689, July 19, Aug. 8, 1690, Byrd to Governor Effingham, March 6, 1689, July 30, 1690, Byrd to John Povey, July 30, 1690, ibid., 1:74, 84, 86, 99, 105, 109, 112, 166–67, 167n; Governor Effingham to William Blathwayt, April 27, 1687, James II to Effingham, Dec. 4, 1687, Billings, *Papers of Effingham,* 302, 332; *EJC* 1:92, 93, 511; Beverley, *History and Present State of Virginia,* 245; Philip A. Bruce, *Institutional History of Virginia* (2 vols., rept. Gloucester, MA, 1964), 2:599–600; Henry Hartwell to LCTP, Sept. 13, 1697, PRO, CO 5/1309.

15. William Fitzhugh to Capt. Roger Jones, May 18, 1685, to George Luke, Oct. 20, 1690, Davis, *Fitzhugh*, 168–69, 284–90.

16. Beverley, *History and Present State of Virginia*, 247–48; Henry Hartwell to LCTP, Sept. 1697, PRO, CO 5/1309; Helen Hill Miller, *Colonel Parke of Virginia: The Greatest Hector in Town* (Chapel Hill, NC, 1989), 76–79; [Evelyn] to My Lord, n.d. [1693–94], PRO, CO 5/ 1308; council members and those to supply vacancies, April 20, 1696, ibid., 1309; see also Francis Nicholson to LCTP, June 10, 1700, ibid., 1311. For other offices, see ibid, 1310, 119, 121–23; Effingham to William Blathwayt, April 27, 1687, Billings, *Papers of Effingham*, 301–2; *EJC* 1:119, 177, 187, 189, 334–35, 350, 364, 379, 383, 383, 393, 394, 411, 412, 443–45; Kukla, *Speakers and Clerks*. On quitrents, see Bruce, *Institutional History* 2:578; William Byrd to My Lord [Francis Howard, Baron Howard of Effingham], July 20, 1690, to Honoured Sir [William Blathwayt], July 30, 1690, Tinling, *Byrd Correspondence*, 127–30; *EJC* 1:251, 256, 343, 2:114.

17. Merchants were Robert Beverley I, William Byrd I, John Carter I, Henry Corbin, John Custis I, William Fitzhugh, Richard Lee I, John Lewis Jr., Thomas Nelson, John Page I, William Randolph, Christopher Robinson I, and perhaps William Tayloe. Attorneys were Robert Beverley I, John Carter I, Henry Corbin, Edward Digges, William Fitzhugh, Edmund Jenings, Richard Lee I, and John Page I. On Beverley, see Kukla, *Speakers and Clerks*, 141–43; *VMHB* 2 (1894–85): 405–13, 3 (1895–96): 49–50 and n. 13. On Byrd, see Tinling, *Byrd Correspondence*, vol. 1; *DVB*, s.v. "Byrd, William I." For the other merchants and lawyers, see, among other sources, Swem, *Virginia Historical Index*, and McIlwaine, *Minutes of Council and General Court*, vol. 1. William Tayloe's son John was a merchant and his brother Robert was the captain of a merchant vessel. See Laura Croghan Kamoie, "Three Generations of Planter Businessmen: The Tayloes, Slave Labor, and Entrepreneurialism in Virginia, 1710–1830" (Ph.D. diss., College of William and Mary, 1999); W. Randolph Tayloe, *The Tayloes of Virginia and Allied Families* (Berryville, VA, 1965); Stephen Loyde (d. 1711) and John Tayloe I (1687–1747) and John Tayloe II (1721–1779), Account and Letter Book, 1708–11, 1714–78, Tayloe Family Papers, 1650–1970, b1, VHS. Philip Lightfoot, whom I do not include, probably was also a merchant; his son Philip was a leading Yorktown merchant. See Francis Jerdone to Messrs. Buchanan & Hamilton, June 28, 1741, *WMQ* (1), 11 (1902–3): 154.

18. For tobacco prices, see John J. McCusker and Russell Menard, *The Economy of British America, 1607–1689* (Chapel Hill, NC, 1985), 120–21. William Fitzhugh reported to John Cooper, April 18, 1687, that tobacco was selling for 9 shillings 6 pence a hundred pounds, which would amount to 1.14 pence a pound; this seems to have the highest price of the decade. Davis, *Fitzhugh*, 220. Fitzhugh wrote Thomas Clayton, April 26, 1686, that he could ship 200 hogsheads at 460 pounds per hogshead. I have used that figure in computing the number of pounds of tobacco shipped by Byrd and Fitzhugh. On tobacco shipped, see Byrd to Perry & Lane, March 5, 7, June 10, 1689, to Arthur North, March 6, 1689, to John Cary, May 29, 1691, Tinling, *Byrd Correspondence*, 99, 101, 103, 105, 150–51; for wheat and corn and pipe staves, see, for example, Byrd to Sadler & Thomas, Oct. 1686, ibid., 64–65; for gristmills and sawmills, see Byrd to Warren Horsmanden, March 1685, to Perry & Lane, Feb. 2, 1685, Jan. 28, 1689, ibid., 5, 29, 91; for diversity of trade and goods shipped, see Byrd to Perry & Lane, June 21, Dec. 30, 1684/ Jan. 9, March 8, 1686, Dec. 11, 1688, June 23, 1689, to Sadler & Thomas, Feb. 10, Oct. 18, 1686, to John Thomas & Co., Feb. 20, May 29, 1689, to Eliakim Hutchinson, May 29, 1689, Aug. 1, 1690, to Arthur North, March 29, June 5, 1685, to Stephanus Van Cortlandt, Aug. 31, 1691, ibid.,

26, 28–29, 49–50, 58–59, 88–89, 110, 50, 64–65, 95, 105, 103, 132, 31, 41, 163–64. For the slave trade, see above and Byrd to Perry & Lane, April 25, Aug. 25, 1684, June 6, 1685, Nov. 10, 1686, to Thomas Grendon, June 21, 1684, to [?], May 10, 1686, [William Popple] to Byrd, June 10, 1700, ibid., 14–15, 42, 65–66, 23, 60, 183–84, 184n; Walter Minchinton, Celia King, and Peter Waite, eds., *Virginia Slave Trade Statistics, 1698–1775* (Richmond, 1984), 5; Louis B. Wright, "William Byrd and the Slave Trade," *Huntington Library Quarterly* 8 (1945): 379–87. On the search for minerals, see Byrd to Robert Coe, May 20, June 21, 1684, to Perry & Lane, June 21, 1684, June 16, 1688, Tinling, *Byrd Correspondence*, 20, 23, 26, 82; see also Byrd's will, *WMQ* (2), 3 (1923): 246–49, and *VMHB* 58 (1946): 331–39. Early mention of wheat is seen in William Fitzhugh to Mrs. Eleanor Cutt and George Jeffries, Feb. 5, 1683, Davis, *Fitzhugh,* 128–29; on the growth of wheat in seventeenth-century Virginia, see also Fairfax Harrison, *Landmarks of Old Prince William: A Study of the Origins of Northern Virginia* (New York, 1924; rept. Berryville, VA, 1964), 397–99.

19. William Fitzhugh to Dr. Ralph Smith, April 22, 1686, to Madam Susanna Letten, Aug. 8, 11, 1690, to Samuel Jefferson, Feb. 18, 1685, to Thomas Clayton, April 26, 1686, April 8, 1687, to John Taylor and Samuel Chue, April 25, 1692, to Cornelius Serjeant, June 21, 1692, July 23, 1693, to John Cooper, June 5, 1682, and [1692?], to Robert Beverley, May 29, 1682, to Sarah Bland, June 5, 1682, to Ralph Wormeley, June 9, 1683, to Nicholas Hayward, May 20, 1686, April 1, 1689, July 10, 1690, July 23, 1692, to Lord Culpeper, June 25, July 10, [1683], Davis, *Fitzhugh,* 175–76, 177–78, 160–61, 180–83, 299–301, 317, 302–3, 303–4, 126, 307–9, 113–14, 116–17, 152–59, 217, 189–91, 248–50, 269–72, 313–15, 146–47. On Fitzhugh's law practice, see ibid., 93n, 114n. For his stores, see "Inventory of the Estate," Aug. 11, 1703, ibid., 383. Chinard, *Huguenot Exile,* 158.

20. Thomas J. Wertenbaker, *The Planters of Colonial Virginia* (Princeton, NJ, 1922), Rent Roll of Virginia, 1704–5, appendix; Christine A. Jones, comp., *John Carter II of Corotoman, Lancaster County, Virginia* (Irvington, VA, 1978), 30–59, 63–69, and Carter tithables in 1700 compiled by Ron Gephart of the Manuscripts Division of the Library of Congress; will of Richard Lee II, March 3, 1715, microfilm edition of the Lee Family Papers, reel 1, UVA; John Custis IV, estate evaluation, c. 1705–6, Custis Family Papers, 1683–1858, MSS 2 p2205 a1, VHS; will of Lewis Burwell II, Oct. 11, 1710, Berkeley Family Papers, box 1, UVA. For Benjamin Harrison III's land and slave holdings, see Hening, *Statutes* 3:538–40. Christ Church Parish, Lancaster County, Wormeley Estate Papers, 1701–10, 1716, photostats, LOV; [Robert Carter] to [Francis?] Lee, July 15, 1702, ibid.; Chinard, *Huguenot Exile,* 142.

21. Will of Henry Corbin, July 25, 1675, Fleet, *Virginia Colonial Abstracts* 4:54–55; will of Edward Digges, Aug., 28, 1669, *VMHB* 14 (1906–7): 305, and inventory of the estate of Mary Digges Page, Aug. 24, 1692, *WMQ* (1), 12 (1893–94): 208–9; will of Benjamin Harrison II, April 16, 1711, ibid., 10 (1901–2): 109–12; Hening, *Statutes* 3:538–40; *VMHB* 21 (1931): 180–82, 277–83; Carole Shammas, "Benjamin Harrison III and the Authorship of *An Essay upon the Government of the English Plantations in the Continent of America,*" ibid., 84 (1976): 167–73; council members and those to supply vacancies, April 20, 1696, PRO, CO 5/1309; *EJC* 1:394, 398, 2:111, 121, 138; Wertenbaker, *Planters,* appendix; *Cavaliers and Pioneers,* vols. 2, 3.

22. The genealogical information comes from a variety of sources but esp. Swem, *Virginia Historical Index,* and the materials in the Library of the Daughters of the American Revolution, Washington, D.C. See also James L. Anderson, "The Governor's Councils of Colonial

America: A Study of Pennsylvania and Virginia, 1660–1776" (Ph.D. diss., Univ. of Virginia, 1967), 234–35. Nicholson to Board of Trade, Dec. 2, 1701, PRO, CO 5/1312.

23. *JHB,* 1659/60–93, 314; Francis Mckemie to Richard Halsey, Sept. 4, 1706, *WMQ* (1), 21 (1912–13): 281–82; Philip Ludwell to Phill, Dec. 20, 1707, Lee Family Papers, 1638–1867, VHS.

24. For Custis, see Answer to Philip Ludwell's Second Petition to the Committee of Foreign Trade and Plantations, Oct. 16, 1689, Billings, *Papers of Effingham,* 423–24; *JHB,* 1659/60–93, 319–20; *EJC* 1:247–48. On Fitzhugh, see Effingham's Answer to Philip Ludwell's Second Petition; Davis, *Fitzhugh,* 31; *JHB,* 1659/60–93, 306; *EJC* 1:509–10. The question of Byrd and illegal slave trading is clouded by insufficient evidence, but in a variety of correspondence from Byrd or others there is no evidence that a license from the Royal African Company, which had a monopoly on the slave trade until 1697, was involved. See, for example, Byrd to Perry & Lane, April 25, 1684, March 29, June 6, 1685, Tinling, *Byrd Correspondence,* 14–15, 31, 42; William Fitzhugh to [John Jackson], Feb. 11, 1683, Davis, *Fitzhugh,* 127–28. Further illegal trade was going on. See Effingham's acknowledgment of receipt from William Cole, May 10, 1688, concerning the seizure of slaves illegally brought into the James River, and instructions from Charles II and James II, Oct. 23, 1683, April 3, 1687, concerning the Royal African Company monopoly, Billings, *Papers of Effingham,* 375–76, 24, 295–96. See also Philip Alexander Bruce, *Economic History of Virginia in the Seventeenth Century* (2 vols., New York, 1895; rept. New York, 1935), vol. 2, chap. 11, esp. pp. 82–89; Morgan, *American Slavery, American Freedom,* 305–7; K. G. Davis, *The Royal African Company* (London, 1957), 46, 109, 295.

25. Billings et al., *Colonial Virginia,* chaps. 4, 5; Morton, *Colonial Virginia,* vol. 1, chaps. 17–20.

26. *EJC* 1:6, 13, 33, 44, 76; Effingham's instructions from Charles II, 1683, Billings, *Papers of Effingham,* 16–17. In these instructions John Custis II and John Page I are not listed as members of the council, but the *EJC* clearly indicates that they were. For Bacon's Rebellion and its aftermath, see Morton, *Colonial Virginia,* vol. 1, chaps. 11–19; Billings et al., *Colonial Virginia,* chaps. 3–5; Wesley Frank Craven, *The Southern Colonies in the Seventeenth Century* (Baton Rouge, LA, 1949), chap. 10; Morgan, *American Slavery, American Freedom,* chaps. 9–14; see also Webb, *End of Independence,* 79–162; "List of Those Whose Services during the Late Rebellion Have Been Reported to the Commissioners as Being Particularly Eminent and Whose Constancy Have Made Them Worthy of Royal Remark," in Samuel Wiseman's Book of Record, Pepysian Library, 2582, Cambridge; Burton J. Hendrick, *The Lees of Virginia: A Biography of a Family* (Boston, 1935), chap. 2; Nagel, *Lees,* 24–25; Rutman and Rutman, *Place in Time,* 79–93. On leadership in the House of Burgesses, see Quitt, *Virginia House of Burgesses,* 313–63. See also Billings, *Virginia's Viceroy,* chaps. 6–7.

27. *JHB,* 1659/60–93, xlix–l, liv, 115, 118, 120, 283, 316–29, 513–15; Morton, *Colonial Virginia* 1:292–98; Thomas J. Wertenbaker, *Virginia under the Stuarts* (Princeton, NJ, 1914), 216–29; Hening, *Statutes* 3:543–71; Philip Ludwell to Sir Joseph Williamson, June 28, 1678, to King and Council, [1688?], Lee Family Papers, 1638–1867, VHS; *EJC* 1:2, 5, 17–21, 24–29, 35–36, 81, 88, 509, 510; Nicholas Spencer to Committee of Trade and Plantations, May 29, 1683, *VMHB* 28 (1920): 222–33, and see also ibid., 3 (1895–96): 225–38, 28 (1920): 120–27; William Byrd to [Thomas Grendon], May 20, 1684, Tinling, *Byrd Correspondence,* 20; William Fitzhugh to Major Robert Beverley, May 29, 1682, to John Cooper, June 5, 1683, Davis, *Fitzhugh,* 113–14,

126; Effingham to Privy Council, Feb. 10, 1685, to Robert Spencer, Feb. 20, 1686, Feb. 22, 1687, from James II, Aug. 1, 1686, April 29, 1688, to Sir John Ernle, [Aug. 16?], 1686, to William Blathwayt, March 7, 1687, April 29, 1688, Billings, *Papers of Effingham,* 237–41, 242, 278–81, 263–64, 373, 267, 284–85, 372–73, and see also 272–73, 410–15.

28. Effingham to William Blathwayt, March 21, April 27, 1687, May 23, 1688, Billings, *Papers of Effingham,* 286–87, 301–2, 383–86; William Byrd to Warham Horsmanden, July 25, 1690, Tinling, *Byrd Correspondence,* 121.

29. *EJC* 1:324, 325, 330, 350, 352, 355–56, 363, 398–99; Edmund Andros to LCTP, June 4, 1695, PRO, CO 5/1308; "Mr. Benjamin Harrison's Memorandum Relating to the Protection of Illegal Traders in Virginia," July 11, 1698, ibid., 1309.

30. Effingham to William Blathwayt, Feb. 6–24, 1686, to Robert Spencer, Feb. 22, 1687, Billings, *Papers of Effingham,* 234–36, 278–79; Francis Nicholson to LCTP, Nov. 13, 1691, Edmund Andros to same, Jan. 5, 1694, PRO, CO 5/1308; *EJC* 1:324, 398–99, 2:87, 93, 186–98. On leading members of the House of Burgesses, see Quitt, *Virginia House of Burgesses,* 361–63. See also Billings, *Virginia's Viceroy,* chaps. 6, 7; Billings et al., *Colonial Virginia,* esp. chap. 5; Billings, *Little Parliament,* chap. 3.

2. Politics, 1700–1737

1. For population, see PRO, CO 5/1313, 70; *JHB,* 1695–1749; Leonard, *General Assembly of Virginia.* For the politics in this era, see David Alan Williams, *Political Alignments in Colonial Virginia Politics, 1698–1750* (New York, 1989).

2. Stephen Saunders Webb, "The Strange Career of Francis Nicholson," *WMQ* (3), 19 (1963): 513–48.

3. Bruce T. McCulley, "From North Riding to Morocco: The Early Years of Francis Nicholson, 1655–1686," *WMQ* (3), 19 (1963): 534–56; *EJC* 2:391–95; Fleet, *Virginia Colonial Abstracts* 7:19–29; Nicholson to Council for Trade and Plantations, Dec. 2, 1700, PRO, CO 5/1312. For Nicholson on the antecedents of the Virginia elite, see *CSP* 22 (1704–5): 423.

4. *EJC* 1:352–53, 357, 360, 433; Nicholson to LCTP, June 24, 1700, Dec. 2, 1701, PRO, CO 5/1312; Parke Rouse Jr., *James Blair of Virginia* (Chapel Hill, NC, 1971), 106–7.

5. For Blair's opposition to Andros, see Rouse, *Blair,* chaps. 5–6; Webb, "Strange Career," 531–33, as well as an affidavit of the council meeting for April 29, 1695, in *An Occasional Bulletin of the Virginia Historical Society,* December 1987 (Blair was temporarily suspended); *EJC* 1:324–25, 350, 352, 355–56, 363; Henry Hartwell, James Blair, and Edward Chilton, *The Present State of Virginia and the College* (London, 1727), ed. Hunter Dickinson Farish (Williamsburg, VA, 1940), 16–20, 25–26, 39; Billings et al., *Colonial Virginia,* 140–55. See also Edmund Andros to Duke of Shrewsbury, April 27, 1697, James Vernon to LCTP, May 31, 1698, Andros to LCTP, June 6, 1698, Ralph Marshall to LCTP, June 15, 1698, LCTP to Privy Council, June 23, 1698, Andros to William Popple, Oct. 31, 1698, PRO, CO 5/1309.

6. Hartwell, Blair, and Chilton, Sept. 13, 1697, PRO, CO 5/1309. See also "Mr. Randolph's Discourse abt. Virginia" to Committee of Trade and Plantations, Aug. 31, 1696, ibid.; *An Essay upon the Government of the English Plantations on the Continent of America . . . By an American* (London, 1701), ed. Louis B. Wright (San Marino, CA, 1945), 8, 34–35, 35, 52. On the author-

ship of the essay, see Shammas, "Benjamin Harrison III and the Authorship of *An Essay upon the Government of the English Plantations,*" 166–73.

7. Leonard W. Labaree, ed., *Royal Instructions to British Colonial Governors, 1670–1776* (2 vols., rept. New York, 1967), 2:589–90, 554, 656–57, 1:47–48, 547–48. See also Nicholson's Instructions, June 8, 1699, Nicholson to LCTP, July 1, 1699, PRO, CO 5/1310; *EJC* 1:399, 420, 442–43, 456–57, 2:95; Hening, *Statutes* 3:195–97; "Mr. Randolph's Discourse abt. Virginia," Aug. 31, 1696, Edmund Andros to LCTP, April 27, 1697, PRO, CO 5/1309; Manning C. Voorhis, "Crown versus Council in Virginia Land Policy," *WMQ* (3), 3 (1946): 503–6.

8. *JHB,* 1695–1702, 199; *EJC* 2:21–22. Charles Scarburgh to [Nicholson], June 8, 1699, Edmund Jenings, J. Lightfoot, Matthew Page, Charles Scarburgh, Richard Lee, William Byrd, Edward Hill, and Benjamin Harrison to Nicholson, June 8, 1699, Nicholson to LCTP, July 1, 1699, PRO, CO 5/1310; *Cavaliers and Pioneers* 3:25–95; William Lowndes to William Byrd, Nov. 22, 1700, Byrd to Philip Ludwell, July 6, 1702, Tinling, *Byrd Correspondence,* 184–85, 185n, 186.

9. Nicholson to LCTP, March 3, 1705, *CSP* 22 (1704–5): 411–26; *EJC* 1:401, 425, 2:25, 98, 300, 330; Kukla, *Speakers and Clerks,* 144–47. Beverley, who replaced Randolph, served only briefly.

10. For Nicholson's instructions, see note 7 above. Hening, *Statutes* 3:207–11; Williams, *Political Alignments,* 19–20; Rouse, *Blair,* 69, 71, 103; Billings et al., *Colonial Virginia,* 162; Polly Cary Legg, "The Governor's Extacy of Troubles," *WMQ* (2), 22 (1942): 391–98. See also Philip Ludwell to Philip Ludwell, Esq., July 26, 1703, Lewis Burwell to Phil. Ludwell, Esq., July 23, 1703, [Nathaniel Burwell] to Phill Ludwell, Esq., Oct. 13, 1703, Copies of Letters Submitted by Philip Ludwell and James Blair to LCTP, PRO, CO 5/1314, 73–77, 72–73, 81–83, for additional comments on the governor's "amour &c."

11. Nicholson to LCTP, July 1, 1699, Dec. 2, 1701, March 1, 1705, PRO, CO 5/1310, 1312; Nicholson to LCTP, March 1, 1705, *CSP* 22 (1704–5): 397–402; George Larkin to LCTP, Dec. 22, 1701, PRO, CO 5/1312; *Essay upon Government,* 13–14.

12. William Byrd to Philip Ludwell, July 6, 1702, Tinling, *Byrd Correspondence,* 186; Nicholson's undated memorandum to Lewis Burwell, [1703?], Legg, "Governor's Extacy," 395; Memorial of J. Lightfoot, Matthew Page, Benja. Harrison, Robert Carter, James Blair, and Phill. Ludwell "concerning the Mal-administrations of his Excelly Francis Nicholson Esqr.," [May 2, 1703], PRO, CO 5/1314, 27–32.

13. William Byrd I to William Blathwayt, May 4, 1700, Tinling, *Byrd Correspondence,* 183; James Blair to LCTP, Dec. 13, 1700, PRO, CO 5/1312, 79; Labaree, *Royal Instructions* 1:429–31; *JHB,* 1695–1702, 267–68, 298–99, 304–5; *EJC* 2:183–89, 196–97, 201, 207; Nicholson to LCTP, Dec. 2, 1701, PRO, CO 5/1312.

14. For Nicholson's speech, see *JHB,* 1695–1702, 304–5. On the courtship, see Legg, "Governor's Extacy," 389–98.

15. The Queen's Most Excellent Majesty in Council, May 18, 1702, PRO, CO 5/1312; *EJC* 2:277, 283; *JHB,* 1695–1702, 1, 393–403; Philip Ludwell to Philip Ludwell, Esq., March 11, 1703, Copies of Letters Submitted by Philip Ludwell and James Blair to LCTP, PRO, CO 5/1314, 61–69; Nicholson to LCTP, March 3, 1705, *CSP* 22 (1704–5): 411–26.

16. *EJC* 2:244, 246; Nicholson to LCTP, n.d., Oct 22, 23, 1703, PRO, CO 5/1313, 161–62,

218–19; [Nicholson] to Madam Lucy, Jan. 7, 1703, Legg, "Governor's Extacy," 394. See also Rouse, *Blair,* chaps. 7–8; Nathaniel Harrison to Mr. Stephen Fouace, July 15, 1702, Philip Ludwell to Philip Ludwell, Esq., July 26, 1703, Copies of Letters Submitted by Philip Ludwell and James Blair to LCTP, PRO, CO 5/1314, 79–81, 73–77; Councillors' Memorial, ibid., 22, 111–13.

17. B[enjamin] H[arrison Sr.] to Philip Ludwell [Sr.?], July 6, 1702, Nathaniel Harrison to Mr. Stephen Fouace, July 15, 1702, Copies of Letters Submitted by Philip Ludwell and James Blair to LCTP, PRO, CO 5/1314, 79–81.

18. Robert Carter to Philip Ludwell, March 1, 1703, Philip Ludwell to Philip Ludwell, Esq., March 11 and 15, 1703, Benjamin Harrison to Philip Ludwell, Esq., March 16, 1703, B.H. to Col. Ludwell, Esq., May 28, 1703, Copies of Letters Submittted by Philip Ludwell and James Blair to LCTP, PRO, CO 5/1314, 48–56, 61–69, 71–79; Williams, *Political Alignments,* 48–51; *EJC* 2:300; *JHB,* 1695–1702, ii–xii.

19. Councillors' Memorial, May 20, 1703, PRO, CO 5/1314, 27–32; Robert Carter to Philip Ludwell, Esq., March 1, 1703, Copies of Letters Submitted by Philip Ludwell and James Blair to LCTP, ibid., 48–56.

20. Councillors' Memorial, ibid., 27–32.

21. On Byrd, see chap. 1 above and Byrd to Philip Ludwell I, July 6, 1702, Tinling, *Byrd Correspondence,* 186–87. On Jenings, see Billings, *Papers of Effingham,* 35; Maurer, "Notes on the Honorable Edmund Jenings," and "Edmund Jenings and Robert Carter"; Edmund Jenings to LCTP, Feb. 21, 1704, PRO, CO 5/1313; Philip Ludwell to Philip Ludwell, Esq., March 11, 1703, Copies of Letters Submitted by James Blair and Philip Ludwell to LCTP, ibid., 1314, 61–69. For William Bassett, see Malcolm Harris, *Old New Kent County: Some Account of Planters Plantations and Places in New Kent County* (2 vols., West Point, VA, 1977), 1:42–44; *JCTP* 1 (1704–9): 320; *EJC* 2:274; Nicholson to LCTP, Dec. 2, 1701, PRO, CO 5/1312; Nicholson to LCTP, March 3, 1705, *CSP* 22 (1704–5): 411–26. Carter to Philip Ludwell, Esq., March 1, 1703, Copies of Letters Submitted by Philip Ludwell and James Blair to LCTP, PRO, CO 5/1314, 48–56.

22. *EJC* 2:334–35, 424, 426; Nicholson to LCTP, Aug. 1, 1703, PRO, CO 5/1313; see also Nicholson to LCTP,, March 1, 2, 3, 6, *CSP* 22 (1704–5): 397–406, 411–26, 429–36; Kukla, *Speakers and Clerks,* 89–94; Philip Ludwell to Philip Ludwell, Esq., March 11, 1703, Copies of Letters Submitted by Philip Ludwell and James Blair to LCTP, PRO, CO 5/1314, 61–69.

23. *JHB,* 1695–1702, 170, 256; "Mr. Treasurer Carter, His Accot," PRO, CO 5/1312, 2; *EJC* 2:369; Beverley, *History and Present State of Virginia,* 93–94; *Cavaliers and Pioneers,* vols. 1–3; see also Rent Roll, 1704–5, Wertenbaker, *Planters of Colonial Virginia,* 183–247; Lancaster County, Order Book 5 (1702–13): 55, 108, 138, LOV microfilm. Lightfoot is a shadowy figure, but his "ill reputation" was much discussed; see *VMHB* 8 (1900–1901): 55–56; *EJC* 1:352; Harris, *Old New Kent* 1:121–22. For Nicholson's comment, see *VMHB* 8 (1900–1901): 55–56.

24. See esp. Copies of Letters Submitted by Philip Ludwell and James Blair to LCTP, PRO, CO 5/1314.

25. Nicholson to LCTP, July 1, 1699, PRO, CO 5/1310; George Larkin to LCTP, Dec. 22, 1701, ibid., 1312; Robert Carter to Thomas Corbin, June 15, 1702, Feb. 26, 1705, Christ Church Parish, Lancaster County, Wormeley Estate Papers, 1701–10, 1716, photostats, LOV; Dr. Blair to LCTP, June 7, 1704, Nicholson to LCTP, March 1, 1705, *CSP* 22 (1704–5): 158–59, 397–

402. For the effect of the Glorious Revolution on the colonies, see Jack P. Greene, *Peripheries and Center: Constitutional Development in the Extended Politics of the British Empire and the United States, 1607–1788* (Athens, GA, 1986), chaps. 1–2.

26. John Lightfoot to James Blair, Oct. 21, 1703, Copies of Letters Submitted by Philip Ludwell and James Blair to LCTP, PRO, CO 5/1314; Councillors' Memorial, ibid.; Kevin Hardwick, "Narratives of Villainy and Virtue: Governor Francis Nicholson and the Character of the Good Ruler in Early Virginia," *JSH* 72 (2006): 39–74, esp. 39–43.

27. Robert Carter to Mr. Thomas Corbin, July 6, 1705, Christ Church Parish, Lancaster County, Wormeley Estate Papers, 1701–10, 1716, photostats, LOV; Dr. Blair to LCTP, June 7, 1704, *CSP* 22 (1704–5): 158–59; *JHB,* 1702–12, xxiii–xxxii, 101–2, 107–9; Robert Carter to Philip Ludwell, Esq., March 1, 1703, B.H. to Col. Ludwell, May 28, 1703, Copies of Letters Submitted by Philip Ludwell and James Blair to LCTP, PRO, CO 5/1314, 48–56; *EJC* 2:334–35; Rouse, *Blair,* esp. chaps. 7–9; Thad W. Tate, "The College, 1693–1792," in Susan H. Godson et al., *The College of William and Mary: A History, 1693–1993* (2 vols., Williamsburg, VA, 1993), 1:35–47.

28. B.H. to Philip Ludwell, July 6, 1702, Copies of Letters Submitted by Philip Ludwell and James Blair to LCTP, PRO, CO 5/1314, 69–70; *EJC* 2:324, 334–35, 336, 391–95. For the memorial and referral to the Board of Trade, see PRO, CO 5/1314, 21–23, 27–32.

29. *JCTP* 1 (April 1704–Feb. 1709): 2–4, 7, 8, 11, 14, 17, 18, 20, 21–22, 23; *CSP* 23 (1706–June 1708): 103–4, 132, 158–59, 166; PRO, CO 5/1314, 34–40.

30. *EJC* 2:414–16, 418–19, 420–22, 422–23, 424–25, 426–29, 436–38, 454, 3:1; Mr. Secretary Hedges to Governor Nicholson, April 17, 1705, *CSP* 22 (1704–5): 485; *JCTP* 1 (April 1704–Feb. 1709): 134, 135; Webb, "Strange Career," 540; [Robert Carter] to Mr. Thomas Corbin, Aug. 26, 1706, Christ Church Parish, Lancaster County, Wormeley Estate Papers, 1701–10, 1716, photostats, LOV; *Papers Relating to an Affadavit by the Reverend James Blair, Clerk, Pretended President of William and Mary College, and Supposed Commissary to the Bishop of London in Virginia, against Francis Nicholson Esq.* (London, 1727). Webb incorrectly stated that Nott was lieutenant governor to George Hamilton, earl of Orkney, but Orkney did not become "Governor general" until 1709. The earl of Sutherland wrote the Board of Trade on Dec. 10, 1709, "to prepare the draught of a commission and instructions for the Earl of Orkney to be Governor of her Majesty's Colony of Virginia." Orkney in turn informed the board that he had nominated Spotswood as of Feb. 21, 1710. *JCTP* 2(1708–15): 105, 106, 131, 132. But the council knew that he had been nominated lieutenant governor as early as Feb. 18, 1710. See *EJC* 3:247. This is the first time that Orkney is mentioned in the council journals as governor. The *DNB,* s.v. "George Hamilton, Earl of Orkney (1666–1737)," incorrectly states that Orkney was appointed governor in 1714. Blair incorrectly reported that Orkney would become governor in 1705. See James Blair to Philip Ludwell, Jan. 6, 1705, and to Dear Brother, Jan. 6, 1705, *WMQ* (1), 3 (1894–95): 15–17, and *VMHB* 5 (1897–98): 53–57. William Byrd II sought to buy the lieutenant governorship from Orkney for £1,000 in 1709, but he reported that the duke of Marlborough quashed it, declaring "no one but soldiers should have a government of a plantation." Louis B. Wright and Marion Tinling, eds., *The Secret Diary of William Byrd Westover, 1709–1712* (Richmond, 1941), 159.

31. Nicholson to LCTP, July 25, 1705, *CSP* 22 (1704–5): 595; *JHB,* 1702–12, 101–2, 107–8, 109.

32. Robert Carter to Philip Ludwell, July 11, 1705, *VMHB* 5 (1897–98): 42–43.

33. *EJC* 3:23, 24, 27.

34. James Blair to Philip Ludwell, Jan. 6, 1705, *WMQ* (1), 3 (1893–94): 15–17; Philip Ludwell I to Phill, Feb. 9, 1706, Lee Family Papers, 1638–1867, VHS.

35. The other councillors were Edmund Jenings, Dudley Digges, John Custis, William Bassett, Henry Duke, William Churchill, and Robert Quary. *EJC* 3:24, 26–27, 29, 30–37, 38–40, 59; Nott to [Mr. Secty Hedges?], Sept. 22, 1705, to the LCTP, Dec. 24, 1705, *CSP* 22 (1704–5): 627, 740.

36. Nott to Mr. Secty Hedges, Dec. 24, 1705, to LCTP, Dec. 24, 1705, *CSP* 22 (1704–5): 742, 737.

37. Labaree, *Royal Instructions* 2:588–89; *EJC* 3:107; Hening, *Statutes* 3:304–7; *JHB*, 1702–12, 234; Voorhis, "Crown versus Council in Virginia Land Policy," 506–7.

38. Col. [Robert] Quary to LCTP, Sept. 11, 1706, *CSP* 23 (1706–June 1708): 63.

39. President of the Council to LCTP, Aug. 29, 1706, ibid., 201–2; Nott to LCTP, Dec. 24, 1705, to [Mr. Secty Hedges], Dec. 24, 1705, ibid., 22 (1704–5): 737, 742; LCTP to President of the Council of Virginia, March 29, 1707, T. Corbin to LCTP, Jan. 11, 1706, LCTP to Nott, March 1, 1706, ibid., 23 (1706–June 1708): 404, 5, 63; *EJC* 3:70, 74, 82; *JHB*, 1702–12, xxviii, 204, 208, 233–35.

40. *EJC* 2:337, 3:113, 116, 117–18, 135, 176, 184, 187, 233, 241; Byrd, *Secret Diary*, 3, 8–9, 11, 21, 32, 33, 36, 37, 39, 42, 45–46, 51; Edmund Jenings to LCTP, Feb. 21, 1704, PRO, CO 5/1313; Philip Ludwell to Philip Ludwell, Esqr., March 11, 1703, Copies of Letters Submitted by Philip Ludwell and James Blair to the LCTP, ibid., 1314, 61–69; B.H. to Col. Ludwell, Esqr., May 28, July 26, 1703, ibid., 77–79, 73–74; Proposal of Edmund Jenings, March 29, 1702, response of Robert Carter, April 6, 1702, Robert Carter to Thomas Corbin, Aug. 20, 1706, Christ Church Parish, Lancaster County, Wormeley Estate Papers, 1701–10, 1716, photostats, LOV; LCTP to Mr. Secretary, Jan. 23, 1706, Col. Quary to LCTP, Sept. 1, 1706, Edmund Jenings to LCTP, Sept. 2, 1706, *CSP* 23 (1706–June 1708): 22, 213–16, 216–17; Nathaniel Blakiston to Philip Ludwell, Dec. 13, 1708, Lee Family Papers, 1638–1867, VHS; Nathaniel Blakiston to Philip Ludwell II, May 28, 1709, *VMHB* 5 (1897–98): 45–47; Maurer, "Edmund Jenings and Robert Carter,"; William Byrd II to William Blathwayt, Sept. 21, 1708, to [John Custis, Dec. 15, 1709], Tinling, *Byrd Correspondence,* 268, 274.

41. Labaree, *Royal Instructions* 2:589–90; *EJC* 3:221, 249–50; Edmund Jenings to LCTP, Oct. 14, 1706, LCTP to Edmund Jenings, Jan. 19, 1710, *CSP* 23 (1706–June 1708): 266, 25 (1710–June 1711): 17–18; Voorhis, "Crown versus Council in Virginia Land Policy," 506–7; *Cavaliers and Pioneers* 3:98–108.

42. On Spotswood, see Leonidas Dodson, *Alexander Spotswood, Governor of Colonial Virginia* (Philadelphia, 1932); Walter Havighurst, *Alexander Spotswood: Portrait of a Governor* (New York, 1967). Byrd, *Secret Diary*, 194; Spotswood to John Spotswood, March 20, 1711, *VMHB* 60 (1952): 228–30. For Orkney, see *DNB*, s.v. "Hamilton, George, First Earl of Orkney"; *JCTP* 2 (1708–15): 105, 106, 131, 132; *EJC* 3:247. The *DNB* incorrectly states that Orkney was appointed governor in 1714.

43. Byrd, *Secret Diary*, 194–95; *EJC* 3:247–48, 254–55.

44. For the intimate relationship of this group, see Byrd, *Secret Diary*. On Byrd's seeking governorships, see ibid., 85, 159; Louis B. Wright and Marion Tinling, eds., *William Byrd of*

Virginia; The London Diary, 1717–1721, and Other Writings (New York, 1958), 259, 263. Jenings, Ludwell, and John Robinson (soon to be on the council) were all, for example, in England in 1713. Byrd went early in 1715. Gawin Corbin was there in 1711 fighting Spotswood's removal of him as naval officer. Spotswood to LCTP, March 6, 1711, Aug. 17, Sept. 13, 1713, to Mr. Blathwayt, June 2, 1713, to Col. Blakiston, Sept. 13, Nov. 16, 1713, R. A. Brock, ed., *The Official Letters of Alexander Spotswood* (2 vols., Richmond, 1882, 1885), 1:63–64, 2:20, 31–32, 38–39, 40–41; Byrd, *Secret Diary,* 319. Byrd's last council meeting was Feb. 23, 1715, and he appeared before the Board of Trade on May 15. *EJC* 3:269, 376, 397; Tinling, *Byrd Correspondence,* 288n; N. Blakiston to Philip Ludwell, Jan. 18, 1711, *VMHB* 4 (1896–97): 21.

45. *JHB,* 1702–12, xx, 43, 1712–26, 111–12; Hening, *Statutes* 3:213–15; Tate, "The College, 1693–1792," 46, 51–53; Hugh Jones, *The Present State of Virginia,* ed. Richard L. Morton (Chapel Hill, NC, 1956), 71. The ordinaries are mentioned in Byrd, *Secret Diary.* Legislation was passed as late as 1713 authorizing the "resurveying and marking out anew the bounds and streets" of Williamsburg. Waverly K. Winfree, comp., *The Laws of Virginia: Being a Supplement to Hening's Statutes at Large, 1700–1750* (Richmond, 1971), 93–97.

46. For the politics of Spotswood's administration, see Williams, *Political Alignments,* chap. 4. See also John M. Hemphill II, "Alexander Spotswood (Lieutenant Governor of Virginia, 1710–1722): Frustrated Imperial Reformer and Successful Virginia Land Baron," MS in my possession.

47. Byrd, *Secret Diary,* 194–95, 230, 249, 297–98, 333, 334, 427–28, 455, 477; Spotswood to LCTP, Aug. 18, 1710, to Mr. Blathwayt, Mar. 6, 1711, Brock, *Letters of Spotswood* 1:8–9, 69; John Custis to Dear Brother, April 30, 1718, Tinling, *Byrd Correspondence,* 315.

48. Spotswood to LCTP, Oct. 24, 1710, March 6, 1711, Oct. 15, 1712, Brock, *Letters of Spotswood* 1:19–24, 49, 2:1–2; Byrd, *Secret Diary,* 257, 264.

49. Williams, *Political Alignments,* 140; Spotswood to LCTP, Dec. 28, 1711, to Lords of Treasury, July 28, 1711, Brock, *Letters of Spotswood* 1:130–32, 98–99; N. Blakiston to Philip Ludwell, July 10, 1711, Lee Family Papers, 1638–1867, VHS.

50. *EJC* 3:351; Spotswood to LCTP, Nov. 16, Dec. 29, 1713, Brock, *Letters of Spotswood* 2:43, 48–50; Winfree, *Supplement to Hening's Statutes,* 75–90; John M. Hemphill II, *Virginia and the English Commercial System, 1689–1733* (New York, 1985), 36–42.

51. Walter Stitt Robinson, "Indian Policy of Colonial Virginia" (Ph.D. diss., Univ. of Virginia, 1950), 180–84; Winfree, *Supplement to Hening's Statutes,* 104–13; Spotswood to Bishop of London, Jan. 27, 1715, to LCTP, Jan. 27, 1715, Brock, *Letters of Spotswood* 2:88–95.

52. Hening, *Statutes* 3:526, 4:37–42; *EJC* 3:255–56, 264, 288, 385; Spotswood to LCTP, July 28, Sept. 5, 1711, to Lords of the Treasury, Dec. 1, 1714, Brock, *Letters of Spotswood* 1:98–99, 110–11, 2:80–82; Williams, *Political Alignments,* 147–48: Voorhis, "Crown versus Council in Virginia Land Policy," 507–9.

53. *EJC* 3:249, 276, 317, 350, 380–81, 417; Spotswood to LCTP, March 9, 1714, Oct. 26, 1720, to My Lord [Bishop of London], March 13, 1714, Brock, *Letters of Spotswood* 2:58–61, 64–65, 243–44; Spotswood to LCTP, Oct. 15, 1711, *CSP* 26 (July 1711–June 1712): 114; Byrd, *Secret Diary,* 542; *JHB,* 1712–26, xxv; "Public Offices in Virginia, 1714," *VMHB* 2 (1894–95): 3–15.

54. Spotswood to LCTP, June 2, 1713, April 15, 1717, to Colonel Blakiston, Aug. 17, 1713, and Council's Representation, received May 1, 1713, Brock, *Letters of Spotswood* 2:25–26, 224–25, 229–30, 221–23; LCTP to Spotswood, June 1, 1716, Aug. 20 and 30, 1717, *CSP* 29 (1716–

July 1717): 111–12, 30 (Aug. 1717–Dec. 1718): 19–20, 22; *EJC* 3:431, 470, 494. The councillors cited a 1705 law concerning criminals being referred to the General Court for trial; Spotswood cited a 1710 law confirming the "Royal prerogative" to create other courts of record. Hening, *Statutes* 3:390–94, 489–90.

55. Spotswood to LCTP, Jan. 27, 1715, Brock, *Letters of Spotswood* 2:100–102; *JHB*, 1712–26, 108–9; *LJC*, Dec. 16, 17, 18, 1714, 584–86.

56. *EJC* 3:385, 389–91; Spotswood to Lords of Treasury and enclosures, Dec. 1, 1714, to LCTP, Jan. 1715, Brock, *Letters of Spotswood* 2:83–87, 94–95; Byrd to Philip Ludwell, July 3, 1717, Tinling, *Byrd Correspondence,* 300–303 and nn; Marambaud, *William Byrd,* 33, 38. The Indian Company did have a monopoly on trade, as Marambaud stated, but it was open to anyone who would subscribe £50 to £100. In testimony before the Board of Trade, July 10, 1716, Byrd said that a massacre in North Carolina and the Yamassee War in South Carolina had slowed trade with the southern Indians but before that time he had exported as many as "50 or 60 hhds" of skins in a year. *JCTP* 3 (1714–18): 163–66.

57. Spotswood to LCTP, Dec. 14, 1714, Jan. 27, 1715, Feb. 16, May 23, July 3, 1716, March 7, 1717, to Lords of Treasury, May 23, 1716, to Mr. Blathwayt, May 24, July 3, 1716, Brock, *Letters of Spotswood* 2:82, 93–103, 139–40, 151–58, 171–72, 265–68, 150–51, 159–62, 172–75; "Observations upon the Mismanagement of the King's Revenues of Virginia with the Lieut-Govern'rs Charge against the Auditor," May 24, 1716, ibid., 2:176–87; *EJC* 3:385, 389–91, 393; [Philip Ludwell], "My Answer to the Govrs Letter and the 29 Instruction," May 24, July 2, 1716, March 29, 1717, Spotswood to Philip Ludwell, Esq., Aug. 20, 1716, Lee Family Papers, 1638–1867, VHS; Williams, *Political Alignments,* 147–48.

58. Spotswood to Mr. Secretary Stanhope, July 15, 1715, to LCTP, Aug. 9, Oct. 24, 1715, May 9, 1716, Brock, *Letters of Spotswood* 2:124, 128, 133–35, 144–50; *JHB,* 1712–26, xxix, xxxiii, 128, 141, 152–53, 159–60, 164–70; *EJC* 3:409, 411; Williams, *Political Alignments,* 163–68.

59. Charges against Spotswood and his reply, Feb. 7, 1716, Jan. 16, 1717, to Mr. Popple, Jan. 16, 1717, Brock, *Letters of Spotswood* 2:190–218, 187; Spotswood to Earl of Orkney, July 1, 1718, *CSP* 30 (Aug. 1717–Dec. 1718): 288–91; Byrd to Philip Ludwell, July 3, 1717, Tinling, *Byrd Correspondence,* 300–303. On Katherine Russell, see, for example, Byrd, *Secret Diary,* 194, 206n, 340, 343, 423, 426, 474; Spotswood to Collo. Blakiston, April 16, 1717, Brock, *Letters of Spotswood* 2:242–44; Lester Cappon, "Correspondence of Alexander Spotswood with John Spotswood of Edinburgh," *VMHB* 60 (1963): 212, 214n.

60. [?] to Richard Beresford, July 4, 1716, Council of Virginia to LCTP, May 4, 1717, William Byrd's report on council relationships, Nov. 16, 1717, Spotswood to LCTP, March 20, Aug. 14, 1718, to Earl of Orkney, Dec. 22, 1718, *CSP* 29 (1716–July 1717): 143, 293–94, 30 (Aug. 1717–Dec. 1718): 218–22, 290–92, 424–25. For examples of the governor's "sharp tongue" and effective arguing, see *EJC* 3:464–65, 479–80, and his speech to the House of Burgesses, Dec. 1, 1718, in which he referred to "malicious Whisperers, Clandestine Informers, and Anonymous Libellers of Government" as well as "a Cataline Crew of Malecontents." *JHB,* 1712–26, 242–43.

61. Memorial of the Virginia Indian Company to Governor Spotswood, April 23, 1716, to LCTP, April 24, 1717, PRO, CO 5/1317 and 1318, LC Transcripts, 405–8, 61–90; Grand Jury Address, October 1716, *CSP* 29 (1716–July 1717): 249; Grand Jury Address, April 18, 1719, *VMHB* 4 (1896–97): 349–53; Edward Porter Alexander, ed., *The Journal of John Fontaine*

(Charlottesville, VA, 1972), 4; William Byrd to Philip Ludwell, Sept. 24, 1717, Tinling, *Byrd Correspondence,* 304–5. On Byrd's contacts and persistence, see, for example, William Byrd to Philip Ludwell, June 30, 1718, ibid., 309–10; Byrd, *London Diary,* 49–50, 52, 53, 55, 87. An example of Spotswood's efforts at building political support can be seen in his courting of the Robinson family. He appointed Christopher Robinson, who accompanied him on his expedition, a naval officer and offered him a council seat that he declined. His brother John was appointed a tobacco agent and ultimately a councillor. Both served in the House of Burgesses. And William Robinson, who may have been a younger brother, served on both grand juries. Spotswood to My Lord, March 13, 1714, Brock, *Letters of Spotswood* 2:64–65; *EJC* 3:276.

62. Spotswood to LCTP, March 20, June 24, 1718, to Earl of Orkney, July 1, Dec. 22, 1718, *CSP* 30 (Aug. 1717–Dec. 1718): 218–22, 272–80, 289–91, 424–25.

63. Mr. Blathwayt to Mr. Popple, Aug. 27, 1716, *CSP* 29 (1716–July 1717): 175; Spotswood to Lords of Treasury, May 23, 1716, to Collo. Blakistone, April 16, 1717, to LCTP, Feb. 27, 1718, Brock, *Letters of Spotswood* 2:150–51, 242–44, 267; N. Blakiston to Philip Ludwell, July 2, 1716, Lee Family Papers, 1638–1867, VHS; William Byrd to Philip Ludwell, July 3, 1717, to John Custis, Oct. 4, 1717, Tinling, *Byrd Correspondence,* 300–303, 305–6; Spotswood to LCTP, June 24, July 1, 1718, to Earl of Orkney, Dec. 22, 1718, *CSP* 30 (Aug. 1717–Dec. 1718): 272–80, 291, 424–25; Philip Ludwell to the Hon'ble Francis Nicholson, Esqr., March 27, 1718, *WMQ* (2), 22 (1942): 396–97. See also John Melville Jenings, ed., "The Lamentations of John Grymes in Four Letters Addressed to William Blathwayt," *VMHB* 58 (1951): 388–94. Byrd appeared before the Board of Trade concerning the tobacco inspection and Indian Company acts on May 8, 15, July 10, 1716, May 10, 1717. The order in council for the repeal of both acts came on Aug. 18, 1717. *JCTP* 3 (1714–18): 137, 139, 163–66, 229–30, 241, 242–43, 244, 255.

64. LCTP to Spotswood, Jan. 29, 1718, Spotswood to LCTP, June 24, 1718, to Earl of Orkney, July 1, 1718, *CSP* 30 (Aug. 1717–Dec.1718): 166–67, 277–80, 289–91; *JHB,* 1712–26, 174–75. The document attacking the Indian Company can be found in Jack P. Greene, ed., "The Opposition to Lieutenant Governor Alexander Spotswood, 1718," *VMHB* 70 (1963): 37–39.

65. *JHB,* 1712–26, 174–75; *EJC* 3:461; Spotswood to LCTP, Feb. 27, 1718, Brock, *Letters of Spotswood* 2:263.

66. Spotswood to LCTP, June 24, July 1, 1718, *CSP* 30 (Aug. 1717–Dec. 1718): 280–91. See also same letter, with some differences, in Brock, *Letters of Spotswood* 2:275–86. *EJC* 3:461; *JHB,* 1712–26, 184, 186, 189–90, 194, 199, 201, 203–5, 208, 210–11, 213–15; *LJC* 2:619; Virginia Indian Company to LCTP, April 24, 1717, PRO, CO 5/1318, 61–90, LC Transcripts; "Journal of the Lieutenant Governor's Travels," *WMQ* (2), 3 (1923): 40–45.

67. *JHB,* 1712–26, 189, 191–92, 196–98, 210, 215–16; Spotswood to LCTP, June 24, 1718, Brock, *Letters of Spotswood* 2:279–80; *EJC* 3:164. It should be noted that the arguments of the House of Burgesses that the instruction concerning trade and shipping bills (suspending clause) and those concerning post office rates being taxes are exactly the same as those set forth in the 1750s and 1760s concerning the Two Penny Act and the Stamp Act.

68. *JHB,* 1712–26, 200–201, 205–6, 207, 209, 212–16, 242; Winfree, *Supplement to Hening's Statutes,* 173–74; Spotswood to LCTP, July 29, Aug. 14, 1718, Brock, *Letters of Spotswood* 2:278–79, 288.

69. *JHB,* 1712–26, 203, 295, 206, 212–14, 229; Spotswood to Earl of Orkney, June 24,

Dec. 22, 1718, March 25, 1719, *CSP* 30 (Aug. 1717–Dec. 1718): 272–80, 424–25, 31 (1719–Feb.1720): 65. See also Graham Hood, *The Governor's Palace in Williamsburg: A Cultural Study* (Chapel Hill, NC, 1991), 38–60.

70. *JHB*, 1712–26, 216–17; *EJC* 3:478–80; Spotswood to LCTP, Aug. 14, 1718, Brock, *Letters of Spotswood* 2:288–89.

71. Spotswood to LCTP, Aug. 14, 1718, Brock, *Letters of Spotswood* 2:292–94; *EJC* 3:482–83; George McLaren Brydon, *Virginia's Mother Church and the Political Conditions under Which It Grew* (2 vols., Richmond, 1947–52), 1:348–49, 352; Jack P. Greene, *The Quest for Power: The Lower Houses of the Assembly in the Southern Royal Colonies, 1689–1776* (Chapel Hill, NC, 1963), 346–54; Bishop William Meade, *Old Churches, Ministers, and Families of Virginia* (2 vols., Philadelphia, 1857), 2: app. 1; William Stevens Perry, ed., *Historical Collections Relating to the American Colonial Church* (5 vols., Hartford, 1870–78), 1:199–242.

72. Spotswood to LCTP, June 24, July 1, 1718, and to Earl of Orkney, July 1, 1718, *CSP* 30 (Aug. 1717–Dec. 1718): 272–80, 291, 289–91, 333; Spotswood to LCTP, Sept. 27, 1718, Brock, *Letters of Spotswood* 2:302–4; Byrd to John Custis, Oct. 2, 1717, Tinling, *Byrd Correspondence,* 293–94.

73. *JHB*, 1712–26, xxxviii–xxxix, xl, 221–24, 227–32, 239–40; Spotswood to LCTP, Dec. 22, 1718, to Earl of Orkney, Dec. 22, 1718, *CSP* 30 (Aug. 1717–Dec. 1718): 425–35, 424–25; Spotswood to LCTP, March 25, 1719, Brock, *Letters of Spotswood* 1:308–16.

74. Spotswood to LCTP, Dec. 22, 1718, to Earl of Orkney, Dec. 22, 1718, *CSP* 30 (Aug. 1717–Dec. 1718): 425–35, 424–25; Spotswood to LCTP, May 26, 1719, Brock, *Letters of Spotswood* 2:320–22; William Byrd to Philip Ludwell, Sept. 24, 1717, Tinling, *Byrd Correspondence,* 305; "Animadversions on a Paper Entituled Virginia Addresses Printed in Philadelphia," Lee Family Papers, 1638–1867, Mss IL51 f82, VHS. See also the testimony of the earl of Orkney before the Board of Trade, Aug. 19, 1718, *JCTP* 3 (1714–18): 425–26.

75. William Byrd to LCTP, Dec. 14, 1718, March 24, 1719, John Custis to Byrd, [March?] 1719, Tinling, *Byrd Correspondence,* 316–17, 319–20, 321–22; Byrd, *London Diary,* 238–39; Spotswood to Mr. Popple, Feb. 5, 1719, Mr. Solicitor General to LCTP, March 5, 1719, LCTP to [the King], April 9, 1719, to Mr. Secretary Craggs, April 10, 1719, Order of Lords Justices in Council, June 25, 1719, *CSP* 31 (1719–Feb. 1720): 23–24, 48, 72–73, 139.

76. Perry, *Historical Collections* 1:199–242; Spotswood to LCTP, March 25, 1719, Brock, *Letters of Spotswood* 2:308–16; Mr. Robertson to Mr. Popple, March 2, 1719, *CSP* 31 (1719–Feb. 1720): 45; P. G. Scott, "James Blair and the Scottish Church: A New Source," *WMQ* (3), 33 (1976): 300–308; Grand Jury's Address and Observations on the Grand Jury's Address of April 18, 1719, *VMHB* 4 (1895–96): 349–56; Virginia Indian Company to LCTP, April 23, 1716, April 24, 1717, PRO, CO 5/1318, LC Transcripts, 61–90, 385–92; Alexander, *Journal of John Fontaine,* 14; lists of sheriffs and tobacco agents, *EJC* 3:92, 338, 371, 380–81, 375, 398, 422, 425, 448.

77. Blair to Bishop of London, n.d., Meade, *Old Churches, Ministers, and Families of Virginia* 2:413–20; Perry, *Historical Collections* 1:199–241, Brydon, *Virginia's Mother Church* 1:351–52; Tate, "The College, 1693–1792," 60–65.

78. Grand Jury's Address and Response, *VMHB* 4 (1896–97): 349–56; "Animadversions on a Paper Entituled Virginia Addresses Printed in Philadelphia," Lee Family Papers, 1638–1867, MSS L51 f82, VHS, see also *VMHB* 22 (1915): 410–16, 23 (1916): 66–71; Nathaniel Harrison to

[Philip Ludwell II], May 15, 1719, William Bassett to Philip Ludwell, Jan. 9, 1720, Lee Family Papers, 1638–1867, MSS L51 f82, VHS; Byrd, *London Diary,* 259.

79. LCTP to Spotswood, June 26, 1719, *CSP* 21 (1719–Feb. 1720): 140–42; Byrd to John Custis, May 16, 1719, to John Campbell, Duke of Argyll, [Nov. 4, 1719], Tinling, *Byrd Correspondence,* 322–23, 324–26; N. Blakiston to Col. Philip Ludwell, May 15, 1719, Lee Family Papers, 1638–1867, VHS; Byrd, *London Diary,* 259, 316, 318–20, 322, 323, 332, 333, 337, 339, 344, 351.

80. *EJC* 3:517, 518, 541; Mr. Solicitor General to LCTP, March 5, 1719, Mr. West to LCTP, June 27, 1719, *CSP* 31 (1719–Feb.1720): 48, 141; Perry, *Historical Collections* 1:197–98.

81. Byrd, *London Diary,* 369–72, 373–78, 385; Spotswood to LCTP, March 5, 1720, Fleet, *Virginia Colonial Abstracts* 14:14.

82. Byrd, *London Diary,* 398–99; *EJC* 3:524.

83. *EJC* 3:524–25; Byrd, *London Diary,* 399–400; Spotswood to LCTP, May 20, 1720, to Secretary Craggs, May 20, 1720, Brock, *Letters of Spotswood* 2:335, 341; Byrd to [John Percival, Baron Percival], June 22, 1720, Tinling, *Byrd Correspondence,* 328.

84. Byrd, *London Diary,* 400n, 400–401; Byrd to [John Percival, Baron Percival], June 22, 1720, Percival to Byrd, Oct. 15, 1720, Tinling, *Byrd Correspondence,* 328, 329–30; Robert Carter to William Dawson, July 14, 1720, Louis B. Wright, ed., *Letters of Robert Carter, 1720–1727: The Commercial Interests of a Virginia Gentleman* (San Marino, CA, 1940; rept. Westport, CN, 1970), 30; *JHB,* 1712–26, 250, 301; testimony of John Bagg, July 17, 1724, Mr. Commissary Blair to Bishop of London, July 17, 1724, Perry, *Historical Collections* 1:314–15, 321–22; Greene, *Quest for Power,* 346–47.

85. Robert Carter to Messrs. Perry, July 22, Sept. 19, 1720, to Perry Sr. and Jr., Nov. 8, 1720, Wright, *Carter Letters,* 35, 47, 58–59; Byrd, *London Diary,* 443, 445, 454–56, 462, 464, 465–67, 469; Spotswood to LCTP, Oct. 22, 1720, Brock, *Letters of Spotswood* 2:343–44; Williams, *Political Alignments,* 200–201.

86. *JHB,* 1712–26, xl, xliii, 249–50, 254, 260, 278, 280, 291–92, 294–95, 298, 300, 308–10, 313–15, 335, 343; *LJC* 2:657, 660; Thomas Lee to Dear Harry and Dear Brother, Nov. 9, 12, Dec. 3, 1720, photostats of originals, Yale University, Ethel Armes Collection of Lee Family Papers, LC, and Richard Bland Lee Papers, 1700–1825, LC; Byrd, *London Diary,* 488, 489, 490.

87. *JHB,* 1712–26, xli–xlii, 315; Hening, *Statutes* 4:77–79; Spotswood to Col. Nathaniel Harrison, March 28, 1724, Drysdale to LCTP, June 6, 1724, *CSP* 34 (1724–25): 115–20, 108–10; *EJC* 3:538–39; Williams, *Political Alignments,* 203–6.

88. Memorandum for His Excellency, [1721?], *WMQ* (2), 10 (1931): 246–50. See also Spotswood to LCTP, June 11, 1722, *CSP* 33 (1722–23): 85–86.

89. *EJC* 3:543. Byrd and Blair's last meeting with the council was on May 6, 1721. John Custis to Gentlemen, [1721], to [James Blair], Aug. 10, 1721, Josephine L. Zuppan, ed., *The Letterbook of John Custis IV of Williamsburg, 1717–1742* (Lanham, MD, 2005), 55–57; Byrd, *London Diary,* 511; Tate, "The College, 1693–1792," 51, 60; Dodson, *Spotswood,* 272–75; John Custis to Byrd, [c. June 24, 1722], Tinling, *Byrd Correspondence,* 331 and n. For Drysdale's commission and presentation to the Board of Trade, see *CSP* 33 (1722–23): 36, and *JCTP* 4 (1718–22): 35; Greene, *Peripheries and Center,* 45–46. Robert Carter stated that at Drysdale's death his wife delivered "all public papers" as well as various letters, including one from Walpole to Orkney

ordering that Spotswood be replaced by Drysdale, and also a letter from Walpole to Drysdale requesting that "Mr. Leheup . . . succeed Mr. [John] Carter in the agency of the countrey." RC Diary, Aug. 6, 1726.

90. Spotswood to Earl of Orkney, July 1, 1718, *CSP* 30 (Aug. 1717–Dec. 1718): 289–91; Greene, *Quest for Power,* 28.

91. Byrd to Charles Boyle, Earl of Orrery, July 5, 1726, Tinling, *Byrd Correspondence,* 355.

92. Spotswood to LCTP, June 23, 1722, *CSP* 30 (Aug. 1717–Dec. 1718): 94; Robert Carter to Philip Ludwell Sr., March 1, 1703, PRO, CO 5/1314, 55–60; Thomas Lee to Henry Lee, Nov. 12, 1720, Richard Bland Lee Papers, 1720–1825, LC; Fairfax Harrison, *Virginia Land Grants: A Study of Conveyancing in Relation to Colonial Politics* (Richmond, 1925; rept. New York, 1979), 93–102; *Cavaliers and Pioneers,* vols. 1–3; Carter Family Papers, 1651–1861, MSS 1 C2468a, 49–52, VHS; Northern Neck Land Grants, 3 (1703–10), 4 (1710–12), LOV; Lancaster County, Order Book 5 (1702–13): 20–22, 259; Jones, *John Carter II,* 33–35, 155; Lancaster County, Order Book 7 (1713–21): 335. For evidence of his building a new home, see Carter to Edward Tucker, July 13, 1720, Wright, *Carter Letters,* 16.

93. *VMHB* 32 (1932): 48; Spotswood to LCTP, June 23, 1722, Commission to John Carter as Secretary of Virginia, June 21, 1722, Drysdale to LCTP, May 16, Nov. 1, 1723, June 29, 1726, Earl of Orkney to LCTP, Jan. 17, 1724, LCTP to King in Council, Jan. 22, 1724, Order of King in Council, Jan. 23, 1724, *CSP* 33 (1722–23): 93, 254, 356, 35 (1726–27): 91–92, 34 (1724–25): 18, 20; *EJC* 4:19, 26, 28, 29–30; John Custis to William Byrd, June 24, 1722, Tinling, *Byrd Correspondence,* 332; RC Diary, Oct. 1, 1723; Robert Carter to Micajah Perry, Oct. 17, July 4, 1723, Jan. 29, 1724, RC Letter Book.

94. LCTP to Drysdale, June 19, 1723, Drysdale to LCTP, Dec. 20, 1722, July 5, Nov. 23, 1723, July 10, 1724, *CSP* 33 (1722–23): 191, 282, 304, 356, 34 (1724–25): 40; *JHB,* 1712–26, xlvii–xlviii, 395; Winfree, *Supplement to Hening's Statutes,* 237–46, 247–53; Edmund Jenings Jr. to John Tayloe, Oct. 28, 1723, Tayloe Family Papers, 1650–1970, 119–20, VHS; Robert Carter to Dear Sir, July 2, 1723, RC Letter Book.

95. John Grimes to [Mr. Leheup], May 25, 1724, *CSP* 35 (1724–25): 24–25; Spotswood to LCTP, June 16, 1724, Drysdale to LCTP, May 16, 1723, June 6, July 10, 1724, ibid., 34 (1724–25): 112–15, 33 (1722–23): 254, 34 (1724–25): 108–9, 140.

96. Spotswood to John Spotswood, Dec. 21, 1724, Cappon, "Correspondence of Alexander Spotswood with John Spotswood of Edinburgh," 239; LCTP to Duke of Newcastle, July 27, 1727, Carter to LCTP, Jan. 14, 1727, *CSP* 35 (1726–27): 278–81, 207; *EJC* 4:155, 208; *Cavaliers and Pioneers* 3:411–12; Dodson, *Spotswood,* chap. 13. On Beverley, see Robert Carter to Philip Ludwell, July 23, 1726, *VMHB* 3 (1895–96): 355–56. On Jenings, see note 101 below.

97. Elizabeth Pratt to Hond Sir [William Pratt, London], Sept. 7, [1725?], Roger Jones Family Papers, LC; Drysdale to LCTP, June 29, 1726, *CSP* 35 (1726–27): 88–92; Robert Carter to William Dawkins, Nov. 29, 1723, RC Letter Book; *EJC* 4:101–2, 108–13; RC Diary, June 24–26, 1726.

98. RC Diary, June 24–26, 1726. Carter's diary is cryptic, and blemishes and tears make it difficult to decipher, but the import is clear. Drysdale's death is reported in the diary, July 23, 1726, and in *EJC* 4:282. Carter's opinion of Grymes can be found, among other places, in his letter to Micajah Perry, Oct. 17, 1723, RC Letter Book. Drysdale's concern about the power of the secretary has already been noted. See also Drysdale to LCTP, July 10, 1726, Governor

Earl of Orkney to Mr. Popple, July 9, 1726, LCTP to Duke of Newcastle, July 14, 1726, king's warrant naming Carter, July 20, 1726, *CSP* 35 (1726–27): 113–14, 108–9, 119–20, 122; *JCTP* 5 (1723–28): 282.

99. [James, Duke of York], to Governor Effingham, Nov. 13, 1683, Billings, *Papers of Effingham,* 307; Maurer, "Notes on the Honorable Edmund Jenings," and "Edmund Jenings and Robert Carter"; conveyance to Robert Carter of "one Messuage or Tenament" in Williamsburg, May 23, 1718, Carter Papers, WM; Robert Carter to Micajah Perry Sr. and Jr., June 17, Feb. 13, 1721, to Right Honorable Lord Fairfax and William Cage, Feb. 13, Aug. 1, 1727, to [Edmund Jenings Jr.], March 8, 1721, John Carter to William Cage, Oct. 2, 1722, Wright, *Carter Letters,* 60–62, 68–70, 88–89, 107–8, 100–111; Robert Carter to Micajah Perry, July 4, 1723, to William Cage, July 4, 1723, Robert Carter to Dear Sr, Sept. 3, 1723, RC Letter Book; Robert Carter will, Aug. 27, 1726, *VMHB* 5 (1897–98): 425, 6 (1898–99): 11, 16.

100. Robert Carter to Philip Ludwell, July 23, 1726, *VMHB* 3 (1895–96): 355–66; RC Diary, July 23, 25, 1726.

101. RC Diary, Aug. 1, 2, 1726; *EJC* 4:113–14; Carter to Philip Ludwell, July 23, 1726, *VMHB* 3 (1895–96): 355–56. Carter incorrectly spelled Le Neve's name "Lemov."

102. Robert Carter to Duke of Newcastle, Jan. 5, 1727, *CSP* 35 (1726–27): 205; RC Diary, Aug. 4, 6, Dec. 22, 1726; John Custis to [James Blair, August 1726?], Zuppan, *Custis Letterbook,* 87; William Byrd to Charles Boyle, Earl of Orrery, Feb. 2, 1727, Tinling, *Byrd Correspondence,* 358–59; *EJC* 4:145–48; Jacob Price, *Perry of London: A Family and a Firm in the Seaborne Frontier, 1615–1752* (Cambridge, Mass., 1992), 76–77; *JCTP* 5 (1725–28): 302–3.

103. John Custis to [Mrs. Drysdale, early 1727?], Zuppan, *Custis Letterbook,* 90–91; RC Diary, March 1–3, 1727; *EJC* 4:128.

104. John Pratt to My Dear Niece, June [1727], Roger Jones Family Papers, LC; Morton, *Colonial Virginia,* 500; William Gooch to Thomas Gooch, Sept. 18, 1727, March 27, June 9, 1728, Gooch Letter Book, 1727–58, transcript, CW; William Byrd to Charles Boyle, Earl of Orrery, Feb. 25, 1728, Tinling, *Byrd Correspondence,* 371; Robert Carter to My Dear Lewis Burwell, June 26, 1729, RC Letter Book; Price, *Perry of London,* 76–77. For the new appellation for the governor's house, the "Pallace," see Thomas Jones to My Dearest Life, Sept. 30, 1728, Roger Jones Family Papers, LC.

105. RC Diary, Sept. 8–12, 1727; *EJC* 4:145–48; Gooch to Thomas Gooch, Sept. 18, Oct. 28, 1727, Feb. 18, March 3, Aug. 27, 1728, Jan. 7, 1730, Gooch Letter Book, 1727–58, CW.

106. Gooch to Thomas Gooch, Feb. 18, March 27, Aug. 27, 1728, Gooch Letter Book, 1727–58, CW; *JHB,* 1727–40, xvi–xvii. On the increasing role of the House of Burgesses, see Williams, *Political Alignments,* chap. 6.

107. John Custis to Hond Madm, [before Dec. 10, 1727], to Mr. Perry, Dec. 10, 1727, and [1730?], Zuppan, *Custis Letterbook,* 98–99, 99–100; Robert Carter to Earl of Orkney, Dec. 12, 1727, to [?], Dec. 16, 1727, to Collo. Page, Dec. 30, 1727, RC Letter Book; Gooch to LCTP, Dec. 13, 1727, to Secretary of State, Dec. 30, 1727, PRO, CO 5/1321, 1327; Duke of Newcastle to Gooch, March 5, 1728, ibid., 324/36; *EJC* 4:182.

108. Instructions to Earl of Orkney, [1727?], Entry Book, 1717–27, PRO, CO 5/1365; Gooch to LCTP, March 26, 1729, Jan 9, 1730, ibid., 1321, 1322; *EJC,* vol. 4; *JHB,* 1727–34.

109. *EJC* 4:155; *JHB,* 1727–40, 28; Gooch to LCTP, Feb. 12, Aug. 9, 1728, LCTP to Gooch, May 7, 1728, May 22, 1729, Gooch to Secretary of State Newcastle, June 9, 1728, Secretary of

State to Gooch, Dec. 1728, PRO, CO 5/1321, 1366, 1337; Gooch to LCTP, June [8?], 1728, April 9, 1730, *CSP* 36 (1728–29): 124, 37 (1730): 77.

110. Robert Carter to Earl of Orkney, Dec. 12, 1727, Aug. 8, 1728, April 11, 1729, to William Dawkins, Dec. 16, 1727, Aug. 29, 1729, to Colo. Page, Feb. 11, 1729, to the Honbl. the Gov., Feb. 11, 1729, RC Letter Book; *EJC* 4:210; John Custis to Mr. Perry, [c. June 1730], Zuppan, *Custis Letterbook,* 108–9.

111. Hemphill, *Virginia and the English Commercial System,* chap. 2; Price, "The Excise Affair Revisited," 271–73; Robert Carter to [Thos.] Evans, Aug. 3, 1723, to James Bradley, Aug. 29, 1729, to John Tayloe, Jan. 19, 1730, RC Letter Book; William Byrd to Micajah Perry, July 23, 1728, Tinling, *Byrd Correspondence,* 377–78; Peter V. Bergstrom, "Markets and Merchants: Economic Diversification in Colonial Virginia" (Ph.D. diss., Univ. of New Hampshire, 1980); Wattenburg, *Statistical History,* 1168; Minchinton et al., *Virginia Slave Trade Statistics,* xiii–xv.

112. Gooch to LCTP, Sept. 7, 1729, Feb. 27, April 9, 1730, PRO, CO 5/1322; Gooch to LCTP, June 29, 1729, *CSP* 36 (1728–29): 418–19.

113. Gooch to LCTP, May 29, 1730, *CSP* 37 (1730): 129; John Custis to Dear Sr [Richard Fitzwilliam, after June 18, 1730], Zuppan, *Custis Letterbook,* 111; *JHB,* 1727–40, 57–59, 61, 70, 74, 75, 75, 76, 78, 80, 82.

114. *LJC,* 708, 771, 772, 775–76, 778–79; *JHB,* 1727–40, 100, 101, 104, 109, 110; *EJC* 4:93–94; John Custis to Dear Sr, [Richard Fitzwilliam, after June 18, 1730], Zuppan, *Custis Letterbook,,* 111; Hemphill, *Virginia and the English Commercial System,* 161–63; Williams, *Political Alignments,* 231–32.

115. Hening, *Statutes* 4:247–71; Hemphill, *Virginia and the English Commercial System,* 156–58; Gooch to LCTP, July 23, 1730, *CSP* 37 (1730): 208.

116. Gooch to Thomas Gooch, July 25, 1730, Gooch Letter Book, 1727–58, CW; Price, *Perry of London,* 80; Price, "The Excise Affair Revisited," 276–77; Gooch to LCTP, Feb. 27, 1731, March 30, 1732, PRO, CO 5/1322, 1323; LCTP to the King, May 19, 1731, to Gooch, May 23, 1731, *CSP* 38 (1731): 106–7, 111–12; *EJC* 4:259–60, 263–64, 269, 281; Ira Peart to Mr. George Gibson, April 15, 1732, Fulham Palace Papers, 13 (1695–1771), Lambeth Palace, London; Robert Carter to Edward Tucker, Aug. 16, 1731, Feb. 28, May 29, 1732, to John Pemberton, Feb. 28, 1732, to Alderman Perry, March 8, May 29, 1732, RC Letter Book; John Custis to Mr. Fitchwms [Fitzwilliam, 1732], to Mr. Perry, [1734], Zuppan, *Custis Letterbook,* 124–25, 142–43; *LJC,* 843–44; *JHB,* 1727–40, 122, 123, 255, 256, 259, 266; Billings et al., *Colonial Virginia,* 239–45. Request for repeal in 1732, for example, came from Lancaster, Prince William, King George, Accomac, Northampton, Middlesex, Stafford, and Richmond counties. For the inspection act, see esp. Janis M. Horne, "The Opposition to the Virginia Tobacco Inspection Act of 1730" (honors thesis, College of William and Mary, 1977).

117. Price, *Perry of London,* 75–76, 82–87; Price, "The Excise Affair Revisited," 278–292; Hemphill, *Virginia and the English Commercial System,* 175–231; Robert Carter to John Stark, May 30, 1728, to Alderman Perry, July 10, 1732, to John Randolph, Esq., [1729?], RC Letter Book; John Custis to Mr. Fitchwms [Fitzwilliam], 1732, to Mr. Loyd [Lionel Lyde, 1732], Zuppan, *Custis Letterbook,* 111, 122–23; Gooch to Bishop of London, Aug. 12, 1732, Church Commissioners for England, Fulham Palace Papers, 13 (1695–1771), Lambeth Palace, London; *EJC* 4:258–59, 267; *JHB,* 1727–40, 146, 152, 159, 160, 161, 164; *LJC,* 808–9, 810, 811, 813.

118. *JHB,* 1727–40, 167; Price, "The Excise Affair Revisited," esp. 271–305; Hemphill, *Vir-*

ginia and the English Commercial System, esp. chaps. 6–7; J. H. Plumb, *Sir Robert Walpole: The King's Minister* (2 vols., London, 1960), 1:257.

119. Cowden, "The Randolphs," chap. 12; Kukla, *Speakers and Clerks,* 113–23; *JHB,* 1727–40, xxiv–xxv, 171–75, 177, 220–21; Hening, *Statutes* 4:433–36.

120. *JHB,* 1727–40, 241–42; Robert Carter to John Carter, July 13, 1720, Wright, *Carter Letters,* 8.

121. Williams, *Political Alignments,* chap. 6, addresses the question of council decline. For a specific example, see Kukla, *Speakers and Clerks,* 22–24, 96, 104–5, on the shift of the office of treasurer from the council to the Speaker of the House of Burgesses.

122. *JHB,* 1727–40, 175–76.

123. Ibid., 241–42.

124. See Jack P. Greene, "Virtus and Libertas: Political Culture, Social Change, and the Origins of the American Revolution in Virginia, 1763–1766," in *The Southern Exposure in the American Revolution,* ed. Jeffrey A. Crowe and Larry E. Tise (Chapel Hill, NC, 1978), esp. 59, 60, 63–65.

3. The Economy

1. Total landholding is difficult to determine. My estimates come from a variety of sources including *Cavaliers and Pioneers,* vols. 1–5. See also Northern Neck Grant Books, LOV, and wills and inventories listed in Swem, *Virginia Historical Index,* as well as family manuscript materials, LOV, VHS, UVA, WM, LC.

2. On John Carter, see *VMHB* 21 (1913): 82, 22 (1914): 48; *DVB,* s.v. "Carter, John."

3. *American Weekly Mercury,* no. 662, Aug. 31–Sept. 7, 1732; Robert Carter's will and codicil, typed transcript by Henrietta G. Goodwin (FHCC, 1988); "Inventory of the Estate of Robert Carter, Esqr.," UVA, transcript by Henrietta G. Goodwin (FHCC, 1983); *Cavaliers and Pioneers,* vols. 1–3; Northern Neck Grants, LOV.

4. See wills of John Carter I and II in Jones, *John Carter II.* On Robert Carter's schooling, see Alan Simpson, "Robert Carter's Schooldays," *VMHB* 95 (1986): 161–88. William Byrd to Micajah Perry, July 3, 1728, Tinling, *Byrd Correspondence,* 378. In 1691 Carter had thirty-four tithables in Lancaster County; see Lancaster County, Order Book 3 (1686–96): 188. *JHB,* 1659/60–93, xiv; names of suitable persons to fill vacancies on council, July 22, 1693, Order in Council, Dec. 14, 1699, PRO, CO 5/1306, 1311.

5. Lancaster County, Order Book 3 (1686–96): 167, 4 (1696–1702): 43, 105–6, 107–8, 6 (1713–21): 45, 7 (1721–29): 304, 8 (1729–43): 48, in Christine A. Jones, comp., "Order Book Entries at Lancaster County Court House Referring to Robert Carter of Corotoman" (FHCC, 1978). *EJC* 2:14, 24; *JHB,* 1695–1702, 171, 256, 259, 1702–12, xxi–xxii; Harrison, *Virginia Land Grants,* 99–104. Edmund Jenings and Thomas Lee held the agency from 1712 to 1719. Robert Carter to Philip Ludwell, March 1, 1703, Copies of Letters Presented by James Blair and Philip Ludwell to LCTP, PRO, CO 5/1314, 55–56; Thomas Lee to Catherine, Lady Fairfax, Sept. 14, 1713, Fairfax Family Papers, 1705–32, LC; Thomas Lee to Henry Lee, Nov. 12, 1720, Richard Bland Lee Papers, 1720–1825, LC. For the Northern Neck Proprietary, see Douglas Southall Freeman, *George Washington: A Biography* (7 vols., New York, 1948–57), vol. 1, app. I-1. For Robert Carter, see ibid., 489–95.

6. Good records on Carter's tobacco shipments exist only for the last twelve years of his life. See Wright, *Carter Letters;* RC Letter Books; RC Diary. For Carter's pride in his tobacco-growing skills, see Carter to William Dawkins, July 3, 1723, RC Letter Book. For evidence on tenant income, see, for example, RC Diary, Sept. 13, 1722; Carter to Richard Hickman, Sept. 17, 1729, RC Letter Book. On estate management, see Carter to Micajah and Richard Perry, July 14, 1720, Wright, *Carter Letters,* 21–22; Carter to Micajah Perry, July 13, 1723, RC Letter Book. For Carter's service as an agent for English and other firms, see Carter to William Dawkins, July 17, 1720, Wright, *Carter Letters,* 12; Lancaster County, Order Book 5 (1702–13): Aug. 11, 1709, 218. For money loaned and store goods sold, see examples in RC Diary, Jan. 31, Feb. 5, Nov. 23, 1723, April 14, July 5, Sept. 21, 1724. See also Carter to Micajah Perry, July 4, 1723, RC Letter Book.

7. Minchinton et al., *Virginia Slave Trade Statistics,* xiv–xv, 5, 49, 62–63; Robert Carter to William Dawkins, to Messrs. Perry, to John Pemberton, and to Messrs. Chamberlayne & Sitwell, July 26, 27, 1720, Wright, *Carter Letters,* 39–43; RC Diary, May 19–24, 1726, Sept. 13–Oct. 3, 1727; Robert Carter to John Pemberton, July 26, Sept. 15, 16, 27, 1727, RC Letter Book.

8. RC Diary, Sept. 24, Dec. 17, 18, 1722, Jan. 19, May 20, 1723, Feb. 13, 1725; "Inventory of Estate of Robert Carter, Esqr.," UVA, Goodwin transcript FHCC; Lancaster County, Order Book 7 (1713–21): May 12, 1714, 51, 8 (1721–29): March 9, 1726, 191; Carter to Alderman Perry, Sept. 10, 1731, to Richard Perry, Aug. 9, 1728, to William Dawkins, Oct. 12, 1728, RC Letter Book. For comments on copper mining, see William Byrd to Micajah Perry, July 3, 1728, Tinling, *Byrd Correspondence,* 278; Carter to Alderman Perry, Sept. 10, 1731, to Edward Athawes, Sept. 10, Nov. 15, 1731, Feb. 28, 1732, RC Letter book.

9. Carter to Richard Perry, July 13, 18, 1720, Wright, *Carter Letters,* 2–3, 31–32; Carter to Micajah Perry, July 4, Aug. 26, 1723, March 24, Dec. 2, 1727, RC Letter Book. On balances with other merchants, see, for example, Carter to William Dawkins, April 16, 1730, ibid.

10. RC Diary, April 8, July 21, Aug. 2, 1723, Sept. 9, Oct. 5, 1724, Dec. 5, 1725.

11. For overseers and "head overseers" as well as skilled servants and slaves, see "Inventory of the Estate of Robert Carter, Esqr.," UVA, Goodwin transcript FHCC. For other employees, see Carter to Capt. Thomas Hooper, Aug. 24, Dec. 28, 1723, to John Stark, Sept. 17, 1723, to Dear Sir, July 2, 1723, to William Dawkins, March 25, 1724, RC Letter Book. For vessels, see RC Diary and the inventory. For head clerk or business manager, see Carter to Dawkins, July 30, 1732, to Philip Perry, March 2, 1732, RC Letter Book; Richard Chapman to Edward Athawes, Aug. 25, 1735, to Micajah Perry, Oct. 13, 1736[3?], and John Carter to Haswell & Brooks, Aug. 11, 1734, Carter Letter Book, 1732–81, UVA, Goodwin transcript FHCC. Richard Chapman to George Carter, Esq., Nov. 16, 1740, letters from the letter book of Richard Chapman, *WMQ* (1), 21 (1913–14): 97–100.

12. See "Inventory of the Estate of Robert Carter, Esqr.," UVA, Goodwin transcript FHCC.

13. RC Diary, Feb. 17, April 6, 7, 1726; Carter to Robert Jones, Oct. 10, 1727, April 16, 1728, RC Letter Book.

14. The figure is arrived at by counting 391.5 field hands and multiplying that figure by £10. The estimate also does not include 26.5 slaves at the home plantation, most of whom performed specialized functions. Children under twelve were not counted, and those between twelve and fifteen were counted as a half share. See Lorena S. Walsh, "Slave Life, Slave Society, and Tobacco

Production in the Tidewater Chesapeake," in *Cultivation and Culture: Labor and the Forming of Slave Life in the Americas,* ed. Ira Berlin and Philip D. Morgan (Charlottesville, VA, 1993), 170–90, esp. 180. "Inventory of the Estate of Robert Carter, Esqr.," UVA, Goodwin transcript FHCC.

15. Kamoie, "Three Generations of Planter Businessmen: The Tayloes," chap. 1; Tayloe, *Tayloes of Virginia,* 2; State of the Case Int: Tayloe and the Lydes of Bristol, Tayloe Family Papers, 1650–1970, 121–22, VHS; John Tayloe to Dear Bro. [James Lyde?], July 22, 1715, to [?, May 1716], to Thomas Crofts & Company, May 11, 1716, and [1716], to Good Cousin [?], 1716, to Messrs. Lyonel Lyde & Company, [1716], to Messrs. Samuel Jacobs & Company, April 2, 1717, July 1719, to [?], July [6], 1717, to Messrs. James and Lyonel Lyde, July 12, 1718, to Mr. John Baker, Aug. 20, 1718, to Messrs. [?], Feb. 2, 1718, to Sir [Mr. Connor], June 18, 1719, to John Baylor, 1720, to Messrs. Lyonel and Cornelius Lyde, [Aug.?] 4, 1720, to Messrs. [?], Sept. 13, 1721, John Tayloe I and II, Account and Letter Book, 1714–78, ibid., b1; Robert Carter to Messrs. Perry, Sept. 27, 1720, Wright, *Carter Letters,* 53–54; Carter to Collo. John Tayloe, Jan. 29, 1729, RC Letter Book; John Tayloe Account Book, 1740–41, and John Tayloe Will, Jan. 3, 1744, Tayloe Family Papers, 1650–1970, a1 and 149, VHS.

16. Kamoie, "Three Generations of Planter Businessmen: The Tayloes," 45–46, 50–51.

17. *DVB,* s.v. "Beverley, William"; William Beverley to John Fairchild, Nov. 26, 1739, July 18, 1743, to Lord Fairfax, April 20, 1743, William Beverley Letter Book, 1737–44, NYPL; see also *WMQ* (1), 3 (1894–95): 232–34; William Beverley Account Books, 1745, 1752, Beverley Family Papers, 1654–1801, MSS 1 B4678 b11, VHS; Robert Beverley to Samuel Athawes, March 3, 1762, Robert Beverley Letter Book, 1761–93, LC; *Cavaliers and Pioneers* 4:118; *EJC* 4:375–76. For land sales, see Robert Mitchell, *Commercialism and Frontier; Perspectives on the Early Shenandoah Valley* (Charlottesville, VA, 1977), 75.

18. Emory G. Evans, *Thomas Nelson of Yorktown: Revolutionary Virginian* (Charlottesville, VA, 1975), chap. 1; Gooch to Board of Trade, Feb. 11, 1738, PRO, CO 5/1324; Francis Jerdone to Messrs. Buchanan, *WMQ* (1), 11 (1902–03): 154; Minchinton et al., *Virginia Slave Trade Statistics,* xiii–xv, 1–135.

19. Holly Brewer, "Entailing Aristocracy in Colonial Virginia: Ancient Feudal Restraints and Revolutionary Reform," *WMQ* (3), 54 (1997): 307–46. Thomas Nelson's will, ibid., (1), 6 (1898–99): 143–45; Robert Carter's will, *VMHB* 5 (1897–98): 408–28, 6 (1898–99): 1–22, but a more accurate version is the transcript by Henrietta G. Goodwin at FHCC. For John Tayloe's will, see Tayloe Family Papers, 1650–1970, 144, VHS. William Beverley's will, *VMHB* 22 (1913): 297–301. For other examples in the first half of the eighteenth century, see the wills of Nathaniel Harrison (1726), Mann Page (1730), John Randolph (1735), and Benjamin Harrison (1743), ibid., 31 (1922):, 278–83, 32 (1923): 39–43, 36 (1928): 376–80, 32 (1923): 98–102; Gawin Corbin (1739), Fleet, *Virginia Colonial Abstracts* 4:54–61; John Custis IV (1749), Custis Family Papers, 1683–1858, a52–53, VHS.

20. Brewer, "Entailing Aristocracy," esp. 324–27; [Robert Carter] to Francis Lee, Dec. 20, 1707, Christ Church Parish, Lancaster County, Wormeley Estate Papers, 1701–10, 1716, photostats, LOV.

21. *EJC* 2:131, 5:227; [Robert Carter] to [Francis?] Lee, July 15, 1702, Christ Church Parish, Lancaster County, Wormeley Estate Papers, 1701–10, 1716, photostats, LOV; Hening, *Statutes* 5:85–89, 277–84; Robert Carter to Philip Perry, March 2, 1732, RC Letter Book.

22. T. M. Devine, *Tobacco Lords: A Study of the Tobacco Merchants of Glasgow and Their Trading Activities, 1740–1790* (Edinburgh, 1975), 56–58; Jacob M. Price, "The Rise of Glasgow in the Chesapeake Tobacco Trade, 1707–1775," *WMQ* (3), 11 (1954): 179–99; Price, *Perry of London*, 64–65, 98; McCusker and Menard, *Economy of British America*, 120–23; Russell R. Menard, "Economic and Social Development of the South," in *The Cambridge Economic History of the United States*, vol. 1, *The Colonial Era*, ed. Stanley L. Engerman and Robert Gallman (New York, 1996), 261–63; Ian K. Steele, *The English Atlantic, 1675–1740: An Exploration of Communication and Community* (New York, 1986), 48–49, 218, 331 n. 33. For a Glasgow firm operating in Virginia, see George Bogle to Matthew Bogle, Oct. 20, 1731, Bogle Papers, 1696–1777, Mitchell Library, Glasgow; David Hancock, *Citizens of the World: London Merchants and the Integration of the British Atlantic Community, 1735–1785* (New York, 1995), 59–62; Account of the Sale of Tobacco of Robert Carter Jr. by Richard Oswald & Brother, Glasgow, Feb. 22, 1733, Carter Family Papers, 1651–1861, MSS 1 C2468a, 102–6, VHS. See also Walsh, "Slave Life, Slave Society, and Tobacco Production in the Tidewater Chesapeake, 1620–1820," 181, 352 n. 26. It should be noted that for the late seventeenth century and the first twenty years of the eighteenth century, most of the elite families benefited from higher prices because they produced sweetscented as opposed to Oronoco tobacco, which sold on the home market at higher prices. For the effect of the decline in demand for sweetscented tobacco, see Darrett Rutman and Anita Rutman, *A Place in Time Explicatus* (New York and London, 1984), chap. 1, esp. the price series on p. 4.

23. Robert Carter to Micajah Perry, July 3, 1723, to Mr. Thomas Evans, July 22, 1723, to Benjamin Grave and to Edward Tucker, July 27, 1723, RC Letter Book; William Byrd to [?], c. July 23, 1728, Tinling, *Byrd Correspondence*, 376; William Nelson to Samuel Athawes, July 5, 1769, to S. Martin, July 2, 1772, Nelson Letter Book, 1766–75, LOV.

24. Price, "Rise of Glasgow," esp. 194–95; Jacob M. Price, "The Last Phase of the Virginia London Consignment Trade: James Buchanan and Co., 1758–1768," *WMQ* (3), 43 (1986): esp. 82–96. William Byrd II, for example, in 1710 had a store at Westover and one in Williamsburg that he operated with Richard Bland. He continued to have a store at Westover as late as 1741. Byrd, *Secret Diary*, 161; Maude H. Woodfin and Marion Tinling, eds., *Another Secret Diary of William Byrd of Westover, 1739–1741* (Richmond, 1942), 157, 161. For the location of Scottish stores, see, for example, the claim of William Cunninghame, March 15, 1784, PRO, AO 13/29.

25. Price, *Perry of London*, chap. 5 and esp. pp. 70–71; *JHB, 1712–26*, 422–24. See also Hemphill, *Virginia and the English Commercial System*, chap. 2, esp. pp. 79–88; George Mason to Patrick Henry, May 6, 1783, Robert A. Rutland, ed., *The Papers of George Mason, 1725–1792* (3 vols., Chapel Hill, NC, 1970), 769–83.

26. For the debt act, see Hemphill, *Virginia and the British Commercial System*, 174–89. *JHB, 1712–26*, 422–24; Gooch to Board of Trade, Feb. 12, 1727, July 10, 1731, PRO, CO 5/1321, 1322; Robert Carter to Alderman Perry, July 10, 1732, RC Letter Book; John Custis to Mr. Loyd [Lyonel Lyde], [1732], Zuppan, *Custis Letterbook*, 122–23.

27. Hemphill, *Virginia and the English Commercial System*, 85–86; John, Charles, and Landon Carter to Alderman Perry, Aug. 27, 1732, Carter Letter Book, 1732–81, UVA, Goodwin transcript FHCC.

28. [Robert Carter] to [?], Aug. 20, 1706, Christ Church Parish, Wormeley Estate Papers, 1701–10, 1716, photostats, LOV; William Byrd to [?], June 27, 1729, Tinling, *Byrd Correspon-*

dence, 418; John Custis to Sir [Mr. Perry], 1724, to Gentlemen, 1721, to Sr, April 2, 1723, to Robert Cary, 1729, Zuppan, *Custis Letterbook,* 53–54, 66–67, 61–63, 101–3; Carter to Mr. Richard Perry, July 13, 1720, Wright, *Carter Letters,* 2; Robert Carter to Edward Athawes, [June 2, 1727? (not clear because he mentioned writing Athawes on Aug. 8, 1728)], to Alderman Perry, July 11, 1732, RC Letter Book; Charles Carter to Messrs. Capel and Osgood Hanbury, Feb. 6, 1760, Carter Letter Book, 1732–81, UVA, Goodwin transcript FHCC; Charles Goore to Mrs. Priscilla Lewis, Dec. 22, 1757, Carter Family Papers, 1651–1861, MSS 1 C2468a, 41–42, VHS.

29. Jacob Price, *Capital and Credit in the British Overseas Trade: The View from the Chesapeake, 1700–1776* (Cambridge, Mass., 1980), 60–61; Hemphill, *Virginia and England's Commercial System,* chap. 2; Robert Carter to Mr. Micajah Perry, May 17, 1727, to Mr. John Starke, July 8, [1729], RC Letter Book; William Byrd to Christopher Smith, Aug. 27, 1735, Tinling, *Byrd Correspondence,* 455; John Custis to Mr. Perry, 1727, Zuppan, *Custis Letterbook,* 91–92.

30. Robert Carter to William Dawkins, July 15, 1720, Wright, *Carter Letters,* 28; George Bogle to Matthew Bogle, Oct. 20, 1731, Bogle Papers, 1696–1777, Mitchell Library, Glasgow.

31. The specifics of the consumer revolution are discussed in chap. 4.

32. John Custis to [Perry & Lane], [spring or summer of 1721], Zuppan, *Custis Letterbook,* 53–54; William Byrd to John Percival, July 12, 1736, Tinling, *Byrd Correspondence,* 487–88; William Dawkins to John and Landon Carter, Jan. 13, 1733, Carter Family Papers, 1651–1861, MSS 1 C2468a, 55–62, VHS; John Carter to Foster Cunliffe, Esq., May 22, 1736, Jan. 8, July 14, 1737, Aug. 1, 1738, John, Charles, and Landon Carter to Foster Cunliffe and Edward Mosely, Aug. 28, 1736, Richard Chapman to Foster Cunliffe and Edward Mosely, Sept. 25, 1736, April 7, 1737, John Carter to Foster Cunliffe and Samuel Powell, Nov. 3, 1737, Aug. 3, 1738, John Carter to Richard Gildart, Aug. 1, 1738, Carter Letter Book, 1732–81, UVA, Goodwin transcript FHCC; [?] to Charles Carter, Esqr., Jan. 6, 1737, folder 32, James Monroe Museum and Memorial Library, Fredericksburg, VA; *Virginia Gazette* (Parks), April 8, 1737, Jan. 8, 1739, (Hunter), Jan. 25, July 3, 1752; Minchinton et al., *Virginia Slave Trade Statistics,* xiv–xv, 14–15, 30–31, 53, 57, 63, 67, 75, 83, 87, 89, 90–91, 100–101, 109, 115, 121, 148–49, 150–51, 153–55, 185, 191, 192; William Beverley to John Fairchild, Nov. 25, 1739, William Beverley Letter Book, NYPL; Cowden, "The Randolphs," chap. 11. The Wayles-Randolph debt ultimately involved Thomas Jefferson as one of the executors of the Wayles estate because his wife Martha was a Wayles heir. In the end it was Randolph's heirs, not Wayles's, that were held responsible for this debt. In December 1797 the U.S. Circuit Court, Virginia District, ruled that $52,881.54 was due. Richard Hanson, the representative of the firm in Virginia, wrote, "In short it is idle to expect a Virginia Jury to find a verdict against Mr. Jefferson." Farrell & Jones to John Wayles, April 6, 1772, April 23, 1773, John Wayles to Farrell & Jones, Sept. 24, 1772, Farrell & Jones to Richard Randolph, Dec. 10, 1773, Aug. 10, 1774, Jan. 27, 1775, U.S. Circuit Court, Virginia District, Ended Cases, Jones, Svg. Ptr., vs. Wayles's Exor., 1797, Jones, Svg. Ptr., vs. Randolph's Exors., U.S. Circuit Court, Virginia District, Record Book 8H, 1797, pp. 51–52, LOV; Richard Randolph to Farrell & Jones, March 8, May 15, 1775, Richard Hanson to Farrell & Jones, July 5, 1786, Sept. 3, 1787, June 2, Dec. 15, 1797, Copies of Letters of Richard Randolph to Farrell & Jones and Extracts of Richard Hanson's Letters as Relate to the African Account, PRO, T 79/30. See also Wayles Executors v. Randolph et al., in Charles Hobson et al., eds., *The Papers of John Marshall* (15 vols., Chapel Hill, NC, 1974–2006), 5:117–60; Debt to Farrell & Jones in Julian P. Boyd et al., eds., *The Papers of Thomas Jefferson* (Princeton, NJ, 1950–), 15:643–77.

33. Morton, *Colonial Virginia,* vol. 2, chaps. 13, 14, 15; Hening, *Statutes* 4:77–79, 81–83; *EJC* 4:92, 160, 223–24, 249, 253, 355–56; Voorhis, "Crown versus Council in Virginia Land Policy," 510–14.

34. *EJC* 4:72, 224, 229, 230, 232, 249–50, 270, 316, 336, 346–47, 365–66, 375–76, 395, 425, 444, 5:133; William Beverley to Dear Sir, April 30, 1732, Milhart Rangdain and others to the Honble William Gooch, 1733, William P. Palmer, ed., *Calendar of Virginia State Papers and Other Manuscripts* (12 vols., Richmond, 1876–93; rept. New York, 1968), 1:217–20; *Cavaliers and Pioneers* 4:118; Mitchell, *Commercialism and Frontier,* 76. On Spotswood and the involvement of Lee and Carter, see chap. 2 above. William Beverley to Capt. James Patton, Aug. 22, 1737, *WMQ* (1), 3 (1894–95): 222–27; Morton, *Colonial Virginia,* 550–51; Robert Beverley to Samuel Athawes, June 5, 1773, Robert Beverly Letter Book, 1761–93, LC.

35. See Byrd, "The Secret History of the Line" and "A Journey to the Land of Eden 1733," *The Prose Works of William Byrd of Westover: Narratives of Colonial Virginia,* ed. Louis B. Wright (Cambridge, Mass., 1966); *EJC* 4:355, 443, 5:38; *Cavaliers and Pioneers* 5:16; Byrd to Governor George Barrington, July 20, 1731, to Gabriel Johnson, [1735?], to John Bartram, Nov. 30, 1738, March 23, 1739, to Christopher Smith, [Sept. 1740?], Tinling, *Byrd Correspondence,* 445–46, 448–50, 465–66, 529–31, 553. See also Morton, *Colonial Virginia,* 560–69. Some of the "Switzers and Germans" did settle on the land, and before Byrd's death he did sell some of it to other people. See Byrd to John Bartram, March 23, 1739, Tinling, *Byrd Correspondence,* 529–31; Byrd, *Another Secret Diary,* 110, 157, 163, 181. *Virginia Gazette* (Parks), June 12, 1739, 4, 1–2; *DVB,* s.v., "Byrd, William III."

36. *EJC* 4:430–31, 5:172–73.

37. Ibid., 5:172–73, 193–95, 6:553, 688–98.

38. Ibid., 6:688–99, 5:138, 141, 156, 167, 243–45, 255, 295–97; Gooch to Board of Trade, Nov. 6, 1747, June 16, 1748, Board of Trade to Gooch, Jan. 19, Sept. 2, 1748, March 4, 1749, PRO, CO 5/1326, 1327, 1366; John Hanbury to the King, [1748], Kenneth P. Bailey, *The Ohio Company of Virginia and the Westward Movement, 1748–1792* (Glendale, CA, 1939), 297–301, see also 24–25, 67, 104–5; Minutes of the Ohio Company, Sept. 25, 1749, Lois Mulkearn, ed., *George Mercer Papers Relating to the Ohio Company of Virginia* (Pittsburgh, 1954), 170–71; Alfred P. James, *The Ohio Company: Its Inner History* (Pittsburgh, 1959), chaps. 2–3.

39. *EJC* 5:436–37, 470, VI, 257, 258, 687; George Washington to John Campbell, Earl of Loudoun, Jan. 10, 1757, to William Crawford, Sept. 17, 1767, and Dismal Swamp Land Company, Articles of Agreement, William W. Abbot et al., eds., *The Papers of George Washington: Colonial Series* (10 vols., Charlottesville, VA, 1983–95), 4:79–80, 7:269–74, 8:26–29; Francis Fauquier to Board of Trade, Dec. 1, 1759, Feb. 13, July 23, 1764, Board of Trade to Fauquier, Feb. 16, 1761, Oct. 10, 1763, George Reese, ed., *The Official Papers of Francis Fauquier, Lieutenant Governor of Virginia, 1758–1768* (3 vols., Charlottesville, VA., 1981), 1:270–77, 2:479, 1037, 3:1078, 1131–32; Palmer, *Calendar of Virginia State Papers* 1:262, 265; Charles Royster, *The Fabulous History of the Dismal Swamp Company: A Story of George Washington's Times* (New York, 1999), chap. 2; Edward T. Price, *Dividing the Land: Early American Beginnings of Our Private Property Mosaic* (Chicago, 1995), 152–58; James, *Ohio Company,* 183–85.

40. Price, *Capital and Credit,* 17–19; Mark Egnal, *New World Economies: The Growth of the Thirteen Colonies and Early Canada* (New York, 1998), chap. 5, pp. 93–98; John Wayles to Farrell & Jones, Aug. 30, 1766, Extracts of Letters of John Wayles as Relate to the Estate of Col.

Peter Randolph, American Loyalist Claims, PRO, T 79/20. A more accessible copy is John M. Hemphill II, ed., "John Wayles Rates His Neighbors," *VMHB* 50 (1958): 301–6.

41. Louis Morton, *Robert Carter of Nomini Hall: A Virginia Tobacco Planter of the Eighteenth Century* (Williamsburg, VA, 1941; rept. Charlottesville, VA, 1964); Carter Letter Book, 1732–81, UVA, Goodwin transcript FHCC; Edward Carter to Thomas Main, June 15, 1791, U.S. Circuit Court, Virginia District, Ended Cases, Thomas Main vs. Carter's Exors., 1797, LOV; Report of W. W. Hening on Claims of Glassford, Gordon, Monteith & Co., PRO, T 79/73; Hening, Statutes 8:214, 218–22; memorandum concerning family property disputes, c. 1765, Carter Family Papers, Sabine Hall Collection, 1659–1797, UVA microfilm.

42. John Sanderson, *Biography of the Signers of the Declaration of Independence* (9 vols., Philadelphia, 1820–37), 8:127–72, is useful; see esp. 168, 170. Clifford Dowdey, *The Great Plantation: A Profile of Berkeley Hundred and Plantation from Jamestown to Appomattox* (New York, 1957), portrayed Benjamin Harrison V correctly, but I believe Benjamin VI was more able than Dowdey suggested. Dowdey's dates of birth for both Harrisons appear to be incorrect. Dowdey said Benjamin VI was thirty in 1785, but in 1787 he wrote he was "near fifty years," which means that his father could not have been born in 1726. He was a signer of the nonimportation association of 1770 and presumably was at least twenty-one at that point. L. H. Butterfield et al., eds., *Diary and Autobiography of John Adams* (4 vols., paperback ed., New York, 1964), 3:367–68, 370–71; Richard Corbin to Edmund Jenings, Nov. 6, 1758, March 15, 1759, Oct. 8, 1760, Richard Corbin Letter Book, 1758–68, CW; Edmund Jenings to Coll. Harrison, July 23, 1759, Edmund Jenings Letter Book, 1753–69, VHS; John Wayles to Farrell & Jones, Aug. 30, 1766, Extracts of Letters of John Wayles as Relate to the Estate of Col. Peter Randolph, American Loyalist Claims, PRO, T 79/20; Hemphill, "John Wayles Rates His Neighbors"; *VMHB* 35 (1927): 89; William J. Van Schreeven, Robert Scribner, and Brent Tartar, eds., *Revolutionary Virginia: The Road to Independence* (8 vols., Charlottesville, VA, 1973–83), 1:83, 2:37–38; Clarence Ver Steeg, *Robert Morris: Revolutionary Financier* (Philadelphia, 1954), 33–34, 190; John E. Selby, *The Revolution in Virginia, 1775–1783* (Williamsburg, VA, 1988), 39, 139; Robert A. East, *Business Enterprise in the American Revolution* (New York, 1958), 131, 138–39; Harry M. Ward and Harold E. Greer Jr., *Richmond during the Revolution, 1775–1783* (Charlottesville, VA, 1977), 123, 142; Tench Coxe to William Tilghman, May 14, 1788, John Kaminski and Gaspar Saladino, eds., *The Documentary History of the Constitution* (17 vols., Madison, WI, 1988–2008), 9:796–97; Benjamin Harrison Jr. to Messrs. Robert Gilman & Co., July 30, 1787, to Charles Herries & Co., April 10, 1788, Feb. 10, March 20, 22, 1791, to David Buchanan, Nov. 30, 1790, and account with Herries & Co., May 30, 1790, Brock Collection, Huntington Library, San Marino, CA; *Tyler's Quarterly Magazine* 2 (1920): 170–75.

43. Cowden, "The Randolphs," chaps. 6, 11, 13, 16, esp. pp. 190–94, 459–70, 638–40; John Wayles to Farrell & Jones, July 9, 1769, Extracts of Letters of John Wayles as Relate to the Estate of Col. Peter Randolph, American Loyalist Claims, PRO, T 79/30; Ryland Randolph to Osgood Hanbury, Aug. 12, 1772, Sept. 3, 1774, Nov. 6, 1783, U.S. Circuit Court, Ended Cases, Hanbury & Lloyd, Svg. Ptrs., vs. Randolph's Admr., 1798, LOV; John J. Reardon, *Edmund Randolph: A Biography* (New York and London, 1974).

44. *DVB*, s.v. "Byrd, William III"; John Wayles to Farrell & Jones, Sept. 24, 1772, Boyd et al., *Papers of Jefferson* 15:653–54.

45. Fifteen of the families appear in Main, "The One Hundred." Main's data come from the

1787 and 1788 tax lists, but this was before the state courts were opened to British debt cases, and most of the real property of the families was still intact. Further, some of his information is incorrect. For example, Robert "King" Carter's youngest son, George, died in 1743 or 1744, and most of his property went to his brother Landon; but George, for unexplained reasons, remained on the tax lists. See George Carter's will, June 7, 1741, Carter Family Papers, Sabine Hall Collection, 1659–1797, UVA microfilm; Hening, *Statutes* 5:301–3; Robert Carter's will, Goodwin transcript FHCC. For Nathaniel Burwell II, see Lorena S. Walsh, *From Calabar to Carter's Grove: The History of a Virginia Slave Community* (Charlottesville, VA, 1997), chaps. 4–7; Morton, *Robert Carter of Nomini Hall.* Charles Carter of Shirley's estate inventory is in the Carter Letter Book, 1732–81, UVA, Goodwin transcript FHCC. For Richard Corbin, see *VMHB* 29 (1921): 380, 382, 520–22, 30 (1922): 309–18, 403–7, 56 (1958): 38–39; see also Richard Corbin Letter Book, 1758–68, CW. For Thomas Nelson Jr., see Evans, *Nelson;* for the Lee family, see Nagel, *Lees.* For the Tayloes, see Richard S. Dunn, "A Tale of Two Plantations: Slave Life at Mesopotamia in Jamaica and Mount Airy in Virginia, 1799 to 1828," *WMQ* (3), 34 (1977): 32–65, esp. 34–35; Kamoie, "Three Generations of Planter Businessmen: The Tayloes." For Robert Beverley III, see *VMHB* 20 (1912): 332–33; *DVB,* s.v. "Beverley, Robert"; Robert Beverley Letter Book, 1761–93, LC. Fitzhugh information is scarce for the eighteenth and nineteenth centuries, but see Davis, *Fitzhugh,* 54–55; *VMHB* 7 (1899–1900): 317–19, 425–27, 8 (1900–1901): 91–95. Leonard, *General Assembly of Virginia,* indicates a very active political role for the nineteenth-century Fitzhughs. For the Masons, see Pamela C. Copeland and Richard K. MacMaster, *The Five George Masons: Patriots and Planters of Virginia and Maryland* (Charlottesville, VA, 1975), chaps. 10–11.

46. Harry J. Carman, ed., *American Husbandry* (London, 1775; rept. New York, 1939), 170–76; William Nelson to Samuel Athawes, July 16, 1770, to Capel and Osgood Hanbury, Feb. 27, 1768, to Edward Hunt & Sons, March 11, June 1, 1769, Nelson Letter Book, 1766–75, LOV; Samuel Athawes to William Dangerfield, March 10, 1768, Palmer, *Calendar of Virginia State Papers* 1:259–60; Richard Corbin to John Roberts, May 13, 1767, Richard Corbin Letter Book, 1758–68, CW; Fauquier to Board of Trade, Nov. 3, 1762, Reese, *Papers of Fauquier* 2:818–19; Robert Beverley to [John Bland?], Aug. 18, 1765, to Samuel Athawes, 1773, Robert Beverley Letter Book, 1761–93, LC; Charles Carter to Mr. Goore, July 25, 1765, to Robert Cary & Company, Feb. 25, 1764, Carter Letter Book, 1732–81, UVA, Goodwin transcript FHCC; Jack P. Greene and Richard M. Jellison, "The Currency Act of 1764 in Imperial Colonial Relations, 1764–1776," *WMQ* (3), 18 (1961): 485–518; Joseph A. Ernst, *Money and Politics in America, 1755–1775* (Chapel Hill, NC, 1973), chap. 3.

47. James Deans to James Buchanan, June 28, 1760, U.S. Circuit Court, Virginia District, Ended Cases, Hyndman's Exors. vs. Dean's Exors. & Yates, 1806, LOV; Robert Carter Nicholas to John Norton, Jan. 13, 1769, John Baylor to John Norton, Sept. 16, 1764, Frances Norton Mason, ed., *John Norton & Sons, Merchants of London and Virginia* (Richmond, 1937), 83, 11–12; Charles Carter to Steward & Campbell, May 25, Aug. 25, 1767, May 5, 1768, Carter Letter Book, 1732–81, UVA, Goodwin transcript FHCC; John Baylor to Lyonel Lyde, [1749–50?], June 9, 1751, Aug. 12, 175[2], John Baylor Letter Book, 1749–65, VHS; Peter Lyons to John Norton, Sept. 15, 1772, John Norton to John Hatley Norton, May 27, 1773, Norton Papers, CW; Robert Beverley to [John Bland], Oct. 10, 1761, to Samuel Athawes, 1773, Robert Beverley Letter Book, 1761–93, LC; Thomas Jones to [William?] Molleson, July 1774, Roger Jones Fam-

ily Papers, LC; William Nelson to Edward Hunt, Sept. 11, 1766, Thomas Nelson Jr. to Thomas and Rowland Hunt, July 29, 1773, Nelson Letter Book, 1766–75, LOV. For an estimate on the size of Virginia indebtedness and the extension of credit, see Price, *Capital and Credit,* 5–19.

48. Samuel Athawes to Edmund Berkeley, 1773, Berkeley Family Papers, UVA; Richard Randolph to Farrell & Jones, Sept. 15, 1773, Copies of Letters of Richard Randolph to Farrell & Jones, American Loyalist Claims, PRO, T 79/30; Robert Beverley to [?], 1764, to John Backhouse, July 25, 1769, Aug. 10, 1775, to Samuel Athawes, 1775, to Messrs. Backhouse & Rutson, June 20, 1793, Robert Beverley Letter Book, 1761–93, LC; William Nelson to James Gildart, Nov. 25, 1767, Thomas Nelson Jr. to Samuel Athawes, July 15, 1775, to Thomas and Rowland Hunt, July 15, 1775, Nelson Letter Book, 1766–75, LOV; Price, *Capital and Credit,* 130; David Klingaman, "The Significance of Grain in the Development of the Tobacco Colonies," *Journal of Economic History* 29 (1969): 268–78; Paul G. E. Clemens, *The Atlantic Economy and Maryland's Eastern Shore* (Ithaca, NY, and London, 1980), conclusion.

4. SOCIETY, 1700–1776

1. Nicholson to Board of Trade, Dec. 2, 1701, PRO, CO 5/1312; *Essay upon Government,* 13–14; Byrd to John Custis, Jan. 31, 1716, Tinling, *Byrd Correspondence,* 290. Carole Shammas, "English Born and Creole Elites in Turn of the Century Virginia," in Tate and Ammerman, *Chesapeake in the Eighteenth Century,* 274–96; Kenneth A. Lockridge, "Colonial Self Fashioning: Paradoxes and Pathologies in the Construction of Genteel Identity in Eighteenth Century America," in *Through the Glass Darkly: Reflections on Personal Identity in Early America,* ed. Ronald Hoffman, Mechal Sobel, and Frederika Teute (Chapel Hill, NC, 1997), 274–339; Michael J. Rozbicki, *The Complete Colonial Gentleman: Cultural Legitimacy in Plantation America* (Charlottesville, VA, 1998), chap. 3.

2. Paul P. Hoffman, ed., *Guide to the Microfilm Edition of the Carter Family Papers, 1659–1797: Sabine Hall Collection* (Charlottesville, VA, 1967); Robert Randolph Carter and Robert Isham Randolph, *The Carter Tree* (Santa Barbara, CA, 1951); Jonathan H. Poston, "Ralph Wormeley V of Rosegill: A Deposed Virginia Aristocrat" (M.A. thesis, College of William and Mary, 1979); Cowden, "The Randolphs"; Tinling, *Byrd Correspondence,* 828; Jane Carson, *Colonial Virginians at Play* (2d ed., Williamsburg, VA, 1989), 138 n. 11; R. C. M. Page, *Genealogy of the Page Family of Virginia* (New York, 1893); Grace L. Chickering, "Founders of an Oligarchy: The Virginia Council, 1692–1722," in *Power and Status: Officeholding on Colonial America,* ed. Bruce C. Daniels (Middletown, CN, 1986), 255–317; *WMQ* (1), 15 (1906–7): 124–25: the editor indicated that this poem was from *Virginia Gazette* (Dixon & Hunter) for 1775; I have been unable to find it, but it could be from a now missing issue.

3. Hening, *Statutes* 3:149–50; Henry Lee to Dear Brother, Feb. 22, 1758, Richard Bland Lee Papers, 1700–1825, LC; William Byrd, "A Progress to the Mines . . . 1732," *Prose Works,* 342–43; A[nne] to Dickey, June 14, 1769, Blair, Braxton, Horner, Whiting Papers, folder 1, WM; Lewis Burwell to Francis Nicholson, Jan. 6, 1703, *WMQ* (2), 22 (1942): 393–94; John Lewis to Charles Carter, July 12, 1742, John Littlepage to Charles Carter, Aug. 22, 1742, Carter Family Papers, Lancaster County, 1718–1833, photostats, LOV; William Beverley to Lord Fairfax, July 22, 1743, *WMQ* (1), 3 (1894–95): 235; John Custis to Dear Brother, March 28, 1717, Tinling, *Byrd Correspondence,* 297–98, and, for dates of marriages of the two Byrd daughters, 828; Lewis

Burwell (1710–1756) to James Burrough, Esq., July 8, 1774, *VMHB* 81 (1973): 412; William Fairfax to George Washington, May 6, 1757, James Kirkpatrick to Washington, Aug. 23, 1758, Abbot et al., *Washington Papers, Col. Ser.* 4:152–53, 5:414; Robert Beverley to Edward Athawes, Oct. 27, 1762, to John Bland or Edward Athawes, Dec. 27, 1762, to John Bland, Feb. 25, 1763, Robert Beverley Letter Book, 1761–93, LC. On the ratio of men to women, see, for example, Alan Kulikoff, *Tobacco and Slaves: The Development of Southern Cultures in the Chesapeake, 1680–1800* (Chapel Hill, NC, 1985), 55; Daniel Blake Smith, *Inside the Great House: Planter Family Life in Eighteenth-Century Chesapeake Society* (Ithaca, NY, 1980), 127–28.

4. William Byrd to Charles Bogle, Earl of Orrery, Feb. 25, 1728, John Tayloe to William Byrd III, April 4, 1758, Maria Byrd to William Byrd III, Nov. 5, 1760, Tinling, *Byrd Correspondence,* 370, 646, 707; *Virginia Historical Register* 1 (1848–49): 119–23; [John Holloway?] to Madam, 1725, Roger Jones Family Papers, LC; Charles Carter to Landon Carter, April 26, 1758, June 24, 1763, Richard Corbin to Landon Carter, May 13, 1763, Carter Family Papers, Sabine Hall Collection, 1659–1797, UVA microfilm; *VMHB* 21 (1913): 29–45; James Kirkpatrick to George Washington, Aug. 14, 1756, Andrew Burnaby to Washington, Jan. 4, 1760, Abbot et al., *Washington Papers, Col. Ser.* 3:352, 6:381. Thomas Nelson to Samuel Athawes, Oct. 8, 1774, Nelson Letter Book, 1766–75, LOV; Louis B. Wright and Marion Tinling, eds., *Quebec to Carolina in 1785–1786: Being the Travel Diary of a Young Merchant of London* (San Marino, CA, 1943), 231.

5. Hening, *Statutes* 3:149–51, 6:81–85. On marriage portions, see, for example, will of Nathaniel Harrison, Dec. 15, 1726, and of William Beverley, 1756, *VMHB* 22 (1913): 278–83, 297–301; Robert Carter's will, 1726, with subsequent additions and deletions, UVA, Goodwin transcript FHCC; William Byrd II's will, Dec. 19, 1743, William Byrd to "Amasia," July 20, 1723, and to "Arranti," July 20, 1723, Tinling, *Byrd Correspondence,* 600, 344–46; Byrd, *Another Secret Diary,* Dec. 5, 6, 1739, and 175 and n. 2; Cowden, "The Randolphs," 695–96; John Custis to Perry, 1731, to Honored Madam, 1732, to Sr, Jan. 4, 1732, to Gentlemen, 1733, Zuppan, *Custis Letterbook,* 116–18, 120–22, 119–20, 132–34; Josephine L. Zuppan, "John Custis of Williamsburg, 1678–1749," *VMHB* 90 (1982): 175–97, and "Father and Son: Letters from John Custis IV to Daniel Parke Custis," ibid., 98 (1990): 84–86. Custis was unable to delay the marriage of his daughter Frances after she was twenty-one but he was not happy about it. Daniel Parke Custis had hoped to marry a "Mrs. Betty" in 1731, but perhaps because of too much fatherly intervention the match did not come to fruition. Subsequently he may have courted Evelyn Byrd, and in 1741 he did court her half sister Annie, but in one of these cases, perhaps both, William Byrd could not come to terms with John Custis, stating that he could not trust such a "phantome as Colonel Custis' generosity" (*Another Secret Diary,* 173 and n. 2). Edmund Berkeley, witnessed statement by John Page, May 26, 1757, Berkeley Family Papers, box 2, UVA; *VMHB* 25 (1917): 34–39; Byrd, *London Diary,* 524–25; RC Diary, Oct. 3, 1722. On the role of fathers, see also J. A. Leo Lemay, *Robert Bolling Woos Anne Miller: Love and Courtship in Colonial Virginia, 1760* (Charlottesville, VA, 1990), introduction. For a somewhat later example of a father's role, see Jack P. Greene, ed., *The Diary of Colonel Landon Carter of Sabine Hall, 1752–1778* (2 vols., Charlottesville, VA, 1965), 939. Carter told a suitor of his daughter Lucy that he might try to dissuade "a child" if he thought there was good reason but that he would never try to "persuade." He informed this suitor, William Colston, that he could provide a marriage portion of £800.

6. Lorena S. Walsh, "The Experiences and Status of Women in the Chesapeake, 1750–1775," in *The Web of Southern Social Relations: Women, Family, and Education,* ed. Walter F. Fraser Jr., R. Frank Saunders Jr., and Jon L. Wakelyn (Athens, GA, 1985), 9–10; Marylyn Salmon, *Women, Property, and the Law in Early America* (Chapel Hill, NC, 1986), chaps. 2, 5; Carole Shammas, "Early American Women and Control over Capital," in *Women in the Age of the American Revolution,* ed. Ronald Hoffman and Peter Albert (Charlottesville, VA, 1989), 13–139; *Virginia Gazette* (Parks), July 29 and December 1737, see also notices of the weddings of Lewis Burwell and Mary Willis, Oct. 29, 1736, Carter Burwell and Lucy Grymes, Jan. 6, 1738, William Nelson and Elizabeth Burwell, Feb. 10, 1738, Robert Tucker and Hannah Corbin, May 18, 1739, and "Fanny" Custis and William Winch, Jan. 29, 1739; Jane Swann to [Elizabeth Jones], Sept. 7, 1757, Roger Jones Family Papers, LC. An example of a premarital contract can be seen in the marriage of the young widow Elizabeth Cocke Pratt to Thomas Jones in early 1726, whereby she continued to have control over £2000, evidently the amount she brought to the union; Jones also gave her 84 slaves valued at £1854; see wills of Thomas Jones, Dec. 16, 1757, and Elizabeth Jones, Dec. 27, 1761, and list of "Negros Invested by Thomas Jones in His Wife Elizabeth for Right of Dower," Feb. 12, 1726, ibid. For an example of a husband assuming control over property brought to the union (Edmund Berkeley and Lucy Burwell), see Statement of Understanding by Lewis Burwell, Feb. 8, 1707, box 2, Berkeley Family Papers, UVA. William Byrd I, writing Arthur North on July 30, 1688, suggested the importance of money in decisions concerning marriage when he said "Now Giles [Webb] being wooeing one of Col. Swans daughters, they are inquisitive what Giles may be worth" (Tinling, *Byrd Correspondence,* 85).

7. *Virginia Gazette* (Parks), April 14, 1738. See three undated letters of Byrd to "Fidelia," c. 1705–6, and one on Feb. 4, 1706, Tinling, *Byrd Correspondence,* 252–59. For a balanced assessment of Byrd's and Lucy Parke's marriage, see Paula A. Treckel, "'The Empire of My Heart': The Marriage of William Byrd II and Lucy Parke Byrd," *VMHB* 105 (1997): 125–56; see also Kenneth Lockridge, *The Diary and Life of William Byrd of Westover* (Chapel Hill, NC, 1987), 49, 66–67, and nn. 69, 70; Lemay, *Robert Bolling Woos Anne Miller,* 52, 55–56.

8. Thomas Jones to Elizabeth Pratt, Sept. 8, Oct. 2, 5, 7, 11, 14, 18, 27, Dec. 19, 1725, and several letters in January 1726, see also "List of Negros Exclusive of the Marriage Settlement," Feb. 14, 1726, Thomas Jones to Elizabeth Jones, Oct. 27, 1736, Roger Jones Family Papers, LC. Elizabeth Pratt's feelings were expressed in a prose poem she wrote c. 1725, misfiled with her will (1761), ibid., reel 4, frames 505–6. For a similar case, see Joseph Ball to Rawleigh Downman, Jan. 16, 1749, to Cousin Joseph Chinn, Feb. 6, 1750, Joseph Ball Letter Book, 1743–59, LC; Lawrence Stone, *The Family, Sex, and Marriage in England, 1500–1800* (New York, 1977), chap. 7; David Cressy, *Birth, Marriage, and Death: Ritual Religion and the Life Cycle in Tudor and Stuart England* (New York, 1997), chap. 10, esp. 260–61.

9. On age at marriage, see, for example, Rutman and Rutman, *A Place in Time: Explicatus,* 64–65; Kulikoff, *Tobacco and Slaves,* 50–51, 56–57. Jones, *Present State of Virginia,* 97; RC Diary, Oct. 3–6, 1722; Wright and Tinling, *Quebec to Carolina,* 205–9; Carson, *Colonial Virginians at Play,* 5–9; *Virginia Gazette* (Purdie & Dixon), Jan. 17, 1771; Hening, *Statutes* 3:149; Tinling, *Byrd Correspondence,* 595.

10. On the legal rights of husbands, see Salmon, *Women and the Law of Property,* chaps. 1, 2; Byrd, *Secret Diary,* 15; William Beverley to Richard Bennett, Feb. 12, 1743, William Beverley Letter Book, 1737–44, NYPL; *Virginia Gazette* (Parks), May 20, 1737. Edmund Berkeley

assumed control over the property his wife, Lucy Burwell, brought to their union; see Lewis Burwell, "Statement of Understanding," Feb. 8, 1707, box 2, Berkeley Family Papers, UVA.

11. Zuppan, "John Custis of Williamsburg," 177–82; draft of Custis marriage agreement, *VMHB* 4 (1896–97): 64–66; Byrd, *Secret Diary*, Aug. 14, 1709, Nov. 19, 27, 1711, March 29, April 21, 1712; Byrd to John Custis, Jan. 31, 1716, Tinling, *Byrd Correspondence*, 291, John Custis to Honored Madam [Mrs. Pepper], 1732, Zuppan, *Custis Letterbook*, 120–21. See also Salmon, *Women and the Law of Property*, 16–17. For Byrd's comments on Lucy, see, for example, *Secret Diary*, March 31, April 5, 6, 7, 8, 9, 21, 27, 29, May 21, June 1, Aug. 14, 1709, Dec. 25, 1710, April 21, Dec. 31, 1711; Byrd to John Custis, Dec. 13, 1716, Tinling, *Byrd Correspondence*, 196. See also Teckel, "Empire of My Heart," esp. 135–36, who stresses what she believes to be Byrd's fear of the "emotional intimacy of marriage" and his need for "power and control." But she does not deny that they loved one another—a love that led her to join him in England in 1715. On Byrd's sexual life see Richard Godbeer, *The Sexual Revolution in Early America* (Baltimore, 2002), chap. 6, 190–208, and 196–97 on his relations with his wife. See also Lockridge, *Diary and Life of William Byrd II*, 49, 57–59, 66–67. A good bit is made of Byrd's need to control his wife, and one incident frequently referred to is his refusal to let her take a book from his library (*Secret Diary*, 461). Kevin Hayes, *The Library of William Byrd of Westover* (Madison, WI, 1997), 44–46, argues that when Byrd and his wife were not disagreeing he had no qualms about her being in the library in which there was at least one book that was hers. Byrd wanted her to read, and Hayes notes that Byrd owned "colonial America's greatest collection of books written by women." Linda L. Sturtz, "The Ladies and the Lottery: Elite Women's Gambling in Eighteenth-Century Virginia," *VMHB* 104 (1996): 165–84, esp. 173–77, makes a good deal of how she sees heated contests, demonstrated in game playing—especially cards—and suggests a larger power struggle between Lucy and William Byrd. "Within the context of the Byrds' battles for domestic ascendancy, their gambling [over cards] seems symptomatic of Lucy's attempts to assert some power in the household" and his "efforts to restrict her self determination" (174). But of the roughly forty occasions of game playing that she cites, there were only three in which they quarreled: Aug. 17, 1709, and Jan. 28 and Nov. 6, 1710. There are, as mentioned, other incidents revolving largely around household management, but in the larger context they too do not appear abnormal. Tradition has it that on one occasion Custis invited Frances to take a ride in the "gig"—they were on the Eastern Shore. He drove to the edge of the Chesapeake Bay and instead of driving along the shore he drove into the water. Frances queried, "Where are you going Mr. Custis?" He replied, "To Hell Madam." Her only comment was "drive on, Sir." He continued until the horse began to swim, replying to her query in the same manner several times. He then turned back to the shore, saying "if I were to go to hell and the devil himself were to come out and meet us, I do not believe you would be frightened." She responded "I know you so well that I am not afraid to go where you go." It was also reported that, frequently, at dinner they communicated through the butler; Whitelaw, *Virginia's Eastern Shore*, 111.

12. Lockridge, *Diary and Life of William Byrd II*; Marambaud, *William Byrd*; Zuppan, "John Custis of Williamsburg," 177–88; Douglas Anderson, "Plotting William Byrd," *WMQ* (3), 55 (1999): 701–22, esp. 711–12; Thomas Jones to My Dearest Life, July 8, 28, Aug. 9, 1728, Roger Jones Family Papers, LC; John Pratt to Elizabeth Jones, Oct. 21, 1728, John Pratt Letters, MSS 2 P8887 b4, VHS; Isaac W. Giberne to Landon Carter, July 8, 1768, Carter Family

Papers, Sabine Hall Collection, 1659–1797, UVA microfilm; Joan R. Gunderson, *The Anglican Ministry of Virginia, 1723–1766: A Study of a Social Class* (New York and London, 1989), esp. 254; Hunter Dickinson Farish, ed., *The Journal and Letters of Philip Vickers Fithian: A Plantation Tutor of the Old Dominion* (3d ed., Williamsburg, VA, 1965), 241; Jonathan Boucher, *Reminiscences of an American Loyalist, 1738–1789* (Boston, 1925), 30. For Richard Corbin, see Harris, *Old New Kent* 1:340–41, and *VMHB* 46 (1936): 38–39. *DVB*, s.v. "Byrd, William III." On separate maintenance, see Julia Cherry Spruill, *Women's Life and Work in the Southern Colonies* (Chapel Hill, NC, 1938; 2d ed., 1972), 333–34; Kathleen M. Brown, *Good Wives, Nasty Wenches, and Anxious Patriarchs: Gender, Race, and Power in Colonial Virginia* (Chapel Hill, NC, 1996), 334–42; Salmon, *Women and the Law of Property*, chap. 4; there are no known cases of separate maintenance among the twenty-one families. *Virginia Gazette* (Parks), Oct. 15, 1735.

13. *Virginia Gazette* (Parks), May 20, June 3, 1737; "Journal of Lord Adam Gordon," in *Travels in the American Colonies*, ed. Newton D. Mereness (New York, 1916), 406.

14. Family size, age at marriage, etc., have been developed from genealogical information. For colonywide levels of age at marriage, see Kulikoff, *Tobacco and Slaves*, 54–63; Rutman and Rutman, *Explicatus*, 73 and, on "positive family limitation," 62–63. William Byrd to Mrs. Jane Pratt Taylor, April 3, 1729, Tinling, *Byrd Correspondence*, 391–92; Greene, *Diary of Landon Carter*, 511, 713; Smith, *Inside the Great House*, chap. 1; Brown, *Good Wives, Nasty Wenches, and Anxious Patriarchs*, 302–3. Jones was certainly feeling the effects of frequent childbirth when she went to England in 1728, but Brown suggests that on a second occasion in 1736 she absented herself to prevent conception and this is not at all clear. See Thomas Jones to My Dearest Life, July 8, 28, 1728, and Oct. 22, 1736, Roger Jones Family Papers, LC; "Life of Secretary William Cocke [the father of Elizabeth Jones]," *VMHB* 5 (1896–97): 189–94; Morton, *Robert Carter of Nomini Hall*, 220.

15. Robert Beverley to Landon Carter, Feb. 26, 1771, Carter Family Papers, Sabine Hall Collection, 1659–1797, UVA microfilm; RC Diary, May 17, 1726, July 14, 19, 1720, June 10, 20, 1724, June 15, 16, 29, 1725; Fithian, *Journal*, 39, 26. By 1773 Robert Carter of Nomini Hall's wife, Frances Tasker Carter, reports that she "has" thirteen children, nine of whom were living—seven at home. Frances [Carter Jones] to Robert Carter, Jan. 4, 1785, Carter Family Papers, 1651–1861, c2468a, 488–89, VHS; Thomas Jones to My Dearest Life, July 8, 27, 28, 1728, Roger Jones Family Papers, LC; *DVB*, s.v. "Byrd, William III."

16. Morton, *Robert Carter of Nomini Hall*, 223–26; Robert Bladen Carter to Robert Carter, June 7, 1786, Carter Family Papers, 1651–1861, MSS 1 C2468a, 289–95, VHS.

17. Greene, *Landon Carter Diary*, 310, 578, 703, 765, 795, 848–49, 869, 956, 1015; Philip Lee to Henry Lee, June 22, 1730, Richard Bland Lee Papers, LC. See also Smith, *Inside the Great House*, chap. 1.

18. William Fitzhugh to Nicholas Hayward, Jan. 30, 1687, Davis, *Fitzhugh*, 203; Richard and Elizabeth Ambler to Edward and John Ambler, Aug. 1, 1748, Lucille Griffith, ed., "English Education for Virginia Youth: Some Eighteenth-Century Ambler Family Letters," *VMHB* 69 (1961): 14–15; Robert Carter to [Thomas Corbin], June 26, 1702, *VMHB* 8 (1900–1901): 180. On the College of William and Mary, see Tate, "The Colonial College, 1693–1782," chaps. 1–13.

19. Robert Carter to Micajah and Richard Perry, July 14, 1720, to John Carter, July 19, 1720,

Wright, *Carter Letters*, 22–23, 32–34; RC Diary, Aug. 1, 1722, June 30, 1724; Charles Carter of Corotoman to Landon Carter [nephew], March 31, 1765, c. 1767, Carter Family Papers, Sabine Hall Collection, 1659–1797, UVA microfilm; Boucher, *Reminiscences of an American Loyalist*, 39, 40–41, 48; William Beverley to John Fairchild, March 9, 1743, *WMQ* (1), 3 (1894–95): 231–32; Alexander Forbes to Bishop of London, July 21, 1724, Papers of Inquiries Sent to the Plantations, Nov. 2, 1723, Fulham Palace Papers, 14 (Misc. Papers, 1679–1771) and 15 (1695–1776), Lambeth Palace, London; John Carter to Micajah Perry, Aug. 12, 1735, Carter Letter Book, 1732–81, UVA, Goodwin transcript FHCC; John Tayloe (1721–1779), Account Book (1748–74), Sept. 5, 1768, and will, May 2, 1773, Tayloe Family Papers, 1650–1970, b5 and 166, VHS; Edward M. Riley, ed., *The Journal of John Harrower; An Indentured Servant in the Colony of Virginia, 1773–1776* (Williamsburg, VA, 1963); Elizabeth Jones to Dear Tom, Jan. 8, 1758, Thomas Jones Jr. to Dear B.W., [1766], Walter Jones to Thomas Jones Jr., Dec. 18, 1766, July 23, 1769, Robert Hamilton to Walter Jones, July 16, 1767, John Warden to Thomas Jones, Dec. 24, 26, 1771, Feb. 8, 10, 1772, Roger Jones Family Papers, LC; Fithian, *Journal*, 20. George Pilcher, *Samuel Davies: Apostle of Dissent in Colonial Virginia* (Knoxville, TN, 1971), said that Davies did not run a school, but Elizabeth Jones told her eldest son that she had put "Walt" with "Davis." She was living in Hanover County, Davies's home base, and there appears to have been no other itinerant named Davis or Davies there. See also Richard Beale Davis, *The Intellectual Life of the Colonial South, 1585–1763* (3 vols., Knoxville, TN, 1978), vol. 1, chap. 3.

20. Robert Carter to William Dawkins, July 14, 1720, Wright, *Carter Letters*, 6; Nathaniel Burwell to Brother, June 13, 1718, *WMQ* (1), 7 (1898–99): 43–44; RC Diary, Mar. 17, 1726; William Dawkins to Robert Carter, Esq., June 16, 1718, Carter Family Papers, Lancaster County, 1716–1837, photostat from James Monroe Memorial Library, Fredericksburg, VA, LOV; *Robert "King" Carter: Builder of Christ Church* (Irvington, VA, 1986), 39; *VMHB* 36 (1936): 17, 161–65; Evans, *Nelson,* chap. 1. For the effects of a long absence, see Ronald Hoffman and Sally Mason, *Princes of Maryland Planters of Maryland: A Carroll Saga, 1500–1782* (Chapel Hill, NC, 2000), chaps. 4, 5, and esp. pp. 210–11, who suggest that Charles Carroll of Carrollton left home a "openly affectionate child" and returned a "remote" reserved man, the emotional impact of his mother's death. See also the ruminations of Lockridge, *Diary and Life of William Byrd II,* 14–15.

21. Tate, "The Colonial College, 1693–1792," 82–121; William Byrd to Perry & Lane, April 1, 1685, July 19, 1690, to Warham Horsmanden, Feb. 26, 1684, ultimo March 1685, Tinling, *Byrd Correspondence,* 12, 22–23, 38, 115, 120; Willard Connelly, "Colonial Americans in Oxford and Cambridge," *American Oxonian* 21 (1942); 6–17, 75–77; *VMHB* 21 (1913): 82, 196–99; George C. Brauer, *The Education of a Gentleman: Theories of Gentlemanly Education in England, 1660–1775* (New York, 1959), 197–201; Rosamande Bayne Powell, *Travelers in Eighteenth-Century England* (London, 1951), 101; William M. Sachse, *The Colonial American in Britain* (Madison, WI, 1956), 52; Cowden, "The Randolphs," 506–10; Robert Carter to Solomon Low, July 5, 1723, to William Dawkins, June 28, 1724, RC Letter Book; William Nelson to John Norton, Feb. 27, 1768, Mason, *Norton & Sons,* 39; Greene, *Landon Carter Diary,* 372–73; Nathaniel L. Savage to John Norton, Sept. 29, 1771, Norton-Dixon-Savage Papers, Brock Collection, Huntington Library; Robert Beverley to Samuel Athawes, 1780, Robert Beverley Letter Book, 1761–93, LC; Richard Henry Lee to William Lee, June 30, 1777, Brock Collection, Huntington Library; see also Alan Simpson, "Robert Carter's Schooldays," *VMHB* 94 (1986): 161–88; Zuppan, "John Custis of Williamsburg," 178–79.

22. Philip Dorey to Madam, Nov. 4, 1737, Roger Jones Family Papers, LC; Richard Ambler to Edward and John Ambler, May 20, 1749, Griffith, "English Education for Virginia Youth," 15–16. See also, much later, William Lee to William Hicks, April 18, 1775, William Lee Letter Book, 1774–75, VHS.

23. Marambaud, *William Byrd,* 17–19; William Byrd I to Christopher Glasscock, March 31, 1685, to Perry & Lane, July 19, 1690, to William Byrd II, July 5, 1690, to [Jacob] Senserff, July 25, 1690, Tinling, *Byrd Correspondence,* 35, 115, 116n, 123, 124.

24. Robert Carter to Dear Lewis, Aug. 22, 1727, Aug. 9, 1728, June 26, 1729, RC Letter Book; Edmund Jenings to Richard Corbin, Nov. 10, 1756, Edmund Jenings Letter Book, 1753–69, VHS; Robert Beverley to [Samuel Athawes], 1780, to William Beverley, Feb. 11, 1781, Feb. 25, 1782, May 24, 1783, to Robert McKenzie, June 1, 1783, to Messrs. Anderson & Co., July 22, 1788, July 13, 1792, to Backhouse & Rutson, Aug. 25, 1792, Robert Beverley Letter Book, 1761–93, LC; Ralph Wormeley to John Grymes, July 12, 1785, Wormeley Letter Book, 1783–1800, UVA; Jane Swan to Thomas Jones, March 8, 1756, Roger Jones Family Papers, LC.

25. Tate, "The Colonial College, 1693–1782," chaps. 4, 5; "Sketches of His Own Family Written by Littleton Waller Tazewell, for the Use of His Children," Norfolk, 1823, 47–48, LOV; Dudley Digges to Bishop of London, July 1, 1767, Fulham Palace Papers, 15 (1695–1776), Lambeth Palace, London. See also James Maury Fontaine to [?], May 11, 1776, Berkeley Family Papers, UVA; Fred Shelley, ed., "The Journal of Ebenezer Hazard," *VMHB* 52 (1954): 405–6. Walter Jones to Dear Brother, July 31, 1762, July 18, 1767, Roger Jones Family Papers, LC; see also *VMHB* 5 (1897–98): 193. Davis, *Intellectual Life of the Colonial South* 3:1607; Dumas Malone, *Jefferson the Virginian* (Boston, 1948), chap. 4.

26. Tate, "The Colonial College, 1693–1782," chap. 4; *VMHB* 21 (1913): 196–99; Robert Beverley to Samuel Athawes, 1780, Robert Beverley Letter Book, 1761–93, LC; Evans, *Nelson,* 16–18; Connelly, "Colonial Americans at Oxford and Cambridge," 6–27, 75–77; *WMQ* (1), 1 (1892–93): 27–41; Louis W. Potts, *Arthur Lee: A Virtuous Revolutionary* (Baton Rouge, LA, 1981), 15–22.

27. *VMHB* 21 (1913): 196–99; *WMQ* (2), 1 (1921): 28–41; Robert Beverley to [Samuel Athawes], 1780, Robert Beverley Letter Book, 1761–93, LC; Ralph Wormeley Jr. to John Grymes, July 12, 1785, Wormeley Letter Book, 1783–1800, UVA. For John Baylor Jr.'s will, Oct. 13, 1807, see U.S. Circuit Court, Ended Cases, Pinkerton & Bell vs. Baylor et al., 1832, LOV. It should be noted that good records of who attended William and Mary before 1750 do not exist.

28. Rosemarie Zagarri, ed., *David Humphreys' "Life of General Washington with George Washington's Remarks"* (Athens, GA, 1991), 6; William Byrd to John Perceval, Earl of Egmont, July 12, 1736, Tinling, *Byrd Correspondence,* 487–88.

29. Philip J. Schwarz, *Twice Condemned: Slaves and Criminal Laws of Virginia, 1705–1865* (Baton Rouge, LA, 1988), 17–23; Philip D. Morgan, *Slave Counterpoint: Black Culture in the Eighteenth Century Chesapeake and Lowcountry* (Chapel Hill, NC, 1998), 261–64; Hening, *Statutes* 3:102–3, 269–70, 4:126–34, 325–27; Nathaniel L. Savage to [John Norton?], July 22, 1766, Norton-Dixon-Savage Papers, Huntington Library; Thomas Jones to My Dearest Life, Oct. 22, 1736, Roger Jones Family Papers, LC; Robert Wormeley Carter to Landon Carter, May 10, 1774, Carter Family Papers, Sabine Hall Collection, 1659–1797, UVA microfilm; Lancaster County, Order Book 5 (1702–12): March 10, 1708; Francis Nicholson to Board of Trade, Oct. 30, 1701, PRO, CO 5/1312; *EJC* 4:243; Gooch to Bishop of London, May 28, 1731, Church

Commissioners of London, Fulham Palace Papers, 15 (1695–1776), Lambeth Palace, London; Gooch to Board of Trade, July 10, 1731, July 18, 1732, *CSP* 38 (1731): 173, 39 (1732): 174. For concern that the increasing numbers of slave baptisms might encourage hopes of freedom, see, for example, James Blair to Bishop of London, June 28, 1729, July 20, 1730, Fulham Palace Papers, 15 (1695–1776) and 13 (1695–1771), Lambeth Palace, London. See also Ira Berlin, *Many Thousands Gone: The First Two Centuries of Slavery in North America* (Cambridge, Mass., 1998), chap. 5. A more recent study is Anthony S. Parent Jr., *Foul Means: The Formation of Slave Society in Virginia, 1660–1740* (Chapel Hill, NC, 2003). I do not find that it adds much to what is already known about slavery in eighteenth-century Virginia.

30. On providing adequately for slaves, see, for example, Robert Carter to Robert Jones, Oct. 12, 1727, to Alderman Perry, Sept. 11, 1731, RC Letter Book; Joseph Ball to Couz. Jos. Chinn, Feb. 18, 1744, Joseph Ball Letter Book, 1743–59, LC; Richard Corbin to James Semple, Jan. 1, 1759, Richard Corbin Letter Book, 1758–68, CW. On patriarchy, see Morgan, *Slave Counterpoint*, chap. 5. William Byrd to Earl of Orrery, July 5, 1726, Feb. 2, 1727, Tinling, *Byrd Correspondence*, 354–56, 358; John Custis IV to Dear Friend [Peter Collinson], 1742, Zuppan, *Custis Letterbook*, 227–28. Fulham Palace Papers, 14 (Misc. Papers, 1679–1771), Lambeth Palace, London. See also, on marriage, Walsh, *From Calabar to Carter's Grove*, 83–85, 285 n. 12; Kulikoff, *Tobacco and Slaves*, 352–53, 374–75. RC Diary, Nov. 30, 1726; Joseph Ball to Couz. Jos. Chinn, Aug. 30, 1746, Joseph Ball Letter Book, 1743–1759, LC; Frederick Jones to Dear Brother, Dec. 21, 1762, Roger Jones Family Papers, LC.

31. Fithian, *Journal,* 86; *EJC* 5:141; York County Deeds, 5 (1741–54): 236–38; John Custis IV will, Nov. 14, 1749, Custis Family Papers, 1683–1858, MSS lc 9698a, 52–53, VHS; "John Blair Diary, 1751," *WMQ* (1), 7 (1898–99): 152; Cowden, "The Randolphs," 469–70; Morgan, *Slave Counterpoint,* 399–405. See also Brown, *Good Wives, Nasty Wenches, and Anxious Patriarchs,* 350–66. I do not find the patriarchs especially anxious in their relationships with their slaves, nor do I find that in their search for domestic tranquillity, their ability to coerce their slaves provided them "with a suitable foil for the serene authority they hoped to wield over wives and children."

32. Nathaniel L. Savage to [John Norton?], July 22, 1766, Norton-Dixon-Savage Papers, Huntington Library; William Byrd to John Perceval, Earl of Egmont, July 12, 1736, Tinling, *Byrd Correspondence,* 487–88; John Custis to Mr. Loyd, 1736, Zuppan, *Custis Letterbook,* 158–59; Robert Beverley to Edward Athawes, July 11, 1761, Robert Beverley Letter Book, 1761–93, LC; Patrick Henry to Robert Pleasants, Jan. 16, 1773, MS Portfolio 17, no. 28, Library of the Society of Friends, London.

33. On the failure to levy additional taxes on slave importation, see Order in Council, Dec. 9, 1770, and Representation to the Board of Trade, Nov. 23, 1770, John C. Van Horne, ed., *The Correspondence of William Nelson as Acting Governor of Virginia, 1770–1771* (Charlottesville, VA, 1975), 76–77, 79–80; Billings et al., *Colonial Virginia,* 281. Joseph Ball to Major William Ball, Feb. 5, 1754, to Joseph Chinn, Feb. 5, 19, April 23, Aug. 31, 1754, Jan. 18, Feb. 21, 1755, Oct. 7, 1758, to Aron, Aug. 31, 1754, Joseph Ball Letter Book, 1743–59, LC. On Joseph Ball, see Douglas Southall Freeman, *George Washington* (7 vols., New York, 1948–57), 1:190–92. On slave jobs and other responsibilities, see, for example, Morgan, *Slave Counterpoint,* chap. 4 and pp. 319–21, 624–26; Greene, *Landon Carter Diary,* 202, 353, 377, 666–67, 946, 947; *Virginia Gazette* (Parks), April 18, 1745, 4–1; *Maryland Gazette,* Sept. 2, 1762, in *WMQ* (1), 3 (1894–95): 267; Theoderick Bland to John Randolph, Esq., June 12, 1772, Bryan Family Papers, 1770–1916,

box 1, UVA; John Self to Robert Wormeley Carter, [1773?], Carter Family Papers, 1651–1861, MSS 1 C2468a, 2355, VHS.

34. Fithian, *Journal,* 89, 90, 131, 133, 134, 156, 184–85; *VMHB* 31 (1923): 60 n. 29; John Carter to Micajah Perry, Esqr., & Co., Aug. 12, 1735, Carter Letter Book, 1732–81, UVA, Goodwin transcript FHCC; Riley, Harrower, *Journal,* 81.

35. Fithian, *Journal,* xxvii–xxx, 19, 21, 22, 25, 26, 28, 31–32, 48, 138, 150; Morton, *Robert Carter of Nomini Hall;* Harrower, *Journal,* 42; Jane Carson, *Colonial Virginia Cookery* (Williamsburg, VA, 1968), 6, 12; Carson, *Colonial Virginians at Play,* 10–11; Byrd, *London Diary,* 456, 458; Byrd, *Secret Diary,* for example, April 1, 1709, Sept. 1, 1710. See also Marambaud, *William Byrd,* chap. 11; William Byrd to John Boyle, Baron of Brogehill, July 28, 1730, Tinling, *Byrd Correspondence,* 432. On easy living and indolent planters, see, for example, Jones, *Present State of Virginia,* 65; Andrew Burnaby, *Travels through the Middle Settlements in the Years 1759 and 1760* (2d ed., 1775; rept. Ithaca, NY, 1960), 18–19.

36. Beverley, *History and Present State of Virginia,* 312–13; Richard Stiverson and Patrick Butler, eds., "Virginia in 1732: The Travel Journal of Hugh Grove," *VMHB* 85 (1977): 31; RC Diary, Jan. 10, 25, 29, 30, 1723, Aug. 31, Sept. 4, 11, 1724. For Byrd, see, for example, *Secret Diary,* April 4, 1709, Jan. 9, Feb. 19–27, Sept. 20, 25, 1710, Jan. 3, 1711, and *Another Secret Diary,* Feb. 2, March 2, May 2–3, 1711. Fithian, *Journal,* 69–70, 89–91, 177, 178–79; Carson, *Colonial Virginians at Play,* 1–4.

37. Fithian, *Journal,* 29, 68, 69, 89, 100, 137, 148, 167–68; see also, for example, Byrd, *Secret Diary,* May 29, June 26, 1709, and *London Diary,* Feb. 28, May 8, June 5, 1720. Dell Upton, *Holy Things and Profane: Anglican Parish Churches in Colonial Virginia* (New York and Cambridge, Mass., 1986), 204–5. The practice of men waiting until after the church service began to enter and men and women visiting before and after church continued in Virginia in rural areas and small towns until at least through World War II.

38. David S. Shields, *Civil Tongues and Polite Letters in British America* (Chapel Hill, NC, 1997), 38, 144–49, 301–2; Nancy L. Struna, *People of Prowess: Sport, Leisure, and Labor in Anglo-America* (Urbana and Chicago, 1996), esp. chaps. 5, 6, 8; Kate Van Winkle Keller, *"If the Company Can Do It": Technique in Eighteenth-Century Social Dance* (Sandy Hook, CN, 1997); Carson, *Colonial Virginians at Play,* 9–13, 107–8; Byrd, *London Diary,* 456, 458, 464, 467, *Secret Diary,* 26, 297, and *Another Secret Diary,* 42; RC Diary, Aug. 23, Sept. 4, 1723; William Byrd to Sir John Randolph, Jan. 21, 1736, Tinling, *Byrd Correspondence,* 471 and n; Fithian, *Journal,* 47, 56–58, 112, 144, 177, 190; William Gooch to Thomas Gooch, Oct. 28, 1728, Gooch Letter Book, 1727–58, transcript, CW; Burnaby, *Travels,* 26; *Virginia Gazette* (Parks), April 27, Nov. 4, 1737, April 7, Nov. 3, 1738, Nov. 2, 1739, Oct. 10, 1745; "John Blair Diary, 1751," July 12, 1751, *WMQ* (1), 7 (1898–99): 151; E. Holloway to Dear Betty [Elizabeth Jones], [1751?], Roger Jones Family Papers, LC; Greene, *Landon Carter Diary,* 659. The *OED* describes "hop" as a dance or a dancing party. Earlier, in 1766, Carter's daughter Judy went to a dance at her "Uncle Beale's" and danced on a "very hot night . . . though sick for her period came on" (Greene, *Landon Carter Diary,* 320). Dances in which the gentry participated included French dances (e.g. minuet, quadrille) and country dances of English origin, as well as jigs of Scottish origin and reels. Burnaby said that "jiggs" were originally borrowed from "the Negroes," but in a footnote to the second edition he commented that he had seen similar dancing in Italy among the "Tuscans." Englishman Robert Hunter reported in 1785 that Virginians danced minuets,

cotillions, Virginia and Scottish reels, and country dances and jigs. He said that the ladies were "perfectly free and easy and at the same [time] elegant in their manners. They would grace any country whatever" (Wright and Tinling, *Quebec to Carolina*, 198–99, 207–8). For balls on public occasions, see Cynthia A. Kierner, "Genteel Balls and Republican Parades: Gender and Early Southern Civic Rituals, 1677–1826," *VMHB* 104 (1996), 185–210.

39. "John Blair Diary, 1751," July 16, 17, Sept. 9, 1751, *WMQ* (1), 7 (1898–99): 142, 145; research report on Peter Pelham, Research Dept., CW; Anne Blair to my Dear Sister, Aug. 7, 21, 1769, Blair, Braxton, Horner Papers, folder 1, WM; Wright and Tinling, *Quebec to Carolina*, 204, 205, 210; John Tayloe (1721–1779), Account Book, 1748–74, accounts for 1767, Tayloe Family Papers, 1650–1970, b5, VHS; Reese, ed., *Papers of Fauquier* 1:xlii; Hood, *Governor's Palace*, 153–54; Carson, *Colonial Virginians at Play*, 14, 105–6. Handel and Vivaldi need no introduction, but Felton may; William Felton (1715–1769) was an English clergyman, organist, and composer, whose compositions were largely for harpsichord and organ. See Stanley Sadie (ed.), *New Grove Dictionary of Music and Musicians* (29 vols., 2nd ed. 1980–2001), 8:662–663; Fithian, *Journal*, 19, 21, 22, 25–26, 30, 50, 57, 79, 138. Much earlier, William Byrd II reported that on one occasion when Governor Spotswood entertained the Council in 1720, the evening ended with "a concert of music" and the drinking of "healths till 11 o'clock" (*London Diary*, 400).

40. Shields, *Civil Tongues and Polite Letters*, 158–60; Carson, *Colonial Virginians at Play*, 22–28. See, for example, Byrd, *Secret Diary*, March 4, April 12, 18, 19, 20, 27, 1709, Jan. 27, March 14, 1710, June 26, 1712, *London Diary*, Sept. 30, 1720, and *Another Secret Diary*, Feb. 5, 7, March 11, 12, 1740, Aug. 20, 21, 1741; RC Diary, Sept. 24, 1723; Mrs. Jane Pratt Taylor to William Byrd II, June 8, [1741?], Tinling, *Byrd Correspondence*, 499–500; Hayes, *Library of William Byrd*, 94, 592; Fithian, *Journal*, Jan. 18, 1774, 57; Wright and Tinling, *Quebec to Carolina*, March 24, 1785.

41. Philip Alexander Bruce, *Social Life of Virginia in the Seventeenth Century* (Richmond, 1907; rept. 1995), 189–93; Carson, *Colonial Virginians at Play*, 19–22; Sturtz, "The Ladies and the Lottery"; Byrd, *Secret Diary*, April 20, 27, May 5, 20, June 3, Sept. 12, Oct. 20, 1709, Oct. 9, 20, 21, 1710, Nov. 23, 24, 1711; Gooch to Board of Trade, June [8?], 1728, *CSP* 36 (1728–29): 117; Hening, *Statutes* 4:214–18, 5:229–31, 6:76–81, 10:205–7; *Virginia Gazette* (Hunter), Sept. 5, 1751; Greene, *Landon Carter Diary*, Sept. 15, Nov. 16, 1771, Feb. 12, 1774, 630, 640, 795; Tinling, *Byrd Correspondence*, 603–4; Louis Morton, ed., "The Daybook of Robert Wormeley Carter of Sabine Hall, 1766," *VMHB* 60 (1960): 301–16; Shelley, "Diary of Ebenezer Hazard," 423; Robert Honyman Diary and Journal, 1772–83, Dec. 23, 1781, LC; T. H. Breen, "Horses and Gentlemen: The Cultural Significance of Gambling among the Gentry of Virginia," *WMQ* (3), 34 (1977): 234–57, esp. 247, 253–54, 257. See also Howard C. Rice Jr., ed., *Travels in North America in the Years 1780, 1781, and 1782 by the Marquis de Chastellux* (2 vols., Chapel Hill, NC, 1963), 603 n.12; Rhys Isaac, *The Transformation of Virginia, 1740–1790* (Chapel Hill, NC, 1983), 118–20.

42. Breen, "Horses and Gentlemen," 257; Carson, *Colonial Virginians at Play*, 51–60; William G. Stanard, "Racing in Colonial Virginia," *VMHB* 2 (1894–95): 293–305; Hening, *Statutes* 4:47–49; Fairfax Harrison, "The Equine FFVs," *VMHB* 35 (1927): 329–70, esp. 367–69; notice of the earliest subscription races in the *Virginia Gazette* (Parks), Oct. 7, Nov. 18, 1737, see also, for example, Jan. 11, 1739, Jan. 11, 1740, May 9, 1745, May 15, Aug. 14, 1746; Abbot et al., *Washington Papers, Col. Ser.* 7:5, 11n, 86.

43. Byrd, *Secret Diary*, Oct. 17, 1709, 244, and *Another Secret Diary*, April 22, May 8, Aug. 7, Oct. 30, 1740, 60, 64, 93, 107; RC Diary, Sept. 20, Nov. 8, Dec. 5, 1733; Fithian, *Journal*, Nov. 25, 1773, April 7, Aug. 25, 1774, 24–25, 94–95, 177–78; *Virginia Gazette* (Dixon), Feb. 10, 1776; John Tayloe to [John Baylor], Nov. 21, 1771, Baylor Family Papers, box 1, UVA; John Tayloe to George William Fairfax, Dec. 14, 1773, Tayloe Family Papers, 1650–1970, 150, typescript, VHS.

44. Beverley, *History and Present State of Virginia*, 308–11; RC Diary, May 28, 1724; Robert Rose Diary, 1747–48, June 14, 1748, Huntington Library; Fithian, *Journal*, Dec. 22, 1773, June 13, March 10, 1774, 37, 54–55, 75; John Clayton to Mr. Samuel Durrent, March 31, 1739, *VMHB* 7 (1899–1900): 172–74; William Nelson to Cousin William Cookson, Nov. 19, 1768, Nelson Letter Book, 1766–75, LOV; Greene, *Landon Carter Diary*, 662, 664, 900, 802, 1087; Donald Jackson and Dorothy Twohig, eds., *The Diaries of George Washington* (6 vols., Charlottesville, VA, 1976–79), vol. 2, esp. 1768 entries; James Thomas Flexner, *George Washington: The Forge of Experience, 1732–1775* (Boston, 1765), 238–49; John Tayloe Account Book, 1748–74, Tayloe Family Papers, 1650–1970, b5, VHS; John Frere to John Hatley Norton, April 1, 1768, Mason, *Norton & Sons*, 43; Peter Martin, *The Pleasure Gardens of Virginia: From Jamestown to Jefferson* (Princeton, NJ, 1991), chap. 3 and pp. 93–95; Barbara Wells Sarudy, *Gardens and Gardening in the Chesapeake, 1700–1805* (Baltimore, 1998), chap. 2; John Custis to Mr. Catesby, June 1730, and to Sr, 1734, Zuppan, *Custis Letterbook*, 109–10, 136–39; Byrd, *Secret Diary*, April 24, 25, May 2, June 13, March 23, 27, 28, July 19, 21, 1710.

45. Carson, *Colonial Virginians at Play*, 87–95, 97–102; Hugh F. Rankin, *The Theatre in Colonial America* (Chapel Hill, NC, 1960), esp. chaps. 2–4, 6–7; Byrd, *London Diary*, April 25, 26, May 2, [1721?], 522, 525; Stiverson and Butler, "Virginia in 1732," 28; *Virginia Gazette* (Parks), Sept. 3–10, 17, 1736, April 22, Oct. 14, Nov. 4, 1737, Nov. 3, 1738, Nov. 2, 30, Dec. 14, 21, 1739, Oct. 10, Dec. 19, 1745, July 18, Aug. 28, 1746, (Hunter), Oct. 3, 17, 1751; Greene, *Landon Carter Diary*, 103; Edmund Jenings to Col. P. L. Lee, June 10, 1754, to Robert Beverley, March 1, 1764, Edmund Jenings Letter Book, 1753–69, VHS; Thomas Jones to My Dearest Life, Sept. 17, 1736, Robert Donald to Mrs. Elizabeth Jones, March 11, June 8, 1758, Roger Jones Family Papers, LC; George Winchester Stone, ed., *The London Stage, 1660–1800* (3 vols., Carbondale, Ill., 1963), 2:649–50, 653, 839; Robert Wormeley Carter to Landon Carter, June [17?], 1770, Carter Family Papers, Sabine Hall Collection, 1659–1797, UVA microfilm; Mary [Burwell] to Dr Betsy [Elizabeth Whiting], Dec. 21, 1781, Blair, Banister, Braxton, Horner Papers, WM.

46. Nancy L. Struna, "Sport and American Leisure," in *Of Consuming Interests: The Style of Life in the Eighteenth Century*, ed. Cary Carson, Ronald Hoffman, Peter J. Albert (Charlottesville, VA, 1994), 438–39; Robert Carter to Ralph Wormeley, Oct. 5, 1771, Robert Carter Letter Book, 1771, VHS; Wormeley to Carter, March 18, 19, 1772, Carter Family Papers, 1651–1861, MSS 1 C2468a, 897, VHS.

47. For recent studies emphasizing the modest nature of Virginia housing and the fact that the elite "supervised or heavily influenced the design and construction of their own houses" rather than relying solely on English pattern books (with the exception of Tayloe's Mount Airy), see Camille Wells, "The Multistoried House: Twentieth-Century Encounters with the Domestic Architecture of Colonial Virginia," *VMHB* 106 (1998): 350–416; Cary Carson et al., "Impermanent Architecture in the Southern American Colonies," and Dell Upton, "Black and

White Landscapes in Eighteenth-Century Virginia," in *Material Life in America, 1600–1860,* ed. Robert Blair St. George (Boston, 1988), 113–58, 357–69; Fraser Neiman, "Domestic Architecture at the Clifts Plantation: The Social Context of Early Virginia Building," and Dell Upton, "Vernacular Architecture in Eighteenth-Century Virginia," in *Common Places: Readings in American Vernacular Architecture,* ed. Dell Upton and John Michael Vlach (Athens, GA, 1986), 292–314, 315–35. For the traditional view of elite houses, see Thomas Tileston Waterman, *The Mansions of Colonial Virginia, 1706–1776* (Chapel Hill, NC, 1945), and Charles E. Brownell et al., *The Making of Virginia Architecture* (Charlottesville, VA, 1992), chap. 1. For specific houses, see ibid., 3, 4, 5, 7, 8, 16–17, 18–19, 24–26; Chinard, *Huguenot in Exile,* 119–20; William Fitzhugh to Ralph Smith, April 23, 1686, Davis, *Fitzhugh,* 175–77; William Byrd to Warren Horsmanden, July 25, 1690, to Perry & Lane, Aug. 8, 1690, Tinling, *Byrd Correspondence,* 135; Jones, *John Carter II,* 58; Camille Wells, "Virginia by Design: The Making of Tuckahoe and the Remaking of Monticello," *ARRIS: The Journal of Southeast Chapter of the Society of Architectural Historians* 12 (2001): 44–73; Alexander, *Journal of John Fontaine,* 85–86, 153 n. 92; Charles E. Hatch Jr., *The Nelson House and the Nelsons: General Study* (Washington, DC, 1969), 68–71. Hatch argues that the house could have been built by 1711 and certainly before 1732. Bishop Meade, *Old Churches, Ministers, and Families of Virginia* 1:205, says that William Nelson (b. 1711) laid the cornerstone "when an infant." The "brick" was "laid in his apron and passed through his little hands", but dendrochronological sampling now indicates that the date was 1720. In their editing, Stiverson and Butler, "Virginia in 1732," *VMHB* 85 (Jan. 1977): 22, 26–29, omit the marginal notation in the description of Yorktown that mentions the Nelson and Ambler houses as two of the brick ones. See William Hugh Grove Diary, 1698–1732, UVA.

48. Robert Carter to Edward Tucker, July 13, 1720, Wright, *Letters of Carter,* 16; Robert Carter will, Aug. 2, 1726, UVA, Goodwin transcript FHCC, for the building of Rosewell and the completion of Corotoman; RC Diary, Jan. 3, 1725; Robert Carter to William Dawkins, June 28, 1729, RC Letter Book; Calder Loth, ed., *The Virginia Landmarks Register* (4th ed., Charlottesville, VA, 1999), 94; Theodore Reinhart, ed., *The Archaeology of Shirley Plantation* (Charlottesville, VA, 1984), 62, 87, 150–55; Richard Guy Wilson, ed., *Buildings of Virginia: Tidewater and Piedmont* (New York, 2002), 356–57. There is a disagreement about Westover. There was a fire there in 1749, and some believe that William Byrd III built the Westover that has survived to the present. William Byrd II said in 1729 that he intended on building "a very good house" (Tinling, *Byrd Correspondence,* 400), and I believe that he did. There is also reason to believe that the house was not entirely destroyed in 1749; for example, all of the portraiture in the house at the time survived. Alden Hatch, *The Byrds of Virginia* (New York, 1969), 193, citing a letter book in the possession of William Byrd of Princeton, NJ, said only the third floor of Westover burned in 1749, which supports the suggestion that the house was built sometime in the preceding twenty years, although most architectural historians disagree. Charles Carter to Landon Carter, July 31, 1738, Carter Family Papers, Sabine Hall Collection, 1659–1797, UVA microfilm, seems to indicate that Cleve had already been built and that Shirley and Sabine Hall were under construction. For Stratford Hall, see Wilson, *Buildings of Virginia,* 333–34; the information on the lower level is from Judy Hynson, Director of Research and Library Collections there.

49. On Richard Corbin and Laneville, see *VMHB* 66 (1958): 38–39; Harris, *Old New Kent,* 340–41, citing the Mutual Insurance Records, 1802, 572–95, LOV. Ivor Noel Hume, *Excavations at Rosewell, Gloucester County, Virginia, 1957–1959,* United States National Museum Bulletin 225, Smithsonian Institution (Washington, DC, 1962), 160–62; *WMQ* (1), 3 (1894–95): 185–89; Camille Wells, "The Eighteenth-Century Landscape of Virginia's Northern Neck," *Northern Neck Virginia Historical Magazine* 37 (1987): 4217–55, esp. 4220. Rosewell was not finished when Mann Page died in 1732. See John and Charles Carter to Messrs. Hayward & Chambers, Madeira Merchants, Nov. 10, 1733, Carter Letter Book, 1732–81, UVA, Goodwin transcript FHCC.

50. Carson, Hoffman, and Albert, *Of Consuming Interests,* and esp. Kevin M. Sweeney, "High Style Vernacular Lifestyles of the Colonial Elite," 1–58, and Lois Green Carr and Lorena S. Walsh, "Changing Lifestyles and Consumer Behavior in the Colonial Chesapeake," 59–166; will and inventory of the estate of Nathaniel Harrison of Surry, 1726, *VMHB* 31 (1921): 279–83, 361–80; list of home furnishings Thomas Jones settled on his wife, 1732, ibid., 26 (1917): 175–76; Alexander, *Journal of John Fontaine,* 86; William Fitzhugh to Nicholas Hayward, July 26, 1689, July 10, 1690, Davis, *Fitzhugh,* 259–63, 269–72.

51. Margaret M. Lovell, "Painters and Their Customers: Aspects of Art and Money in Eighteenth-Century America," in Carson, Hoffman, Albert, *Of Consuming Interests,* 285–300; Richard H. Saunders and Ellen G. Miles, eds., *American Colonial Portraits, 1700–1776* (Washington, DC, 1987), 17, 35, 47, 53, 107, 157–58, 251–52, 284–86, 296–97; William Fitzhugh to John Cooper, July 26, 1698, and Fitzhugh's will and inventory, Davis, *Fitzhugh,* 367, 379; T. H. Breen, "The Meaning Likeness: Portrait Painting in Eighteenth-Century Consumer Society," *The Portrait in Eighteenth-Century America,* ed. Ellen G. Miles (Newark, 1993), 54; Richard K. Dowd, "The Fitzhugh Portraits by John Hesselius," *VMHB* 75 (1967): 159–73; Edmund Berkeley of Barn Elms, will and inventory, 1718, *VMHB* 35 (1925): 37; Robert Carter will, 1726, 25, UVA, Goodwin transcript FHCC; Graham Hood, *Charles Bridges and William Dering: Two Virginia Painters, 1735–1750* (Charlottesville, VA, 1978), 5, 62, 82, 88, 97–98, 109–14, 118–22; William Gooch to Thomas Gooch, May 26, 1735, Gooch Letter Book, 1727–58, transcript, CW; William Byrd II to Alexander Spotswood, Dec. 22, 1735, Tinling, *Byrd Correspondence,* 468; Evans, *Nelson,* between pp. 22–23; will of Mary Willing Byrd, 1813, *VMHB* 38 (1928): 145–54; Jackson and Twohig, *Washington Diaries* 3:108–9; George Washington Cash Accounts, May 1772, and George Washington to Jonathan Boucher, May 21, 1772, Abbot et al., *Washington Papers, Col. Ser.* 9:36, 49; Richard Henry Lee to Landon Carter, Oct. 9, 1772, Carter Family Papers, Sabine Hall Collection, 1659–1797, UVA microfilm.

52. Lovell, "Painters and Their Customers," 285–85, 287–88, 299–300; Timothy Clayton, *The English Print, 1688–1802* (New Haven, 1997), xi, 13–14, 106–7, 122–23, 195, 198–99, 262; Byrd, *Secret Diary,* 324, and *London Diary,* 89; Fithian, *Journal,* 83; John Custis to Gentlemen, 1717, to Mr. Cary, 1734, Zuppan, *Custis Letterbook,* 34–35, 140–41; Joseph Ball to Benjamin Waller, Sept. 10, Dec. 6, 1757, Sept. 8, 1758, April 10, 1759, Ball Letter Book, 1743–59, LC; Benj. Dod to William Dawson, March 28, 1751, William Dawson Papers, 1728–75, LC; Robert Wormeley Carter to Landon Carter, March 16–19, 1764, Carter Family Papers, Sabine Hall Collection, 1659–1797, UVA microfilm; Mary Willing Byrd, Will, 1813, *VMHB* 38 (1928): 148–49; William Nelson to John Norton, Sept. 4, 1769, to Samuel Waterman, Sept. 3, 1770,

to Samuel Athawes, March 25, 1771, Nelson Letter Book, 1766–75, LOV; [Thomas Jones?] to [Walter Jones], [Jan. 1770], Roger Jones Family Papers, LC; Edmund Berkeley of Barn Elms, will and inventory, 1718, *VMHB* 35 (1925): 34–38.

53. Karen Calvert, "The Function of Fashion in Eighteenth-Century America," in Carson, Hoffman, and Albert, *Of Consuming Interests,* 252–83, esp. 260–69, 274–75; Mary Stanard, *Colonial Virginia: Its People and Its Customs* (Philadelphia, 1917), esp. 186–202.

54. Byrd, *Secret Diary,* 298, 463; Robert Carter to John Carter, July 13, 1720, Wright, *Letters of Carter,* 8; Robert Wormeley Carter to Landon Carter, Nov. 16–19, 1764, June 8, 1770, Carter Family Papers, Sabine Hall Collection, 1659–1797, UVA microfilm; Fithian, *Journal,* 69–70.

55. Calvert, "The Function of Fashion," 264–69; Stanard, *Colonial Virginia,* 187–88; Robert Carter to James Bradley, Aug. 26, 1729, July 26, 1731, RC Letter Book; William Byrd II to John Hanbury, Oct. 22, 1735, Tinling, *Byrd Correspondence,* 463; M. Stith to Madam [Elizabeth Jones], May 7, 1728, Roger Jones Family Papers, LC; Thomas Lee to Henry Fitzhugh, Nov. 13, 1716, Richard Bland Lee Papers, 1700–1825, LC; Edward Athawes to John and Charles Carter, Jan. 12, 1735, Carter Family Papers, Sabine Hall Collection, 1659–1797, UVA microfilm; Charles Carter, invoice of goods from William Dawkins, Dec. 1731, Nov. 30, 1733, bill from James Currie, hairdresser, 1753–58, clothes bought from John Priestman of Craven Court, Craven Street, London, June 2, 1760, Carter Family Papers, Lancaster County, 1718–1833, LOV; John Baylor to [Edward] Athawes, Dec. 12, 1749, John Baylor Letter Book, 1749–65, VHS; Robert Beverley to John Martin Jordan, March 3, 1762, to Mr. Scot, Tailor, July 1762, to John Smither (taylor Arundel Street), [1773?], Robert Beverley Letter Book, 1761–93, LC; John Custis to Hugh Howard, 1725, Zuppan, *Custis Letterbook,* 81–82; Arthur Lee to Richard Henry Lee, Aug. 19, 1766, Lee Family Papers, UVA microfilm; Robert Wormeley Carter to Landon Carter, June 8, 1770, Carter Family Papers, Sabine Hall Collection, 1659–1797, UVA microfilm; London invoice, 1716, Bristol invoice, 1717, and invoices 1719, 1721, 1724, John Tayloe I and II Account and Letter Book, 1714–78, Tayloe Family Papers, 1650–1970, VHS; Robert Carter to Thomas Evans, July 22, 1723, RC Letter Book; Robert Carter will, 1726, UVA, Goodwin transcript FHCC. Supplies for caring for wigs were readily available; see *Virginia Gazette* (Parks), July 31, 1746.

56. Davis, *Intellectual Life in the Colonial South,* vol. 2, esp. 501–14, 538–61, 579–95; Wright, *First Gentlemen of Virginia,* pt. 2, 95–347; Hayes, *Library of William Byrd,* 1–103; W. Preston Haynie, comp., *A Northumberland County Bookshelf, or A Parcel of Old Books* (Bowie, MD, 1994); John Clayton to Honour'd Doctor, April 24, 1684, Berkeley and Berkeley, *The Reverend John Clayton,* 3–5; Jones, *John Carter II,* 42–43, 49–50; "Library of Colonel Ralph Wormeley, Esq., of Rosegill," *WMQ* (1), 2 (1893–94): 169–74 and evaluation of £250 for the library of Peyton Randolph, 175; will and inventory of the estate of Nathaniel Harrison of Surry, 1726, *VMHB* 21 (1933): 361–79, esp. 365; "Inventory of the Estate of Robert Carter, Esqr.," UVA, Goodwin transcript FHCC; will of Sir John Randolph, *VMHB* 36 (1916): 378; William Beverley to Micajah Perry, July 12, 1737, July 11, 1738, to Benjamin Hone, Aug. [25?], 1738, to Charles Smyth, March 2, 1744, William Beverley Letter Book, 1737–44, NYPL; John Carter library, *Tyler's Quarterly and Historical Magazine* 8 (1926): 143. For the Custis libraries, see Abbot et al., *Washington Papers, Col. Ser.* 6:284–300. For Thomas Nelson Jr.'s library, see Joseph Hall Jr. to Mrs. Hannah Nice, [1775?], *WMQ* (1), 22 (1913–14): 158–59. For Philip Ludwell III's substantial library, see Charles Carroll of Carrollton to Richard Corbin and Robert Carter Nicholas, Nov. 8, 1767, "Books Chosen by Charles Carroll of Carrollton," Ronald Hoffman et al., eds.,

Dear Papa Dear Charlie: The Papers of Charles Carroll of Carrollton, 1748–1782 (3 vols., Chapel Hill, NC, 2001), 3:1564–69. For Secretary Thomas Nelson's library, see Thomas Nelson Sr. to Thomas Jefferson, March 6, 1770, Boyd et al., *Papers of Jefferson* 1:37; see also Account of Thomas Nelson Sr. with Samuel Waterman, PRO, T 79/26. A catalog of the library of Robert Carter of Nomini Hall is in Fithian, *Journal,* 221–29. Libraries were, of course, not limited to our twenty-one families, or for that matter to the elite. See, for example, Will and Inventory of the Estate of Edmund Berkeley of Barn Elms, 1718, *VMHB* 35 (1925): 31–38; Joseph Ball to Couz. Jos. Chinn, July 17, 1745, March 14, 1746, Jan. 18, 1755, Joseph Ball Letter Book, 1743–59, LC; Francis Jerdone to Capt. Archb. Crawford, June 24, 1756, Francis Jerdone to Capt. Hugh Crawford, Jan. 5, 1757, Francis Jerdone Letter Book, 1756–63, WM; Inventory of the Estate of Mr. John Herbert, 1761, *VMHB* 38 (1910): 181–185; Books ordered by Thomas Jones, May 7, 1769, Jones Family Papers, LC; John Baylor Will, Feb. 15, 1770, Baylor Family Papers, box 2, UVA; and the will as it appears in U.S. Circuit Court, Ended Cases, Pinkerton and Bell vs. Baylor & als, 1832, LOV. It is stated in this version of the will that Baylor had between 1,200 and 1,300 volumes.

57. See James Raven, "The Importation of Books in the Eighteenth Century," in *The Colonial Book in the Atlantic World,* ed. Hugh Amory and David D. Hall (Cambridge, 2000), 185–86, 188–89, 194; Calhoun Winton, "The Southern Book Trade in the Eighteenth Century," ibid., 228–30, 232, 238–39. See also Davis, *Intellectual Life in the Colonial South* 2:601–2, 609–18. *Virginia Gazette* (Parks), Oct. 24, 1745. On Scots' stores, see, for example, William Allason to James Knop, July 22, 1771, Allason Letter Book, 1770–89, LOV; Estate of James Walker, Oct. 19, 1773, U.S. Circuit Court, Ended Cases, Cunninghame & Co. vs. Walker's Admr., 1797, LOV; James Hughes in account with W. Cunninghame & Co. and Walker Trent, Nov. 29, Dec. 22, 1773, Cunninghame Papers, Huntington Library. On magazines and newspapers, see, for example, Robert Carter to Micajah Perry, Aug. 7, 1728, RC Letter Book; William Beverley to Micajah Perry, July 12, 1737, to Charles Smyth, March 2, 1744, William Beverley Letter Book, 1737–44, NYPL; Francis Jerdone to Flowerdew & Norton, April 10, 1760, Francis Jerdone Letter Book, 1758–63, WM; William Nelson to John Norton, Sept. 6, 1766, Mason, *Norton & Sons,* 16; Greene, *Landon Carter Diary,* 250, 581, 785, 786, 787, 805, 914, 954, 957. For ordering books, see ibid., 337, 785–87, 910, 912, 953–54; George Wythe to John Norton, May 15, 1768, Norton Papers, CW; Robert Carter Nicholas to John Norton, May 20, 1768, William Nelson to John Norton, Aug. 27, 1768, Sept. 4, 1769, Mason, *Norton & Sons,* 52, 66, 105–6; Walter Jones to Dear Brother, Aug. 12, 1769, Roger Jones Family Papers, LC; William Fitzhugh to Ralph Wormeley, Aug. 2, 1682, Davis, *Fitzhugh,* 124; William Byrd to Perry & Lane, July 23, 1689, Tinling, *Byrd Correspondence,* 111; William Beverley to Charles Smyth, March 2, 1744, William Beverley Letter Book, 1737–44, NYPL.

58. Davis, *Intellectual Life in the Colonial South* 2:526–95; Wright, *First Gentlemen of Virginia,* 117–285, esp. chap. 5; Hayes, *Library of William Byrd,* introduction. For England, see John Brewer, *The Pleasure of the Imagination: English Culture in the Eighteenth Century* (New York, 1997), chap. 4, esp. 171–73, 181, 186; Neil McKendrick, John Brewer, and J. H. Plumb, *The Birth of a Consumer Society; The Commercialization of Eighteenth-Century England* (Bloomington, IN, 1982), introduction; "Inventory of the Estate of Robert Carter, Esqr.," UVA, Goodwin transcript FHCC; Fithian, *Journal,* 221–29; Joseph Ball to Couzn Jos. Chinn, July 1745, Nov. 14, 1746, Jan. 18, 1755, Joseph Ball Letter Book, 1743–49, LC. On book sharing, see, for

example, books loaned by Stephen Loyde, summer 1711, Stephen Loyde, Account and Letter Book, 1708–11, Tayloe Family Papers, 1650–1970, b1, VHS; Ralph Wormeley to Landon Carter, Feb. 6, 1771, Carter Family Papers, Sabine Hall Collection, 1659–1797, UVA microfilm; Greene, *Landon Carter Diary*, 720. Roger Atkinson to Samuel Gist, July 30, 1770, Roger Atkinson Letter Book, 1769–76, UVA.

59. Edward L. Bond, "Anglican Theology and Devotion in James Blair's Virginia, 1685–1743: Private Piety in the Public Church," *VMHB* 104 (1996): 313–40, esp. 315–16, 317, 318, 320, 322–23, 326, 328–29, 337, 340, see also Edward L. Bond, ed., *Speaking the Gospel in Colonial Virginia* (Lanham, MD, 2005), 75–97, on John Page to his son; John K. Nelson, *A Blessed Company: Parishes, Parsons, and Parishioners in Anglican Virginia., 1690–1776* (Chapel Hill, NC, 2001), 205–7, 252, 290–94; Gunderson, *Anglican Ministry of Virginia*, 159–63; Dell Upton, *Holy Things and Profane: Anglican Parish Churches in Colonial Virginia* (New York, 1986). See also Jon Butler, *Awash in a Sea of Faith: Christianizing the American People* (Cambridge, Mass., 1990), chap. 6, esp. 167–68; Patricia Bonomi, *Under the Cope of Heaven: Religion, Society, Politics in Colonial America* (New York, 1986), 104.

60. Marambaud, *William Byrd*, 63; Byrd, *Secret Diary*, xxviii, May 30, 1709, 41; Kenneth Berland, Jean Christian Gilliam, and Kenneth A. Lockridge, eds., *The Commonplace Book of William Byrd II of Westover* (Chapel Hill, NC, 2001), 58–64, 88, no. 349, p. 159, no. 526, pp. 197–99, 244–95; Robert Carter to William Dawkins, July 14, 1720, Wright, *Carter Letters*, 25.

61. William Gooch to Bishop of London, July 8, 1735, Fulham Palace Papers, 13 (1695–1771), Lambeth Palace, London; James Blair to Bishop of London, March 11, 1737, ibid., 15 (1695–1776); will of Sir John Randolph, Dec. 23, 1735, *VMHB* 36 (1926): 376–80. Randolph's views were also published, probably at his direction, in the *Virginia Gazette* (Parks), April 29–May 6, 1737. On John Custis, see [William Dawson] to [Thomas Wilson?], Aug. 21, 1750, William Dawson Family Papers, 1728–75, LC.

62. Greene, *Landon Carter Diary*, 26–27, May 10, 1752, 81, May 10, 1774, 809; Isaac W. Giberne to Landon Carter, May 13, 1774, Carter Family Papers, Sabine Hall Collection, 1659–1797, UVA microfilm. On the influence of Tillotson, see Meade, *Old Churches, Ministers, and Families of Virginia* 2:354–55; Norman Fiering, "The First American Enlightenment: Tillotson, Leverett, and Philosophical Anglicanism," *New England Quarterly* 54 (1981): 307–44.

63. Nelson, *Blessed Company*, 205–7, 252; Byrd, *Secret Diary*, May 3, 1709; RC Diary, Feb. 23, 1723; Robert Carter to John Falconer, Dec. 16, 1727, RC Letter Book; Greene, *Landon Carter Diary*, 26–27; Upton, *Holy Things and Profane*, 104. For the clergy's feelings about dissenters, see, for example, the Reverend Patrick Henry's correspondence with Commissary William Dawson, Feb. 13, 1745, April 29, 1747, Aug. 22, 1751, and James Maury to Dawson, Oct. 6, 1755, *WMQ* (2), 1 (1921): 265–66, and (1) 2 (1893–94): 261–63, 278; Petition of Virginia Clergy to Speaker of the House of Burgesses, [1745?], Church Commissioners for England, Fulham Palace Papers, 14 (Misc. Papers, 1679–1771), Lambeth Palace, London; William Dawson to Bishop of London, July 27, 1750, ibid., 13 (1695–1771); John Leland to Thomas Dawson, Oct. 12, 1758, George Trash to Dawson, Dec. 9, 1758, William Dawson Family Papers, 1728–75, LC; Fithian, *Journal*, April 3, 1774, 89. On seating, see Upton, *Holy Things and Profane*, 176–83; Gunderson, *Anglican Ministry of Virginia*, 155; Byrd, *Secret Diary*, Dec. 18, 1710, 273; Benjamin Waller to Thomas Jones, June 2, 1750, Roger Jones Family Papers, LC; C. G. Chamberlayne, ed., *The*

Vestry Book of Stratton Major Parish, King and Queen County, Virginia, 1729–1783 (rept. Richmond, 1989), 166–67, on the seating of the Robinson and Corbin families.

64. See T. H. Breen, *The Marketplace Revolution: How Consumer Politics Shaped American Independence* (New York, 2004), esp. 39, 52,60, 90, 121–23; McKendrick, Brewer, and Plumb, *Birth of a Consumer Society,* pt. 1; Carr and Walsh, "Changing Lifestyles and Consumer Behavior in the Colonial Chesapeake," and Cary Carson, "The Consumer Revolution in Colonial America: Why Demand?" in Carson, Hoffman, Albert, *Of Consuming Interests,* 59–166, 483–697, esp. 134–45, 490–524; T. H. Breen, "The Empire of Goods: The Anglicanization of Colonial America, 1690–1776," *Journal of British Studies* 25 (1986): 467–99.

65. Jacob M. Price, "New Time Series for Scotland's and Britain's Trade with the Thirteen Colonies and States, 1740–1791," *WMQ* (3), 33 (1975): 307–25; Wattenburg, *Statistical History,* 1117; PRO, Customs 3 (1696–1780), 50–75. See W. E. Minchinton and C. J. French, introduction, *British Records Relating to America in Microform, Customs 3, 1696–1780* (1974), for the seventeen luxury items.

66. "Observations in Several Voyages and Travels in America in the Year 1736," *WMQ* (1), 15 (1906–7): 222–23; Francis Jerdone to Mr. William Hamilton, Sept. 20, 1753, ibid., 12 (1902–3): 238; bill to Daniel Parke Custis from Robert Cary & Co., Feb. 5, 1750, Custis Family Papers, 1683–1858, MSS 1, C9698a, 61, VHS; Robert Beverley to John Bland, Oct. 10, 1761, and instructions to Mr. Page, Nov. 10, 1761, Robert Beverley Letter Book, 1761–93, LC; William Nelson to John Norton, July 25, 1766, Mason, *Norton & Sons,* 14; William Nelson to Rowland Hunt, May 16, 1771, Thomas Nelson to Samuel Athawes, Sept. 14, 1773, Nelson Letter Book, 1766–75, LOV; Nathaniel Littleton Savage to John Norton, Aug. 24, 1768, Norton-Dixon-Savage Papers, 1764–96, Brock Collection, Huntington Library. Thomas Jones is not among our families but he was certainly among the gentry. After he married Elizabeth Cocke Pratt he began to refurbish his coach and chariot. He wrote Elizabeth, who was in England, that he was sending over "Brasses belonging to the coach 4 coats without the crest and 2 Crests for the Coach and 8 Crests for the Harness' as well as 4 Toppings for the Horses" which he supposed should be the "Colour of the lining of the Coach." Similar instruction was given concerning the chariot; the "Brass plates of the Chariot" should "be of the same dimensions to cover the places the old ones were taken from" and there "must be four Coats and two Coats for the Chariot and eight Crests for the Harness." He was also sending "three Toppings for the horses" to be refurbished. She was to check at the Herald's Office to find out what "Livery is proper." Thomas Jones to My Dearest Life, July 8, 22, 1728, Roger Jones Family Papers, LC.

67. Fithian, *Journal,* Dec. 27, 1773, March 4, April 7, July 13, 15, Sept. 12, 1774, 41–42, 78, 94, 141, 146, 189; will of Charles Carter of Cleve, *VMHB* 31 (1921): 64–65; Robert Fairfax to Rev. Denny Martin, Aug. 24, Sept. 29, 1768, Kent Archives Office, Kent, Eng., U23620; *Virginia Gazette* (Purdie & Dixon), Aug. 27, 1768; Wright and Tinling, *Quebec to Carolina,* 209. Some house servants also wore livery; see Greene, *Landon Carter Diary,* 295.

68. Lawrence and Jean Fawther Stone, *An Open Elite? England, 1540–1800* (Oxford, 1984), 8–9; Rozbicki, *Complete Colonial Gentleman,* 39–40, 44–45, 48–49, 50, 58, 62–65, 137–43; *Virginia Gazette* (Parks), March 4–11, 1737; Fithian, *Journal,* March 12, 1774, 76, and Fithian to Rev. Enoch Green, Dec. 1, 1773, 27; Charles Yates to George McCall, Sept. 30, 1773, Charles Yates Letter Book, 1773–83, UVA. See, for example, Clifford Dowdey, *The Golden Age: A Climate of Greatness, Virginia, 1732–1775* (Boston, 1970).

69. Robert Beverley to [John Bland], Oct. 10, 1761, Robert Beverley Letter Book, 1761–93, LC; James Dean to James Buchanan, June 28, 1764, U.S. Circuit Court, Virginia District, Hyndman's Exors. vs. Dean's Exors. & Yates, 1806, LOV; Cowden, "The Randolphs," 167–73, 189–206; Robert Carter to Samuel Athawes, Feb. 21, 1764, Robert Carter Letter Book, 1764–68, CW; William Nelson to Samuel Athawes, Nov. 15, 1768, Sept. 1, 1772, Nelson Letter Book, 1766–75, LOV. Nelson also told merchant Edward Hunt that he was "too general in your suspicions" about "advancing a little Money for a Correspondent in such a way to lose his consignment." Caution was certainly appropriate but "it hurts me to have your ship go out without being fully loaded." William Nelson to Edward Hunt, Sept. 11, 1766, ibid. There also appears to have been some concern about family antecedents. Who were "our first ancestors in this Country?" Robert Carter asked his uncle Landon in 1765. And more pointedly, Thomas Jones asked his brother Walter, who was in London, to go by "the heralds office & search for" the family coat of arms because "we are in Virginia of late years say'd to be descendants of convicts & the refuse of Goals," and "I think it necessary know from whence we are sprung." Walter Jones was unsuccessful because of "a peculiar Difficulty in tracing Welch arms." [Thomas Jones] to [Walter Jones], n.d. [June 1770?], Walter Jones to Thomas Jones, June 20, 1770, Roger Jones Family Papers, LC; Robert Carter to Landon Carter, Dec. 27, 1765, Carter Family Papers, Sabine Hall Collection, 1659–1797, UVA, microfilm.

70. John F. D. Smyth, *A Tour in the United States of America* (2 vols., London, 1784), 1:65–70; St. John Shropshire to Coll. [Robert] Carter, Aug. 16, 1705, Carter Family Papers, folder 16, WM; RC Diary, July 26, 28, 1725; Francis Makemie to Mr. Robert Harley, Feb. 4, 1706, *WMQ* (1), 21 (1913–14): 281–82; "The Fisher History," Louise Pecquet du Bellet, *Some Prominent Virginia Families* (4 vols., Lynchburg, VA, 1907), 2:774–77; John Carter to Landon Carter, Aug. 12, 1737, Carter Family Papers, Sabine Hall Collection, 1659–1797, UVA microfilm.

71. [Elizabeth Jones] to Madam [Susanna Randolph], Aug. 11, 1740, Roger Jones Family Papers, LC; Henry Lee to Richard Lee, Feb. 16, 1767, Richard Bland Lee Papers, 1700–1825, LC; William Gooch to Thomas Gooch, July 5, 1735, Gooch Letter Book, 1727–58, transcript, CW; William Byrd to Governor William Gooch, Sept. 1, 1728, Tinling, *Byrd Correspondence,* 387; *WMQ* (1), 22 (1914–15): 223; James A. Servies and Carl R. Dolmetsch, eds., *The Poems of Charles Hansford* (Chapel Hill, NC, 1961), 58, 62–64.

72. Isaac, *Transformation of Virginia,* chap. 11; Fithian, *Journal,* Aug. 25, 1774, 178; Owen Griffith to Landon Carter, Dec. 21, 1771, Dr. Walter Jones to Landon Carter, June 17, 1774, Carter Family Papers, Sabine Hall Collection, 1659–1797, UVA microfilm; John Dixon to Robert Carter III, July 3, 1772, Carter Family Papers, folder 18, WM; Greene, *Landon Carter Diary,* 326n, 392, 475, 505, 552, 1030–31; Glenn Curtis Smith, "On John Randolph's Considerations," *VMHB* 59 (1959): 108–11; "Deposition of Sir John Randolph," [1775?], ibid., 15 (1907–8): 149; John Randolph, "Considerations on the Present State of Virginia," Van Schreeven et al., *Revolutionary Virginia* 1:204–18.

EPILOGUE

1. Williams, *Political Alignments,* chap. 8; Jack P. Greene, "Political Power in the House of Burgesses, 1720–1776," *WMQ* (3), 15 (1958): 485–505; Richard M. Jellison, ed., *Society, Freedom, Conscience: The American Revolution in Virginia, Massachusetts, and New York* (New

York, 1976), 37–43; Leonard, *General Assembly of Virginia,* 76–77, 78–80, 81–82, 83–85, 88–90, 94–96, 99–100, 102–4, 105–7; *JHB,* 1727–40, 321–22, 393–94, 1742–47, 5–7, 236, 258–59, 1752–58, 6–7, 58, 107–8, 111, 127, 234–35, 328, 417–19, 1758–61, 7, 57–58, 199, 201–2, 1761–65, 8, 69–70, 230–31, 1766–69, 14–16, 143, 190–91, 228–29, 1773–76, 75–76, 177–78; Billings et al., *Colonial Virginia,* 251–59.

2. Gooch to Board of Trade, May 24, 1748, PRO, CO 5/1338; Frank L. Dewey, "New Light on the General Court of Colonial Virginia," *William and Mary Quarterly Law Review* 21 (Fall 1979): 2–8; Karen L. Peacock, "The Council of Colonial Virginia, 1750–1776" (honors thesis, College of William and Mary, 1977), esp. 20–27, 34–38, 45, 48–53; Jackson Turner Main, *The Upper House in Revolutionary America, 1763–1788* (Madison, WI, 1967), 43–49.

3. Greene, *Quest for Power,* 17; Billings et al., *Colonial Virginia,* 254–56, 261–66.

4. On the Proclamation Line and the land problem, see Woody Holton, *Forced Founders: Indians, Debtors Slaves, and the Making of the Revolution in Virginia* (Chapel Hill, NC, 1999), chap. 1; Edmund and Helen Morgan, *The Stamp Act Crisis* (Chapel Hill, NC, 1953), chap. 5; Robert J. Chaffin, "The Townshend Act Crisis, 1767–1771," in *The Blackwell Encyclopedia of the American Revolution,* ed. Jack P. Greene and J. R. Pole (Cambridge, Mass., 1991), 126–45.

5. Ernst, *Money and Politics,* chap. 6; David J. Mays, *Edmund Pendleton, 1721–1803* (2 vols., Cambridge, Mass., 1950), 1:358–69.

6. Leonard, *General Assembly of Virginia,* 91–96; Fauquier to Board of Trade, June 5, 1765, April 7, 1766, to Earl of Shelburne, April 27, 1767, Reese, *Papers of Fauquier,* 3:1250, 1353, 1443; Jack P. Greene, ed., "'Not to Be Governed or Taxed, But by . . . Our Representatives': Four Essays on Opposition to the Stamp Act by Landon Carter," *VMHB* 76 (1968): 259–300, quote from 296; *JHB,* 1766–69, 3–16.

7. William Nelson to Cousin William Cookson, Nov. 26, 1767, to Farrell & Jones, Nov. 19, 1768, Nelson Letter Book, 1766–75, LOV.

8. *JHB,* 1766–69, 190–91, 214–15, 218, 1770–72, xxvii–xxxi, 85; Van Schreeven et al., *Revolutionary Virginia* 1:67–84; Breen, *Marketplace Revolution,* 245–46; Chaffin, "The Townshend Act Crisis," 138–40; PRO, Customs 3 (1696–1780), in Minchinton and French, *British Records Relating to America on Microform,* 50–75; Price, "New Time Series," *WMQ* (3), 32 (1975): 307–25.

9. John Selby, *Dunmore* (Williamsburg, VA, 1977); Richard Henry Lee to John Dickinson, April 4, 1773, to Samuel Adams, April 24, May 8, June 16, 1774, to Landon Carter, April 25, 1774, James C. Ballagh, ed., *The Letters of Richard Henry Lee, 1767–1794* (2 vols., New York, 1911), 1:83–84, 106–8, 110, 111–13; *JHB,* 1773–76, xi–xii, xv, 28, 31, 36, 124, 126; Van Schreeven et al., *Revolutionary Virginia* 1:93–95; Merrill Jensen, *The Founding of a Nation: A History of the American Revolution* (New York, 1968), 422–33 and chap.17.

10. Van Schreeven et al., *Revolutionary Virginia* 1:89–92, 96–100.

11. Council to Dunmore, June 10, 1774, PRO, CO 5/1352; *EJC* 6:574, 577–78, 656–57; *Virginia Gazette* (Purdie & Dixon), June 17, July 14, 1774; Hening, *Statutes* 8:515–16; James Parker to Charles Steuart, June 17, 1774, Charles Steuart Papers, National Library of Scotland; John Tayloe to Duncan Campbell, July 20, 1774, Notarial Copies of Sundry Letters to Duncan Campbell, American Loyalist Claims, PRO, T 79/120.

12. Van Schreeven et al., *Revolutionary Virginia* 1:109–68; Thomas Nelson's address is on pp. 165–66. Evans, *Nelson,* 36.

13. Greene, *Landon Carter Diary*, 842, 847; Van Schreeven et al., *Revolutionary Virginia* 1:219–39.

14. Van Schreeven et al., *Revolutionary Virginia* 1:204–18, 235; Dunmore to Secretary of State, June 25, 1775, PRO, CO 5/1353; Richard Corbin to Edmund Jenings, Feb. 1, 1766, Richard Corbin Letter Book, 1758–68, CW; Robert Calhoon, ed., "'A Sorrowful Spectator of These Troublesome Times': Robert Beverley Describes the Coming of the Revolution," *VMHB* 73 (1975): 42–45; Barbara A. Sorrill, "The Lightfoot Family of Yorktown," ibid., 75 (1967): 280–81; Fauquier to Earl of Shelburne, June 4, 1767, Reese, *Papers of Fauquier* 3:1481–82, 1:844 n. 7. For the Lees, see Nagel, *Lees,* chap. 1. For Thomas Nelson Jr., see Evans, *Nelson,* chap. 3.

15. Van Schreeven et al., *Revolutionary Virginia* 2:101–246; Thomas Nelson to Thomas and Roland Hunt and to Samuel Athawes, Aug. 7, 1774, Nelson Letter Book, 1766–75, LOV; Robert Beverley to Samuel Athawes, Sept. 6, 1774, Robert Beverley Letter Book, 1761–93, LC; Charles Yates to Samuel Martin, Sept. 28, 1774, to Gale Fearon & Co, Dec. 2, 1774, Charles Yates Letter Book, 1773–83, UVA; William Carr to James Russell, Sept. 27, Dec. 1774, Jan. 9, 1774 [1775], Russell Papers 2, Coutts & Co. Bankers, London; Greene, *Landon Carter Diary,* 813; *Virginia Gazette* (Rind), Nov. 24, 1774; James Parker to Charles Steuart, Nov. 27, 1774, Charles Steuart Papers, National Library of Scotland; Dunmore to Secretary of State, Dec. 24, 1774, PRO, CO 5/1353; Richard Henry Lee to Samuel Adams, Feb. 4, 1775, Ballagh, *Letters of Lee,* 127–28.

16. Van Schreeven et al., *Revolutionary Virginia* 2:101–4; Jensen, *Founding of a Nation,* chap. 19.

17. *JHB,* 1773–76, 169; Van Schreeven et al., *Revolutionary Virginia* 2:245, 334–37, 347–67, n. 8, 368. The Lee brothers were kept abreast of developments in London by their brothers Arthur and William. See Lewis W. Potts, *Arthur Lee: A Virtuous Revolutionary* (Baton Rouge, LA, 1981); William Lee to Francis Lightfoot Lee and Richard Henry Lee, Dec. 24, 1774, Jan. 13, Feb. 10, 1775, William Lee Letter Book, 1774–75, VHS.

18. Van Schreeven et al., *Revolutionary Virginia* 2:347–86, 358–70 nn. 8, 9; *Virginia Gazette* (Rind), April 1, 1775; James Parker to Charles Steuart, April 6, 1775, Charles Steuart Papers, National Library of Scotland; Edmund Randolph, *History of Virginia,* ed. Arthur H. Shaffer (Charlottesville, VA, 1970), 209–17; Mays, *Pendleton* 2:4–8.

19. William Reynolds to George F. Norton, April 20, May 25, 1775, William Reynolds Letter Book, 1771–79, LC; John Selby, *The Revolution in Virginia, 1775–1783* (Williamsburg, VA, 1988), 19–22; Selby, *Dunmore,* 20–22; Van Schreeven et al., *Revolutionary Virginia* 3:3–5, 34–37, 45–46, 48–49, 61–63; Robert Donald to Patrick Hunter, April 16, 1775; U.S. Circuit Court, Ended Cases, Buchanan & Milliken vs. Robert Donald, LOV.

20. Van Schreeven et al., *Revolutionary Virginia* 3:5–10, 54–55, 63–67, 77–82, 85–86 n. 2; Evans, *Nelson,* 47, *EJC* 6:589–83. For John Page Jr., see *Virginia Historical Register* 2 (1850–51): 143–51. For Robert Carter, see Morton, *Robert Carter of Nomini Hall; DVB; EJC* 6:584; *JHB,* 1773–76, 198, 239. Morton has Carter retiring from politics as early as 1774, but he was in Williamsburg through most of June 1775 and participated in Council business. *Virginia Gazette* (Dixon & Hunter), May 11, 1775, (Purdie), May 5, 1775, supplement; Charles Yates to Samuel Martin, May 11, 1775, Charles Yates Letter Book, 1773–83, UVA; Michael Wallace to Gustavus B. Wallace, May 14, 1775, Wallace Family Papers, 1775–81, UVA; Dunmore to Secretary of

State, March 14, June 25, 1775, PRO, CO 5/1353. For Dunmore's letter to Dartmouth of May 15, see *JHB,* 1773–76, xvi–xviii.

21. *JHB,* 1773–76, 171, 173–77, 189, 193–94, 199, 201–3, 214–15, 219–21, 228–36, 245, 248–51, 253–62, 270–71, 279, 280, 283; *Virginia Gazette* (Dixon & Hunter), June 10, 1775, (Purdie & Dixon), June 9, 1775, supplement; Selby, *Revolution in Virginia,* 41–45.

22. Selby, *Revolution in Virginia,* 44–47. For Richard Corbin and his family, see my short biography, originally written for *DVB,* in my possession; *Virginia Gazette* (Dixon & Hunter), May 20, 1775; memorial of Richard Corbin Jr., Feb. 12, 1787, PRO, AO 12/56; *VMHB* 14 (1907): 311; Van Schreeven et al., *Revolutionary Virginia* 6:147 n. 4. For Ralph Wormeley Jr., see James Laverne Anderson, "The Virginia Councilors and the American Revolution," *VMHB* 82 (1974): 13; Van Schreeven et al., *Revolutionary Virginia* 6:437 n. 18, 7:47–48, 102–3, 142. For William Byrd III, see *DVB,* s.v. "Byrd, William III"; *Virginia Gazette* (Pinkney), June 1, 1775; Byrd to Sir Jeffrey Amherst, July 30, 1775, to Ralph Wormeley, Oct. 14, 1775, Tinling, *Byrd Correspondence,* 812–13 and n, 814–16. For John Randolph, see Cowden, "The Randolphs," 668–772. For John Randolph Grymes, see *VMHB* 18 (1910): 375n; Ralph Wormeley to John Randolph Grymes, April 4, 1776, Van Schreeven et al., *Revolutionary Virginia* 6:325–27 n. 20, 331 nn. 11, 15, 402, 7:8, 571–72, 572 n. 1. Robert Beverley to Samuel Athawes, Sept. 6, 1774, to Mr. Charles Page, [fall 1791], Robert Beverley Letter Book, 1761–93, LC; Robert Calhoon, ed., "Robert Beverley Describes the Coming of the Revolution," *VMHB* 73 (1965): 41–55.

23. Van Schreeven et al., *Revolutionary Virginia,* vol. 3, esp. 304–96, 314, 351, 400–401, 418–19, 446–47, 451–52, 456–57, 457–59, 471–72, 478, 485, 503–4, 508 n. 26; see also ibid., 4:3–4; Hening, *Statutes* 9:49–53, 53–60; Cowden, "The Randolphs," 647; *Virginia Gazette* (Dixon & Hunter), Nov. 11, 1775; Selby, *Revolution in Virginia,* 49–53.

24. Selby, *Dunmore,* 41–49; Selby, *Revolution in Virginia,* 55–74; Van Schreeven et al., *Revolutionary Virginia* 4:334, see also ibid., 5:15–17; *Virginia Gazette* (Purdie), Nov. 10, 1775, (Dixon & Hunter), Nov. 16, 1775.

25. Selby, *Revolution in Virginia,* 75–79, 90–91; Van Schreeven et al., *Revolutionary Virginia* 5:3–5, 25–28, 33, 150, 158, 164–65 n. 15, 383, 386–87 n. 6, 435–37; *DVB,* s.v. "Byrd, William III"; John Adams, Notes of Debates in the Continental Congress, Feb. [16], 1776, Butterfield et al., *Diary and Autobiography of John Adams* 2:229; see also Paul H. Smith et al., eds., *Letters of Delegates to Congress, 1774–1789* (25 vols., Washington, D.C., 1976–99), 3:261; Randolph, *History,* 233.

26. Selby, *Revolution in Virginia,* 89–95; Van Schreeven et al., *Revolutionary Virginia* 6:3–9; Dunmore to Richard Corbin, Jan. 27, 1776, Edmund Pendleton to Corbin, Feb. 10, 1776, Extract from a Letter from Williamsburg, Feb. 27, 1776, Freeholders of James City County to Delegates Robert Carter Nicholas and James Norvell, April 21, 1776, ibid., 29–30, 112–13, 144–45, 353 n. 2, 458; Edmund Pendleton to Richard Henry Lee, April 20, 1776, David J. Mays, ed., *The Letters and Papers of Edmund Pendleton, 1734–1803* (Charlottesville, VA, 1967), 163–65; Randolph, *History,* 251; Thomas Nelson to John Page, Feb. 13, 1776, Francis Lightfoot Lee to Landon Carter, March 19, 1776, Richard Henry Lee to Patrick Henry, April 20, 1776, to Robert Carter Nicholas, April 22, 1776, Smith et al., *Letters of Delegates* 3:248–49, 407–8, 571–72, 607–8; Thomas Nelson to Member of the Convention, May 8, 1776, Charles Campbell, *History of the Colony and Ancient Dominion of Virginia* (Philadelphia, 1860), 645–46.

27. Van Schreeven et al., *Revolutionary Virginia* 6:287, 290, 300 n. 7, 423 n. 11, 7:20–25; Edmund Pendleton to Richard Henry Lee, May 7, 1776, Mays, *Papers of Pendleton* 176–77; Greene, *Landon Carter Diary,* 1008–9; Charles Carter to William Fitzhugh, July 1, 1775, *VMHB* 17 (1909): 257; Landon Carter to George Washington, May 9, 1776, William W. Abbot et al., eds., *The Papers of George Washington: Revolutionary War Series* (Charlottesville, VA, 1985–), 4:235–39; Roger Atkinson to Samuel Pleasants, Nov. 20, 1776, Roger Atkinson Letter Book, 1776–77, UVA; Leonard, *General Assembly of Virginia,* 119–23.

28. Van Schreeven et al., *Revolutionary Virginia* 7:2–3, 26–29, 46–48. For Ralph Wormeley, see ibid., 6:325–27, 437, 7:46, 102–3, 142.

29. Ibid., 7:2–4, 26–29, 46–48, 122–23, 141–42 and n. 8, 146–47; Pendleton's compromise resolution, Mays, *Papers of Pendleton,* 178–79; Randolph, *History,* 250–51; Selby, *Revolution in Virginia,* 95–99.

30. Selby, *Revolution in Virginia,* 106–10; Van Schreeven et al., *Revolutionary Virginia* 7:9–10; George Mason to Richard Henry Lee, May 18, 1776, Rutland, *Papers of Mason,* 271–72; Randolph, *History,* 252–55; Selby, *Dunmore,* 55–62.

31. Van Schreeven et al., *Revolutionary Virginia* 7:594–98, 636–39, 649–54; Selby, *Revolution in Virginia,* 116–21; Main, *Upper House in Revolutionary America,* 124–31; Roger Atkinson to Samuel Pleasants, Nov. 23, 1776, Roger Atkinson Letter Book, 1769–76, UVA; Randolph, *History,* 253–60.

32. Greene, *Landon Carter Diary,* 46–47; Landon Carter to George Washington, May 9, 1776, Abbot et al., *Washington Papers: Rev. War Ser.* 4:235–39; George Mason to Richard Henry Lee, May 18, 1776, Rutland, *Papers of Mason,* 177–272; Randolph, *History,* 255–60; Richard Henry Lee to Edmund Pendleton, May 12, 1776, Ballagh, *Letters of Lee* 1:192; Van Schreeven et al., *Revolutionary Virginia* 1:165–66, 7:654.

33. *DVB,* s.v. "Byrd, William III."

34. Robert Munford to William Byrd III, April 20, 1775, Tinling, *Byrd Correspondence* 2:805–6; Michael A. McDonnell, "World Turned 'Topsy Turvy': Robert Munford, *The Patriots,* and the Crisis of the Revolution in Virginia," *WMQ* (3), 61 (April 2004): 235–70, esp. 245, 254, 255, 257, 262–63, 264, 265, 267, 268–69, 270; Royster, *Fabulous History of the Dismal Swamp Company,* 221, 240, 241, 284–85.

35. On legislative service, see Leonard, *General Assembly of Virginia,* 122–82; *JHD,* 1776–90. On committee membership, see Martha W. Hiden, *How Justice Grew: Virginia Counties: An Abstract of Their Formation* (Williamsburg, VA, 1957), 32–46, 83–87; see also Daniel P. Jordan, *Political Leadership in Jefferson's Virginia* (Charlottesville, VA, 1983), 13–17; Jackson Turner Main, *Political Parties before the Constitution* (Chapel Hill, NC, 1973), chap. 9 and pp. 442–48; Kaminski and Saladino, *Documentary History of the Constitution,* 9:561–631; H. R. McIlwaine et al., eds., *Journals of the Council of State of Virginia* (5 vols., Richmond, 1933–82), 5:375–410; *Virginia Gazette and American Advertizer,* Oct. 7, 1784; *Virginia Independent Chronicle,* April 25, Aug. 8, 1787 (poem). See also Michael A. McDonnell, "Class War? Class Struggle during the American Revolution in Virginia," WMQ (3), 63 (2006): 305–44, which argues for a more fluid definition of class and class struggle based on people's different socioeconomic backgrounds.

36. Emory G. Evans, "Planter Indebtedness and the Revolution in Virginia," *WMQ* (3), 28 (1971): 349–79; Main, *Political Parties before the Constitution,* 256; *JHD,* 1781–86, 41, 45, 46,

54, 72–73, 74–75, 81, 1786–90, 51–52, 55, 57, 77, 79–86; Hening, *Statutes* 12:528; John Rose to Duncan Campbell, Nov. 14, 1784, Claims of Duncan Campbell in Virginia, American Loyalist Claims, PRO, T 79/12; Robert Beverley to Samuel Gist, Oct. 2, 1784, Robert Beverley Letter Book, 1761–93, LC; William Lee to Francis Gildart, June 3, 1786, William Lee Letter Book, 1783–87, VHS.

37. Robert Beverley to William Beverley, May 24, 1783, [June 1783?], May 27, [1789], Robert Beverley Letter Book, 1761–93, LC; Menard and McCusker, *Economy of British America*, 369–70, 374–76; Allan Schaffer, "Virginia's 'Critical Period,'" in *The Old Dominion: Essays for Thomas Perkins Abernethy*, ed. Darrett B. Rutman (Charlottesville, VA, 1964), chap. 10, esp. 165–68; Lucille Griffith, "Brother of the Revolution: The Career of William Lee, Virginian," (Rockefeller Library, CW, 1984), 211–12; William Lee to Thomas Nelson, Oct. 1783, *VMHB* 38 (1938): 43; Lee to Luke Stavely, Aug. 10, 1784, William Lee Letter Book, 1783–87, VHS; William Allason to Henry Ritchie, Dec. 22, 1784, Allason Letter Book, 1770–89, LOV; Ralph Wormeley to Welch & Son, Sept. 20, 1785, Wormeley Letter Book, 1783–91, UVA; Petition to Virginia Assembly of Norfolk Inhabitants, *Virginia Gazette or American Advertiser* (Richmond), Oct. 15, 1785; Philip Hamilton, *The Making and Unmaking of a Revolutionary Family: The Tuckers of Virginia, 1752–1836* (Charlottesville, VA, 2003), 78. See also Albemarle County Legislative Petitions, 1776–90, Nov. 3, 1787, LOV.

38. Rice, *Chastellux Travels*, 435, 437, 441, 442.

39. Thomas Nelson to George Washington, June 30, 1778, Washington Papers, LC; pay for a recruit, 1781 and March 6, 1781, Carter Letter Book, 1732–81, UVA, Goodwin transcript FHCC; Hening, *Statutes* 10:25–27, 259–62; [George Braxton] to [sister Elizabeth Whiting], March 13, 1781, Blair, Bannister, Braxton, Horner, Whiting Papers, WM; Edmund Pendleton to James Madison, May 17, 1783, Mays, *Papers of Pendleton,* 446; William Lee to Samuel Thorpe, June 6, 1785, William Lee Letter Book, 1783–87, VHS; Archibald Stuart to Thomas Jefferson, Oct. 24, 1785, Boyd et al., *Papers of Jefferson* 8:645, 687; Report of W. W. Hening on Claims of Glassford, Gordon, Monteith & Co., concerning Charles Carter, June 15, 1802, PRO, T 79/73; Extracts of Such Parts of Richard Hanson's Letters as Relate to Archibald Cary's Account, 1784–90, ibid., 30; Nagel, *Lees,* 131–32. For the elite's lack of enthusiasm for supporting the war effort and the reaction to the 1780 draft law, see McDonnell, "Class Struggle during the American Revolution," 317, 323, 329–30.

40. Leonard, *General Assembly of Virginia,* 179–218, 469–73; Emily J. Salmon and Edward D. C. Campbell, eds., *Hornbook of Virginia History* (Richmond, 1994), 109–11.

41. Lorraine E. Holland, "Rise and Fall of Antebellum Virginia Aristocracy: A Generational Analysis" (Ph.D. diss., Univ. of California–Irvine, 1980), chap. 4.

42. Jan Lewis, *The Pursuit of Happiness: Family and Values in Jefferson's Virginia* (New York, 1984), chaps. 2, 4, 6, esp. pp. 65–68, 108–9, 134–36, 164–68, 209–11, 220–30; Francis Corbin to Henry Lee, Feb. 1798, Brock Collection, Huntington Library.

43. Royster, *Fabulous History of the Dismal Swamp Company,* 317–18, 369, 415–16; Hamilton, *Making and Unmaking of a Revolutionary Family,* 107–8, 167; Evans, *Nelson,* 137–48; York County, Will and Inventories, 23 (1781–1811): 661–63, LOV; "List of Creditors of Genl. Thomas Nelson Taken from a Book Left by R. Andrews," 1795, and Thomas Nelson Jr. to Micajah Crew, Dec. 7, 1801, to James Rawlings, July 22, 1817, Brock Collection, Huntington Library.

44. Hamilton, *Making and Unmaking of a Revolutionary Family,* 74, 99–106, 180; Cowden, "The Randolphs," 471–84.

45. Nagel, *Lees,* 160–87, 212, 301.

46. Hamilton, *Making and Unmaking of a Revolutionary Family,* 99–101; John Randolph to Thomas Forman, Oct. 29, 1813, Feb. 23, April 17, 1814, *VMHB* 49 (1941): 202–4; Anthony F. Upton, "The Road to Power in Virginia in the Early Nineteenth Century," ibid., 64 (1954): 259–80, esp. 271–74; Robert Dawidoff, *The Education of John Randolph* (New York, 1979), 30, 40, 56, 70, 71, 72, 73, 75–76, 77, 88–89.

47. Byrd, *Prose Works,* 355–56, 358–59; Thomas L. Kane to Elizabeth Kane, c. 1840s, Kane Collection, Clements Library, University of Michigan; Hening, *Statutes* 7:323–30, 445–52.

Index

Page numbers followed by a t *indicate tables.*